The Benjamin PSI Series

Consulting Editors

Fred S. Keller

Ben A. Green, Jr.

W. A. BENJAMIN, INC.

Menlo Park, California • Reading, Massachusetts • London • Amsterdam •
Don Mills, Ontario • Sydney

Personalized System of Instruction

41 Germinal Papers

Edited by

J. Gilmour Sherman

Georgetown University

A Selection of Readings on the Keller Plan

ISBN 0-8053-8791-9
CDEFGHIJK–AL–798765

To Christina C. Stockman
the great lady who was on my side as I
learned at my own pace.

Preface

When we first presented papers on PSI (or "Keller Plan"), it was only in the context that this method of teaching might be appropriate for an introductory course in psychology, limited perhaps to an experimental-behavioral orientation. The effective use of PSI has become broader than anticipated and already extends to a wide range of disciplines.

The time has come for a collection of germinal papers. As PSI is adopted to new subject matter and to different levels of education, it is modified to fit new conditions. There is the danger that PSI enthusiasts will claim credit for any, and all, successful educational innovations. There is the corresponding danger that a broad definition will tend to discredit PSI for the failures of some quite different approach.

This collection of papers is designed to serve as a guide to those who wish to explore PSI in new environments, by defining through example what it is and how it works. The papers provide an outline of method, some data, some potential extensions, and the history of PSI. The collection will also attempt to delimit the field so that PSI does not deprive others of their deserved credit or blame. This does not imply that modifications are not appropriate. The *form* of PSI is not critical; some of its *functions* are.

Unlike some educational innovations, PSI is rooted in a system: learning-reinforcement theory. The basic law of that theory, Thorndike's *law of effect* states, "responses followed by reinforcement increase in frequency." The law dictates one critical function, essential for effective instruction, the response-reinforcement contingency. That is, there is a relationship between behavior and its consequences. Instruction which casts the student in a spectator role, the receiver of a presentation, or, leaves the results of active participation to chance, ignores the law of effect, neglects the functional relation it specifies, and breaks the most fundamental law of learning. The traditional lecture system is an example—too often it is not working.

PSI has been used too widely and too successfully to doubt that, in its original form, it works. This is not to advocate that PSI is suitable for all education. The form is too restrictive for many situations; the functions too poorly delineated to insure successful adaptations to all areas. There is nothing here that should be slavishly followed, no claim of an answer to all of education's ills, no final format. But if the critical functions of what has worked well are understood, present use and future extension will be most efficient.

What these papers present, then, is a state-of-the-art report on an innovation that has already out-performed all expectations. If PSI took shape on March 29, 1963 (see the introduction to Section V), it was within a group whose orientation was "better education can come from experimentation." Hopefully this is still the case.

Contents

List of Authors

Sam M. Austin
Article 12

Cyclotron Laboratory, Physics Department, Michigan State University, East Lansing

Stanley E. Ball
Article 27

Department of Mathematics, The University of Texas at El Paso

George D. W. Berry
Article 21

Department of Philosophy, Boston University

Joel J. Blaustein
Article 5

Department of Psychology, Queens College, New York City

David G. Born
Articles 6, 10, 28

Center to Improve Learning and Instruction, University of Utah, Salt Lake City

Olgierd Celinski
Article 31

Faculty of Pure and Applied Science, University of Ottawa, Canada

Brett K. Cole
Article 5

Department of Psychology, Queens College, New York City

Jeffrey R. Corey
Articles 2, 3

Department of Psychology, C. W. Post College of Long Island University, Greenvale, New York

Michael L. Davis
Article 10

Department of Psychology, Dickinson College, Carlisle, Pennsylvania

A. J. Dessler
Article 15

Professor of Space Science, Rice University, Houston, Texas

John Farmer
Article 5

Department of Psychology, Queens College, New York City [deceased]

C. B. Ferster
Article 34

Department of Psychology, American University, Washington, D.C.

Howard F. Gallup
Article 25

Department of Psychology, Lafayette College, Easton, Pennsylvania

K. E. Gilbert
Article 12

Cyclotron Laboratory, Physics Department, Michigan State University, East Lansing

Stephen M. Gledhill
Article 10

University of Utah, Salt Lake City

Ben A. Green, Jr.
Articles 11, 22

Center for Personalized Instruction, Georgetown University, Washington, D.C.

Joel Greenspoon
Article 30

Chairman, Department of Psychology, The University of Texas of the Permian Basin, Odessa

Lee Harrisberger
Article 36

Dean, Science and Engineering Department, The University of Texas of the Permian Basin, Odessa

Emily W. Herbert
Article 6

Department of Human Development, University of Kansas, Lawrence

John H. Hess, Jr.
Article 26

Chairman, Psychology Department, Eastern Mennonite College, Harrisonburg, Virginia

Lawrence L. Hoberock
Articles 8, 14

Department of Mechanical Engineering, The University of Texas at Austin

Fred S. Keller
Articles 1, 37, 38

Center for Personalized Instruction, Georgetown University, Washington, D.C.

John J. Knightly
Article 19

Graduate School of Library Science, The University of Texas at Austin

Billy V. Koen
Articles 8, 13

Department of Mechanical Engineering, The University of Texas at Austin

Gerald D. Lachter
Article 5

Department of Psychology, C. W. Post College of Long Island University, Greenvale, New York

Micah Wei-Ming Leo
Article 17

Department of Chemistry, Barrington College, Barrington, Rhode Island

H. G. MacDermot
Article 9

University of Oregon, Eugene

Harlley E. McKean
Article 16

Department of Statistics, University of Kentucky, Lexington

James S. McMichael
Articles 2, 3

Department of Psychology, C. W. Post College of Long Island University, Greenvale, New York

Robert F. Morgan
Article 33

Dean for Faculty Affairs, California School of Professional Psychology, San Francisco

William A. Myers
Article 4

Veterans' Hospital, Minneapolis, Minnesota

Terry F. Nelson
Article 7

Center for Behavioral Modification, Minneapolis, Minnesota

Frederick L. Newman
Articles 16, 27

Eastern Pennsylvania Psychiatric Institute, Philadelphia

S. N. Postlethwait
Article 35

Department of Biology, Purdue University, West Lafayette, Indiana

Paul Protopapas
Article 18

Department of Biology, Lowell State College, Lowell, Massachusetts

Ronald Purtle
Articles 16, 27

Director of Research, Yoke Crest, Inc., Harrisburg, Pennsylvania

Charles H. Roth
Article 8

Department of Electrical Engineering, The University of Texas at Austin

John L. Sayre
Article 19

Director of University Libraries, Phillips University, Enid, Oklahoma

David W. Scott
Article 7

Orchard Park, New York

W. C. Sheppard
Article 9

Department of Psychology, University of Oregon, Eugene

J. Gilmour Sherman
Articles 23, 29, 39, 40, 41

Center for Personalized Instruction, Georgetown University, Washington, D.C.

Clarence C. Smith
  Article 27

Department of Education, New Mexico State University, Las Cruces

Elizabeth Poplin Stanfield
  Article 20

Department of Foreign Languages, Georgia State University, Atlanta

P. P. Szydlik
  Article 24

Department of Physics, State University College, Plattsburgh, New York

Sivasailam Thiagarajan
  Article 32

Center for Innovation in Teaching the Handicapped, Indiana University

Thomas B. Toy
  Article 33

North Carolina State University, Raleigh

Gerald R. Wagner
  Article 8

Department of Mechanical Engineering, The University of Texas at Austin

Paul Whelan
  Article 28

University of Utah, Salt Lake City

Dennis L. Young
  Article 27

Department of Mathematics, New Mexico State University, Las Cruces

Section I

Method, Data, and Evaluation

Keller's "Good-bye Teacher" stands alone as the "classic" description of PSI. As the introductory paper it serves to describe the method and to introduce a series of research reports. Keller's five distinguishing features are the best definition of PSI and its essential characteristics. McMichael and Cory's paper [Article 2] presents results so universally reported, it too could stand alone as the definitive data paper, if confirmation and replication were not so much a part of the experimental tradition.

While each paper in this section adds its own special contribution, a theme does emerge. In study after study, the data show (1) PSI changes the grade distribution for the better and (2) this style of teaching is preferred by the majority of students. These two findings recur in studies using different measures, from universities of very different character and tradition, from courses designed for students at different stages in the academic hierarchy, and from courses in different disciplines (see Myers [Article 4]; Hoberock *et al.* [Article 8]; and also the papers in Section II). The constraints of educational practice appear to preclude educational research from attaining the purity and elegance of design characteristic of research in the "hard" sciences. However, despite acknowledged methodological flaws, there comes a time when a finding appears so often, under such disparate conditions, that it is strengthened in generality rather than weakened by the loose controls that continue to produce it.

For the sake of argument let us take the opposite view and adopt the position of those who may prefer not to accept a weak proof. Certainly there is little here, or elsewhere, that could make a case for the conclusion that students in PSI courses learn less. Even the most conservative view suggests that students learn at least as much as in traditionally taught courses—and with a considerable gain in satisfaction. This alone may be enough to recommend PSI. The data are compelling, if not definitive, that this is indeed a "worst case" analysis. This is not to suggest that the method is perfect and that there are no problems—but that is the subject of Section III.

As the Nelson and Scott paper [Article 7] points out, " . . . comparisons of personalized courses with other course formats has well enough demonstrated the advantages of the personalized model to make further collection of this sort of data redundant." Increasingly, research reports are now directed toward defining and evaluating the critical features of PSI. From Keller's list of five essential features, self-pacing (Nelson and Scott) and the proctor function (Farmer *et al.* [Article 5]; Born, 1971 [Article 10]) have received the most attention. The importance of the removal of penalties for errors has been almost totally neglected. From what we know of the crippling and supressive effects of punishment, a system that depends upon an active, responsive student might well give more attention to this aspect of PSI, perhaps making it a sixth essential feature.

The reader should note that the procedures of the Sheppard and MacDermot paper [Article 9] rely heavily on oral interviews. Their course was more akin to Ferster's technique and the reader may want to turn to Section IV at this point and read Ferster's paper [Article 34]. In classroom practice the two procedures appear to be converging. PSI's reliance on written material, written tests, and written answers has obvious advantages for the integrity and quality-control of the response-reinforcement contingency. Increasingly those following Ferster's lead base interviews on some written core, presumably from some recognition of those advantages. On the other hand, Ferster's oral interview recognizes the importance of establishing a fluent verbal repertoire in the subject matter. The oral interview is more flexible and results in rapid feedback on the adequacy of written materials. Perhaps most important, the interview is the occasion of immediate, powerful, and subtle reinforcers. An increasing recognition of those advantages has led to an expansion of the proctor role in the PSI system. The expanded proctor function approximates Ferster's oral interview within a highly structured context.

Data can take us only so far. Any teacher worthy of the title knows we know more about our students than we can put in numbers. It is our student who will ultimately determine, by preference and achievement, the merits and fate of PSI.

"GOOD-BYE, TEACHER. . . ." [1]

Fred S. Keller [2]

When I was a boy, and school "let out" for the summer, we used to celebrate our freedom from educational control by chanting:

Good-bye scholars, good-bye school;
Good-bye teacher, darned old fool!

We really didn't think of our teacher as deficient in judgment, or as a clown or jester. We were simply escaping from restraint, dinner pail in one hand and shoes in the other, with all the delights of summer before us. At that moment, we might even have been well-disposed toward our teacher and might have felt a touch of compassion as we completed the rhyme.

"Teacher" was usually a woman, not always young and not always pretty. She was frequently demanding and sometimes sharp of tongue, ever ready to pounce when we got out of line. But, occasionally, if one did especially well in home-work or in recitation, he could detect a flicker of approval or affection that made the hour in class worthwhile. At such times, we loved our teacher and felt that school was fun.

It was not fun enough, however, to keep me there when I grew older. Then I turned to another kind of education, in which the reinforcements were sometimes just as scarce as in the schoolroom. I became a Western Union messenger boy and, between deliveries of telegrams, I learned Morse code by memorizing dots and dashes from a sheet of paper and listening to a relay on the wall. As I look back on those days, I conclude that I am the only living reinforcement theorist who ever learned Morse code in the absence of reinforcement.

It was a long, frustrating job. It taught me that drop-out learning could be just as difficult as in-school learning and it led me to wonder about easier possible ways of mastering a skill. Years later, after returning to school and finishing my formal education, I came back to this classical learning problem, with the aim of making International Morse code less painful for beginners than American Morse had been for me (Keller, 1943).

During World War II, with the aid of a number of students and colleagues, I tried to apply the principle of immediate reinforcement to the early training of Signal Corps personnel in the reception of Morse-code signals. At the same time, I had a chance to observe, at close hand and for many months, the operation of a military training center. I learned something from both experiences, but I should have learned more. I should have seen many things that I didn't see at all, or saw very dimly.

I could have noted, for example, that instruction in such a center was highly individualized, in spite of large classes, sometimes permitting students to advance at their own speed throughout a course of study. I could have seen the clear specification of terminal skills for each course, together with the carefully graded steps leading to this end. I could have seen the demand for perfection at every level of training and for every student; the employment of classroom instructors who were little more than the successful graduates of earlier classes; the minimizing of the lecture as a teaching device and the maximizing of student participation. I could have seen, especially, an interesting division of labor in the educational process, wherein the non-commissioned, classroom teacher was restricted to

[1]President's Invited Address, Division 2, Amer. Psychol. Ass., Washington, D.C., Sept., 1967.

[2]Currently on leave of absence at the Institute for Behavioral Research, 2426 Linden Lane, Silver Spring, Maryland.

From *Journal of Applied Behavior Analysis*, 1968, *1*, 78–89; copyright 1968 by the Society for the Experimental Analysis of Behavior, Inc.

duties of guiding, clarifying, demonstrating, testing, grading, and the like, while the commissioned teacher, the training officer, dealt with matters of course logistics, the interpretation of training manuals, the construction of lesson plans and guides, the evaluation of student progress, the selection of non-commissioned cadre, and the writing of reports for his superiors.

I did see these things, of course, in a sense, but they were embedded deeply within a special context, one of "training" rather than "education". I did not then appreciate that a set of reinforcement contingencies which were useful in building simple skills like those of the radio operator might also be useful in developing the verbal repertories, the conceptual behaviors, and the laboratory techniques of university education. It was not until a long time later, by a very different route, that I came to such a realization.

That story began in 1962, with the attempt on the part of two Brazilian and two North American psychologists, to establish a Department of Psychology at the University of Brasilia. The question of teaching method arose from the very practical problem of getting a first course ready by a certain date for a certain number of students in the new university. We had almost complete freedom of action; we were dissatisfied with the conventional approaches; and we knew something about programmed instruction. We were also of the same theoretical persuasion. It was quite natural, I suppose, that we should look for fresh applications of reinforcement thinking to the teaching process (Keller, 1966).

The method that resulted from this collaborative effort was first used in a short-term laboratory course[3] at Columbia University in the winter of 1963, and the basic procedure of this pilot study was employed at Brasilia during the following year, by Professors Rodolfo Azzi and Carolina Martuscelli Bori, with 50 students in a one-term introductory course. Professor Azzi's report on this, at the 1965 meetings of the American Psychological Association and in personal correspondence, indicated a highly satisfactory outcome. The new procedure was received enthusiastically by the students and by the university administration. Mastery of the course material was judged excellent for all who completed the course. Objections were minor, centering around the

relative absence of opportunity for discussion between students and staff.

Unfortunately, the Brasilia venture came to an abrupt end during the second semester of its operation, due to a general upheaval within the university that involved the resignation or dismissal of more than 200 teachers. Members of the original psychology staff have since taken positions elsewhere, and have reportedly begun to use the new method again, but I am unable at this time to report in detail on their efforts.

Concurrently with the early Brazilian development, Professor J. G. Sherman and I, in the spring of 1965, began a series of more or less independent applications of the same general method at Arizona State University. With various minor changes, this work has now been tried through five semesters with an increasing number of students per term (Keller, 1967 [b]; Sherman, 1967). The results have been more gratifying with each successive class, and there has been as yet no thought of a return to more conventional procedures. In addition, we have had the satisfaction of seeing our system used by a few other colleagues, in other courses and at other institutions.[4]

In describing this method to you, I will start with a quotation. It is from a hand-out given to all the students enrolled in the first-semester course in General Psychology (one of two introductions offered at Arizona State University) during the past year, and it describes the teaching method to which they will be exposed unless they elect to withdraw from the course.

> "This is a course through which you may move, from start to finish, at your own pace. You will not be held back by other students or forced to go ahead until you are ready. At best, you may meet all the course requirements in less than one semester; at worst, you may not complete the job within that time. How fast you go is up to you.
>
> "The work of this course will be divided into 30 units of content, which correspond roughly to a series of home-work assignments and laboratory exercises. These units will come in a definite numerical order, and you must show your

---

[3]With the aid of (Dr.) Lanny Fields and the members of a senior seminar at Columbia College, during the fall term of 1963-64.

[4]For example, by J. L. Michael with high-school juniors on a National Science Foundation project at Grinnell College (Iowa), in 1965; and by J. Farmer and B. Cole at Queens College (New York) in a course similar to the one described here.

mastery of each unit (by passing a "readiness" test or carrying out an experiment) before moving on to the next.

"A good share of your reading for this course may be done in the classroom, at those times when no lectures, demonstrations, or other activities are taking place. Your classroom, that is, will sometimes be a study hall.

"The lectures and demonstrations in this course will have a different relation to the rest of your work than is usually the rule. They will be provided only when you have demonstrated your readiness to appreciate them; no examination will be based upon them; and you need not attend them if you do not wish. When a certain percentage of the class has reached a certain point in the course, a lecture or demonstration will be available at a stated time, but it will not be compulsory.

"The teaching staff of your course will include proctors, assistants, and an instructor. A proctor is an undergraduate who has been chosen for his mastery of the course content and orientation, for his maturity of judgment, for his understanding of the special problems that confront you as a beginner, and for his willingness to assist. He will provide you with all your study materials except your textbooks. He will pass upon your readiness tests as satisfactory or unsatisfactory. His judgment will ordinarily be law, but if he is ever in serious doubt, he can appeal to the classroom assistant, or even the instructor, for a ruling. Failure to pass a test on the first try, the second, the third, or even later, will not be held against you. It is better that you get too much testing than not enough, if your final success in the course is to be assured.

"Your work in the laboratory will be carried out under the direct supervision of a graduate laboratory assistant, whose detailed duties cannot be listed here. There will also be a graduate classroom assistant, upon whom your proctor will depend for various course materials (assignments, study questions, special readings, and so on), and who will keep up to date all progress records for course members. The classroom assistant will confer with the instructor daily, aid the proctors on occasion, and act in a variety of ways to further the smooth operation of the course machinery.

"The instructor will have as his principal responsibilities: (a) the selection of all study material used in the course; (b) the organization and the mode of presenting this material; (c) the construction of tests and examinations; and (d) the final evaluation of each student's progress. It will be his duty, also, to provide lectures, demonstrations, and discussion opportunities for all students who have earned the privilege; to act as a clearing-house for requests and complaints; and to arbitrate in any case of disagreement between students and proctors or assistants. . . .

"All students in the course are expected to take a final examination, in which the entire term's work will be represented. With certain exceptions, this examination will come at the same time for all students, at the end of the term. . . . The examination will consist of questions which, in large part, you have already answered on your readiness tests. Twenty-five percent of your course grade will be based on this examination; the remaining 75% will be based on the number of units of reading and laboratory work that you have successfully completed during the term."

(In my own sections of the course, these percentages were altered, during the last term, to a 30% weighting of the final examination, a 20% weighting of the 10 laboratory exercises, and a 50% weighting of the reading units.)

A picture of the way this method operates can best be obtained, perhaps, by sampling the activities of a hypothetical average student as he moves through the course. John Pilgrim is a freshman, drawn from the upper 75% of his high-school class. He has enrolled in PY 112 for unknown reasons and has been assigned to a section of about 100 students, men and women, most of whom are also in their beginning year. The class is scheduled to meet on Tuesdays and Thursdays, from 9:15 to 10:30 a.m., with a laboratory session to be arranged.

Together with the description from which I quoted a moment ago, John receives a few mimeographed instructions and some words of advice from his professor. He is told that he should cover two units of laboratory work or reading per week in order to be sure of taking an A-grade into his final examination; that he should withdraw from the course if he doesn't pass at least one readiness test within the first two weeks; and that a grade of Incomplete will not be given except in special cases. He is also advised that, in addition to the regular classroom hours on Tuesday and Thursday, readiness tests may be taken on Saturday forenoons and Wednesday afternoons of each week—periods in which he can catch up with, or move ahead of, the rest of the class.

He then receives his first assignment: an introductory chapter from a standard textbook and two "sets" from a programmed version of similar material. With this assignment, he receives a mimeographed list of "study questions", about 30 in number. He is told to seek out the answers to these questions in his reading, so as to prepare himself for the questions he will be asked in his readiness tests. He is free to study wherever he pleases, but he is strongly encouraged to use the study hall for at least part of the time. Conditions for work are optimal there, with other students doing the same thing and with an assistant or proctor on hand to clarify a confusing passage or a difficult concept.

This is on Tuesday. On Thursday, John comes to class again, having gone through the sets of programmed material and having decided to finish his study in the classroom, where he cannot but feel that the instructor really expects him. An assistant is in charge, about half the class is there, and some late registrants are reading the course description. John tries to study his regular text, but finds it difficult to concentrate and ends by deciding to work in his room. The assistant pays no attention when he leaves.

On the following Tuesday, he appears in study hall again, ready for testing, but anxious, since a whole week of the course has passed. He reports to the assistant, who sends him across the hall, without his books and notes, to the testing room, where the proctor in charge gives him a blue-book and one of the test forms for Unit 1. He takes a seat among about 20 other students and starts work. The test is composed of 10 fill-in questions and one short-answer essay question. It doesn't seem particularly difficult and, in about 10 min John returns his question sheet and is sent, with his blue-book, to the proctor's room for grading.

In the proctor's room, in one of 10 small cubicles, John finds his special proctor, Anne Merit. Anne is a psychology major who passed the same course earlier with a grade of A. She receives two points of credit for about 4 hr of proctoring per week, 2 hr of required attendance at a weekly proctors' meeting, and occasional extra duty in the study hall or test room. She has nine other students besides John to look after, so she will not as a rule be able to spend much more than 5 or 10 min of class time with each.

Anne runs through John's answers quickly, checking two of them as incorrect and placing a question mark after his answer to the essay question. Then she asks him why he answered these three as he did. His replies show two misinterpretations of the question and one failure in written expression. A restatement of the fill-in questions and some probing with respect to the essay leads Anne to write an O.K. alongside each challenged answer. She congratulates John upon his performance and warns him that later units may be a little harder to master than the first.

John's success is then recorded on the wall-chart in the proctors' room, he is given his next assignment and set of study questions, and sent happily on his way. The blue-book remains with Anne, to be given later to the assistant or the instructor for inspection, and used again when John is ready for testing on Unit 2. As he leaves the room, John notices the announcement of a 20-min lecture by his instructor, for all students who have passed Unit 3 by the following Friday, and he resolves that he will be there.

If John had failed in the defense of one or two of his answers, he would have been sent back for a minimal period of 30 min for further study, with advice as to material most needing attention. If he had made more than four errors on his test, the answers would not have been considered individually; he would simply have been told that he was not ready for examination. And, if he had made no errors at all, he would probably have been asked to explain one or two of his correct answers, as a way of getting acquainted and to make sure that he was the one who had really done the work.

John did fail his first test on Unit 2, and his first two tests on Unit 4 (which gave trouble to nearly everyone). He missed the first lecture, too, but qualified for the second. (There were seven such "shows" during the term, each attended by perhaps half of the students entitled to be there.) After getting through his first five units, he failed on one review test before earning the right to move on to Unit 6. On the average, for the remainder of the course, he required nearly two readiness tests per unit. Failing a test, of course, was not an unmixed evil, since it permitted more discussion with the proctor and often served to sharpen the concepts involved.

In spite of more than a week's absence from school, John was able, by using the Wednesday and Saturday testing sessions, to complete his course units successfully about a week before the final examination. Because of his cramming for other courses during this last week, he did not review for his psychology and received only a B on his final examination. His A for the course was not affected by this, but his pride was hurt.

Sometime before the term ended, John was asked to comment on certain aspects of the course, without revealing his identity. (Remember, John is a mythical figure.) Among other things, he said that, in comparison with courses taught more conventionally, this one demanded a much greater mastery of the work assignments, it required greater memorization of detail and much greater understanding of basic concepts, it generated a greater feeling of achievement, it gave much greater recognition of the student as a person, and it was enjoyed to a much greater extent.

He mentioned also that his study habits had improved during the term, that his attitude towards testing had become more positive, that his worry about final grades had diminished, and that there had been an increase in his desire to hear lectures (this in spite of the fact that he attended only half of those for which he was qualified). When asked specifically about the use of proctors, he said that the discussions with his proctors had been very helpful, that the proctor's non-academic, personal relation was also important to him, and that the use of proctors generally in grading and discussing tests was highly desirable.

Anne Merit, when asked to comment on her own reactions to the system, had many things to say, mostly positive. She referred especially to the satisfaction of having the respect of her proctees, of seeing them do well, and of cementing the material of the course for herself. She noted that the method was one of "mutual reinforcement" for student, proctor, assistant, and instructor. She suggested that it ought to be used in other courses and at other levels of instruction. She wondered why it would not be possible for a student to enroll in a second course immediately upon completion of the first, if it were taught by the same method. She also listed several changes that might improve the efficiency of the course machinery, especially in the area of testing and grading, where delay may sometimes occur.

In an earlier account of this teaching method (Keller, 1967), I summarized those features which seem to distinguish it most clearly from conventional teaching procedures. They include the following:

"(*1*) The go-at-your-own-pace feature, *which permits a student to move through the course at a speed commensurate with his ability and other demands upon his time.*

"(*2*) The unit-perfection requirement for advance, *which lets the student go ahead to new material only after demonstrating mastery of that which preceded.*

"(*3*) The use of lectures and demonstrations as vehicles of motivation, *rather than sources of critical information.*

"(*4*) *The related* stress upon the written word *in teacher-student communication; and, finally:*

"(*5*) *The* use of proctors, *which permits repeated testing, immediate scoring, almost unavoidable tutoring, and a marked enhancement of the personal-social aspect of the educational process.*"

The similarity of our learning paradigm to that provided in the field of programmed instruction is obvious. There is the same stress upon analysis of the task, the same concern with terminal performance, the same opportunity for individualized progression, and so on. But the sphere of action here is different. The principal steps of advance are not "frames" in a "set", but are more like the conventional home-work assignment or laboratory exercise. "The 'response' is not simply the completion of a prepared statement through the insertion of a word or phrase. Rather, it may be thought of as the resultant of many such responses, better described as the understanding of a principle, a formula, or a concept, or the ability to use an experimental technique. Advance within the program depends on something more than the appearance of a confirming word or the presentation of a new frame; it involves a personal interaction between a student and his peer, or his better, in what may be a lively verbal interchange, of interest and importance to each participant. The use of a programmed text, a teaching machine, or some sort of computer aid within such a course is entirely possible and may be quite desirable, but it is not to be equated with the course itself." (Keller, 1967.)

Failure to recognize that our teaching units are not as simple as the response words in a programmed text, or the letter reactions to Morse-code signals, or other comparable atoms of behavior, can lead to confusion concerning our procedure. A well-known critic of education in America, after reading an account of our method, sent me a note confessing to "a grave apprehension about the effect of breaking up the subject matter into little packages." "I should suppose," he said, "it would prevent all but the strongest minds from ever possessing a synoptic view of a field, and I imagine that the coaching, and testing, and passing in bits would amount to efficient training rather than effectual teaching."

Our "little packages" or "bits" are no smaller than the basic conceptions of a science of behavior and cannot be delivered all at once in one large synoptic parcel. As for the teaching-training distinction, one needs only to note that it is always the instructor who decides what is to be taught, and to what degree, thus determining whether he will be called a trainer or a teacher. The method he uses, the basic reinforcement contingencies he employs, may be turned to either purpose.

Many things occur, some of them rather strange, when a student is taught by a method such as ours. With respect to everyday student behavior, even a casual visit to a class will provide some novel items. For example, all the students seated in the study hall may be seen studying, undistracted by the presence or movements of others. In the test room, a student will rarely be seen chewing on his pencil, looking at a neighbor's blue-book, or staring out the window. In the crowded proctors' room, 10 pairs of students can be found concurrently engaged in academic interaction, with no couple bothered by the conversation of another, no matter how close by. Upon passing his assistant or instructor, in the corridors or elsewhere, a student will typically be seen to react in a friendly and respectful manner—enough to excite a mild alarm.

More interesting than this is the fact that a student may be tested 40 or 50 times in the course of one semester, often standing in line for the privilege, without a complaint. In one extreme instance, a student required nearly two terms to complete the work of one (after which he applied for, and got, permission to serve as a proctor for the following year).

Another unusual feature of our testing and grading is the opportunity given to defend an "incorrect" answer. This defense, as I noted earlier, may sometimes produce changes in the proctor's evaluation, changes that are regularly checked by the assistant or the instructor. Occasionally, a proctor's O.K. will be rejected, compelling the student to take another test, and sensitizing the proctor to the dangers of leniency; more often, it produces a note of warning, a correction, or a query written by the instructor in the student's blue-book; but always it provides the instructor with feedback on the adequacy of the question he has constructed.

Especially important, in a course taught by such a method, is the fact that any differences in social, economic, cultural, and ethnic background are completely and repeatedly subordinated to a friendly intellectual relationship between two human beings throughout a period of 15 weeks or more. Also, in such a course, a lonesome, ill-favored underprivileged, badly schooled, or otherwise handicapped boy or girl can be assured at least a modicum of individual attention, approval, encouragement, and a chance to succeed. The only prerequisite for such treatment is a well-defined amount and quality of academic achievement.

Another oddity of the system is the production of a grade distribution that is upside down. In Fig. 1, are the results from a class of 208 students at Arizona State University during the past semester. Note the diminishing relative frequency as one moves from A to D. The category of E, indicating failure, is swollen by the presence of 18 students who failed to take up their option of W (withdrawal from the course). Grades of C and D were due to the failure of students to complete all the units of reading or laboratory before going into the final examination.

Figure 2 shows data from the class 1 yr earlier. Essentially the same distribution holds, except for the category of Incomplete, which was then too easily obtainable. Discouraging the use of the Incomplete, together with the provision of more testing hours, apparently has the effect of regularizing study habits and equalizing the number of tests taken per week throughout the term.

In Fig. 3 (filled bars), the grade distribution is for a section of 25 students in an introductory course at Queens College (N. Y.) during the second semester of the past school year.

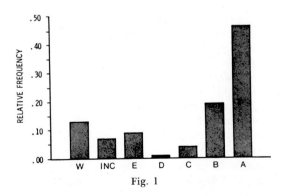

Fig. 1

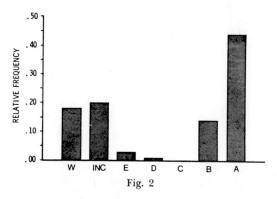

Fig. 2

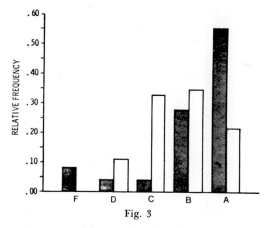

Fig. 3

The same method of teaching was employed as at Arizona State, but the work requirement was somewhat greater in amount. The distinctive feature here is the relative infrequency of low grades. Only four students received less than a B rating. Professor John Farmer, who provided me with these data, reports that the two students receiving F had dropped out of the course, for unknown reasons, after seven and eight units respectively.

With this teaching method, students who are presumably inferior may show up better upon examination than presumably superior students taught by more conventional procedures. Figure 4 shows two distributions of grades on a mid-term examination. The empty bars represent the achievement of 161 students of an Ivy League College, mainly sophomores, in the first semester of a one-year lecture-and-laboratory course in elementary psychology. The filled bars represent the achievement of 66 Arizona State University students, mainly freshman, on an unannounced mid-term quiz prepared by the Ivy League instructor and from which 13% of the questions had to be eliminated on the grounds of differential course coverage.

Relevant to this comparison is that pictured in Fig. 3. The grade distribution obtained by Professor Farmer (and his associate, Brett Cole) is here compared with one obtained from a section of 46 students in the same course, taught in the conventional manner by a colleague who is described as "a very good instructor". The filled bars show the Farmer-Cole results; the empty ones are those from Professor Brandex.

Such comparisons are of some interest and may relieve the tedium of a lecture, but they raise many questions of interpretation, and their importance should not be over-emphasized. The kind of change needed in education today is not one that will be evaluated in terms of the percentage of A's in a grade distribution or of differences at the 0.01 (or

0.001) level of confidence. It is one that will produce a reinforcing state of affairs for everyone involved—a state of affairs that has heretofore been reached so rarely as to be the subject of eulogy in the world's literature, and which, unfortunately, has led to the mystique of the "great teacher" rather than a sober analysis of the critical contingencies in operation.

Our method has not yet required a grant-in-aid to keep it going. On one occasion we tried to get such help, in order to pay for mimeograph paper, the services of a clerk, and one or two additional assistants. Our request was rejected, quite properly, on the grounds that our project was "purely operational". Almost any member of a present-day fund-granting agency can recognize "research" when he sees it. I do think, however, that one should be freed, as I was, from other university demands while introducing a system like ours. And he should not be asked to teach more than two such courses regularly, each serving 100 students or less, unless he has highly qualified assistants upon whom he can depend.

Neither does the method require equipment and supplies that are not already available to almost every teacher in the country. Teaching machines, tape recorders, and computers could readily be fitted into the picture. Moving pictures and television could also be used in one or two ways without detriment to the basic educational process. But these are luxuries, based on only partial recognition of our problem, and they could divert us from more important considerations. (Proctors, like computers, may go wrong or break down, but they can often be repaired and they are easily replaced, at very little expense.)

The need for individualized instruction is widely recognized, and the most commonly suggested way of filling this need is automation. I think that this solution is incomplete,

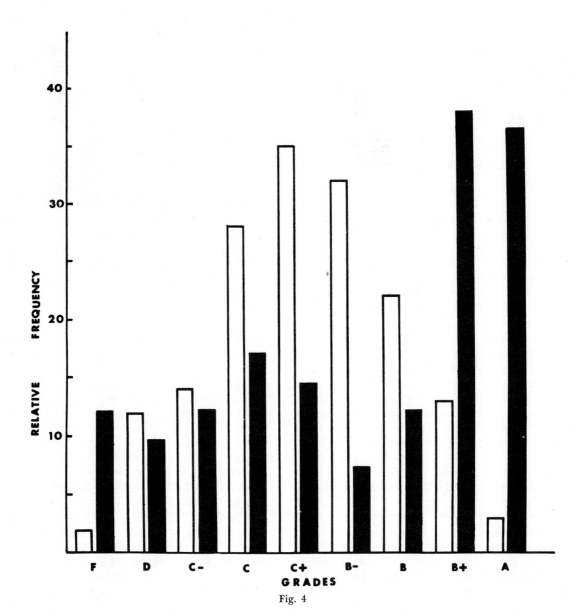

Fig. 4

especially when applied to the young; and I'd like to mention a personal experience that bears upon the matter.

In the summer of 1966, I made numerous visits to a center for the care and treatment of autistic children.[5] One day, as I stood at the door of a classroom, I saw a boy get up from his chair at the end of a class period and give a soft pat to the object on the desk in front of him. At the same time, he said, with a slight smile, "Good-bye, Teaching Machine!"

This pseudo-social behavior in this fundamentally asocial child amused me at the time. It reminded me of Professor Moore's description of the three-year-old who became irritated

when his "talking typewriter" made a mistake, called the device a "big bambam", requested its name, and ended by asking, "Who is your mother?" Today, however, I am not so sure that this is funny. It does suggest that affection may be generated within a child for an electromechanical instrument that has been essential to educational reinforcement. Unfortunately, such a machine, in its present form, is unlikely to generalize with human beings in the boy's world, giving to them a highly desirable reinforcing property. In fact, the growth of this type of student-machine relation, if it were the only one, would be a poor substitute for a directly social interaction.

In an earlier report upon our method, I mentioned that it had been anticipated, partially or *in toto*, in earlier studies and I de-

----

[5]At the Linwood Children's Center, Ellicott City, Maryland.

scribed one of these in some detail. As for current developments by other workers in our field, I have not made any systematic attempt to examine the offerings, even those that deal with college or university instruction. However, I have been impressed by several of them which seem to have points in common with ours, which have met with some success, and which will probably be increasingly heard from in the future.

One of these is the Audio-Tutorial Approach to the teaching of botany, developed by S. N. Postlethwait at Purdue University (Postlethwait and Novak, 1967). Another is the Socratic-Type Programming of general psychology by Harry C. Mahan (1967) and his associates at Palomar College, in California; and a third is the Interview Technique recently applied by C. B. Ferster and M. C. Perrott (1968) in teaching principles of behavior to graduate students in education at the University of Maryland.

Professor Postlethwait's method places great emphasis upon "independent study sessions" in which students carry out each individual work assignment in the course at their own pace, by means of the extensive use of tapes and films. Teaching assistants provide for oral quizzing on major concepts and help the students with difficult assignments. Weekly "small assembly sessions" are used primarily for recitation and the discussion of problems or small research projects; and "general assembly sessions" deal mainly with motivational materials. Postlethwait reports high student interest and greatly improved performance with the use of this technique. "Grades have risen from 6% A's under the conventional system to as high as 25% A's in some semesters. Failures have decreased from 20% in the conventional system to as few as 4%."

"Socratic-Type Programming" is described by Professor Mahan as "a philosophy and technology of instruction which emphasizes student response rather than presentations by the teacher. Its basic media consist of exercises made up of questions and short answers covering the content of a standard text, the text itself, tapes for recording the questions in the exercises, a classroom tape recorder for administering tests, tape duplicating facilities, a listening center in the college library, and student owned tape recorders for home use whenever possible. Classroom time is devoted largely to the discussion of points covered by the questions. All examinations are the short-answer type and are presented aurally on tape." Students must pass three periodic tests with a score of 85% or better before they are permitted to take a comprehensive final examination. The method does not yet permit "multiple exit" from the course, but Mahan says it is "tending very much in that direction." (1967.)

The Interview Technique, as described by Ferster and Perrott, does permit students to complete the course at different times, and it also approximates the student-and-proctor feature. Progress through the course is possible by verbalizing successive units of course content in a lengthy series of short interviews. The interviews are conducted mainly between students currently enrolled in the course, and any student is free to leave the course when all of his reading assignments have been adequately covered. The interviewer may sometimes be a staff member, as at the beginning of the course, but generally he is a student who has already been interviewed by someone else on the topic in question. The interviews are highly formalized, with the interviewer playing the role of the listener, checker, appraiser, and summarizer. Each interview is an open-book affair, but of such short and sharply-defined duration (10 min, as a rule) that the student can do no more than cue himself by reference to the printed page.

The goal of this method is nothing less than fluency with respect to each main feature of the course. Lectures, group discussions, and demonstrations are available at certain times, contingent upon a given stage of advance. Inadequate interviews are rejected, in whole or part, without prejudice, and with suggestions for further study. A product of high quality is guaranteed through staff participation at critical points. A modification of this procedure, which is to include written tests and the employment of advanced-student proctors, is planned by Professor Ferster for the introductory course in psychology at Georgetown University during the coming semester.

In systems like these, and in the one I have centered on, the work of a teacher is at variance with that which has predominated in our time. His public appearances as classroom entertainer, expositor, critic, and debater no longer seem important. His principal job, as Frank Finger (1962) once defined it, is truly "the facilitation of learning in others." He becomes an educational engineer, a contingency manager, with the responsibility of serving the great majority, rather than the small minority, of young men and women who come to him for schooling in the area of his competence. The teacher of tomorrow will not, I think, continue to be satisfied with a 10% efficiency (at best) which makes him an object of contempt by some, commiseration by others, indifference by many, and love by a few. No longer will he need to hold his position by the exercise of functions that neither transmit culture, dignify his status, nor encourage respect for learning in others. No longer will he need to live like Ichabod Crane, in a world that increasingly begrudges him room and lodging for a doubtful service to its young. A new kind of teacher is in the making. To the old kind, I, for one, will be glad to say, "Good-bye!"

I started this paper on a personal note and I would like to end it on one. Twenty-odd years ago, when white rats were first used as laboratory subjects in the introductory course, a student would sometimes complain about his animal's behavior. The beast couldn't learn, he was asleep, he wasn't hungry, he was sick, and so forth. With a little time and a handful of pellets, we could usually show that this was wrong. All that one needed to do was follow the rules. "The rat," we used to say, "is always right."

My days of teaching are over. After what I have said about efficiency, I cannot lay claim to any great success, but my schedule of rewards was enough to maintain my behavior, and I learned one very important thing: *the student is always right.* He is not asleep, not unmotivated, not sick, and he can learn a great deal if we provide the right contingencies of reinforcement. But if we don't provide them, and provide them soon, he too may be inspired to say, "Good-bye!" to formal education.

REFERENCES

Ferster, C. B. and Perrott, M. C. *Behavior principles.* New York: Appleton-Century-Crofts, 1968. Pp. 542.

Finger, F. W. Psychologists in colleges and universities. In W. B. Webb (Ed.), *The profession of psychology.* New York: Holt, Reinhart and Winston, 1962. Pp. 50-73.

Keller, F. S. Studies in international morse code: 1. a new method of teaching code reception. *Journal of Applied Psychology*, 1943, **27**, 407-415.

Keller, F. S. A personal course in psychology. In R. Ulrich, T. Stachnik, and J. Mabry (Eds.), *The control of behavior.* Glenview, Ill.: Scott, Foresman, 1966. Pp. 91-93. [Article 37]

Keller, F. S. Neglected rewards in the educational process. *Proc. 23rd Amer. Conf. Acad. Deans*, Los Angeles, Jan. 1967 [a]. Pp. 9-22.

Keller, F. S. Engineering personalized instruction in the classroom. *Rev. Interamer de Psicol.*, 1967 [b], **1**, 189-197.

Keller, F. S. and Schoenfeld, W. N. The psychology curriculum at Columbia College. *American Psychologist*, 1949, **4**, 165-172.

Mahan, H. C. The use of Socratic type programmed instruction in college courses in psychology. Paper read at West. Psychol. Ass., San Francisco, May, 1967.

Postlethwait, S. N. and Novak, J. D. The use of 8-mm loop films in individualized instruction. *Annals N. Y. Acad. Sci.*, Vol. **142**, Art. 2, 464-470.

Sherman, J. G. Application of reinforcement principles to a college course. Paper read at Amer. Educ. Res. Ass., New York, Feb., 1967. [Article 39]

Received 27 October 1967.

2

CONTINGENCY MANAGEMENT IN AN INTRODUCTORY PSYCHOLOGY COURSE PRODUCES BETTER LEARNING [1]

James S. McMichael and Jeffrey R. Corey

For the contingency management techniques first devised by Keller (1966, 1968) to become a widely accepted teaching method, it is necessary that they be shown (1) to be applicable to general subject matter and (2) to be superior to traditional lecture methods. The present study demonstrated (1) by successfully teaching the material from a standard psychology text. The superiority of contingency management was established by direct comparison of final examination scores from comparable groups taught the same subject matter by either Keller's method or traditional methods. Students taught by Keller's method also rated the course more favorably.

Since Keller (1968) first introduced the systematic application of principles of learning derived from laboratory studies to the teaching of a college subject, his techniques have seen increasing use. Several studies have been done or are in progress to determine the factors most critically responsible for the effectiveness of the method (*cf.* Farmer, Lachter, and Blaustein, 1968). But certain basic questions remain to be answered, questions which would be among the first to be asked by a professor who is considering adopting these techniques.

The first concern would be: can the techniques be applied to any organized body of knowledge? Many of those who now employ the techniques either use textbooks that focus upon the area of the experimental analysis of behavior (*e.g.*, Farmer *et al.*, 1968) or have prepared materials that they deem particularly appropriate to the use of contingency management techniques (*e.g.*, Malott, personal communication). Since most introductory courses,

including those in psychology, rely upon a general textbook, one purpose of the present study was to test whether contingency management techniques could be used to teach the subject matter of a standard textbook, Kendler's *Basic Psychology* (1968).

Secondly, and of fundamental importance, the question naturally arises as to whether students will learn more when these techniques are used. Ancillary to this is the question as to whether students would, by their own criteria for a good course, rate a course using these techniques higher than they would a course taught by traditional methods. Thus, the second major purpose was to assess the effectiveness of contingency management techniques in these respects.

Before the experiment itself, a feasibility study was conducted. During the summer of 1968, a general introductory course based on Kendler's *Basic Psychology* (1968) was administered to 165 students in five separate classes. It was found that: (1) general material, *i.e.*, statistics, physiological psychology, verbal learning, forgetting, *etc.*, could be presented using Keller's method. (2) Students tended to achieve relatively high grades on objective final examinations. (3) The students rated the course very highly. We were favorably impressed with these results but felt that more data were needed to justify the expansion of this program to our regular introductory course. Consequently, the purpose of the present study was to compare directly the results of a course section using contingency manage-

[1] Authorship is considered equal. Reprints may be obtained from either author at the Department of Psychology, C. W. Post College, Greenvale, New York 11548. The authors wish to thank Andrew P. Spiegel, Dean of the College, for his encouragement and for providing financial assistance where it was needed to carry out the project. We also wish to thank the graduate students, Mr. George Dos Santos, Mr. William D. Siegfried, and Mr. George Whitehead, who helped supervise the undergraduate proctors and who aided in the collection and analysis of the data. Professor Richard M. Malott of Western Michigan University provided us with valuable advice in the initial stages of this project.

ment techniques to results obtained by comparable students in conventional lecture sections covering the same material.

METHOD

Subjects

Students. 880 students at C. W. Post College registered in four introductory psychology sections without prior knowledge of what method would be used to teach the course. The initial registration figures were as follows: Experimental class, 221; Control class A, 229; Control B, 213; and Control C, 217. Twenty-seven students withdrew from the experimental class, 36 from Control A, 29 from Control B, and 20 from Control C before the final exam.

Staff. In the experimental class, one of the authors supervised two graduate assistants and 19 undergraduate proctors. The proctors received academic credit for their duties; each proctor was responsible for about 12 students (range 7 to 18).

In each of the control sections, the instructor was assigned one graduate assistant. Nine additional graduate assistants were available, when needed, from a grading pool.

Procedure

Specific details of procedure used in the experimental class may be found in Keller (1968). The course was the first of a two-semester introductory sequence. To make the course compatible with the second semester, which was to be taught by conventional techniques, the second edition of Kendler's *Basic Psychology* (1968) was divided into twelve 20-page units, with the assignments covering chapters 1, 3, 4, and 7 through 11. The control classes used the same textbook and covered the same material.

The control classes met three times a week for 50-min lectures and were tested three or four times; the experimental students were assigned two 50-min proctoring sessions a week in which to take unit tests and to receive a proctor's help.

Students were required to pass, with a perfect score, each unit test, consisting of 10 fill-in questions, before receiving a study guide for the next unit. Each study guide was designed by the authors to call the students' attention to concepts we considered central to the topic of the unit. On the average of once a week the instructor presented a lecture, demonstration, or film. It was stated that only those students who had passed the appropriate number of units were to attend these presentations, but no attempt was made to enforce this ruling.

At the end of the semester, the instructors from all the sections selected 50 multiple-choice questions from the instructor's manual for use as a common final exam. All items were agreed to be appropriate and representative of the material covered in each course. While some of these items had previously appeared on 1-hr examinations in all the control sections, none had been seen by the experimental class. All final examinations were given at the same time and were closely proctored. To guard against contamination of the results by cheating, alternate forms of the exam were appropriately distributed. The exams were graded by graduate students using a punched answer key and were spot-checked by the instructors. Before the exam date, students were told how the final exam would weigh in the determination of course grades as follows: Experimental group, 40%; Control A, 40%; Control B, 50%; Control C, 50%.

Included with the exam was an anonymous rating sheet, handed in separately from the exam. The students were asked to rate the overall quality of the course on a 0 to 10 scale, with 0 labelled as "extremely poor" and 10 as "extremely good". Other scales were included to provide more detailed information for the individual instructor.

RESULTS

The distribution of final exam scores in the experimental and control groups appears in Fig. 1. The mean score out of 50 possible points for each of the groups was: Control A, 35; Control B, 34; Control C, 34; Experimental, 40.

An analysis of variance showed the overall effect to be highly significant (F = 35.5, df = 3, 764; p < 0.005). *Post hoc* t-tests revealed that the most substantial differences among groups existed between the experimental group and each of the control groups (p < 0.0001 for each comparison). By contrast, the differences among the control groups were slight, with none reaching the 0.01 level of significance in spite of the large number of subjects.

Likewise, the student ratings showed that the experimental group rated the course higher than did the control groups. These data are seen in Fig. 2, and an analysis of variance showed the overall effect to be highly significant (F = 78.9; df = 3, 706; p < 0.005). The mean ratings were: Control A, 6; Control B, 7; Control C, 5; Experimental, 9. *Post hoc* t-tests again showed that the experimental-

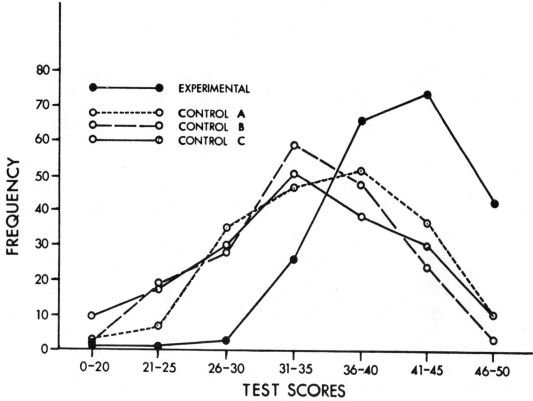

Fig. 1. Distribution of test scores for the three control classes and the experimental class. The mean score for the experimental class was 40; for Control A, 35; Control B, 34; and Control C, 34.

group ratings were higher than each of the control-group ratings ($p < 0.0001$). At the same level of significance Control B was higher than either of the other control groups, which did not differ significantly from each other ($p = 0.31$).

DISCUSSION

The data indicate that students in the experimental group learned more and rated the course higher than did comparable students taught by conventional methods. The data from the final examination are especially convincing in light of several aspects of the procedure which, if anything, would have favored students in the control groups. First, the questions on the final examination were multiple-choice items selected by the instructors from the commercial test-item file. Students in the control groups had been given multiple-choice tests throughout the semester and, therefore, would have been more practiced in studying for this kind of final exam. Second, some of the items on the final examination had previously been given to the control groups on 1-hr examinations. Third, while bias could not be introduced by students selectively reg-

istering for sections of their choice, students could drop the course from their schedules. If there were greater numbers of dropouts in the experimental group than in the control groups, a bias favoring the experimental group could have been introduced by leaving students who were better able to handle the material or more favorably disposed toward the course. To the contrary, the experimental course was dropped by fewer students than on average dropped the control sections.

One aspect of the experimental design produced a confounding which cannot entirely be dismissed. There were different instructors for the various groups, and it is possible that the instructor for the experimental group was a substantially "better teacher". However, we do not think this to be a likely explanation of the data, since his students in the previous year had achieved scores on objective examinations which were no higher than those of the present control groups. The instructors varied considerably in factors which could relate to teaching effectiveness (*e.g.*, orientation toward the field of psychology, amount of teaching experience, and sex). Since no substantial differences were seen among the control groups on final examination scores, we

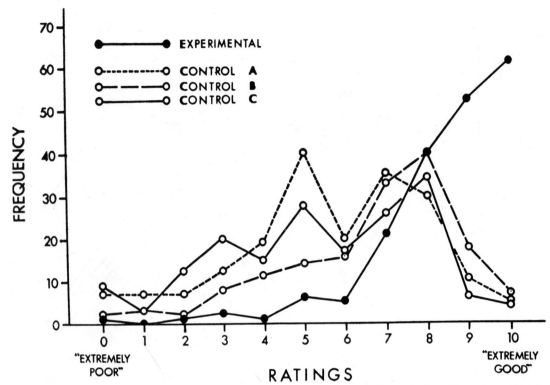

Fig. 2. Distribution of ratings for the three control classes and the experimental class. The mean rating for the experimental class was 9; for Control A, 6; Control B, 7; and Control C, 5.

conclude that the method, rather than such confounded factors, produced the present results.

From the data which showed that the students in the experimental section rated the course highly, we merely conclude that students will readily accept the use of contingency management techniques. Clearly, there are many possible sources of variability in students' ratings of courses, and these were not systematically studied in this experiment.

Since this study was designed to compare two teaching methods, our data do not bear directly on the question of which factors are responsible for the efficacy of contingency management techniques. However, in the course of this study, certain potential improvements in technique were suggested. For example, to reduce procrastination, attendance at all proctoring sessions is strongly encouraged for students who are behind in unit tests. A further contingency now allows accelerated students to perform a laboratory experiment or to write a paper on an area of special interest. After the initial investment of time and institutional resources, this course now functions smoothly and with no additional costs as part of our general introductory psychology program.

REFERENCES

Farmer, J., Lachter, G. D., and Blaustein, J. J. *The effect of proctoring in a structured teaching situation.* Paper presented at the meetings of the Eastern Psychological Association, Washington, D.C. 1968.

Keller, F. S. A personal course in psychology. In R. Ulrich, T. Stachnik, and J. Mabry (Eds.), *Control of human behavior.* Glenview, Ill.: Scott, Foresman, Inc., 1966. Pp. 91-93. [Article 37]

Keller, F. S. "Goodbye, teacher......" *Journal of Applied Behavior Analysis*, 1968, **1**, 79-89. [Article 1]

Kendler, H. H. *Basic psychology.* 2nd ed.; New York: Appleton-Century-Crofts, 1968.

Received 25 February 1969.
(Revised 12 May 1969.)

3

RETENTION IN A PSI INTRODUCTORY PSYCHOLOGY COURSE [1]

Jeffrey R. Corey and James S. McMichael

The retention of material learned by students in a PSI introductory psychology course was found to be superior to the retention of the same material by students in a conventionally-taught section. Retention tests were administered at the end of the semester to all students and to randomly drawn samples ten months later.

The Personalized System of Instruction (PSI) is a set of techniques developed by Keller (1968) to improve the quality of instruction at the college level. Most of the studies which demonstrated that PSI students learn more than conventionally-taught students (McMichael and Corey, 1969 [Article 2]; Sheppard and MacDermot, 1970 [Article 9]; Witters and Kent, 1972; Morris and Kimbrell, 1972) typically assessed student achievement during the course or at the final examination, but did not measure long term retention of the material. Superior final exam performance *and* better performance on a retention test five months later was found by Cooper and Greiner (1971) who employed a behaviorally-based instructional system attributed to Jack Michael.

Evidence for superior retention after completion of a PSI course was provided by a study in which samples of students were given the same final examination 19 weeks after the completion of the course described in McMichael and Corey (1969). PSI students still scored significantly higher than did conventionally-taught students. This retention study (Corey, McMichael, and Tremont, 1970), as well as that of Cooper and Greiner (1971), suffered from possible sources of sampling bias, in that only students who were available at the time of the retention test served as the sample. In our study, only 30 percent of the PSI students and 24 percent of the controls were in the retention sample, while the Cooper and Greiner (1971) study sampled 40 percent of the original students. Also,

anonymous scoring procedures in both studies made it impossible to determine the amount forgotten by individual subjects.

The question of individual student forgetting (or retention) is an important one since any instructional technique which produced only transitory improvements in student mastery would be of limited value. Consequently, the present study was designed to assess mastery of course material in PSI and conventionally taught introductory psychology courses at the end of the semester and to measure retention of the information ten months later in randomly selected samples.

METHOD

Subjects. Two classes of introductory psychology with 141 students in the PSI section and 223 students in the control section comprised the original groups. Twenty-one students from the PSI course and 19 from the control section dropped the course before the final exam. Random samples of 24 students were drawn from each class list for the retention exam. Of these, 18 controls and 19 PSI students agreed to participate; the others could not be contacted. One PSI student was dropped from the sample because he was serving as a proctor at the time of the retention test.

Procedure. All students were assigned the same readings from *Basic Psychology* (Kendler, 1968). Controls were taught by a conventional lecture and hour-exam format. The procedure for the PSI students has been described previously (McMichael and Corey, 1969). The 100 item comprehensive final examination, which made up 50 percent of all students' final grades, was selected from the publisher's test item file by the control instructor. The exams were given at the same time and were

[1] Research supported by a grant from the Esso Educational Foundation. Originally reported in "Personalized Instruction: A Symposium in Honor of Fred Keller" at the 79th annual meeting of the American Psychological Association in 1971 at Washington, D.C. We wish to thank Richard Valente, Nancy K. Shamow, and Paul Tremont who assisted in the collection of these data.

closely proctored. Tests were graded and double checked by graduate assistants.

Ten months after the final examination, the two samples of students were contacted and offered $5 for "about an hour's work." The same 100 item final exam was then given and graded.

RESULTS

On the original final exam, the whole PSI group achieved a mean of 78.2; the controls, 65.1; ($t = 10.325$; $df = 322$, $p < .0001$). Those PSI students who subsequently were given the retention test had a mean of 78.9 on the original exam; the sample of controls had a mean of 67.7. On the retention test, the PSI sample achieved a mean score of 69.4; the controls, 54.0. These data appear in Figure 1. An analysis of variance yielded the following: the effect of teaching method was highly significant ($F = 18.44$, $df = 1,34$, $p < .0001$) as was the effect of test time ($F = 97.11$, $df = 1,34$, $p < .0001$), and the interaction of method by test time was not ($F = 3.18$, $df = 1,34$, $p = .085$).

The Pearson r correlations between scores on the original exam and retention test were +.83 for the PSI students and +.69 for the controls ($p < .001$ in each case).

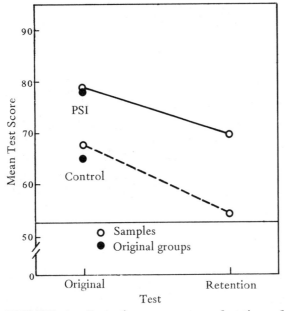

FIGURE 1. Retention scores as a function of teaching method and test time. The filled circles represent the mean test scores of each class at the end of the semester. The open circles represent the mean test scores of randomly drawn samples of students at the end of the semester and ten months later.

DISCUSSION

The results of this study show that, relative to students in a lecture section, students in a PSI course do better on a comprehensive final exam and that they maintain their superiority when retested ten months later. While both groups of students forgot some of what they learned, there was no evidence to suggest that the PSI students forgot more; in fact, the direction of the (nonsignificant) interaction effect is inconsistent with such a conclusion.

The 13.1 percent difference between the entire PSI and control groups on the original test (filled data points in Figure 1) replicates the finding reported by McMichael and Corey (1969) and other investigators. The present experiment differed from the 1969 study in that the examination was longer and all items were selected by the instructor of the conventionally taught class. However, the PSI class in the present study suffered more attrition than did the control class (c.f., Born and Whelan, 1973 [Article 28]). In addition, information was available concerning instructional techniques to be used prior to registration. We neither know how many students used this information nor do we know what effect, if any, this potential self-selection would produce.

The procedure employed to generate samples of students for the retention test appeared to be appropriate, since the sample means were not significantly different from the original populations. Thus, the finding that PSI students retain more (Corey, McMichael, and Tremont, 1970) should not be seen as an artifact of the sampling procedures used in that study.

The high correlations between final examination performance and performance on the retention test is consistent with the stress placed upon the mastery aspect of the personalized system of instruction. Students who master units of course material tend to recall more of that material at a later time, whether the test is given at the end of the semester or ten months later. How much students will know a semester or year later depends on how well they mastered the material originally.

REFERENCES

Born, D. G. and Whelan, P. Some descriptive characteristics of student performance in PSI and lecture courses. *The Psychological Record*, 1973, *23*, 145-152. [Article 28]

Cooper, J. L. and Greiner, J. M. Contingency management in an introductory psychology course produces better retention. *The Psychological Record*, 1971, *21*, 391-400.

Corey, J. R., McMichael, J. S., and Tremont, P. J. Long term effects of personalized instruction in an introductory psychology course. Paper presented at the 41st annual meeting of the Eastern Psychological Association, Atlantic City, New Jersey, April 1970.

Keller, F. S. "Good-bye, teacher. . . ." *Journal of Applied Behavior Analysis,* 1968, *1,* 79–89. [Article 1]

Kendler, H. H. *Basic Psychology,* 2nd edition; New York: Appleton-Century-Crofts, 1968.

McMichael, J. S. and Corey, J. R. Contingency management in an introductory psychology course produces better learning. *Journal of Applied Behavior Analysis,* 1969, *2,* 79–83.

Morris, C. J. and Kimbrell, G. McA. Performance and attitudinal effects of the Keller method in an introductory psychology course. *The Psychological Record,* 1972, *22,* 523–530.

Sheppard, W. C. and MacDermot, H. G. Design and evaluation of a programmed course in introductory psychology. *Journal of Applied Behavior Analysis,* 1970, *3,* 5–11. [Article 9]

Witters, D. R. and Kent, G. W. Teaching without lecturing: Evidence in the case for individualized instruction. *The Psychological Record,* 1972, *22,* 169–175.

4

OPERANT LEARNING PRINCIPLES APPLIED TO TEACHING INTRODUCTORY STATISTICS [1]

William A. Myers [2]

A grade of A was given in an introductory statistics course for meeting a set of contingencies that included no work outside of class (except by request), near-perfect performance on exams following each unit of work in a programmed text, correction of all exam errors, self pacing of work, and the chance to finish the course early. A grade of incomplete was given otherwise. Correlations among performance measures failed to show any meaningful relationships between time taken to finish the course, errors made on exams, and errors made in the programmed text. Responses to a five-part questionnaire were overwhelmingly favorable to the course, but did not vary as a function of grade point average, time taken to finish the course, or number of errors made on exams. The uniformly high level of performance, the students' lack of interest in social contact with the instructor during class, and the absence of drop-outs are all attributed to the contingencies employed, chief among which, according to the instructor's judgment and student rankings, were self-pacing, frequent non-punitive exams and a guaranteed grade of A for near-perfect work at every stage.

Persons interested in the application of operant methods to instruction are familiar with such implied criticisms as: does the student feel deprived of personal contact with the instructor? Does the student feel he is being treated as an object or is not recognized as an individual? Was the material so easy that a sense of excitement and adventure was totally missing? Does the student think the grading system was fair? Would the student voluntarily take another course taught by similar methods? Were the bright students bored an appreciable part of the time? In addition to these attitudinal questions, there is the question of the quality of objectively measured performance in a course taught by operant methods.

Answers to the above questions have so far been favorable for an operant approach to instruction (Keller, 1968; McMichael and Corey, 1969), but additional data are needed, particularly from students.

There is another whole set of attitudinal questions which, since they do not impugn operant techniques, are not asked by critics; namely, are there features of the operant approach to instruction which students actively like?

The main purpose of the introductory statistics course described here was to arrange the conditions of learning so that a group of students with varied background and ability would master the course content. Performance and attitudinal data were collected to determine whether that purpose was realized and to evaluate the set of learning conditions employed.

The methods used were similar enough to those described by Keller (1967) to be considered as a partial replication of his methods. Certain departures from his methods were deliberately introduced in the hope that they would reduce the number of students failing to complete the course, the major flaw in Keller's approach.

The course was given at the University of Wisconsin in an eight-week summer session in 1968. Of the 38 students enrolled, there were seven sophomores, 15 juniors, 10 seniors, and six adult specials. Most were in the college of liberal arts, with a scattering from business, agriculture, and education.

METHOD

Contingencies

At the first class meeting, the instructor explained the rules of the course and gave a brief rationale for them. Students were told that they could work only in class; that the

---

[1] I am grateful to Barry Bragg (now Dr. Bragg) who, as teaching assistant in the course, worked harder than I had a right to expect.

[2] Now at the Minneapolis, Minnesota, Veterans' Hospital.

From *Journal of Applied Behavior Analysis*, 1970, *3*, 191–197; copyright 1970 by the Society for the Experimental Analysis of Behavior, Inc.

time allowed for work was continuous 2.5 hr period each weekday; that they could arrive and leave whenever they chose, but the text book (Elzey, 1968) could not be taken out of class; that each unit of the book and the exercises following it had to be completed in writing before taking the exam for that unit; that each exam must be passed with fewer than three errors before beginning the next unit; that all errors on exams had to be corrected whether the exam was passed or not; that a grade of A would be given for passing all 24 unit exams and a grade of Incomplete for anything less; that individual tutoring could be had anytime by raising a hand or while an exam was being graded, but it had to be initiated by the student himself; that the instructor and teaching assistant were to be considered equals insofar as grading exams was concerned, and that the course was over when the last unit exam in the book was passed.

Unit exams varied in length and type of question depending on the nature of the material covered in the corresponding unit of the text. An effort was made, however, to include a number of questions requiring calculation from each unit. Students moved freely between the classroom and another room containing desk calculators.

Daily Study Sessions

A session began when the instructor unlocked the storeroom where the texts and exams were kept between sessions. Students found their own books and began work. When they were ready for an exam, they took it from a folder after showing the instructor or teach-

ing assistant that the unit and the book exercises had been done. When they finished an exam, they had the option of bringing it either to the instructor or the teaching assistant for grading.

When they left for the day, books were left in the classroom, except in cases where the instructor gave the student the option of taking the book home for the weekend. This option was offered when a student needed more time to complete the work.

When asked on several occasions if they wanted lectures to supplement the text, only a handful said yes. Accordingly, no lectures were given.

RESULTS

Performance

Figure 1 indicates that there were large individual differences in the time taken to complete the course, in the number of errors made on exams, and in the number of errors made in working through the text. The Pearson Product-Moment correlation between number of days to finish the course and errors made on the exams was 0.414 ($P < 0.05$); between number of days to finish and errors made in the book, $r = 0.43$ ($P < 0.05$); and between errors in the book and errors on exams, $r = 0.04$ (n.s.).

Work done in class was generally intensive. Although it was not prohibited, there was virtually no eating, sleeping or magazine reading. When asked why they did not take advantage of the freedom to leave class for a break, most students said they were acutely conscious of a time pressure, even though, objectively, there was more than enough time.

Questionnaire

There were five parts to the questionnaire. In the first part were 15 items comparing the course as taught against what they imagined it would have been under the lecture method. Each item was rated on a seven-point scale whose midpoint was "no difference between the course as it was given and a lecture course" and whose end points were "a lot more by the course as it was given" and "a lot less by the course as it was given." Since they did not actually take the course by the lecture method (except for four students who had previously failed or dropped the course when it was given by the lecture method), their judgments were necessarily between the course as it was taught and their impression of the lecture method from past experience.

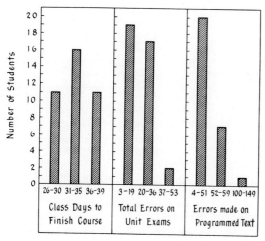

Fig. 1. Performance among students in time taken to finish the course, number of errors made on unit exams, and number of errors made in the programmed text.

Out of 18 items in Part I, 16 elicited relatively extreme judgments, all favoring the course as taught. Some of the judgments most favorable to the course were (1) "the amount of material fully understood" (x = 2.03: the verbal equivalent lies between "a lot more" and "a moderate amount more" by the course as given); (2) confidence in solving statistical problems (x = 2.11); (3) amount of time bored in class (x = 6.62: the verbal equivalent lies between "a lot" and "a moderate" amount less by the course as given); (4) the extent to which natural differences of ability among the students were taken into account (x = 2.00); (5) the extent to which the course failed to recognize you as an individual (x = 6.22). All of these findings agree with Keller's (1967).

In Part II, the students ranked a list of 13 features of the course in the order of "their importance to you". The fact that students have very different past histories of academic performance is reflected by the high variability of the rankings. The item receiving the highest mean rank (x = 2.65) and the lowest variability was "Being able to work at your own pace". The item receiving the next highest rank (x = 4.89) was "Taking an exam on each set", followed by "Not being penalized for mistakes on exams by lowering the grade (x = 5.54)".

Table 1 shows which features of the course received the first five ranks as a function of cumulative grade point average. All groups agree that self-pacing is most important. Al-

though agreement is close on the remaining four items shown in the table, there are important differences. While all groups consider grading contingencies important, those who have been well rewarded in the past value means (Item 3) above ends (Items 11 and 12), whereas those who have been poorly rewarded in the past value ends (Items 11 and 12) above means (Item 3).

Section III asked for absolute judgments on a five-point scale concerning the difficulty of exams, amount of work required for exams, adequacy of book, and amount of vocal instruction. The mid-point was "about right" and the extremes were "much more than necessary" and "much less than necessary". The means of the judgments were all within half a scale point of the midpoint and the variability was very small (range of the Average Deviation was 0.05 to 0.63).

Section IV asked for personal evaluations of the teaching assistant and instructor on strictness of grading, extent to which they were helpful and encouraging, and their skill in explaining material. With one exception, the means of the judgments were close to but on the favorable side of the mid-point of a seven-point scale. The exception occurred on the item concerning the instructor's grading of exams. The mean judgment was 3.54, which deviates slightly from the midpoint towards the "too strict" end of the scale.

The results of Section V, which asked the students to predict their future choices between the type of course as given and the lecture method, are shown in Table 2. Their responses favored the operant method, but did not show a willingness to give up the lecture method entirely.

Table 1

Features of the course receiving the first five ranks as a function of students' cumulative grade point average (on a four-point grading scale).

	GPA	
3.0 and Above	2.5 and Above	Below 2.5
8	8	8
3	3	11
11	12	12
12	11	3
13	13	1

Note—The numbers designate the following items in the list of features to be ranked.
1. Being able to move around or take a break when you felt like it.
3. Taking an exam on each set.
8. Being able to work at your own pace.
11. Not being penalized for mistakes by lowering the grade.
12. Knowing you would get an A if you did everything asked of you.
13. Being asked to correct mistakes on exams.

Table 2

The number of students willing to take future courses taught by operant versus lecture method.

Question	Yes	No
Would you take another course like this one in statistics?	29	6
Would you take another course by the lecture method in statistics?	10	26
Would you take another course in psychology by the lecture method?	34	1
Would you take another course in psychology taught like this one?	27	6
Would you take another course like this one in subjects besides statistics and psychology?	29	6

Note—The responses do not add to the same total for each question due to several missing answers.

In answer to the question, "What did you like most about the course?", 19 of 37 mentioned self-pacing. Other frequent responses were "receiving positive reinforcement for each unit" and "having immediate knowledge of results". Only one of the students mentioned something other than a programmed contingency.

By contrast, many answers to the question, "What did you like least about the course?", were irrelevant to the teaching method used (*e.g.,* "having to take the course in the psychology building, which is extremely ugly and sterile").

The final section, entitled simply "Comments", contained many remarks favorable to the course, the instructor, and the teaching assistant. The most frequent theme of these comments and also of conversations before class was the need for more courses taught by these methods. The enthusiasm of students for the method used, although it is not as easily interpreted as numerical data to specific questions, was astonishing in its volume and repetitiveness. One student asked three days in a row if he was really going to get an A for meeting the instructor's demands.

In order to answer questions concerning the effects of individual performance differences on attitudes towards the course, the students were divided into groups based on their cumulative grade point averages, the number of class days required to complete the course, and the number of errors made on the unit exams.

The data in Table 3 do not show any discernible effect of grade point average or number of class days to complete the course on questionnaire ratings. The number of errors made on exams is a different story. On most of the items in Part I, the groups (C2 and C3) that made the most errors on the exams had mean ratings more favorable to the course than the group (C1) that made the fewest errors on exams. To complete the symmetry of this relationship between number of errors and attitude towards the course, the group (C3) with the most errors gave ratings more favorable to the course than the group (C2) that made an intermediate number of errors on 11 of the 18 items of Part I.

Item 6 of Part I deserves special mention because of the high frequency with which boredom is ascribed to operant methods of instruction. The item asks ". . . what per cent of the time were you bored in class?" A rating of seven means "a lot less by the course as given". The group with the highest grade point average had a mean rating of 6.92 with an average deviation of 0.15 ($N = 12$) The middle and lowest groups had mean ratings of 6.38 (A.D. $= 0.95$) and 6.58 (A.D. $= 0.62$) respectively.

Of 38 students taking the course, 37 received As, one received a B[3], and no one received an Incomplete.

DISCUSSION

In Keller's course (1967) 20% of the students took Incompletes and another 19% failed or dropped the course. In McMichael and Corey's course (1969), 12% of the contingently-managed group dropped the course. The fact that there were no dropouts in the course described here is probably due in part to its being given in summer school when many students attempt to meet curriculum requirements.

Another reason may have been the contingencies used in grading. The over-all requirement for an A may be thought of as a second-order multiple schedule in which the student had to complete a fixed number of work units (24), each requiring a variable amount of work [FR24(VRx)]. The consequence of completing each unit may be a combination of events including (1) the satisfaction of passing the unit exams (2) the opportunity to proceed, (3) the confidence produced by near-perfect performance and (4) advancing faster than other students. Meeting the overall requirement produced three academic credits of A and, to judge from the questionnaires, various pleasant affective states. Failure to complete the course not only produced an undesirable grade, but it negated all the work done before quitting. Many students said they would have been satisfied with a grade lower than A, so the contingencies should thwart the option of mediocre performance, providing the instructor has chosen to require A-quality work and has made this clear in his work contract with the students. The perseverance usually seen in ratio schedules (Ferster and Skinner, 1957, pp. 39-41) coupled with an unwelcome event contingent on quitting may have been sufficient to prevent dropping-out in this course.

The frequently heard charge that programmed texts are boring, particularly to students may or may not be true, but a distinction should be made between the boredom attributable to the text itself and that attributable to a set of contingencies that includes a programmed text. As a record of feelings about

---

[3] Of 38 students, 37 received an A and one, who went through the course in his own way without consulting the instructor, received a B.

Table 3

Comparisons of mean ratings on Part I of the questionnaire as a function of grade-point average, time taken to complete course, and number of errors on exams. Entries are the number of items from a total of 18 on which the mean rating of one group favored the course more than the mean rating of another.

Grade-Point Average		Time to Finish Course		Errors on Exams		
$A_1 > A_2$	$A_1 > A_3$	$B_1 > B_2$	$B_1 > B_3$	$C_1 > C_2$	$C_1 > C_3$	$C_2 > C_3$
9	11	9	9	3	4	7

A_1—grade-point average of 3.0 or greater
A_2—grade-point average between 2.5 and 3.0
A_3—grade-point average less than 2.5
B_1—up to 35 days
B_2—between 36 and 40 days
B_3—between 41 and 45 days
C_1—between 4 and 15
C_2—between 16 and 25
C_3—between 26 and 53

the set of contingencies used in this course, the questionnaire data indicate that no one was bored, least of all the students with the highest grade-point averages. A related criticism is the charge that programmed learning is too easy, but all three grade-point groups judged that they had done a moderate to a lot more work than they would have done in a lecture course, and none of the groups thought the grading of exams was lenient, so it is safe to conclude that none of the groups thought the course too easy. The questionnaire items dealing with (1) the amount of personal contact with the instructor, (2) the extent to which natural differences of ability was taken into account, and (3) the extent to which the student was treated as an individual all received highly favorable ratings regardless of grade point average, time taken to finish the course, or number of errors made on exams. The agreement among students, given these differences, was the most surprising finding in the questionnaire data. It seems highly likely that the favorable attitudes reported were a function of the success that all but one student experienced. Providing that the success is earned in a way that meets acceptable academic criteria, this would seem to be an uncontroversial outcome. The experience of success may also explain the paradoxical result recorded in Table 3. Those who made the most errors liked the course most; perhaps because they were successful in spite of their errors.

The behavior of the students in this course also bears on the much discussed issue of student-faculty contact. Although they were friendly and talkative (especially about the teaching method being used) outside of class hours, they chose to limit their contacts with the instructor during class hours to matters concerning the content of the course, in spite of the fact that they could have had conversation with the instructor at any time simply by raising their hand. The great majority refused the offer of supplementary lectures and most students cut short attempts by the instructor to talk about anything but the subject matter. As one student put it, "With the chance of finishing the course early, why should we waste time talking to you?" Keller (1965) also reported that attendance at lectures given as supplements to his course in introductory psychology were poorly attended. This raises the possibility that the amount and kind of contact that students seek from faculty is not some sort of behavioral invariant, but rather a function of the learning conditions operative in a given course. At the very least, this finding falsifies the generalization that social contact between student and instructor during class is a necessary condition for effective learning.

The correlations between performance measures were much smaller than would be expected on the view that these measures are largely determined by the students' personalities. Knowing how many errors a student made on the programmed text, for example, was not useful in predicting his rate of progress or his exam performance. The fact that planned contingencies can produce low correlations among performance measures shows that performance is not an invariant beyond the instructor's ability to change, but rather an outcome that can be made sensitive to classroom conditions. This implies that the instructor bears a good part of the responsibility for arranging the conditions that produce high-level perform-ance.

The view that the student bears some re-sponsibility for his own performance is equi-vocally supported by the present data. Table 1 shows that students can identify the major conditions of learning that led them to high levels of performance. Of 13 features of the course given to them for ranking, the students ranked them in nearly the same order of im-portance as the instructor. This finding is equivocal, however, because it is possible that students do not know how to put these condi-tions of learning into an effective combination. It is also an open question whether they would have identified the important contingencies at all without at least one exposure to their effec-tiveness.

There were, of course, sizable individual dif-ferences in performance, but these were not considered in assigning grades. Their value to the students is evident, however, in that the brighter and harder working students finished the course earlier. As part of the instructor's explanation to the students of the contingen-cies in the course, it was announced that per-formance differences were relevant to grades only if a student failed to do quality work even under optimal conditions. It could then be justifiably said that a student was not capa-ble of earning an A. It was further explained, however, that (1) the conditions for this course were probably not optimal, and (2) given university entrance requirements, every-one present could do A-level work. In conse-quence of this rationale, it was decided that a grade of B or C would mean only that a stu-dent had not done the work, not that he could not do it. Under the conditions of the course, therefore, the practice of employing grades to designate ability levels could not be justified and was not used for that purpose. Instead, either a student did all the work required and received an A, or he failed to do some of the work and got an Incomplete.

The number and role of staff in this course with 38 students was very different from the staffing of similar efforts aimed at large groups. Both Keller (1967) and Malott (1969) em-ployed a hierarchy of personnel while, in the present case, there were only two staff mem-bers and the hierarchical distinction between them was deliberately minimized. It would ap-pear that staffing can take many forms, pro-viding basic contingencies are met.

The most frequent argument in favor of operant methods in education is that with ever-increasing student populations they are a fiscal necessity. The fact that an operant ap-proach worked well in a small group should help to highlight its educational value as well.

REFERENCES

Elzey, F. F. *A programmed introduction to statistics.* Belmont, Calif.: Wadsworth, 1966.

Keller, F. S. "Goodbye Teacher . . ." *Journal of Ap-plied Behavior Analysis,* 1968, **1**, 79-89. [Article 1]

Keller, F. S. Neglected rewards in the educational process. Proceedings 23rd American Conference of Academic Deans, Los Angeles, Jan., 1967. Pp. 9-22.

Keller, F. S. In a talk given to the Center for Research in Human Learning at the University of Minnesota, 1965.

Ferster, C. B. and Skinner, B. F. *Schedules of rein-forcement.* New York: Appleton-Century-Crofts, 1957.

Malott, R. W. and Svinicki, J. G. *Contingency man-agement in an introductory psychology course for 1000 students.* Western Michigan University. Un-published.

Skinner, B. F. *The technology of teaching.* New York: Appleton-Century-Crofts, 1968.

McMichael, J. S. and Corey, J. R. Contingency man-agement in an introductory psychology course pro-duces better learning. *Journal of Applied Behavior Analysis,* 1969, **2**, 79-83.[Article 2]

Received 27 August 1969.
(Revised 7 June 1970.)

5

THE ROLE OF PROCTORING IN PERSONALIZED INSTRUCTION [1]

John Farmer[2], Gerald D. Lachter,
Joel J. Blaustein, and Brett K. Cole

The effect of amount of student-proctor interaction was investigated within the framework of Keller's (1968) method of personalized instruction. College students enrolled in introductory psychology were randomly assigned to five groups: 0%, 25%, 50%, 75%, and 100%, reflecting the percentage of units on which each student was proctored. The results indicated that (a) the proctored students were superior to the nonproctored students as measured by final examination performance, (b) for the proctored groups, the amount of proctoring did not differentially affect final examination performance, and (c) the major effect of increased proctoring was an acceleration of the rate of progress through the course.

The variables emphasized in traditional teaching methods have recently been subjected to critical scrutiny. Both in the laboratory and the classroom, behavior change can be effectively evaluated and controlled only after some objective behavior has been selected and reliably measured. Such objective or active responding is not emphasized in the lecture system in which the student is treated as a passive recipient of information (Corey and McMichael, 1970). More importantly, events or procedures capable of producing those changes in behavior that are the concern of any teaching method have seldom been detailed in terms of their schedule of presentation; nor have investigators described the effects of these procedures on the behavior of the individual student, behavior from which academic achievement is then inferred (Skinner,

1968). Personalized instruction (Keller, 1966), however, focuses upon the specific objective behaviors of the individual student. These behaviors are differentiated and maintained by presentation schedules of classroom events (such as a passing test grade) that function as reinforcers. Recent investigations of personalized instruction have shown this procedure to be more effective than the traditional lecture system in the following ways: (a) students earned higher grades in personalized instruction courses than in lecture courses (Keller, 1966, 1968); (b) final exam performance was better after personalized instruction courses than after lecture courses (McMichael and Corey, 1969); (c) in a retest one full semester after completion of the course, superior performance was maintained among students who had received personalized instruction (Corey, McMichael, and Tremont, *unpublished*).

The use of proctors is essential to the success of personalized instruction. The indispensable functions of proctors have been described in detail by Keller (1968). The most important tasks of proctors include: (1) the careful scheduling of reinforcing events, which, to be effective, must immediately follow the desired variant of a student's behavior; (2) increasing the chances that the desired variants will appear in the indi-

---

[1]Portions of this paper were presented at the meetings of the Eastern Psychological Association, Washington, D. C., April, 1968.

[2]The final version of this manuscript was completed without the guidance of its originator, Dr. John Farmer. His untimely death deprived his co-authors and colleagues of his innovative and constructively critical approach to the teaching methods discussed and evaluated here. The co-authors wish to acknowledge their immeasurable debt, express their gratitude for this opportunity of collaboration, and assume full responsibility for the statements to which any criticism may be addressed.

From *Journal of Applied Behavior Analysis,* 1972, *5,* 401–404; copyright 1972 by the Society for the Experimental Analysis of Behavior, Inc.

vidual student's repertoire of behavior. Basically, this is done by explaining the course material and detailing the cues on which correct differential responses depend.

The present investigation attempted to ascertain the relative effectiveness of various proportions of proctored instruction.

METHOD

Subjects

The experimental subjects were 124 undergraduate students in two sections of Introductory Psychology at Queens College of the City University of New York. No knowledge of the procedure to be used was available to these students before the first course meeting. During the course of the term, seven students dropped the course. Three were from the 0% group, one from the 50% group and three from the 100% group. The data of these students were not included in the analyses.

Procedure

The course material, which was taken from *Principles of psychology* by F. S. Keller and W. N. Schoenfeld (1950), and *Analysis of behavior* by J. G. Holland and B. F. Skinner (1961), was divided into 20 units of approximately 20 pages each. Each unit consisted of a reading assignment, study guide, and test. A unit was passed only when a student had achieved a perfect score on the test associated with that unit; he was then allowed to proceed to the next unit. Each student was required to take as many alternate forms of each test as was necessary to achieve a perfect score. Students were permitted to take only one test per class session, each test being graded during that class session. Proctors were students from previous semesters who had demonstrated mastery of the course material. The experimental subjects were randomly assigned to each of the five proctoring conditions: 0% (N = 25), 25% (N = 24), 50% (N = 25), 75% (N = 24), and 100% (N = 19), indicating the percentage of 20 units on which the student was proctored. The tests of the 0% group were never proctored. These students were informed that they had passed or failed a test by the end of the class session in which the test was taken. The correct answers were written in the test booklets, and the booklets were redistributed during the next class session. The other groups were treated exactly like the 0% group, except that a certain percentage of the units (*i.e.,* all tests for those selected units) were graded by a proctor in the student's presence. For the 25, 50, 75, and 100% conditions, all tests taken on 5, 10, 15, and 20 units respectively, were graded in the student's presence.

The final examination consisted of a total of 120 questions, 61 multiple choice and 59 true-false, and was designed to sample equally the material from the 20 units comprising the course without repeating questions already used on unit readiness quizzes.

RESULTS

The Newman-Keuls method (Winer, 1962) for tests of differences between pairs of means revealed that all the proctored groups (25% to 100%) required significantly fewer tests for unit mastery than did the unproctored group (0%). The q values (4112) obtained for the several comparisons were as follows: 0% *versus* 100%, $q = 4.91$, $p < 0.05$; 0% *versus* 75%, $q = 4.43$, $p < 0.05$; 0% *versus* 50%, $q = 4.70$, $p < 0.05$; 0% *versus* 25%, $q = 3.95$, $p < 0.05$. All other comparisons were non-significant. That is, none of the proctored groups differed significantly from one another. Since the frequency of test-taking was fixed at one test per class session, the data in Figure 1 also indicated acceleration in class progress when any amount of proctoring greater than 0% was employed. The final exam performance shown in Figure 1 was also clearly improved by proctoring. Among the proctored groups, different proportions of proctoring did not differentially effect exam scores $F(3.88) < 1.00$). The proctored students, however, were significantly superior to the non-proctored students in final exam scores ($p < 0.02$, $F(1115) = 5.73$). The final exam questions were selected from sources other than the unit tests used throughout the course in an effort to prevent any ceiling effect that might have obscured differences among proctored and unproctored groups.

In addition, at the beginning of the next semester the same final exam was given to 100 students registered in Introductory Psychology courses before they had received any course material or any course instruction. This "operant-level" determination yielded chance performance on the test (a score of 45) by this uninstructed group. The value of the scores reported in Figure 1 thus represented improvements in test performance resulting from either proctored or unproctored class activities.

DISCUSSION

The clearest conclusion to be drawn from these results is that some proctoring (25% or

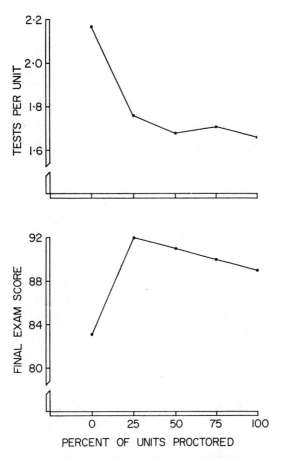

Fig. 1. Tests per unit and final examination score as a function of per cent of units proctored. The points for the tests per unit function were obtained by dividing the total number of tests taken by the total number of units passed for each group. The final exam score function represents the average score for each group, on a test with a possible maximum score of 120.

more of the units taken) is both necessary and sufficient to improve a student's rate of progress. With proctoring, the student achieved a required level of mastery (in the current study, a perfect score on a test for each unit) with less exposure to test materials, and in less time than he would have without proctoring. The greater achievement in a fixed time period, such as a semester, is clearly linked to the use of proctors. However, in cases where less-definitive conditions are ostensibly responsible for progress, slow, and therefore less progress by a student during a fixed time is often interpreted as a chronic deficit in the student's ability or motivation. Since proctoring, as opposed to total lack of proctoring, can be clearly shown to affect rate of student's progress, arguments that attribute lack of progress to incontrovertible deficits on the part of the student may lose plausibility.

While some proctoring is both necessary and sufficient to improve a student's rate of progress in a course, proctoring of all units (100% group) is not necessary for such improvement. Lesser proportions of proctoring allow intermittent scheduling of proctoring without sacrificing the benefits of such assistance. Proctors can thus accelerate the progress of more students in the same amount of time and with no loss in effectiveness.

In addition to being associated with slow rates of progress in the course, the no-proctoring condition was inefficient from a manpower or cost standpoint. The subjects in the no-proctoring condition required an average of 42 tests, whereas subjects in the 50% proctored condition required only 30 tests on the average, 15 of which (assuming the mean number of tests per unit was taken on each proctored unit) were graded in the student's presence. Thus, in this example, when the number of proctored tests was reduced by changing the per cent of proctored units from 50% to 0%, for every test not proctored, an average of one more test had to be given to each student.

Once shown to be feasible, intermittent proctoring may be desirable for reasons other than minimizing the number of personnel to staff a course adequately. The purpose of proctoring is not, nor should it be, to make the student dependent on unique information or service from the proctor. The advantage of proctoring is to provide training that enables the student to maintain and extend his academic achievement even in the absence of proctoring assistance. That proctoring should foster such independence is its most prominent recommendation. With intermittent proctoring comes, first, the means to increase academic progress, and second, a technique that determines the maintenance of progress over those periods when proctoring does not occur. It is, in essence, a self-evaluating system and can be measured directly to substantiate the adequacy and effectiveness of that technique.

Finally, the use of students as proctors under the guidance of professional teachers, clearly extends the efficiency and effectiveness of the teaching staff. This extension, together with intermittent yet efficacious use of proctors, may provide the means to relieve overburdened teachers.

REFERENCES

Corey, J. R. and McMichael, J. S. *Using personalized instruction in college courses.* New York: Appleton-Century-Crofts, 1970.

Corey, J. R., McMichael, J. S., and Tremont, P. J. *Long-term effects of personalized instruction in an introductory psychology course.* Unpublished paper presented at the meetings of the Eastern Psychological Association, Atlantic City, N.J., 1970.

Holland, J. G. and Skinner, B. F. *The analysis of havior.* New York: McGraw-Hill, 1961.

Keller, F. S. A personal course in psychology. In R. Ulrich, T. Stachnik, and J. Mabry, (Eds), *Control of human behavior.* Glenview, Illinois: Scott Foresman, 1966. [Article 37]

Keller, F. S. "Goodbye, teacher . . ." *Journal of Applied Behavior Analysis.* 1968, 1, [Article 1]

Keller, F. S. and Schoenfeld, W. N. *Principles of psychology.* New York: Appleton-Century-Crofts, 1950.

McMichael, J. S. and Corey, J. R. Contingency management in an introductory psychology course produces better learning. *Journal of Applied Behavior Analysis,* 1969, 2, [Article 2]

Skinner, B. F. *The technology of teaching.* New York: Appleton-Century-Crofts, 1968.

Winer, B. J. *Statistical principles in experimental design.* New York: McGraw-Hill, 1962.

Received 12 July 1971.
(Revised 18 January 1972.)

6

A FURTHER STUDY OF PERSONALIZED INSTRUCTION FOR STUDENTS IN LARGE UNIVERSITY CLASSES[1]

David G. Born and Emily W. Herbert [2]

The 161 students enrolling in a beginning psychology course were taught using a variant of Keller's personalized instructional procedures. Course material was divided into twelve units and complete mastery of the material in each unit was demonstrated with a short written examination and a brief interview conducted by a more advanced student. Students could progress through the course material at their own rate. Data are reported on the number of students who withdrew from the course, when they withdrew, and characteristics of their performance prior to withdrawal. For students who completed the course, data on rate of completion of course requirements and level of mastery of course material are presented. Furthermore, student evaluation of various facets of the course are summarized. Of special interest is the finding that student test evaluators were rated as a very favorable feature of the course, and that there was no apparent distinction made between graduate-student and undergraduate evaluators. This suggests that the instructional manpower pool might be extended through the careful use of undergraduates in the college classroom.

RECENTLY, Keller (3, 4) described a set of procedures for providing individualized (personalized) instruction to students in large university classes. Although there are a great many ways in which Keller's course procedures differ from traditional procedures, most important would seem to be a de-emphasis of the lecture method, in which the instructor engages in all of the important behaviors, and an emphasis on procedures which make students engage in the important behaviors. The course includes several interesting features: (a) course material is divided into units and a student must pass a written examination on each unit of material with a perfect score before receiving the next unit of material, (b) students may progress through the course at their own rate, and (c) evaluation of student examinations is done by students who have earlier mastered the course material. A recent comparison of the Keller method with the lecture method has been reported by McMichael and Corey (5), and the results indicate that the Keller procedures generate a higher quality of student performance than the more traditional lecture-discussion techniques. Also, Ferster and Perrott (2) have described a similar set of course procedures, and Ferster (1) has reported data showing how some aspects of the Ferster and Perrott procedures affect student rate of progress and level of mastery of course material. It is the purpose of the present paper to report still other effects of the Keller procedures on the performance of students in a Keller-type course.

METHOD

Student Composition and Teaching Personnel

The 161 students who enrolled in the introductory psychology course during the 7-week summer session, 1968, had no prior knowledge that an unconventional teaching format would be used in the course. The teaching personnel included the course instructor and ten student proctors. Five of the student proctors were graduate students and five were undergraduates, all psychology majors.

Procedure

Although the course described in this paper was similar in principle to the course described by Keller (4), there were many differences in procedural detail and course materials. Some of the more important features of this course follow.

Materials. The course material was presented to students mainly in the form of textbooks, lectures, and movies. In addition, there were discussion opportunities during which information about course related subjects, additional examples of principles, and tutoring of assigned material was provided at student request.

The primary text was J. R. Millenson's Principles of Behavioral Analysis (7). Additionally, students were required to read Ellen Reese's Analysis of Human Operant Behavior (9), and selected readings from Control of Human Behavior by Ulrich, Stachnick, and Mabry (10).

A lecture was given once a week. The lecture topic was selected on the grounds that it would be of interest to both students and the lecturer and that it would provide students with an opportunity to hear descriptions of psychological principles being used in a different context than in their assigned readings. The lectures were concerned almost exclusively with the application of psychological principles to a variety of topics, and therefore served primarily to supplement the more formal written materials.

A movie was scheduled once a week and provided an opportunity for students to observe many psychological principles in action. As with lectures, a schedule of movie topics was published and distributed early in the quarter so students would know in advance exactly what topics were covered in each movie.

The weekly discussion session provided the students with an opportunity to acquire additional information about a topic, get coaching around sections

From *The Journal of Experimental Education*, Vol. 40, No. 1, Fall 1971.

of the course material with which they were having difficulty, or discuss any of the readings, course procedures, or related topics.

On the first day of class the students were informed that they would be required to pass a series of examinations over all of the written course material, but that they would not be tested over the contents of movies, lectures, or discussion sections. However, they were encouraged to attend movies, lectures, and discussions on the grounds that these events provided an opportunity to learn something "extra" in the course.

Examinations and Grading

Figure 1 is a flow chart showing the sequence of activities for students progressing through a personalized instruction course. The course material was divided into twelve study units, each accompanied by a unit examination. A final exam sampled materials covered in all twelve study units. A study guide, which identified new terms and concepts and introduced the reading assignment, was prepared for each unit and given to the students. Each unit examination, consisting of a mixture of ten to fifteen fill-in, sentence completion, and short answer essay questions, could only be passed with a "perfect" score; errors on examinations resulted in the student being asked to do additional studying before he returned to take a different examination over the same material. It should be noted that there was no penalty associated with less than perfect performance except that the student was not allowed to progress in the course; the unit examinations had to be taken in numerical order.

Upon completing an examination a student brought his exam directly to his student proctor who judged each answer correct or incorrect, asked the student to clarify any answer too ambiguous to evaluate, and generally queried the student for information related to the reading assignment (this was especially true when examination answers appeared to have been memorized). For each unit examination successfully passed, a student earned points toward his final grade. A total of 70 points was earned by passing all twelve unit examinations, and the final examination was worth 30 points. The total points required for the various letter grades were: 95 or higher, A; 90-94.9, B; 85-89.9, C; 80-84.9, D; below 80, E. Although the final examination could be taken only once (i.e., was not repeatable) two early examining dates were scheduled for students who finished the unit examinations and wanted to complete the course early. One of these early examinations was given at the end of the sixth week, and the other at the end of the seventh week. The regular final examination was scheduled on the last day of the eighth week.

RESULTS AND DISCUSSION

Course Withdrawals

Of the 161 students who originally registered in the course, eighteen withdrew. Five withdrew during the first week of the quarter, and the remainder withdrew between the third and sixth weeks. Eleven of these eighteen students filled out a questionnaire asking for reasons for their withdrawal. Of the eleven, only one said she didn't like the way the course was conducted, and five said the course was too much work when added to their other class and work requirements. The other reasons given for withdrawal were irrelevant to the course itself. Of the thirteen

FIGURE 1.

FLOW CHART SHOWING PROCEDURES FOR PROGRESSING THROUGH A PERSONALIZED INSTRUCTION COURSE

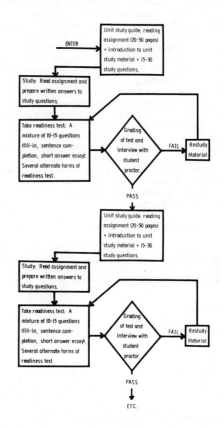

students withdrawing after the first week of the quarter, all students were behind the minimum rate of progress required to successfully complete course requirements by the end of the academic quarter. Five of the thirteen students had not successfully passed the examination on the first unit of material at the time of withdrawal, and only three of the students had completed as much as 25 percent of the material (i.e., three unit examinations). Of the five students who had not successfully passed the first unit examination at the time of withdrawal, only one of them had actually attempted to take that examination. Of the other eight students who withdrew from the course after the first week, only one appeared to be having difficulty with course material as determined by the number of examinations repeated; although several of these students had failed one test, only one student had failed as many as two tests. Thus, the reasons for withdrawal would appear to be more closely related to difficulty in preparing for examinations than to difficulty in passing examinations.

Attendance

Figure 2 shows attendance at various course activities. The uppermost figure shows attendance on days set aside for testing. (To be recorded as in attendance, a student had to take a unit exam.) As may be seen from the figure there is little difference in the attendance on the Tuesday and Thursday weekdays and a generally lower level of attendance on the Saturday testing day. Furthermore, it may be noted that there is a slight increase in the number of tests taken over the entire quarter. This increase contrasts sharply with a similar record of student attendance over successive weeks of t h e academic quarter at films, lectures, and scheduled discussion sections. These data may be seen in the lower half of Figure 2. Based on these data it would a p p e a r that student interest in taking tests increased slightly as the quarter continued, whereas student interest in extra events decreased steadily during the quarter. Some of the reasons for this difference in attendance will be discussed in a later section of this paper. In passing, it is of at least nominal interest that students who withdrew from the course after the first week generally had not attended lectures, films, or discussion sessions. Why students who are having difficulty preparing for examinations would not come to discussion sessions at which they had opportunities to get help with presumably difficult material is only a matter of conjecture. However, it is at least possible that these students had not made the effort to prepare for the tests, and as a result their attendance at discussions sessions would not be especially meaningful.

Course Completion

Of the 121 students taking the final examination seventeen of them had not completed the twelve study units. Among the students completing the c o u r s e there was considerable variation in rate of comple-

FIGURE 2.

ATTENDANCE AT CLASS ACTIVITIES*

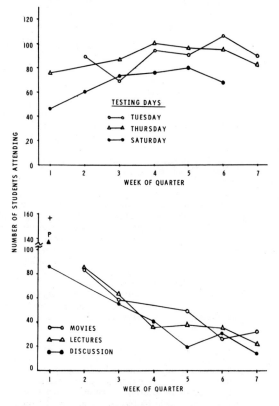

*The upper panel shows the number of students attending class on testing days; the lower panel shows the number attending weekly movies, lectures, and discussion sections as the quarter progressed

FIGURE 3

FREQUENCY DISTRIBUTION OF FINAL LETTER GRADES

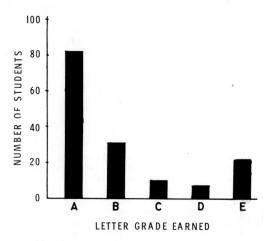

tion. One student took an examination on each testing day and passed successfully. This student completed the usual 8-10 week course at the start of the fifth week. Most students completed the course at the lowest possible rate. These rates are reflected in the number of students finishing the unit examinations in successive weeks of the course. The number of students finishing during the fifth week of the course was three, the number finishing during t h e sixth week was fifteen, the number finishing during the seventh week was thirty-seven, and the number of students finishing the course during t h e eighth week was sixty-six.

Of the possible points in t h e c o u r s e, thirty percent could be earned on the f i n a l examination. The final exam, it will be recalled, was not repeatable. This examination was made up of a mixture of multiple choice (50% of the items), short answer, and sentence completion items. A student who had successfully completed each unit examination needed a score on the final examination of at least 83 p e r cent to receive an A grade, 82-67 percent to receive a B grade, 66-50 percent to receive a C grade, 49-34 percent to receive a D grade. That the examination was not difficult for students having already successfully passed each unit examination with a perfect score is shown by the frequency distribution of letter grades in Figure 3. This distribution of grades is markedly skewed, and is clearly atypical of the distribution most commonly associated with c o l l e g e course grading. At first glance, one puzzling point about this distribution is the number of lower grades in the course. These can be explained when one remembers that each unit examination was w o r t h a number of points, and all students did not pass all unit examinations. Students who received E grades did not earn the number of points necessary for higher grades and this group, with one exception, w a s made up of people who did not take the final examination, had not been in attendance for some time, and about which no withdrawal information from the registrar's office had been received at t h e t i m e grades were reported. The single exception in the E category was a girl who had completed ten units of material and wrote a very poor final examination. Grades of C and D were earned, without exception, by students who had not completed the necessary twelve unit examinations prior to taking the final. This distribution of grades is similar to that r e - ported by Keller (4).

Course Evaluation

Upon arriving for the final examination, each student was given a lengthy questionnaire asking for an evaluation of several features of the course. The questionnaire was administered prior to receipt of the final examination and prior to final grade assignments in the course.

Student evaluation of proctors. The procedures used in this course depend importantly upon student assistants in large numbers. Thus, it is crucial that students taking the course respond favorably to the student proctors. The questions asked about performance of proctors deliberately included terms (e. g., "challenging," "competent," etc.) which are often described as essential to high quality teaching performance. Figure 4 includes the distribution of student ratings on a variety of questions about proctor performance. This figure is somewhat complicated by the fact that there is an attempt to show similarities and differences between graduate student proctors and undergraduate proctors on these questions. In constructing this figure the graduate students who received the highest and the poorest overall student ratings are shown along with the undergraduates receiving the highest and lowest ratings. Beneath each set of frequency distributions may be seen the specific question to which the students responded, and the anchors on each end of a scale from 1-7 along which they could respond.

Perhaps the most striking thing about this figure is the similarity in ratings earned by the best graduate student and the best undergraduate. This similarity is made more striking when it is revealed that the best graduate student was a person one year from receiving her PhD, and the best undergraduate was a sophomore. Thus, although 5 years of training separated the best undergraduate and the best graduate proctor it is clearly the case that the students were not making their evaluations on matters which had to do with amount of college training. The poorest graduate proctor was in his second year of training and the poorest undergraduate was a college senior. In no case however, would one say that these poorer proctors were bad. Since the ratings were generally on the very high end of the scale, one can only conclude that the proctors were extremely successful in challenging students, helping students, etc. Interestingly, and perhaps most important, student evaluation of proctor competence was very favorable, without exception. Thus, in summary, from a student's point of view it would seem that other students can perform an important role in assisting in college instruction.

Student evaluation of lectures, movies, and discussion session. As previously mentioned, the lower half of Figure 1 shows the number of students attending class on lecture, movie, and discussion days. It may be seen that the manner in which attendance at these events drops over the course of the quarter

FIGURE 4.

FREQUENCY DISTRIBUTIONS OF STUDENT RATINGS OF THE MOST AND LEAST FAVORED GRADUATE AND UNDERGRADUATE PROCTORS*

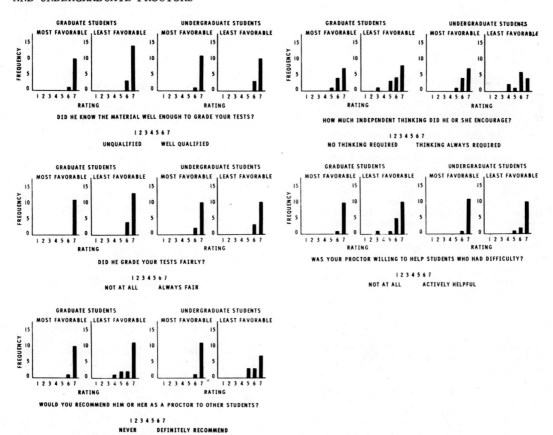

*Beneath each set of histograms is the question which was rated and the anchors provided for the 7-point rating scale

is very similar regardless of the event scheduled. At least one explanation of these data is that none of these events were interesting. Contrary to this suggestion is the data drawn from the questionnaire completed at the end of the course. In response to the question "Were the lectures interesting?" frequencies of student responses, on a 7-point scale ranging from not at all interesting to very interesting, were as follows: 1 - 0 students, 2 - 3 students, 3 - 8 students, 4 - 10 students, 5 - 22 students, 6 - 29 students, 7 - 40 students. Although the lectures were rated slightly more interesting than movies and discussion sessions, these latter events received favorable ratings, with discussions rated least interesting of the three. Apparently, making events such as lectures interesting is not a guarantee that even a modest number of students will regularly attend. Most likely, by making grades independent of lecture content, and by providing students with handouts which identified the most important aspects of the reading assignments, we had taken from lectures at least two of the important reasons for regular attendance. Experimental verification of the importance of these two factors in maintaining attendance at lectures in large classes remains to be obtained.

General course evaluation. In response to the question, "Would you recommend this course to other students?" only seven of the 145 students completing the course responded "no." For all but one of the seven students not recommending the course, the proctors were evaluated very favorably and the complaints centered around the course material being uninteresting and too much work. Also, of the seven students not recommending the course, none reported attending more than one movie, and four reported attending none at all. Three of these students did not attend a lecture and two of them reported attending as many as four lectures. Also, four of these students had not attended a discussion session, but one of them had attended six times.

The most frequent complaint about the course had to do with the very large amount of work required. Many students reported that the course demanded so much effort that it interfered considerably with their performance in other courses. An estimate of the actual work time was obtained from the separate unit examinations. For purposes of equalizing the unit work requirement, students were asked to estimate the time they spent preparing for each unit examination, and this estimate was entered at the top of each test form. Thus, for each student we had a record of the amount of time he estimated spending in preparation for each unit examination. The average reported time of preparation for each unit examination was approximately 4 hours. Recalling that there were twelve unit examinations to be passed, the average total preparation time for the course was approximately 48 hours. This turns out to be roughly comparable to the number of hours students would normally expect to spend in this course sitting in classroom lectures. It will be recalled that the course requirements included passing twelve unit examinations, which meant that students also had to come to class at least twelve days out of the academic quarter. Combining these figures it may be seen that average course requirements were approximately 60 hours. From these data it would seem that the amount of time required by the course was not more, and was probably less, than students would normally have spent taking the same course taught by the lecture method. (In this regard, it should be recalled that students generally did not attend lectures, movies, and discussion periods.) It should also be noted that in this course the average grade was A, where-

as in the usual lecture course the average grade is C. Thus, for at least a comparable number of hours invested in the course students achieved better letter grades than they would get in other courses. It is at least interesting that students complain about "difficulty" under these circumstances. It would appear that preparing for a course with a study guide and a textbook is considerably more "difficult" than preparing with a lecturer and a textbook. Indeed, students ranked this introductory psychology course as difficult, or nearly as difficult, as courses in chemistry, physics, and mathematics. From the present data it would appear that "difficulty" may be equated with hours required to fill course requirements.

CONCLUSIONS

The present paper reports several kinds of information about the effects of Keller's personalized instructional method which have not previously been available. Of special interest is the student evaluation of proctors and the very favorable ratings they received. This result, combined with what appears to be higher levels of student performance resulting from these procedures than with lecture procedures (5), suggest that through the use of student proctors the instructional manpower pool may be greatly increased to the advantage of all concerned.

Perhaps the most important advantage of personalized instruction, which may be seen in this paper and others (e.g., 1, 4, 8), is that with the lowered student/instructor ratios achieved by using student proctors, it becomes possible to gather information about individual student performance which is unobtainable in the large lecture hall. From this sort of information it should be possible to design educational techniques appropriate for today's students. At the very least, with data we may be able to justify our classroom activities to ourselves and to the general community.

FOOTNOTES

1. A majority of the credit for the education of students enrolled in this course must be given to Phil Christiansen, Bob Elton, J. D. Gill, Emily Herbert, John Jenkins, Rick Keller, Ron Menlove, Paula Nasfell, Joann Norton, and Howard Parker, the student proctors who volunteered their time and efforts.

2. Now at the Department of Human Development, University of Kansas, Lawrence.

REFERENCES

1. Ferster, C.B., "Individualized Instruction in a Large Introductory Psychology Course," The Psychological Record, 18:521-532, 1968.[Article 34]

2. Ferster, C.B.; Perrott, M.C., Behavior Principles, Appleton-Century-Crofts, New York, 1968.

3. Keller, J.S., "A Personal Course in Psychology," in Ulrich, R.; Stachnik, T.; Mabry, J., (eds.), Control of Human Behavior, Scott, Foresman, Inc., Glenview, Illinois, pp. 91-93, 1966. [Article 37]

4. Keller, F.S., "Goodbye, Teacher . . ." Journal of Applied Behavior Analysis, 1:79-89, 1968. [Article 1]

5. McMichael, J.S.; Corey, J.R., "Contingency Management in an Introductory Psychology Course Produces Better Learning," Journal of Applied Behavior Analysis, 2:79-83, 1969. [Article 2]

6. Mallott, R.W.; Whaley, D.L.; Ulrich, R.E., Analysis of Behavior: Principles and Applications, Wm. C. Brown and Co., Dubuque, Iowa, 1967.

7. Millenson, J.R., Principles of Behavioral Analysis, The Macmillan Co., New York, 1967.

8. Pennypacker, H.S., "Precision Teaching of an Undergraduate Program in Behavior Principles," paper reported at the meetings of the Midwestern Psychological Association, May, 1969.

9. Reese, Ellen, The Analysis of Human Operant Behavior, Wm. C. Brown and Co., Dubuque, Iowa, 1966.

10. Ulrich, R.; Stachnik, T.; Mabry, J. (eds.), Control of Human Behavior, Scott, Foresman, Inc., Glenview, Illinois, pp. 91-93, 1966.

7

PERSONALIZED INSTRUCTION
IN EDUCATIONAL PSYCHOLOGY*

Terry F. Nelson and David W. Scott

The recent introduction of personalized instruction, sometimes called "PSI" or the "Keller System," into the curricula of American colleges and universities has brought about a small-scale but important revolution in teaching methods at the college level. Inspired by the Experimental Analysis of Behavior and systematized in the experimental work and writings of Keller (1963, 1967, 1968, and 1970), personalized instruction involves a radical departure from most traditional and contemporary models of college teaching. Small, sequential units of work, each of which is mastered before further units are attempted, immediate grading of tests with opportunity for tutoring and remedial work, self-pacing, the minimal use of lectures for transmitting information, study objectives for each unit, and the involvement of undergraduate proctors in the teaching-learning process are the main features of personalized instruction.

The present study deals with the organization of a course in educational psychology within a personalized format and the results of its Winter, 1971, implementation within the Kalamazoo College curriculum. Texts used were Meachum and Wiesen, *Changing Classroom Behavior* (1969); Mager, *Developing Attitude Toward Learning*

*The authors wish to thank Kay Schichtel, who, with the second author, served as a teaching assistant in the course. We also wish to thank Professors Fred S. Keller and Jack L. Michael, both of Western Michigan University, for their invaluable assistance throughout the project.

(1968); Homme, et al., *How to Use Contingency Contracting in the Classroom* (1969); and Skinner, *The Technology of Teaching* (1968). Additional course readings from Michael (1970), Mager (1962), and Staats (1968) were included as well.

The course, through a major emphasis on applications of behavior principles to the classroom, was an effort to provide a scientific approach to classroom phenomenon. As was stated in the course syllabus, given to students on the first day of the course:

This course is designed to help the future teacher acquire a way of thinking about behavior. Our main concern will be the study of educational problems within the systematic framework of behavior theory as derived from the experimental analysis of behavior. This conceptual model will encourage you to make relevant observations that you would not ordinarily make and help you to formulate hypotheses that can be checked systematically against additional observation. This approach is based on the assumption that the beginning teacher cannot resort to a recall of detailed bits and pieces of research findings and "facts," as derived from traditional approaches to educational psychology, in order to understand behavior, deal with problems, and facilitate the learning process of pupils. Rather, we assume that you are forced to fall back on the economy of a theory; one which is functional and of relevance to behavior and educational practice.

Moreover, performance criteria and precise behavioral specifications were

From *Michigan Academician*, Vol. IV, No. 3, Winter 1972.

not only taught as essential to pedagogic success, but were inherent in the course structure itself. This alone may represent a minor breakthrough; consistency of this sort between a course content and course structure has been, at best, rare in traditional teacher education courses.

Former efforts in the implementation of personalized college instruction, in particular comparisons of personalized courses with other course formats, has well enough demonstrated the advantages of the personalized model to make further collection of similar data redundant (Green, 1969; Koen, 1970; McMichael and Corey, 1969; Nelson, 1970; Sheppard and MacDermot, 1970; Witters and Kent, 1970). We saw fit rather to devote our efforts to evaluating the effectiveness of each of the features of personalized instruction along with several traditional course features, and to isolating factors which might contribute to the continued improvement of the personalized format. As such, data were collected on patterns of student pacing, student achievement, and student reaction to the course material and to the teaching method.

METHOD

Seventy Kalamazoo College undergraduates enrolled for the course, listed in the college catalogue as Psychology 115: Educational Psychology. Prerequisite to the course is a one-quarter course in general psychology. The distribution of students by class was as follows: 8 freshmen, 30 sophomores, 13 juniors, 19 seniors. Of the 62 non-freshmen in the course, 15 were declared majors in psychology. Of the 32 juniors and seniors, 9 had declared an intention to secure secondary school teaching certification from the State of Michigan, toward which credit from Psychology 115 could be applied. A variety of different major fields were represented in the class enrollment.

In addition to the instructor regularly assigned to Psychology 115, two teaching assistants (TA's) were employed in the administration of the course. Each TA was a senior, and each had taken Psychology 115 at an earlier date. One TA received one unit (5 quarter hours) of course credit for her participation; the other received a small financial remuneration.

The duties performed specifically by the instructor were to lecture once per week; to organize, select, or write study and discussion materials for the course; to establish testing and grading policies; to evaluate term projects; and to assign final grades. The balance of instructional duties, including proctoring unit examinations and leading discussion groups, were shared fairly equally by the instructor and the two TA's.

To supplement the instructor's regularly assigned office and the lecture room assigned to Psychology 115, space was made available in the form of a large room containing several moveable tables and chairs, which was used both for testing and discussion. Attached to this large room were several smaller rooms, two of which served as offices for the TA's. The entire area was open and accessible to students and TA's during most of the entire day, Monday through Friday, and on Saturday mornings.

Reading material from the five texts and two additional sources was divided into twelve discrete units of work. A study guide was drawn up for each unit which included supplementary notes, objectives, and study questions which, if answered correctly, were to ensure adequate comprehension of the material in the unit. A unit examination and alternate examinations, each of which tapped the material covered in the study guide as completely and succinctly as possible, were also written for each unit. The examinations were chiefly of the short essay variety, requiring paragraph answers to five or six questions over the unit material. Multiple-choice and fill-in questions were interspersed where it was considered appropriate.

After the fourth, eighth, and twelfth units, hour-long review examinations were required of each student. The first review examination covered material from the first third of the course, and included questions which required integration of materials from each of the first four units. The second review examination similarly covered the second third, units five through eight, of the course. Material from all twelve units was included on the third or "final" review examination.

Students were required to purchase the five texts in the course. Other materials, including study guides, supplemental readings, and discussion materials were provided free of charge.

On the first day of class, students were given a syllabus which described the format of the course. It was made clear that they would have the opportunity to proceed through the twelve units of reading assignments, the twelve unit exams, and the three review exams at their own pace. Thus, they would not be held back by other students or forced to go ahead until they were ready to do so. In addition, the mastery criterion for unit advancement was explained and the reexamination policy stated. Students were given a sheet of Examination Guidelines also, describing the conditions under which they would be writing the unit exams. They were asked to respond to the exam questions in terms of their own understanding without the aid of notes or text since the objective of testing was to determine their readiness to proceed to further material. They were told to return the completed exam immediately to the instructor or TA who would evaluate and discuss it in their presence, and then determine whether they could proceed to the next unit or needed to restudy and take an alternate exam over the same material. They were also told that it would take approximately 30 to 40 minutes to write the exam to their satisfaction and have it discussed afterwards.

Additional course credit was available through attendance at weekly discussion sessions. To earn a discussion point, a student was required to read a selected article, respond to a series of study questions over the article, and hand the answered study questions in to the discussion leader. These discussion papers were then read by the instructional staff, commented upon, and handed back to the students the following week. It was thus possible to carry on written interaction between students and instructional staff as a supplement to the day-by-day testing operations and weekly discussion sessions. Lectures, given once per week, were designed to further explain, integrate, and supplement the text material and, perhaps, to "inspire" students to excel in the subject matter. Lectures generally lasted one hour. Discussions immediately followed them, and lasted a second hour.

A special interest project was also required of each student, due the tenth week of the quarter. Typical projects included research proposals based on the course readings, pilot studies including data collection and analysis, papers investigating the relevance of the course material to special problem areas in education, the writing of programmed units for particular subject matters, and designing courses or extended units of study on topics of major interest.

Grades for the course were determined on an absolute basis as follows: *1* the number of passed unit exams (12 exams, 5 points each, for a possible 60 points), *2* performance on the three one-hour review exams (3 exams, 5 points each, for a possible 15 points), *3* attendance, preparation, and participation in the discussion sessions (10 discussions, 1 point each, for a possible 10 points) and *4* the quality of the special interest project (1 project, worth 15 points, for a possible 15 points). Students accumulating points in the 90 to 100 range earned the grade of *A*, 80 to 89 points, *B*, 70 to 79 points, *C;* 60 to 69 points, *D;* and below 60 points, *F* (no credit).

The instructional staff kept explicit records of passed and failed examinations for each student, and the dates on which these examinations were taken. Data of this sort attest to the adequacy of both the instructional materials themselves and their sequential arrangement, and reveal information about how students are pacing themselves throughout the course.

Further data were obtained in the form of responses to a questionnaire given to the 49 students attending the last lecture-discussion session of the quarter. These 49 students included a representative cross section of the total enrollment; those who had completed all of the unit assignments by that date and those who had not. The questionnaire requested information of the students as to their attitudes toward the course and toward psychology, the amount of work the course required of them relative to other courses, and their feelings about the various features of the course and of the personalized system of instruction. A brief assessment of specific unit examinations, study guides, lectures, and discussion topics was included for use primarily in reviewing course materials for subsequent administration of the course.

RESULTS

Self-pacing is a feature of personalized instruction designed to respect individual differences in student ability and to respect the other outside demands placed upon students' time. The question of pacing as a dependent variable becomes crucial when students are allowed this freedom to proceed at their own rate through a course of instruction. Figure 1 shows a cumulative account of each review examination taken throughout the duration of the course, plotted against days

tests were available. Over the initial ten weeks of the quarter, testing took place six days a week. During the eleventh week, "finals week," testing was possible for the first three days. As such, after 21 days, or 3-1/2 calendar weeks, one-third of the total 63 testing days were over. After 42 days, or 7 calendar weeks, two-thirds of the available testing days had passed. As Figure 1 shows, after the 21st day of testing only 29 students, about 41 percent of the class, had taken the first review examination. After 42 days, 22 students, or 31 percent of the class, had taken the second review examination. At the end of the quarter, 63 students (90 percent), and as many as would do so, had taken the final review examination. Thus, although all unit tests and review exams were successfully completed by most students by the time testing was stopped and final grades computed, student procrastination was heavy.

It is interesting that, despite the procrastination, the self-pacing feature figured highly in the students' enjoyment of the course (see Table I). Moreover, 57 percent of the students responding to the evaluation questionnaire reported that they found themselves working "harder" than they did in most courses. The fact that the questionnaire was administered at a time when only 7 testing days remained may have influenced this result; Figure 1, particularly with respect to the later weeks, does seem to reflect a race by many students with the college calendar. The procrastination problem did not seem to lie, however, in subject matter difficulty; 88 percent of the students felt that the course material was either "about average in difficulty" or "quite easy to master." Sixty-nine percent of the students felt that there was "more" material presented in the course than is presented in most courses.

The grade distribution for the 70 students enrolled in Psychology 115 was negatively skewed with grades of *C* and *D* almost nonexistent. The

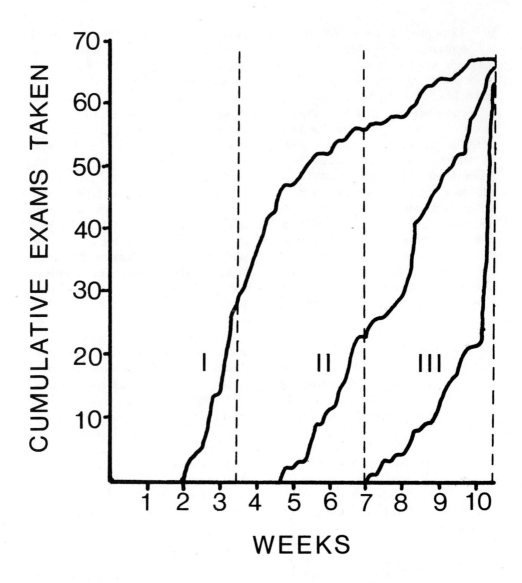

FIG. 1. Cumulative review examinations taken, plotted against testing days. The line marked "I" denotes first review examinations; that marked "II" denotes second review exams; that marked "III" denotes final review exams.

grade of *A* was earned by 54 percent of the students, the grade of *B* by 31 percent, while 3 students failed to receive credit for the course. This finding seems to be fairly common for personalized courses. Keller (1968) and Koen (1970) report very similar grade distributions.

Students were given a list of 12 features of the course and were asked to rank them, 1 to 12, in terms of *1* their importance to enjoyment and *2* their importance to learning during the presentation of the course. Table I presents all 12, with the mean and stan-

dard deviation of the "enjoyment" rankings each received. As was mentioned above, the "self-pacing" feature was most popular, followed closely by interactions with teaching personnel and the "small-step" feature of the course. Table II similarly presents "learning" rankings. Study guides and frequent testing received high average rankings, although these features were not ranked high for "enjoyment." In addition, 100 percent of the students responding to the questionnaire felt that the unit study guides were "helpful."

TABLE I
RANKING OF THE IMPORTANCE OF COURSE FEATURES
TO ENJOYMENT

FEATURE	ORDINAL RANKING	MEAN RANKING	SD
Self-pacing*	1	3.8	2.58
Interactions with the teaching assistants*	2.5	4.0	2.06
Interactions with the instructor*	2.5	4.0	2.38
Small steps*	4	4.1	2.02
Discussions	5	6.1	3.52
Study guides*	6	6.7	2.98
Special interest project	7	6.9	3.77
Films	8	7.2	3.48
Frequent tests*	9	7.6	2.77
Mastery criterion*	10	8.1	2.82
Lectures	11	9.4	1.84
Review examinations	12	10.0	2.26

*Features of personalized instruction.

Of special note is the rather poor showing, on both rankings, of such traditional classroom practices as lectures, discussions, films, and term projects. Students often rated each of these features, taken independently, "as good as" or "better than" those in most other courses. Only 27 percent of those responding to the questionnaire, however, felt that the lecture-discussion sessions "aided my progress and understanding," while 53 percent felt that they "had some positive effect" and 20 percent felt that they "were of little or no value." The students were also asked to pick from among the words "boring," "entertaining," "inspirational," "worthless," and "informative" the word which best described the lectures. "Informative" was chosen by 57 percent while only two respondents chose "inspirational" and only one picked "entertaining." The presentation of the material in the course, which de-emphasized the instructor's role as lecturer, was rated "quite good" by 77 percent. No respondent felt that the course was presented "poorly." The course was reported to be "quite interesting" by 87 percent and no student reported that he thought the course was "dull."

General attitudes toward the course and toward psychology seemed encouragingly favorable after the completion of the course. Most students, 73 percent, found themselves talking about the course "a lot" outside of class and 83 percent of the students were "quite interested" in learning more about psychology. Ninety percent said they definitely intend to take another course in psychology and in 84 percent of these cases, this course influenced their decision to do so. Ninety-five percent reported that they would take another self-paced course, if given the opportunity. If they had to do it all over again, 87 percent said they "would gladly" take Psychology 115.

DISCUSSION

The success of self-pacing, small steps of work, and interactions with the teaching personnel in positively influencing student enjoyment of Psychology 115—and the success of the study objectives and frequent tests in enhancing student learning—speaks well for personalized instruction as a means of imparting more than just a set of facts to be learned. In addition to acquiring a sound knowledge repertoire, students in the course received—

TABLE II
RANKING OF THE IMPORTANCE OF COURSE FEATURES
TO LEARNING.

FEATURE	ORDINAL RANKING	MEAN RANKING	SD
Study guides*	1	3.4	2.45
Small steps*	2	3.7	2.15
Frequent tests*	3	4.1	2.32
Mastery criterion*	4	5.2	3.45
Self-pacing*	5	5.4	3.38
Interactions with the teaching assistants*	6	5.9	2.53
Interactions with the instructor*	7	6.4	2.86
Review examinations	8	7.4	2.73
Special interest project	9	8.3	3.26
Lectures	10	8.9	2.45
Discussions	11	9.1	2.52
Films	12	10.1	2.03

*Features of personalized instruction.

in their own words—an "interesting course," "well-prepared," and one in which they were willing to "work harder" than usual. The students' final attitudes toward personalized instruction and toward the field of psychology speak for themselves. The overwhelming majority of students said they wanted, if possible, to take other personalized courses and courses in psychology. This finding has many implications for the problem of imparting "approach tendencies," ie, positive attitudes, toward college-level subject matters. As Mager (1968) has phrased it, "People tend to avoid the things they are hit with, whether it be a club, a stick, or a subject matter assignment." Personalized instruction may well provide a solution.

The apparent disfavor with which lectures, term papers, discussions, films, and other more traditional components of college instruction were received by Psychology 115 students should not necessarily be seen as an indictment of these college course features. Keller (1968) has alluded to the possible reinforcing value of special lectures and presentations (or the right to attend them) as consequences of success in self-paced course

work. It is not inconceivable, though it is unusual to think so, that term papers and other "special interest" type projects can be employed similarly as consequences for mastery of required material. It is important to recognize, however, that these aspects of college teaching are not necessary to an enjoyable, effective course of instruction, but may be more appropriately viewed as supplementary to it. New functions for lectures and term papers, as components of an instructional program administered according to established principles of behavior, may well be discovered and tested in future personalized courses.

Student procrastination in self-paced courses remains an interesting problem, especially since most personalized courses must currently be implemented within a college calendar involving grade deadlines and other time considerations. Future administration of self-paced courses can institute other contingencies designed to enhance steady and more consistent student progress. A program of differential reinforcement of minimal rates of progress, perhaps in the form of extra course credit for keeping up with a minimal, pre-determined schedule, might have a positive effect on student pacing. It might also be possible to allow students who finish early to proctor late-finishing course members. Besides any reinforcement value to students of such a privilege, the administrative advantages of this arrangement in dealing with a possible overload of testing at term's end are clear.

Analysis of the major independent variables in personalized instruction represents only a beginning in a potentially valuable field of study. Effective programming is no less important to college-level courses than it is to more basic instructional situations. As such, techniques for the preparation and evaluation of materials for personalized college courses must develop to a level of sophistication appropriate to a technology of college instruction.

SUMMARY

Characteristics of personalized instruction are examined for their relative contributions to student achievement and attitudes towards psychology. Frequent tests and study objectives were found to rank high as contributors to student achievement. Self-pacing, small units of work, and frequent interactions with the teaching personnel appear to contribute most to favorable attitudes toward the instruction and toward psychology in general. Lectures, term papers, discussions, and films were viewed with disfavor relative to features of personalized instruction. Data on student pacing patterns were presented with suggestions for additional contingencies to deal effectively with the problem of procrastination. Personalized instruction is viewed as an effective means of overcoming deficiencies common to college instruction.

REFERENCES CITED

GREEN, B. A., JR. 1969. A self-spaced course in freshman physics. Paper presented at the Education Research Center Colloquium, M.I.T., April.

HOMME, L., A. P. CSANYI, M. A. GONZALES, and J. R. RECHS. 1969. *How to use contingency contracting in the classroom.* Champaign, Ill.: Research Press.

KELLER, F. S. 1963. A personal course in psychology. Paper presented at the meeting of the American Psychological Association, Philadelphia, August. [Article 37]

———. 1967. Neglected rewards in the educational process. *Proceedings of the 23rd American Conference of Academic Deans,* Los Angeles, January.

———. 1968. "Goodbye, teacher . . ." *Journal of Applied Behavior Analysis, 1,* 79–89. [Article 1]

———. 1970. Science education in the seventies. Paper presented at the meeting of the American Association for the Advancement of Science, Chicago, December.

KOEN, B. V. 1970. Self-paced instruction in engineering: a case study. Paper presented at the American Society for Engineering Education, Columbus, Ohio, June. [Article 13]

MAGER, R. 1962. *Preparing instructional objectives.* Palo Alto, Calif.: Fearon Publishers.

MAGER, R. 1968. *Developing attitude toward learning.* Palo Alto, Calif.; Fearon Publishers.

MCMICHAEL, J. S. and J. R. COREY. 1969. Contingency management in an introductory psychology course produces better learning. *Journal of Applied Behavior Analysis, 2,* 79–83. [Article 2]

MEACHUM, J. L. and A. E. WIESEN. 1969. *Changing classroom behavior: a manual for precision teaching.* Scranton, Pa.: International Textbook Co.

MICHAEL, J. L. 1970. Principles of effective usage. In R. Ulrich, T. Stachnik, and J. Mabry (eds.), *Control of Human Behavior.* Vol. II Glenview, Ill.: Scott, Foresman, pp. 28–35.

NELSON, T. F. 1970. Teaching and learning at Kalamazoo College. Report to the Faculty Development Committee, Kalamazoo College, June.

SHEPPARD, W. C. and H. G. MACDERMOT. 1970. Design and evaluation of a programmed course in introductory psychology. *Journal of Applied Behavior Analysis. 3,* 5–11. [Article 9]

SKINNER, B. F. 1968. *The technology of teaching.* New York: Appleton-Century-Crofts.

STAATS, A. W. 1968. *Learning, language, and cognition.* New York: Holt, Rinehart, and Winston.

WITTERS, D. R. and G. W. KENT. 1970. An experimental evaluation of programming student study behavior in undergraduate courses. Research project under HEW Grant 9-C-040, Bridgewater College.

8

THEORY OF PSI EVALUATED
FOR ENGINEERING EDUCATION*†

Lawrence L. Hoberock, Billy V. Koen,
Charles H. Roth, and Gerald R. Wagner

The objective of this paper is to evaluate from experimental data and observation five theoretical features of F. S. Keller's Personalized-Proctorial System of Instruction (PSI) for engineering education. This system was tested in courses in nuclear, mechanical, electrical, and operations research engineering at The University of Texas at Austin. We have found that students easily take advantage of the unique features of PSI and adapt them to their own needs, that they enjoy learning by this method, and that they learn more than in conventional courses. Our results indicate that the self-pacing and unit perfection features of PSI are extremely appropriate for engineering education; that the emphasis on written-word learning and the use of proctors are definite assets; and that the motivational lecture feature is of lesser value.

INTRODUCTION

A Personalized-Proctorial System of Instruction (PSI), based on well-known principles of positive reinforcement in learning theory,[1] has been designed by F. S. Keller,[2] a modern learning theoretician. The techniques of this system appear to match very closely some unique characteristics of engineering courses. This has prompted the authors to systematically test its utility in four different engineering courses at The University of Texas at Austin. This paper presents the results of these tests and evaluates the major theoretical features of PSI for applicability in engineering education.

Different subject areas were used for each of the tests: Nuclear Engineering, Mechanical Engineering, Electrical Engineering, and Operations Research. We feel that the level, type, time span, and size of the courses used provides a sufficiently broad sample space to draw relevant conclusions about PSI for engineering courses in general. Specifically, the courses were:

1. Nuclear Engineering: "Nuclear Reactor Theory I"—An elective senior level course with 21 students taught over a regular fourteen week term.
2. Mechanical Engineering: "Kinematics and Dynamics of Machinery"—A required junior level course with 12 students taught over a six week summer term.
3. Electrical Engineering: "Digital Systems Engineering I"—A required junior level course with 40 students taught over a regular fourteen week term.
4. Operations Research: "Applied Statistics"—An elective graduate level course with 25 students taught over a regular fourteen week term.

THE THEORETICAL FRAMEWORK

Extensive descriptions of PSI and details of how to apply it are ably presented elsewhere.[3, 4, 5]

*Paper delivered at the American Society for Engineering Education Annual Meeting, June 21-24, 1971, at the United States Naval Academy, Annapolis, Maryland.

†The authors appreciate the support of the PSI course experiments by their departmental chairmen, Dr. J. Parker Lamb and Dr. Archie W. Straiton. Credit also goes to Dr. James E. Stice, Director of the Bureau of Engineering Teaching, who encouraged and supported this collective effort.

[1] Skinner, B. F., *The Technology of Teaching*, Appleton-Century-Crofts, 1968.

[2] Keller, F. S., "Engineering Personalized Instruction in the Classroom," *Revista Interamericana de Psicologia*, 1967, I, pp. 189-197.

[3] Keller, F. S., "Good-Bye, Teacher. . .", *Journal of Applied Behavior Analysis*, No. 1, Spring, 1968. [Article 1]

[4] Koen, B. V., "Self-Paced Instruction in Engineering: A Case Study," Paper No. 84, presented at the American Society for Engineering Education Annual Meeting, June 22-25, 1970, Ohio State University, Columbus, Ohio. Modified Version in *IEEE Transactions on Education*, February, 1971. [Article 13]

[5] Hoberock, L. L., "Personalized Instruction in Mechanical Engineering," *Engineering Education*, Vol. 61, No. 6, March 1971. [Article 14]

From *IEEE Transaction on Education*, Vol. E-15, No. 1, February 1972.

However, we briefly describe the five major features of the system, as given by Keller, that provide the essential links to learning theory. Our study consists of evaluating individually each of these features. They are as follows:[3]

1. "The go-at-your-own-pace feature, which permits a student to move through the course at a speed commensurate with his ability and other demands upon his time."
2. "The unit-perfection requirement for advance, which lets the student go ahead to new material only after demonstrating mastery of that which preceded."
3. "The use of lectures and demonstrations as vehicles of motivation rather than sources of critical information."
4. "The related stress upon the written word in teacher-student communication."
5. "The use of proctors, which permits repeated testing, immediate scoring, almost unavoidable tutoring, and a marked enhancement of the personal-social aspect of the educational process."

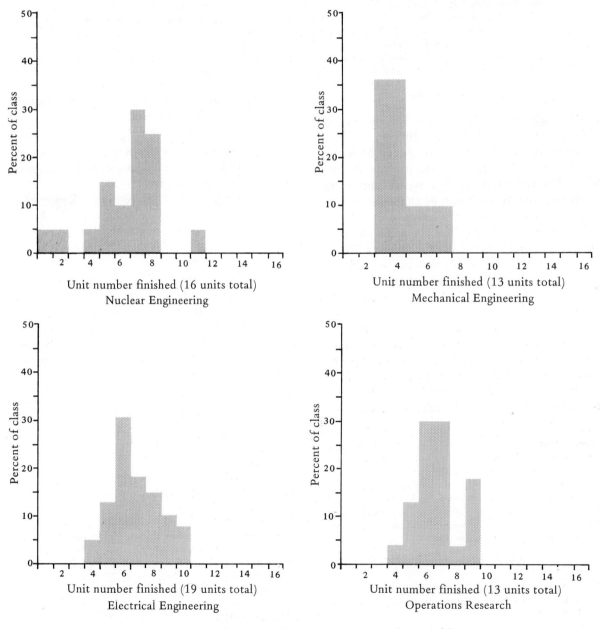

FIGURE 1.   Distribution of students among units at midterm.

The literature on PSI to date gives little evidence that these features are all equally important for engineering courses. Neither does it substantiate for which type of course PSI would be most or least useful. In what follows, we present our combined experience in addressing these problems.

THE GO-AT-YOUR-OWN PACE FEATURE

Our evidence supports Keller's view that students quickly take advantage of the self-paced feature. Figure 1 gives the distribution of students among the various units halfway through each of the courses. Table 1 presents the data discussed below. During the progress of the four courses, the maximum spread between least units completed and most units completed, expressed as percent of total units, were (listed in the order, Nuclear Engineering, Mechanical Engineering, Electrical Engineering, and Operations Research): 75%, 54%, 42%, and 54%. The fastest students completed all the units early: 75%, 93%, 89%, and 80% of the way through the respective courses. This indicates that the slower students, when not forced to catch up with a "class average," took their necessary time and used the available learning resources to completely learn the material; and that the faster students, when not forced to hold back for a "class average," made more efficient use of their time in learning the material. On the other hand, the average learning rate was found to be strongly affected by other factors. In the M.E., E.E., and O.R. courses, a poorly programmed early unit that was too difficult or too lengthy, not only retarded progress over that unit, but also produced discouragement and frustration that slowed average progress during succeeding units. In the N.E. course, it was found that the learning rate was considerably less if the students had no opportunity to interact with the professor.

Contrary to a commonly held belief in engineering, the majority of students did not find pacing themselves unpleasant. When asked if they found self-pacing frustrating, the following percentages said no or definitely no: 100%, 55%, 72%, and 68%. On the other hand, a substantial number of students, when not specifically encouraged or provided with suggested unit schedules or "benchmarks," found difficulty in getting started or sustaining consistent progress.

Student opinion of self-pacing was quite favorable. When asked to compare the PSI courses with all other courses they had taken, the following percentages of students said they look forward more or much more to the PSI class activities: 89%, 70%, 78%, and 50%. Furthermore, 72%, 64%, 91%, and 59% of the students, respectively, considered the self-paced mode of instruction to be better than the traditional lecture method.

The self-pacing feature also has advantages for the instructor. Since each student proceeds at his own rate, a student's speed in learning and test taking is removed from the grading process. Effectively, only final proficiency is measured. This feature also allows the instructor to realistically evaluate what the students can learn in a given time period. Such information can be invaluable in curriculum and course design.

We conclude that the self-paced feature, when properly programmed and augmented by professorial encouragement, is extremely effective for both good and poor engineering students. Furthermore, it provides a pleasant, student-favoring medium of teaching and supports a positive attitude toward learning.

UNIT PERFECTION FEATURE

One of the major difficulties with conventional instruction in engineering is that a typical C stu-

TABLE 1.   DATA ON THE GO-AT-YOUR-OWN-PACE FEATURE.

Course	N.E.	M.E.	E.E.	O.R.
Percent maximum spread among units	75%	54%	42%	54%
Percent of total term time at which first student finished the course	75%	93%	89%	80%
Percent of students who found self-pacing unfrustrating	100%	55%	72%	68%
Percent of students who looked forward to PSI more than lecture courses	89%	70%	78%	50%
Percent of students who considered PSI better than the lecture method	72%	64%	91%	59%

TABLE 2.   DATA ON THE UNIT PERFECTION FEATURE.

Course	N.E.	M.E.	E.E.	O.R.
Percent of students who were undisturbed by the absence of conventional grading of tests and papers	100%	73%	94%	96%
Percent of students who spent above average effort in the PSI courses	89%	90%	78%	68%
Average number of attempts to pass readiness tests	1.71	1.68	1.51	1.24
Percent of students who felt they obtained more than they expected from the PSI courses	78%	54%	84%	59%

dent ends with large gaps in his knowledge. Furthermore, since engineering instruction is usually cumulative, a student who does only C work at the beginning of a course is penalized, de facto, in his learning of material appearing later in the course. This observation has not been lost on the students themselves. In answer to the question "Did it disturb you that your achievement was not evaluated in the usual manner (i.e., test, papers, etc.)?," students said no or definitely no in the percentages: 100, 73, 94, and 96. These positive results, summarized with other data in Table 2, were obtained in spite of the fact that the unit perfection requirement demands of the students considerably more time than they devote to other courses. Several of the slower students reported that they spent two or three times as much time on the PSI courses than on conventional courses. On our surveys, 89%, 90%, 78%, and 68%, respectively, of our students said that their effort in the PSI courses was above or well above average when compared to the effort they usually put into other courses. Furthermore, when a student in a conventional course is tested over a block of material, he usually has only one chance to demonstrate his knowledge. In the PSI courses, however, we demand that a student achieve perfection, regardless of the number of attempts he makes. Although this demands more of the student's time, it is not necessarily excessive. In each course, the average number of attempts to pass readiness tests for unit perfection were 1.71, 1.68, 1.51, and 1.24.

In the Mechanical and Electrical Engineering courses, the amount of material covered (or "traveled through") was 5% to 10% less when taught by PSI than when taught conventionally. In the Nuclear Engineering and Operations Research PSI courses more material was covered. However, in all four courses, the amount of material *learned* was greater as a result of the perfection require-

ment. This is indicated in Figure 2 by the grade distributions of each of the PSI courses compared with conventionally taught courses. In the E.E. course, which had previously been taught several times by the same instructor using the same textbooks and essentially the same course content, a final exam was given that was comparable in difficulty and scope to final exams used in previous semesters. The final exam average for the PSI course was 84%, compared with 75%, 74%, and 73% the last three times the course was taught by the lecture method. In addition, the students *felt* that they learned more. Compared with what they hoped to get from the PSI courses, 78%, 54%, 84%, and 59% of the students said that they obtained more or far more than they expected from these courses. In the O.R. course, students were asked if they felt the PSI method would result in a longer retention of the material; 95% said yes or definitely yes.

THE USE OF LECTURES AND DEMONSTRATIONS AS MOTIVATIONAL DEVICES RATHER THAN INFORMATION SOURCES

The most significant aspect concerning lectures in the PSI method to date is their virtual absence. In three of the four courses, only one to three lectures were given. They were well attended and added interest to the courses, but we feel that they probably could have been eliminated without any serious loss. This was not true, however, in the Operations Research course. One of the objectives in this course was for students to develop a conversational ability with technical material so as to effectively explain it to non-technical managers. To teach this skill, the professor should orally communicate with his students in more detailed

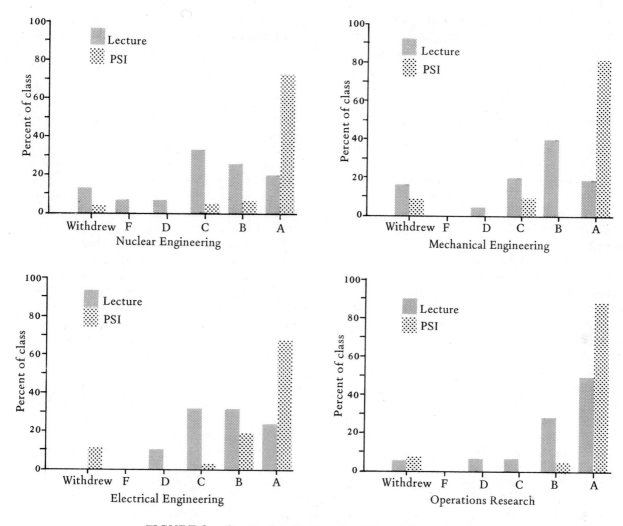

FIGURE 2.   Grade distributions for PSI and Lecture classes.

fashion than merely "motivational." Five lectures were given, and all were well attended and accepted. The essential difference between this application of lectures and the others was its use as a source of information. We feel, however, that most engineering courses do not require this type of learning, and the motivational lectures appear to be of doubtful value. On the other hand, it has been documented in the Nuclear Engineering course that complete absence of the professor from the learning process significantly lowers the rate of learning by the students. We therefore question only the value of the lecture in the PSI method, not the personal activity of the professor with his students.

The students in the Nuclear, Mechanical, and Electrical Engineering courses did not feel that the absence of lectures was deleterious. When asked if they considered communication between students

and the PSI staff to be a major problem, 88%, 90%, and 91% of the students said no or definitely no.

STRESS ON THE WRITTEN WORD

Since the majority of learning in PSI comes from written materials, these must be well prepared, whether they are textbooks, instructors notes, or problem manuals. Students quickly become frustrated over weaknesses in these materials, since there are no lectures to compensate for them. Hence an inadequate or poorly written textbook requires considerable effort from the instructor in preparing supplementary notes and study units. On the other hand, PSI removes the student from possible frustration from idiosyncrasies of a professor in lecture and removes the burden of having to analyze a lecturer to figure out what is to be learned. The stress on the written word forces the instructor to be less ambiguous in what he expects the students to learn, and the unit readiness tests provide excellent feedback on what material is difficult or easy for the students.

One of the goals of PSI is to have the student learn to learn by himself. This is particularly important for technical people, who face a rapid technological obsolescence after they leave formal schooling. It is mandatory that they be able to learn on their own in order to remain technically competent. The stress on the written word enhances self-learning. In the Nuclear Engineering course, students indicated some transference of study habits developed in the PSI course to other conventionally taught courses. Our results show that students did become more efficient with written word learning. Since a score of 100% was necessary to pass a test, students tended to satisfy themselves that they thoroughly knew the material before taking the tests. Given the perfection requirement, we considered the average number of attempts to pass readiness tests (1.71, 1.68, 1.51, and 1.24 from Table 2) to be relatively small. These numbers indicate that students were quite capable of learning from textbooks and supporting written material. Furthermore, when forced to learn by themselves, students were more exploratory in their thinking. Compared with other courses, the PSI courses were ranked above average or one of the best by 89%, 54%, 87%, and 73% of the students for purposes of stimulating new ideas.

THE USE OF PROCTORS

Keller[3] has stated that the use of proctors permits repeated testing and immediate scoring. The value of repeated testing is its provision of extensive feedback to both the student and the instructor on what the student has learned. Contrast this with the rather limited amount of test feedback in a conventional course. Furthermore, the immediate scoring provides the opportunity for a student to defend an incorrect answer, which provides additional feedback to the instructor concerning both the student and the adequacy of his test questions. This aspect also gives the student an opportunity to "think on his feet," and it supports a friendly intellectual exchange in the learning process. As indicated in Table 3, the students found this advantageous. In answer to a survey question, 88%, 67%, 75%, and 68% of the students considered proctoring sessions interesting. They also felt that the proctors were sensitive to their difficulties with the material. When asked whether their proctors listened to them in such a way to know whether or not they understood the ideas and concepts, 94%, 100%, 87%, and 87% said yes or definitely yes. Furthermore, 94%, 100%, 94%, and 100% of the students felt free to ask questions of, disagree with, and express their ideas to their proctors. Perhaps the most interesting statistics are those which indicate that proctoring helps to generate an extra enthusiasm and interest in the course material. The students were asked whether the course materials, student proctor interaction, and interaction with the PSI staff stimulated them to work beyond the actual requirements of the course. The answer yes or definitely yes were given by 57%, 80%, 68%, and 34% of the students. Given that the *actual* requirements of the courses were 100% learning of the prescribed material, we feel that it would have been significant if only 10% of the students had worked beyond those requirements.

Since the proctors are almost always students themselves, it seems appropriate to evaluate the effect PSI has for them. Whereas most "graders"

TABLE 3.   DATA ON THE USE OF PROCTORS FEATURE.

Course	N.E.	M.E.	E.E.	O.R.
Percent of students who considered proctoring sessions interesting	88%	67%	75%	68%
Percent of students who felt proctors listened to their understanding of ideas and concepts	94%	100%	87%	87%
Percent of students who felt free to question, disagree with, and express ideas to their proctors	94%	100%	94%	100%
Percent of students who felt they were stimulated to work beyond the actual course requirements	57%	80%	68%	34%
Percent of students who felt proctors were enthusiastic about proctoring	100%	100%	84%	89%

for a conventional engineering course find their work tedious, the PSI proctors enjoyed their work. Such pleasure is certain to have advantageous effects upon the students they help, as well as positively effecting the proctors' attitude toward learning. Of all the proctors used to date in the four courses, more than half of them were volunteers who served without pay. Furthermore, the students themselves observed that the proctors enjoyed their work. They were asked if the proctors revealed enthusiasm about their work with the course, and 100%, 100%, 84%, and 89% said yes or definitely yes.

CONCLUSION

The results of our experiments show that PSI is an extremely effective method for use in many types of courses in engineering education. These types include those in which the material to be learned is structured in a definite hierarchy with well defined objectives, is largely available from written materials, and is amenable to individual, rather than group, learning. Our tests further show that students readily take advantage of the special features of the PSI method, that they find the learning experience considerably more pleasurable than in conventional courses, and that they learn more than in conventional courses. On our surveys, 94%, 82%, 94%, and 77% of the students ranked the PSI courses above average or one of the best when compared with all other courses they had taken. Furthermore, 89%, 82%, 93%, and 85% of the students stated that if given the opportunity, they would take another course taught by PSI.

Of the five features peculiar to PSI, the self-pacing and unit perfection features appear to be the most valuable. The stress upon the written word and the use of proctors are definite assets to engineering learning and support both the unit perfection and the self-pacing features. However, the fifth feature of motivational lectures appears to be of considerably less value, and our results indicate that it might be eliminated without serious consequences.

9

DESIGN AND EVALUATION OF A PROGRAMMED COURSE IN INTRODUCTORY PSYCHOLOGY [1]

W. C. Sheppard and H. G. MacDermot

The design of a programmed course in introductory psychology, utilizing an interview procedure, is described. The performance of students in this course was compared with that of students covering the same subject matter but taught in a more conventional manner. Students in the experimental course scored significantly higher on objective and essay final examinations and rated the course more positively.

A technology of teaching (Skinner, 1968; Keller, 1969) is being developed, utilizing principles derived from an experimental analysis of behavior. The technology has been applied at the university level, most appropriately, to teach courses in the experimental analysis of behavior (Ferster, 1968; Keller, 1967a, b; Kent, 1965; Lloyd and Knutzen, 1969; Malott, 1968). This report describes the design and evaluation of a programmed teaching procedure applied to a large undergraduate course in the psychology of learning. The design of this experimental teaching procedure was patterned after the approach taken by Keller (1968) and elaborated by Ferster (1968). The performance of students taught using this experimental teaching procedure was compared with the performance of students covering the same subject matter but taught in a more conventional manner (see also McMichael and Corey, 1969).

METHOD

Subjects

Students registered for an introductory course entitled Psychology of Learning without prior knowledge that they would be involved in an experimental program. A total of 301 students enrolled and were assigned to either of two groups based on the first initial of their last name. Two hundred and three students, whose last names began with the letters A through O, were assigned to the section using the experimental teaching procedure; 98 students, whose last names began with the letters P through Z, constituted the conventional instruction, or control group.

Procedure

The fundamental feature of the experimental teaching procedure was the interview. The interview involved an interaction between two persons. A student participated in an interview as a speaker after studying a small section of the assigned text, typically five to 15 pages. The listener in the interview was, at various times, the course instructor, a teaching assistant, or, most often, another studen who had previously studied and successfully passed an interview on that section of the text. During the interview, the speaker was required to describe fluently and in detail to the listener the material contained in that section of the text within a 10-min period. The listener attended to the speaker without interruption, took notes on his performance and timed him. Both the speaker and listener were permitted to refer to the text or notes during the interview. After the speaker stopped speaking, the listener had the responsibility for asking questions to probe an omission or inaccuracy, comment upon the speaker's performance, and engage the speaker in a discussion of some aspect or implication of the section.

The decision as to whether the speaker's performance was satisfactory or not was jointly determined by both the speaker and listener. If both the speaker and listener were satisfied

[1] This research was supported by a grant from the Esso Education Foundation. The authors wish to thank Ruth Clifford, Carmen Collias, Dennis Culver, Julie Curtin, Steven Ellis, Kenneth Himes, Mary Himes, Daniel Hursh, Dennis Lee, Harold MacDermot, Charles Ryberg, and Dean Stites who served as teaching assistants in the course.

From *Journal of Applied Behavior Analysis*, 1970, *3*, 5–11; copyright 1970 by the Society for the Experimental Analysis of Behavior, Inc.

that the speaker's performance demonstrated mastery of the section, they recorded the fact on an individual progress chart, which the listener signed.

On those occasions when a speaker's performance was judged to be not satisfactory, which was usually self-evident because of difficulties the speaker would have in completing the interview within the allotted time period, the listener and speaker discussed those difficulties. The speaker then restudied the same material for at least 10 min before repeating the interview. When the repeated interview was successfully completed, which could involve more than one repetition, the fact was recorded and the student continued without any penalty.

Each student was required to serve alternately as a speaker or listener a designated number of times during the course. This number was determined by the grade the student wished to earn. An additional requirement was that for every student, a teaching assistant serve as a listener on the average of once every five interviews. After completing three to five interviews, a chapter or two, the student took a written exercise, lasting approximately 20 min, that consisted of four or five short-answer essay questions. The essay questions were randomly selected from either a list of study questions that had previously been given to the student or from questions included at the end of each section of the text.

A teaching assistant read the answers, discussed them with the student, and made a decision as to whether the student's performance on the written exercise was satisfactory or not. A satisfactory performance required that all responses be functionally correct. If they were, the student continued on to the next assignment; if they were not, the student and teaching assistant jointly determined where errors existed, the student then reviewed the material for at least 10 min and took an alternative form of the same exercise. There was no penalty for repetition of a written exercise.

The course content consisted of the text, *Behavioral Principles,* written by Ferster and Perrott (1968). The text covered in depth the principles of respondent and operant conditioning. The text was divided into 36 sections; each section comprised the material to be covered in a single interview. The student's grade in the course was determined by how far he progressed through the material. To earn a grade of "A", the student was required to complete successfully 36 interviews and 11

written exercises. To earn a "B" in the course required completion of approximately three-fourths of the material needed for an "A"; coverage of approximately one-half of the material necessary for an "A" earned the student a grade of "C", and a "D" grade required coverage of approximately one-third of the amount necessary for an "A". There were no penalties imposed for repeating either interviews or written exercises.

The three-credit hour course met for 1 hr three times a week for nine weeks. During the class period, students either studied the text, participated in interviews as a speaker or as a listener, or were engaged in answering the essay questions that comprised the written exercise. In addition to the regularly scheduled class period, students could participate in these same activities in a small classroom staffed by at least two teaching assistants from 12 P.M. to 5 P.M. each weekday. This provided a total of 45 class days during the term.

The students were assigned to one of 12 teaching assistants who were upperclass undergraduate students who had covered the material using the interview procedure under the supervision of the course instructor. The teaching assistants received 3 hr of academic credit for performing their duties. The teaching assistants certified student progress by recording the results of interviews and written exercises as they were completed, listened to interviews, selected questions for the written exercises, discussed the material with students and met weekly as a group with the instructor to analyze the course. The instructor organized the course, observed the class procedures, listened to occasional interviews, held individual discussions, and met with students having special problems.

Three lectures were presented during the term by the course instructor, attendance at which was optional.

The procedures followed with the conventional instruction, or control group, were designed to make the two groups as comparable as possible in respect to the amount of time students from each group spent speaking, listening, writing, and conversing with the teaching assistants or the instructor.

Students placed in the control group were assigned the same text as the experimental group. They were required to meet weekly for one 2-hr period to take part in small (five to 10 person) group discussions, and to meet once a week for an hour as a class with the instructor or a teaching assistant. Specific sections of the text were assigned to be covered during the small group-discussion meetings. The same study questions provided to the experimental group were given to the control group. The weekly class hour was devoted to a question and answer period. In addition, each student in this group was required to write a short, one to two page, paper every other week on some aspect of the material being covered in the text at that time.

The same three lectures made available to the experimental group were also presented to the control group; again attendance was optional. The teaching assistants and course instructor were the same for the experimental and conventional groups.

The students in both the experimental and conventional instruction groups were given the same objective final examination at the end of the course, consisting of 100 multiple-choice questions with each section of the text being equally represented. In addition, there was an essay examination consisting of five questions. Since a high level of student performance was anticipated, both the multiple choice and essay questions were designed by the course instructor to be more difficult than any similar examination questions he had ever given to undergraduate students before.

Students in the experimental group were told that the purpose of the final examination was not to determine grades but rather to ascertain the effectiveness of the procedures used in the course in helping them to master the course material. Students in the control group were told that 50% of their final grade in the course would be determined by their performance on the final examination. These instructions might be expected to bias performance on the final examination strongly in favor of the control group.

Immediately before the final examination, both groups were asked to complete an unsigned attitude survey in connection with the course.

RESULTS

Of the 203 students assigned to the experimental group, 168 remained after the first three weeks, the university "drop" period. Fifty-five of these students progressed to the "A" level, 58 completed the work necessary to earn a "B", 51 earned a grade of "C", only two students received "D" grades, and two failed the course.

Figure 1 shows that students in the experimental group progressed through the material at different rates. In general, students earning A's completed the first interview earlier and

progressed at a more rapid rate than those students earning B's; students earning B's started before those earning C's and also progressed at a more rapid rate.

Six per cent of all interviews were judged to be unsatisfactory and were repeated once; less than 1% of all interviews were repeated more than once. Students serving as listeners were just as likely as teaching assistants to judge an interview unsatisfactory.

Attendance during the class periods varied from approximately 40 to 70%. Many students were able to complete the interviews and written exercises required for an "A" during the regularly scheduled class periods. Other students preferred to take advantage of the times teaching assistants were available in the small classroom and consequently did not attend the regularly scheduled class. Several students were able to complete the course at the "A" level within six weeks and a large number of students had reached this level before the end of the nine-week period. Upon reaching the "A" level, students were excused from further class participation.

In the control group, 92 of the original 98 students were still enrolled after the first three weeks of the term. Thirty-five of 203 students dropped from the experimental group as compared to six of 98 from the control group. Was it possible that any differences in performance between the experimental and control groups could, perhaps, be accounted for by poorer students dropping the experimental section? In order to examine this question, the cumulative grade-point average of each student was obtained. The average grade point for all of the students remaining in the experimental group was 2.72, the average for those remaining in the conventional group was 2.69, and the

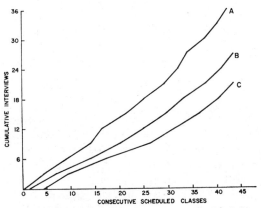

Fig. 1. Cumulative curves of mean completed interviews as the term progressed for students earning "A's", "B's", and "C's" in the experimental course.

grade point average for those students who dropped the experimental section was 2.67. Since the GPAs of these groups are extremely similar, the possibility that differences in performance between students in the two groups could be accounted for by a bias introduced by students dropping the course is highly unlikely.

On the 100-question objective final examination, the mean score for the experimental group was 73.1 with a standard deviation of 12.1, and the mean score for the control group was 66.8 with a standard deviation of 11.9. The difference between means is significant, using a t test, beyond the 0.01 level of confidence. The Kuder-Richardson estimate of reliability for the objective final examination was 0.89.

Since the students in the experimental group had already earned their grade, based upon the number of interviews and written exercises they completed, it is possible to compare their scores on the objective final examination as a function of the amount of course material completed. Those students who completed the material necessary to obtain an "A" averaged 82.5 on the objective final examination; the students who progressed to the "B" level averaged 71.7; those who progressed to the "C" level averaged 65.3; and those who progressed to the "D" level averaged 52.5. The performance of students in the experimental group is directly related to the amount of material they had covered.

A five-question essay examination was also used as an evaluative instrument to determine whether there was a difference between the two groups in their ability to verbalize the course material. Three readers independently scored the essay examinations from both the experimental and control groups using a 25-point scale. The names on the examinations were covered so that the readers did not know to which group each examination belonged. The reliability of the scores assigned to the essay examinations by the three readers was as follows: between readers one and two there was a reliability of 0.92; reliability between readers one and three was 0.78; and reliability between readers two and three was 0.83. The average scorer reliability was 0.85.

On the essay examination, the mean score for the experimental group was 17.4, with a standard deviation of 5.9, and the mean score for the control group was 13.9, with a standard deviation of 6.5. The difference between means is significant, using a t test, beyond the 0.01 level of confidence. Again it is possible

to compare the scores of the students in the experimental group on the essay final examination as a function of the amount of course material completed. Those students who completed the material necessary to obtain an "A" averaged 21.3 on the essay final examination; the students who progressed to the "B" level averaged 17.0; those who progressed to the "C" level averaged 14.4, and those who progressed to the "D" level averaged 6.0. The performance of students in the experimental group on the essay final examination is directly related to the amount of material they had covered.

Single measures of student satisfaction with the experimental teaching procedure and the conventional instruction procedure were obtained from a weighted composite of the student ratings on the following three items, which were part of the attitude survey both groups were asked to complete:

1. How satisfied are you at the present time with this course? Nine-point scale ranging from extremely satisfied to extremely dissatisfied.
2. What is your reaction to the manner in which this course was taught? Seven-point scale ranging from very delighted to very disappointed.
3. How does the probable long-range value for you of this course compare with all other courses you have had in college? Five-point scale ranging from highest 10% of other courses to lowest 10% of other courses.

The composite measure of student satisfaction for the experimental teaching procedure was significantly higher ($P < 0.01$), using a t test, than the conventional instruction procedure.

The correlation between the composite measure of student satisfaction for each student and the achievement as measured by each student's score on the objective final examination was $r = 0.46$ for the experimental group and $r = 0.30$ for the control group.

In response to the question, how effective was the interview method in helping you to master more material in greater depth in comparison with the traditional lecture-examination method?, 94% of the students in the experimental group rated the interview method more effective, 6% rated both methods the same, and no student rated the interview method less efficient.

In addition, the attitude survey revealed

that students in the experimental group, in comparison to students in the control group, rated the course: as being more organized, as allowing more opportunity to proceed at an individual pace, as providing more stimulation to work in comparison to the level at which they usually work, as providing more effective interactions with other students in increasing learning, as stimulating more of an interest in pursuing further study in this area, as no more difficult, as more enjoyable, as utilizing a teaching procedure that they would prefer to be used in other courses, and as utilizing a text that was better and less difficult.

DISCUSSION

Two strong biases were introduced in this study which would favor higher achievement by students in the conventional instruction or control group on the final examination. First, 50% of the final grade in the course for students in the conventional instruction group was based on their performance on the final examination; students in the experimental group had already earned their grade before the final examination. Second, all of the students in the conventional instruction group were required to study the entire text, their grade for the course depended upon this; however, only those 55 students in the experimental group who earned "A's" completed the entire text, the 58 students earning "B's" completed approximately three-fourths of the text, and the 51 students earning "C's" completed only approximately one-half of the text. These biases were introduced to subject the experimental teaching procedure to an extremely difficult test. Given these biases it is impressive that students in the experimental group achieved significantly higher scores on both the objective and essay final examinations than students in the conventional instruction group. The greatest difference in performance between the two groups was on the essay examination. This is expected because the interview procedure is designed to facilitate the development of verbal fluency. It is probable that the average achievement of students in the experimental group could be substantially increased by arranging the experimental course so that more of the students would complete a greater proportion of the course material. This could perhaps be achieved by reducing the total number of interviews required to cover the text, by increasing the number of interviews required to earn a "C" or "B", by encouraging students to begin tak-

ing interviews earlier in the course, or by increasing the duration of the course.

In addition to their superior achievement, students in the experimental group also expressed more positive attitudes regarding the course. These positive attitudes are probably a reflection of many of the positive features of the experimental teaching procedure, for example: the student is actively involved in the course, he is either speaking, listening, taking written exercises, or studying; the student progresses at his own pace, he is not forced to go ahead before he is ready, or held back by others; the student progresses in small steps and receives immediate feedback regarding the adequacy of his performance, this frequent evaluation teaches the student the level of study required in the course; the student's study behavior is reinforced by his own performance during the interview, as he is speaking he is also listening and differentially responding to the fluency of his verbal performance; the student progresses only after achieving complete mastery over a section, his repertoire is tested in detail during the interview, not merely sampled; the student is not penalized for the repetition of unsatisfactory interviews or written exercises, this provides opportunities for remediation; the student is motivated by arranging an environment within which his progress is immediately reinforced, the aversive control exercised by the threat of tests and grades is minimized; the student's study is paced throughout the course, he does not concentrate his study toward the end of the course; the student does not compete with others for grades, he can cooperate with and assist other students without threatening his own grade; and the student's study habits are improved because the interview procedure teaches the student how to study effectively.

One possible objection to the experimental teaching procedure could be the 17% drop rate for the course. Students dropping the experimental course were interviewed to ascertain their reasons for not continuing. The most common response was that the course appeared to be too difficult and to involve too much work. This was stated succinctly by one student when he said: "Why should I go through all of that effort to learn this material when I can take a similar course from another professor and just cram the night before the final and get a "C" or a "B" without having to bother to learn anything." Several points can be made regarding the drop rate. First, most of the students in the course were sophomores; in two other courses, Developmental Psychology and Psychology of Learning, that the author has subsequently taught to juniors and seniors using the same experimental teaching procedure, the drop rate has been 9% and 6%, respectively. Second, the average drop rate for introductory psychology courses taught by the author in a conventional manner has ranged from 10 to 15% from year to year. Third, Ferster (1968) and McMichael and Corey (1969) reported drop rates of 13% and 12% respectively, for students enrolled in programmed courses.

The programming principles utilized in the design of the experimental teaching procedure are similar to those employed by McMichael and Corey (1969) in their experimental course, although the specific formats differ. The basic conclusion of this study is in agreement with McMichael and Corey (1969), who found the experimental teaching procedure to be superior to conventional instruction procedures as measured by student achievement and student satisfaction. In addition, subsequent experience by the author and his colleagues in applying the experimental teaching procedure to courses in Developmental Psychology, Psychology of Learning, Behavioral Technologies, and Personality provide support for Mc-Michael and Corey's (1969) statement that these procedures have wide generality and are applicable to general subject matter.

One of the most important features of the experimental teaching procedure was the employment of undergraduate teaching assistants. The significance of this experience for the undergraduate teaching assistant is difficult to assess. However, of the 12 teaching assistants in the course, nine of whom were seniors, eight of the nine were accepted into graduate programs in Psychology. Only three of these eight students were undergraduate psychology majors and only two had planned, before this experience as a teaching assistant, to enter graduate programs in psychology.

This study has convinced the author that the greatest untapped resource in the university today is the undergraduate student. By actively involving the undergraduate student in the teaching and learning process it is possible to individualize instruction, at no additional cost to the institution, even in introductory courses of 500 students or more. This is now being done as an accepted part of our introductory psychology program.

REFERENCES

Ferster, C. B. Individualized instruction in a large introductory psychology college course. *Psychological Record*, 1968, 18, 521-532. [Article 34]

Ferster, C. B. and Perrott, M. C. *Behavior principles*. New York: Appleton-Century-Crofts, 1968.

Keller, F. S. Engineered personalized instruction in the classroom. *Revista Interamericana de Psicologia*, 1967, 1, 189-197. (a)

Keller, F. S. *Neglected rewards in the educational process.* Proceedings of the 23rd American Conference of Academic Deans, Los Angeles, 1967 (b)

Keller, F. S. "Good-bye teacher . . ." *Journal of Applied Behavior Analysis*, 1968, 1, 79-89. [Article 1]

Keller, F. S. A programmed system of instruction. *Educational Technology Monographs*, 1969, 2, 1-26.

Kent, N. D. Aspirations, successes and failures teaching the experimental analysis of behavior. *American Psychologist*, 1965, 20, 542.

Lloyd, K. E. and Knutzen, N. J. A self-spaced programmed undergraduate course. *Journal of Applied Behavior Analysis*, 1968, 1, 79-90.

Malott, R. W. *Contingency management in an introductory psychology course for 1000 students.* Paper presented at the American Psychological Association Convention, 1968, San Francisco.

McMichael, J. W. and Corey, J. R. Contingency management in an introductory psychology course produces better learning. *Journal of Applied Behavior Analysis*, 1969, 2, 79-83. [Article 2]

Skinner, B. F. *The technology of teaching*. New York: Appleton-Century-Crofts, 1968.

Received 30 September 1969.
(Revised 19 December 1969.)

10

EXAMINATION PERFORMANCE IN LECTURE-DISCUSSION AND PERSONALIZED INSTRUCTION COURSES[1]

David G. Born, Stephen M. Gledhill, and Michael L. Davis

Students enrolled in a Psychology of Learning course were assigned to either a lecture section, one of two similar personalized instruction sections, or a fourth section that rotated across all three teaching procedures. All students took identical midterms and a final examination. After correcting test performance for differences in the cumulative grade point average of students in the four sections, examination performance of students in the personalized sections was found to be superior to that of students in the lecture section. An analysis of class section examination performance by item type revealed that students in the lecture section scored lower on all item types, but the greatest differences occurred on items that required written responses (essay and fill-in items) rather than recognition responses (multiple choice items). A gross analysis of student performance in the class rotated across the instructional procedures suggests that personalized instruction had its greatest impact on students with "average" to "poor" academic records.

Following the outline and subsequent elaboration of Keller's "personalized system of instruction" (Keller, 1966, 1968) several persons (e.g., Ferster, 1968; Gallup, 1969; McMichael and Corey, 1969; Malott and Svinicki, 1969; Pennypacker, 1969; Sheppard and MacDermot, 1970; Born and Herbert, 1971) have implemented courses that are in some way or other variations on Keller's basic theme. Although many important questions remain to be answered about the effects of various procedures within the Keller course format, among the more pressing and important questions are those related to the general effects of these procedures on the quality of student performance in comparison with the quality of performance generated under more traditional lecture-discussion procedures.

Comparisons of examination performance following instruction with traditional lecture procedures and personalized instruction procedures have been reported by both McMichael and Corey (1969) and Sheppard and MacDermot (1970). In both comparisons, the results showed that students educated with personalized procedures performed at a significantly higher level on final examinations than students attending daily lectures over the same material. The present investigation attempted a similar comparison and also attempted to identify additional ways that the resulting student performance differed. A secondary objective was to determine further the impact of these two general procedures on rates of withdrawal from the courses, and how opportunities for additional flexibility in progress through a personalized course affects student performance in that course.

METHOD

Subjects

The 60 students enrolled in a Psychology of Learning course at the University of Utah during Spring Quarter, 1969, participated.

[1]This research was completed without support during Spring Quarter, 1969. The writers express their gratitude to the following students who volunteered to serve as proctors: Phillip Christiansen, John Jenkins, Mark Lundstrom, Scott Moffat, Marilynn Moffitt, and Kim Wheatley.

From *Journal of Applied Behavior Analysis*, 1972, 5, 33–43; copyright 1972 by the Society for the Experimental Analysis of Behavior, Inc.

Procedure

The fact that different instructional procedures would be used in the course was first announced at the initial class meeting. At this time, each student was also told where to report for subsequent classes, but students were not told about the different instructional procedures to be used in the various class sections.

Before the first class meeting, the cumulative grade point average (GPA) was calculated for each of the students assigned to the Learning course through computer pre-registration. These cumulative GPAs were subsequently used as a partial basis for assigning students to the different class sections in an attempt to equate the levels of academic skills in the various sections; *i.e.,* the students were rank ordered on the basis of GPA, and the students in each successive set of four were randomly assigned to one of the four class sections.

Lecture-discussion section. Since the course was scheduled to meet on Monday, Wednesday, and Friday of each week, a 1-hr lecture was delivered on each of these days unless the instructor was out of town. Students were informed that attendance was optional and would not influence their grade, even though attendance was recorded each class meeting by asking the students to sign their name to a paper passed around the room at the start of each lecture. The lectures were prepared and delivered by the senior author who has had 8 yr of university level teaching experience and is thoroughly familiar with the course content. These lectures were designed to supplement the reading assignments but not be a "re-hash" of them. During the first lecture of the course, and after each midterm examination, students were given the reading assignments that would be covered by the next examination, and a list of the lecture topics for each class day. The reading assignments were repeated at student request, but no special attempt was made to exert pressure on students to keep up with the reading assignments.

Keller section. Provisions were made for students to attend class at the regularly scheduled time for 1 hr on Monday, Wednesday, and Friday. On class days, proctors (advanced psy-

chology majors who were familiar with the course material) were available for giving unit tests, handing out new study units, or supplying tutorial help as required. Each student in this section was assigned a proctor at the first class meeting. The student reported to this proctor each day he attended class.

The specific course format consisted of dividing the reading material into 16 study units each of which corresponded to the first 16 chapters of the Ferster and Perrott (1968) book, and selected readings from the text by Malott, Whaley, and Ulrich (1968). Each student was held responsible for knowing thoroughly the written material in each unit. This could be demonstrated by passing a unit test with a perfect score. Unit tests consisted of 8 to 10 sentence completion or fill-in items, and 2 to 3 short answer essay questions. To aid the students in preparing for these examinations, they were given a study unit for each chapter that contained the reading assignment for the unit, and questions to direct their reading. Generally, these study questions were a sample from those provided by Ferster and Perrott (1968). The student was instructed that when he felt that he had mastered the material, he should report to his proctor and ask for a unit test. If he passed the unit test with a perfect score he was given the next study unit; if his performance was unsatisfactory, he was asked to study the material again and take a different unit test over the same material. This was continued until all 16 units had been completed.

Although there were more testing days than unit tests to be taken, and there was some opportunity for students to progress at their own rate, it should be noted that a pacing requirement was imposed upon students in this section. To be eligible to take a midterm examination, students were required to complete all study units covered by that midterm. Because midterms and the final examination were scheduled the same day for all four classes, the go-at-your-own-pace feature was therefore modified, but not eliminated.

Modified-Keller section. The modified-Keller section followed essentially the same format as the Keller section with a few notable exceptions. First, each student determined the size of each of his study units. The major text, *Behavior Principles,* was written with each chapter divided into three to five parts or subdivisions. This provided 57 convenient segments of reading material for which individual study units and test questions were written. The student could, then, determine the size of his study unit by combining in sequential order the number of study questions for which he felt he could conveniently prepare. Following mastery of the material he could be given a unit test that corresponded in length to the unit for which he had prepared.

Students in the modified-Keller section were also allowed to earn a maximum of 100 extra points—the maximum number of points that could be earned from a midterm examination. These points could be earned by doing a small experiment, reading and writing a report on material related to the course in an area of special interest to the student, *etc.* The only restriction imposed was that the subject matter of the project must relate to the course content and the project must be approved by the course assistant.

As in the Keller section, a student in the modified-Keller section was assigned a proctor, and received the same study guide questions. When the student felt he had completely mastered the material he wished to be tested on, he would report to the proctor for a unit test. If his performance was satisfactory, he would select the reading assignment and receive the study questions for his next study unit. If his performance was unsatisfactory, he was asked to review the reading material and then take another unit test over the same material. This was continued until all 57 segments of the course were completed. The pacing requirement discussed regarding the Keller section also applied to the modified-Keller section.

Rotating section. The final class section was exposed to all three of the teaching procedures previously described. This group of students started in the Lecture-Discussion section and were then re-assigned to the other sections after the first midterm examination. At this time, half of these students were assigned to the

Keller section and the remaining half were asked to report to the modified-Keller section. After the second midterm examination, these students were again re-assigned, and those in the Keller section now reported to the modified-Keller class and those in the modified-Keller section reported to the Keller class. Regardless of the section to which they were assigned, the instructional procedures in effect were those appropriate to the particular class they were attending.

Testing procedure. The primary measures of course effectiveness were the midterm and final examinations common to all sections. These examinations consisted of multiple choice items in which one, some, or all of the choices could be correct, fill-in items, and short answer essay or definition items. Each midterm included about 30 test items, and the final examination had 60 items. These examinations were constructed by the senior author without prior knowledge of the study questions assigned to students in the Keller and modified-Keller classes.

All examinations were given in the same room to all students at the same time. Each student was given a test to which a numbered slip of paper had been attached. The students were instructed to write only their name on the numbered slip, detach it, and return it to the course assistant. To prevent grader bias these slips were placed in an envelope until grading of the examinations was completed.

Scoring of the completed examinations was done independently by the three authors. Each exam reader scored each item on each examination and recorded his scores on a separate sheet for each student. When exam scoring was completed, a total score for each summary sheet was obtained and a mean of the three totals for each student was computed. This mean score served as the numerical grade the student received for the examination. Only at this stage were the numbered slips matched with the examinations so that the names and sections of the students were revealed to the authors.

At the conclusion of the course, the scores from the two midterms and the final examination were summed for each student and a distribution of total scores was obtained for those students in the lecture-discussion section. This distribution was divided in the traditional way into letter grades of A, B, C, D, and E (failing) by the senior author. Generally speaking, the location of a cut-off line in this distribution was based upon a number of considerations; *e.g.,* the senior author's personal standards of excellence for certain letter grades, relative student standing in the distribution, and gaps in the distribution. The total examination scores of the Keller, rotating, and modified-Keller sections were then compared with this distribution from the lecture section and final letter grades for all students were assigned using the cut off lines from the lecture-discussion section.

RESULTS

Examination Performance

Inter-grader agreement. To evaluate inter-grader agreement of total scores assigned each midterm and final examination, each grader's scores were correlated with those of each of the other two graders. Over the three examinations these Pearson *r* correlations ranged from $+0.79$ to $+0.96$, with a median correlation of $+0.83$.

Examination scores. Because of variation in the total number of points that could be earned on midterm examinations and the final examination, each student's score on each of the examinations was converted to a percentage score; that is,

$$\frac{\text{points earned}}{\text{points possible}} \times 100.$$ This conversion permitted a direct comparison of examinations and facilitated further statistical analysis.

Unfortunately, the initial assignment of students to the four class sections was based on a list of students who pre-registered for the course, and not on the list of students who actually attended the first day of class. Eleven of the students who pre-registered failed to appear in the classroom and these pre-registration withdrawals quite markedly altered both the number of students and the distribution of GPAs in each of the class sections. In an attempt to adjust the class sections for initial differences in student quality, the data were subjected to anal-

yses of covariance, with cumulative GPA the covariate. The data included in each of the following analyses were from students who completed the entire course; *i.e.,* partial data obtained from students who withdrew from the course or who failed to take one of the examinations for other reasons have been excluded from the following analyses.

A 3×4 (tests $\times$ class sections) analysis of covariance revealed a statistically significant main effect of both class sections ($F_{3, 36} = 4.18$, $p < 0.05$) and examinations ($F_{2, 74} = 5.02$, $p < 0.05$). A comparison of the four adjusted class section means using the Duncan Multiple Range Test showed the lecture-discussion section statistically different ($p < 0.05$) from each of the other sections, with no other statistically reliable differences. The statistically significant main effect of examinations is of little interest, and shows only that the three examinations were not of equal difficulty.

Table 1 shows, for each class section, the number of students completing the course, the mean GPA of those students and the standard deviation of that distribution of GPAs, the unadjusted mean score on each of the three examinations and the standard deviation of those exam scores, and the adjusted mean score for each examination. Although the lack of a statistically significant interaction ($F_{6, 74} = 1.36$, $p > 0.05$) between instructional procedures and examinations prevents a thorough analysis of the class section means over the three examinations, there is sufficient *a priori* interest in similarities and differences among the four sections on the first examination to warrant making comparisons of these means. A Duncan Multiple Range Test of the four class section means on the first examination revealed the Keller and modified-Keller sections were both statistically different ($p < 0.05$) from the Lecture and Rotating sections, with no other statistically reliable differences.

To evaluate how students in each of the four class sections scored on each of the three test item types, a percentage score for each item type was obtained for each student on each examination, and these percentage scores were combined to produce for each student a mean mul-

Table 1

Means and Standard Deviations of GPA and Adjusted and Unadjusted Scores on Each Examination for Each Class Section

Class Section	n	$\overline{X}$ GPA	σ GPA	$\overline{X}$ Exam Score			σ Exam Score			Adj. $\overline{X}$ Exam Score		
				Exam 1	Exam 2	Exam 3	Exam 1	Exam 2	Exam 3	Exam 1	Exam 2	Exam 3
Lecture	12	2.52	0.56	72.8	69.8	65.2	12.2	13.8	13.1	74.5	71.5	66.9
Rotating	10	2.88	0.49	75.0	77.4	82.1	13.8	9.1	8.3	73.1	75.5	80.2
Mod-Keller	12	2.82	0.63	83.0	77.9	78.8	6.6	7.0	10.6	81.7	76.6	77.5
Keller	7	2.50	0.64	84.0	79.6	78.1	10.4	8.7	15.9	85.9	81.5	80.0

Table 2

Means and Standard Deviations of GPA and Adjusted and Unadjusted Scores on Each Item Type for Each Class Section

Class Section	n	$\overline{X}$ GPA	σ GPA	$\overline{X}$ Exam Score			σ Exam Score			Adj. $\overline{X}$ Exam Score		
				MC	FI	ESS	MC	FI	ESS	MC	FI	ESS
Lecture	12	2.52	0.56	77.6	69.9	60.3	10.4	14.9	13.8	79.3	71.6	62.0
Rotating	10	2.88	0.49	84.4	82.2	73.5	6.5	10.1	10.0	82.5	80.3	71.6
Mod-Keller	12	2.82	0.63	85.6	81.8	71.1	5.6	6.1	13.4	84.3	80.5	69.8
Keller	7	2.50	0.64	80.4	82.4	78.8	8.4	9.9	15.4	82.3	84.3	80.7

tiple choice (MC), a mean fill-in (FI), and a mean essay score (ESS). These mean scores were then entered into a 3 × 4 (test item type × class section) analysis of covariance, with cumulative GPA again the covariate. This analysis revealed a statistically significant item type × class section interaction ($F_{6, 74} = 2.26$, $p < 0.05$) and a significant main effect of both instructional procedure ($F_{3, 36} = 4.18$, $p < 0.05$) and item type ($F_{2, 74} = 35.35$, $p < 0.05$).

A comparison of the adjusted means making up the interaction revealed no statistically reliable differences among the four class sections on multiple choice items, but the lecture-discussion section scored poorer than each of the other three sections on both fill-in and essay items. In addition, on essay items the mean score of the Keller section was statistically higher than the mean essay score of both the rotating and modified-Keller sections. The relevant means and standard deviations are shown in Table 2.

Total scores and letter grades. Upon completion of the course, mean scores obtained on each midterm and the final examination were summed for each student. Perfect performance in the course was shown by a score of 400 points; 100 points for each midterm examination, and 200 points for the final examination. Before examining the total scores obtained by students in the Keller, modified-Keller, and rotating sections of the course, the senior author examined the distribution of points in the lecture-discussion section and determined the cut-off for the various letter grades. As mentioned earlier, once these cut-off points were determined for students in the lecture-discussion section they were also employed in assigning letter grades to students in the other three sections of the course. Figure 1 shows the distribution of total points earned in each section of the course and the frequency with which letter grades of A, B, C, D, and E were earned by students in each of the four class sections.

Student Withdrawals

Excluding students who never attended class, the pattern of withdrawals from the various

sections of the course was as follows. One student (GPA = 1.80) withdrew from the Keller section after obtaining passing grades on both midterm examinations because he fell far behind after the second midterm. One student (GPA = 2.24) in the modified-Keller section insisted on attending class with students in the lecture-discussion section after he had successfully passed unit tests over approximately three chapters of material. This student subsequently attended lectures, earned a low C grade on the first midterm, and finally withdrew from the course. None of the students in the rotating section withdrew until they were assigned to the

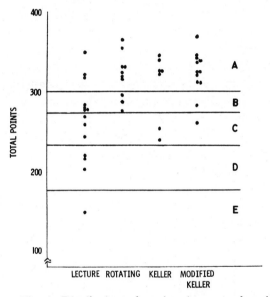

Fig. 1. Distribution of total points earned and final grade assigned to students in each of the four class sections.

Keller or modified-Keller sections. Following re-assignment, two students (GPA's = 1.21 and 2.00) dropped out of the rotating group after spending one and three weeks (respectively) in the non-lecture sections. One of these students (GPA = 1.21) insisted that he could not do well under the Keller procedures and was subsequently granted permission to remain with the lecture group. He performed poorly on each examination and earned a final grade of E. The other student officially withdrew from the course. There were no withdrawals from the lecture-discussion section.

*Student Examination Performance
Within the Rotating Section*

The rotating section was included in the design of the present investigation to determine the feasibility of making an intra-subject evaluation of the teaching procedures used. Unfortunately, intra-subject variability in examination scores was sufficiently great to preclude an analysis at the level of individual students. However, in an attempt to determine whether the various teaching procedures affected good students and poorer students in this section similarly, each of the three sets of examination scores for the entire class was rank ordered, with the lowest score receiving a rank of 1. The rotating class was then divided and the ranks of the five students scoring at the top of the class on the first examination were averaged for each of the two remaining examinations, and the ranks of the five students scoring in the lower half of the class on the first examination were similarly averaged. These mean ranks are shown in Figure 2. Generally speaking, the examination performance of students in the upper half of the class was not differentially affected by the different teaching procedures, possibly because of a

ceiling on the test scores. However, the change to personalized instructional procedures produced an increase in the lower half of the rotating class. From these data it would appear that the major contribution of personalized instructional procedures is that they develop higher levels of excellence in "good" to "poor" students—a result that tends to justify "top-heavy" letter grade distributions (like those in Figure 1) to skeptical colleagues.

Patterns of Progress Through the Course

The students in the modified-Keller course might have been expected to show a variety of patterns of progress through the reading assignments. One student in the modified-Keller section attended class only on alternate testing days and consistently completed two chapters at a time; *i.e.,* the equivalent of two units of work in the Keller section. Another student in the modified-Keller section employed the contrasting provision and took one complete unit and a part of another to make up for missed classes at the end of the course. Other than these two exceptions, all students in the modified-Keller section elected to study and take examinations over one chapter at a time. Therefore, although there were opportunities for differences in individual rate of progress, the students in the modified-Keller section tended to progress through the course in a manner like the students in the Keller section where a study unit corresponded to a single chapter in the book.

One further difference between the modified-Keller and Keller sections is of interest. Although students in the modified-Keller section were allowed to design and execute their own projects for academic credit, only three students took advantage of this option, and all three contracted to turn in a paper for extra points. In all three instances, the students had earned A grades on the basis of their examination performance, and additional points from the project were not needed to obtain a grade of A.

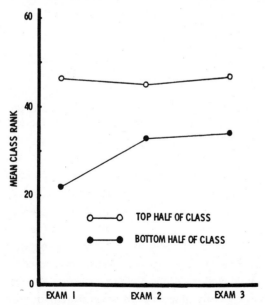

Fig. 2. Mean class standing on each exam of students scoring in the upper and lower half of the rotating class on the first examination. The reader should note that the lowest exam score was assigned a rank of 1, and that higher ranks are associated with higher examination scores.

DISCUSSION

Earlier reports of the impact of Keller-type instruction on students in university level classes have indicated a higher withdrawal rate than usually occurs in more traditionally taught courses (Keller, 1968; McMichael and Corey, 1969; Sheppard and MacDermot, 1970; Born, 1971). In the present investigation, there is also slight evidence of a higher drop rate. Excluding pre-registration withdrawals, no students withdrew from the Keller section, one student withdrew from the modified-Keller section, and two students withdrew from the revolving section. Interestingly, the two students who withdrew from the revolving section did not withdraw until they were requested to rotate to Keller-type classes. The fact that the median GPA of students withdrawing from the personalized sections was 1.91 (range from 1.21-2.42), whereas the median GPA of students completing the course was 2.66 (range 1.21-4.00), is important considering the claim that personalized instructional procedures generate higher quality student performance than more traditional lecture-discussion techniques. The possibility exists that performance in personalized courses is superior on the average because academically poorer students tend to withdraw from classes taught in this manner.

Evidence that the additional effectiveness of the Keller instructional method cannot be accounted for solely on the basis of differential withdrawals was obtained from an analysis of examination scores earned in the various sections of the present course. Since the analysis of covariance presumably corrected the class section means for differences in the GPA distributions, the obtained differences are not simply a consequence of the fact that poorer students tend to remain in the lecture-discussion section of the course.

The finding that academically less successful students withdrew from the personalized courses is at odds with findings of Sheppard and Mac-Dermot (1970), who reported that the average GPA of students withdrawing from their personalized courses was comparable to the average GPA of students completing the course. In the past few years the senior author has taught several personalized beginning psychology courses, and students withdrawing from these courses have typically come from the pool of poor to mediocre students (Born, 1971). For example, in the most recent course, the average GPA of the 27 students who withdrew was 1.99, and the average GPA of the 71 students completing the course was 2.62. Thus, withdrawal by poorer students seems to be characteristic of our classroom procedures, and it would be important to know precisely which features of the Sheppard and MacDermot course alter this pattern of withdrawals. As in the case of Sheppard and MacDermot, the most frequent comment by students withdrawing from our courses was that they are "too much work" (Born and Herbert, 1970), and we have assumed that withdrawals are related to study habits; *i.e.,* students who typically study regularly tend to carry a higher GPA and find the personalized course procedures require no special change from their regular study routine, whereas students who study infrequently might tend to earn a lower GPA and find the course demands considerably more work. The Sheppard and MacDermot finding suggests there may be other interpretations of the higher withdrawal rate associated with personalized courses.

At the time of the second midterm examination, two students were absent because of illness and were allowed to take the same exam several days later. Both of these students were in the lecture section. On the last day of class, in discussing the course procedures and preliminary results in lecture, both of these students indicated that they were not in fact ill at the time of the second exam, but rather that they had not finished reading all of the assigned material and feigned illness to gain additional time to study. Although each of them had read the major textbook, a study of the related readings, the content of which was also included on the examinations, had not been completed. Also, two other students from the lecture class who took the examination at the regularly scheduled time reported that in spite of intensive "cramming" they also did not have time to study the related readings carefully, but did manage to skim read that portion of the assigned course work. Since students were required to complete unit examinations before taking the midterms in the personalized classes, the need for intensive cramming was eliminated. Likely, the forced pacing of study behavior in the personalized classes is a major factor in the differences in examination performance obtained in the present experiment.

Although valuable data were gathered by including the rotating section in the present experiment, some problems developed with students in this section which should be considered in future classroom investigations employing intra-subject designs. These problems were associated with complaints about the course from several students. A potential source of these complaints comes from the fact that students in this section were subjected to a different teaching procedure about every three weeks. One consequence of this frequent re-assignment to a new classroom and teaching staff was that these students failed to develop the personal friendships with the teaching staff that emerged in each of the other sections. Thus, although their instruction was "individualized" it was not necessarily "personalized".

Generally speaking, the data related to how different class sections scored on different examination item types confirm and extend the findings of other investigators. Both McMichael and Corey (1969) and Sheppard and McDermot (1970) found that personalized procedures produce better student performance on multiple-choice items, and the latter investigators found these same students perform better on essay questions as well. Although there were no statistically reliable differences among the class sections on multiple choice items in the present experiment, the lowest mean performance was obtained from students in the lecture section. On fill-in and essay items, however, the lecture section was significantly poorer than each of the other sections. Possibly superior performance by students in the non-lecture sections on items that required written responses resulted from the fact that unit tests in the personalized classes required students to compose written answers, and there were, therefore, many opportunities for proctors to "shape" examination writing skills. Because there were no multiple choice questions on unit tests there were no similar opportunities to develop skills in answering multiple choice items. Not inconsistent with

this suggestion is the fact that students in the Keller section performed better than students in all sections on essay items. Because there were fewer students in this section, proctors presumably had more time to spend with each individual student and could do a more thorough evaluation of student mastery of course material.

Although not previously mentioned, an extensive questionnaire was completed by each student at the end of the course. Generally, the questionnaire revealed the same general findings reported by Gallup (1969) and Sheppard and MacDermot (1970); the personalized courses were judged to be a great deal of work, virtually free of cheating, and demanding a higher level of mastery than would be required in a similar class taught with the lecture method. Eighty five per cent of the students completing the personalized classes indicated that they enjoyed the class and would recommend it highly to their friends; only about half of the students in the lecture section indicated they would make a similar recommendation. Among students in the rotating section, the only group exposed to both lecture and personalized procedures, four out of 10 indicated a preference for lecture. However, for reasons mentioned previously these latter data should be interpreted cautiously. All things considered, personalized instruction would appear to be an important step in the direction of solving some of the serious problems in higher education.

REFERENCES

Born, D. G. and Herbert, Emily W. A further study of Keller's personalized system of instruction. *Journal of Experimental Education*, 1971, *in press*. [Article 6]

Born, D. G. *Student withdrawals in personalized instruction courses and in lecture courses.* In F. Newman (Chm.), Personalized Instruction: A national trend moves into the rocky mountain region. Symposium presented at the meeting of the Rocky Mountain Psychological Association, Denver, May, 1971.

Ferster, C. B. Individualized instruction in a large introductory psychology course. *Psychological Record*, 1968, **18**, 521-532. [Article 34]

Ferster, C. B. and Perrott, Mary C. *Behavior principles.* New York: Meredith Corp., 1968.

Gallup, H. F. *Personalized instruction in introductory psychology.* Paper presented at the meeting of the Midwestern Psychological Association, Chicago, Illinois, May, 1969.

Keller, Fred S.   A personal course in psychology. In R. Ulrich, T. Stachnik, and J. Marbry (Eds.), *Control of human behavior.* Glenview, Illinois: Scott Foresman, Inc., 1966. Pp. 91-93. [Article 37]

Keller, Fred S.   "Goodbye, teacher. . ." *Journal of Applied Behavior Analysis,* 1968, **1**, 79-89. [Article 1]

Malott, R. W. and Svinicki, J. G.   Contingency management in an introductory psychology course for one thousand students. *Psychological Record,* 1969, **19**, 545-556.

Malott, R. W., Whaley, D. L., and Ulrich, R. E. *Analysis of behavior: principles and applications.* Dubuque, Iowa: Wm. C. Brown Co., 1967.

McMichael, J. S. and Corey, J. R.   Contingency management in a introductory psychology course produces better learning. *Journal of Applied Behavior Analysis,* 1969, **2**, 79-83. [Article 2]

Pennypacker, H. S.   *Precision teaching of an undergraduate program in behavior principles.* Paper presented at the meeting of the Midwestern Psychological Association, Chicago, Illinois, May, 1969.

Sheppard, W. C. and MacDermot, H. G.   Design and evaluation of a programmed course in introductory psychology. *Journal of Applied Behavior Analysis,* 1970, **3**, 5-11. [Article 9]

Winer, B. J.   *Statistical principles in experimental design.* New York: McGraw-Hill, Inc., 1962.

Received 16 March 1971.
(Revised 1 August 1971.)

Section II

Other Disciplines

Probably the first PSI course in a subject matter other than psychology was a physics course given by Dr. Ben A. Green, Jr., at M.I.T. in the spring of 1969. Article 11 reporting on PSI at M.I.T. begins this section.

A summary of PSI courses in the June 1972 issue of the *PSI Newsletter* indicated that, after psychology and physics, PSI courses have been given most frequently in engineering, math and statistics, chemistry, and biology, in that order. Brief reports of applications in these disciplines are included here. Astronomy, Spanish, library science, and philosophy are also represented. Since these extensions of PSI to new subject areas have all occurred within the past two years, several of the reports are preliminary and informal.

The diversity of subject matter represents more than just a laundry list of disciplines. A significant question emerges when we note that as the course content diverges from the sciences, the course procedures follow the PSI format less closely. It is simply too early to state with certainty whether this trend represents the caution and successive approximations characteristic of early attempts or whether it represents necessary changes reflecting real differences between the sciences and humanities.

For those contemplating using PSI in new subject matter areas, it must be stated very clearly that this method requires detailed behavioral objectives which can be specified in advance. This by no means limits the goals to rote learning of facts. Recent texts (for example Julie S. Vargus *Writing Worthwhile Behavioral Objectives* New York: Harper and Row, 1972) suggest success with goals directed toward achievements as complex as concept formation and creativity. While many report that the attempt to state objectives is beneficial in itself, it clearly is not an easy task in many disciplines.

We might approach the matter of PSI's limitations from a different direction. When an instructor finds himself repeating the same information to a large number of students, he has found something predictable. The predictable can be passed on to a proctor, leaving the instructor's more valuable time for what cannot be predicted. As a result, the instructor trades boredom for challenge, the student gains greater access to the talents of a less harried teacher when help is needed most, and the proctor is able to instruct on standard material with a first-time freshness, while he is also learning. This seems to be one of those rare instances where everyone wins.

From this view the applicability of PSI is not limited by a line dividing the arts and sciences, nor by the overused distinction between rote learning and "something more creative," nor even by stereotyped versus unique properties of the subject matter itself. Rather, the limitations seem better described in terms of the amount of redundancy in the *teaching,* whatever the topic. This approach suggests that the prospective user should first evaluate how often he repeats himself, perhaps also considering how often he feels there was no time to get beyond fundamentals. When every student-teacher interaction is totally unique, PSI is not applicable.

One final comment on the papers in this section. The reader should note that the grade distribution and preference data closely follow the results reported in Section I.

11

PHYSICS TEACHING
BY THE KELLER PLAN AT MIT*

Ben A. Green, Jr.

The Keller plan (a self-paced, student-tutored, mastery-oriented instructional system) has spread widely in the six years of its existence, but mainly in teaching psychology. The paper reports experience with the plan in introductory physics. The results are strongly favorable; students report that they learn material more thoroughly and more efficiently. Lectures are used sparingly and mainly for motivation. Students may take as many as 20 written tests in a semester without complaint. Sophomore tutors grade the tests on the spot and have proven to be extremely valuable. The instructor's role is not to broadcast information but to manage a system and to write the necessary tests and other materials, as well as to give personal help to individuals in unusual cases.

The conventional system of lectures, laboratories, recitations, problem sets, and examinations works pretty well for many physics students. For convenience and economy it is hard to beat, although the convenience is to the teacher and the economy is to the administration.

Nonetheless, many of us have sensed that there might be a better way to teach. We remember from our days as students how boring it was to sit through a lecture on something we understood perfectly well, or to wait out an explanation repeated for someone who was too busy writing down the previous remark to catch the current one. We chafed under the necessity of attending a nine o'clock class when we had spent the night on a term paper due in another subject. If we cut the class, we worried about what was covered. Even when we felt we knew the material, we often worried about the exam, for we remembered other occasions when we had walked into an unexpected question and realized too late that our understanding had only touched the surface.

Most innovations in physics teaching have naturally tended to center on things of interest to the physicist. A new apparatus to demonstrate conservation of angular momentum, a cheaply producible accelerometer, a beautiful film show-

ing examples of geometrical symmetry, a way to draw Lissajous figures with sand, and, on the theoretical side, a simpler way to derive a difficult result—all of these things are inherently interesting to the teacher as physicist (and to his physicist colleagues).

But there are other constituencies which the innovationally inclined teaching physicist must serve—constituencies which have different needs. One such constituency is the students. At a minimum, the students want to learn what will gain them access to useful professions, whether that be grades or understanding. Another, the administration, wants this to happen at minimum expense; and if an external funding agency is paying for the educational innovation, it would like to be assured that the new thing is effective and exportable.

Evaluation in these terms has been difficult. The instructional effect of ingenious apparatus, of a new film, or even of a new textbook depends on the instructional system into which it fits. Each of those innovations is, in fact, only a component of a system, and it is, finally, a whole system which succeeds or fails.

The purpose of this paper is to report our experience at MIT with an instructional system designed to exploit what has been found about learning from the perspective of "reinforcement theory." Before describing this particular system, let us consider instructional systems in general from this point of view.

The concept of an instructional system is not useful until we distinguish between teaching and the transmission of information. It is obvious that one does not teach violin playing merely by transmitting information to the student about how to play the violin. The student must do his part, and the teacher must evaluate and respond to the student's efforts. The student is an active element in a process, not merely a receiver of

From *American Journal of Physics*, Vol. 39, No. 7, July 1971.

information. In verbal learning (as opposed to skill acquisition) the "receiver model" of the student appears to work better, but that is mainly because the other phases of the learning process are not usually made explicit. They are still there.

In the view taken here, learning is a three-step process: presentation, response, and consequence.[1] *Presentation* is the sending of signals (including "course content"), whether by lecture, textbook, film, or live demonstration. *Response* is what the student does after the presentation. Thinking about what was just said is a minimal response; working a problem is a more visible one. But a response dies out unless it is followed by a favorable *consequence* at least occasionally. After thinking, one suddenly understands. After working a problem, one sees that the answer is right. After taking a test, one gets an A. Occurrence of the consequence completes a cycle.

To design an instructional system is to arrange a sequence of these three-element cycles in such a way as to optimize learning. This can be done at various levels of detail. At the finer end of the scale there is programmed instruction of the short-question, quick-answer, quick-confirmation type. On the coarse end there is a semester plan of lectures (presentation), final exam (response), and course grade (consequence), which constitute only one giant cycle. Most good college courses fall somewhere between these extremes.

It seems important to avoid both these extremes. The small-frame program tends to get monotonous; a student needs more variety in his response mode if his interest is to be sustained through a period of months. Besides, such small-frame programs are expensive to create and tend not to take advantage of the self-teaching skills many college students have acquired in high school. The "one-big-final-exam" course, on the other hand, is notoriously ineffective. Most courses have at least a mid-term exam and if the grades are fed back to the students, this completes a first half-term cycle. The instructional system to be described below has its most prominent cycles about one week in length.

The system I now wish to describe has been called "self-paced study," but self-pacing is only one feature. It has been called variously "personalized" and "programmed" by its inventors, Fred S. Keller and J. G. Sherman. Perhaps the best choice is to call it the "Keller plan" in honor of the senior member of this team, a distinguished psychologist who was for many years chairman of the psychology department at Columbia University.

A visitor observing sessions of a Keller-plan course finds it hard to see what is going on. He wants to know how often the class meets and what hours the students are required to attend. There is a puzzling bustle and confusion in scheduled rooms at scheduled hours. People are busy talking, writing, walking around. There may be more than one room in use; one where people are writing, another filled with pairs of people talking. The instructor may be talking with one or two students, or he may be idly reading a newspaper. Students are continually entering or leaving with no particular notice taken of the fact.

What is going on is basically this: The subject matter of the course has been divided into *units* of work, in our practice about one week's work of a conventional course. For each unit there is a *study guide* and a set of perhaps four short *tests*, hopefully equivalent. The instructor has bought his ease by preparing these materials in advance.

A student works from the study guide, which states what he should learn and suggests a way to go about it. When the student feels that he can do what he is supposed to be able to (such as work problems of a given type, explain certain apparent paradoxes, give an account of certain historical developments), he asks the instructor for a test. He writes out his answers in the classroom and takes the paper to his *tutor*, an undergraduate who attends class sessions regularly for this purpose and who is responsible for 10 students. The tutor examines the paper and marks it (after discussion with the student) pass or fail: If pass, the student gets the next unit's study guide from the instructor. If fail, the student must work further on the same unit and try again.

The apparent confusion in the classroom reflects the fact that some of the students there are just studying alone, some are taking tests, and some are consulting their tutors on difficult points. Sometimes the instructor is asked to review a paper on which the student and tutor disagree. Sometimes he substitutes as tutor himself.

Some students may be working on Unit 9 while others are still on Unit 2. The pace is up to the student, within limits. Some students make rapid progress in spite of failing many tests; others are more cautious and never fail, although their pace is slow. (The usual equation "fast" equals "good" breaks down.) What counts is progress, no matter how fast or slow. Failures on unit tests do not affect one's course grade.

If the visitor to the course comes on one of the rare days when lectures are given, he will notice that attendance is small, but that those attending are awake and alert to participate. He may be surprised to hear that the day's lecture is intentionally "off on a tangent" to the main course content. In fact, students are promised that attending the lecture will *not* help them gain a higher grade. Even more strange, the students may have had to earn the right to attend the lecture by having passed a critical number of units. There may be only one lecture every two or three weeks.

Depending on the subject matter, the student may have a variety of other things to do besides studying from books and papers. He may have facilities to view film or film loops. He may be able to check out take-home kits for doing experiments. But, in each case, he decides whether to engage in the activity according to whether he thinks that to do so will help him achieve the unit's objectives, as stated in the study guide.

I first read of this instructional system in an article by Keller[2] which was detailed enough to enable me to try out the scheme with 20 students in the spring term of 1969. The subject was 8.02, meaning physics (8), second semester (02), which includes special relativity and an introduction to electromagnetism. We used the same texts[3] as were used in the regular course; only the method was changed. I broke 8.02x (x meaning the experimental section) into 18 units of work and for each unit, I wrote a study guide and four tests. The guides were between two and 10 pages double-spaced. I stated objectives as operationally as I could in a few lines, and I made up a "suggested procedure" consisting of reading, working a few problems, answering a few questions, and sometimes viewing a film. In areas where my conception of the subject matter differed from that of the text, I wrote some prose discussion, and often I made up short programmed sequences of questions.

Of the 1000 students enrolled in 8.01 in the preceding fall term, about 600 heard my brief announcement of an experimental course, about 150 came to that evening's meeting at which the course was described, and 100 applied for the 20 places I could offer. I tried to choose equally between those who were bored with the "slow"

pace of 8.01 and those who were hopelessly left behind by its "swift" march.

It has become cliche in educational innovation to report that "the students were enthusiastic." I enjoyed giving the course. I found that I got to know the students much better. I knew they were learning more because I had in hand the 18 tests which each student wrote out by the end of the term. I discovered difficulties and had to repair several units. How the students experienced the course is reflected in their comments, some of which are quoted below.[4]

The success of 8.02x in that spring term 1969 led me to try 8.01x in the fall, again with only 20 students. My colleague, Edwin Taylor, decided to offer 8.04x at the same time. Jay Walton of Civil Engineering offered a computer course 1.00x as well. Each of these new Keller-style courses were kept small so as to give us a chance to prove our study guides. If something were not good enough, we could teach it "by hand" if necessary. In the following term (spring, 1970) we gave 8.02x again to 100 students, under the leadership of Daniel Kleppner and Berol Robinson; and Edwin Taylor again gave 8.04x, this time for 75 students. At this writing (fall, 1970), all of 8.01x, 8.02x, 8.03x, and 8.04x are available, and 8.05x is being prepared.

Obviously we are pleased. We can see students working hard and enjoying it. We know from previous experience that they are learning fully as much as students in the regular versions of these courses.

We have not collected comparative test data. (Others who have tried the Keller plan[2,5,6] and have published such data find an *inverted* normal distribution of grades: more A's than C's.) Such comparisons are debatable and usually do not convince skeptics anyway. Instead, let us report the comments students make about our Keller courses. In addition to students' responses to questionnaires, we have Freshman Performance Evaluation sheets which each freshman must fill out twice a semester for each of his courses. Although they are asked to rate themselves on these sheets, many freshmen comment on the course as well as on their own performances.

We report these comments by category, since it is of great interest to see what features of the course students see as important, positively or negatively. First the global judgments:

A rave review:

FANTASTIC. I wish all my courses could be like this. I personally enjoy this more than any other course I take. It is more satisfying than anything else. Every department in the Institute should be required to offer self-paced options in each subject.

I am very glad I took part and would enjoy taking similar courses not only to learn the material but also to examine the educational aspects of the things worked. I'm interested in education and this is really great. Keep up the good work—but remember you're writing for dummies—not fellow professors.

Freedom, understanding, without pressures for problem solving skill.

Rather than the 8.01 emphasis on solutions, 8.01x places its emphasis on understanding, with solutions coming as a logical extension.

You'll have to pay me to take 8.02 when 8.02x is available.

Here is our only global bad review:

8.01x is a teach-and-learn course and turned out to be as inefficient as all its competitors. The human mind does not learn efficiently or permanently when it is told something, read something, deduces something, etc.

This last comment probably refers to the highly structured nature of the course. The subject is laid out in serial order of topics, and the student is advised just how to study for each one. This is not to everyone's taste, but the objection occurs more often to teachers than to students. So far I have had only two students out of about 50 who felt this reaction strongly. I advised these students to switch back to the regular class. In fact, neither of them did so. One continued with us and then enrolled in the succeeding 8.02x; the other got permission to pursue independent study, in which he performed very well.

The specific feature of our experiment which received most comment was freedom of pace.

I go at my own speed; I have no pressure put on me by other people; people don't try to make a jackass out of me when I don't know something.

For the student who wishes to study without being paced by an instructor, it is ideal.

If I don't finish an 8.02 problem set by the due date, that is too bad, but in this course, one can procrastinate *ad infinitum,*

if necessary. I have just taken a two-week vacation from physics but am not behind at all.

I think one of the benefits of self-study is the freedom to set your own pace and define your own interests. Regular courses tend to bring the horizons of a topic too close, hemming you in.

If I were in 8.01 and had troubles . . .I'd be behind by the time I got it figured out. Here I'm not, and when I catch onto something I don't have to wait around for others to hold me back.

Time to dwell on a subject if I wanted to.

I found I had gone quickly through the first few units and was able to spend more time later on parts that were unclear.

Closely related to freedom of pace were comments focusing on the freedom to study when and where one wishes.

I like to work on them [units] when not in the mood for too much work. I am especially glad to be free of problem sets and lectures.

Not the regular hum-drum. It was nice to be able to do it when you wanted—not when you were supposed to.

Free work schedule was the best thing.

Not getting up at 9 for lecture, no problem sets (to submit formally), or deadlines.

The tutors were valued:

. . . tutors—most effective part of program (if tutor is good).

(Most of our sophomore tutors have been very good.)

They [tutors] are very helpful when self is insufficient for self-study.

A comment on what we call "mastery as a criterion for advancement":

This type of program is just what is needed for P–F grading. If you don't know it, you get an F, but have a chance to keep at it until you get a P; then, you know you know it—and no half measures, either.

Another student put his finger on the response–consequence phases of the learning cycle:

The structure of the course is such that one can see the immediate effect of one's labors. Each unit test gives one a sense of accomplishment.

A prime payoff to the student from the self-paced format is that it makes his work more efficient:

> My time was used more effectively.

> I have gone through the material quite rapidly, not because there is less to do but because the presentation agrees with me.

> I have not had to work at all hard, however, and sometimes doubt that I am learning as much as the people who spend endless hours on regular 8.01 problem set and reading. If all my courses were like this one, I would be learning more and spending less time on useless homework assignments.

> When I see the other students on the [dormitory] floor slaving over 8.01 problem sets three nights a week, and not getting too far at that, I take pity.

This efficiency results from a number of factors, but most prominent among them is probably the fact that the objectives of each unit's work are defined explicitly. The student does not spend time on other matters unless he is interested in them for their own sake. While this saves a student time, it may cost him the many other things he might have learned if he had chosen topics more randomly. Some students complain about this. Actually, a student still has freedom to explore in self-paced study and we encourage him to use it. We do *require* a specified minimum which is easy to acquire. If this minimum is interesting, other exploration becomes self-rewarding.

We come now to the most troublesome aspect of self-pacing: What if the pace is too slow? We have all had the experience of working better under deadlines than without them. When the problem sets do not have to be turned in precisely on Wednesdays, it is easy to put off the work. In the students' words:

> I feel I could have done better and delved more deeply into the material had I been self-motivated. But because of the nature of the course and pressure from other subjects, I did only an adequate amount of work.

> The temptation to loaf when on the self-paced program was too much and I fell units behind. However, in the past week or so, I have made up most of the work.

Procrastination is a problem only with some students. The average rate of work in our freshman course 8.01x in the present term can be seen in Fig. 1, which shows the total number of tests passed versus time (class days) in the fall term, 1970. If everyone eventually passed all the units, the curve would coincide with the straight line at the right-hand side of the graph; and if everyone passed units at a steady rate, the curve would *be* the straight line. Thus the gap between the curve and the line is a measure of either procrastination or (toward the end of the term especially) withdrawal. The curve shows that, on the average, the freshmen keep up well.

It is interesting to compare the two sophomore courses 8.03x and 8.04x in this respect. Edwin Taylor, who ran 8.04x in the fall term, 1970, was not particularly concerned with the procrastination problem. If a student wanted to finish the work during the following term, that was okay. In my 8.03x, on the other hand, I announced that "I's" would be hard to get, and that grades would be given on the basis of work accomplished. Furthermore, I (a) published a recommended schedule of dates of passing units which would yield a steady rate of work, (b) made admittance to "fun" lectures contingent on having passed units, and (c) offered early final exams for students who finished the units early. (The final is required in order to get higher than a B grade. The passing schedule contained a normal pace

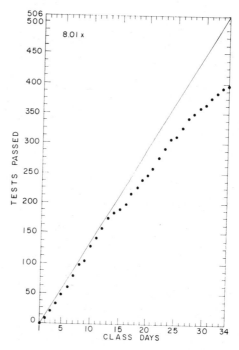

Fig. 1. Total tests passed by class in subject 8.01x vs class days, fall 1970. (The straight line would result if all students worked at a steady rate and finished on time.) The students were freshmen.

and an accelerated pace, the latter finishing in time for the early final.)

The results of these different policies is shown in Figs. 2 and 3, which show the test-passing history of 8.03x and 8.04x. The schedules were published on Day 9, which may account for the jump in the 8.03x curve at that point, although that was also the day just before the first fun lecture.

SOME QUESTIONS AND ANSWERS ABOUT HOW THE COURSES ARE RUN

How many tutors are needed?

We find that a tutor should be responsible for about 10 students, certainly no more than 12. If there are fewer tutors, then the waiting time to get a test graded gets too long. If there are more, a tutor can get too bored waiting for a student to talk with.

How is time scheduled during the week?

We have tried five 1-h periods, three 2-h periods and two 2-h periods (during which the tutors and instructors are available in the study area). A 1-h period is wasteful, since no tutors are needed until students have had time to write out their tests. Also, failure costs a day's delay. With a 2-h period, one has a second chance to pass a test, and the load on tutors tends to even

out over the period. We have settled on three 2-h periods.

How do you keep track of what students are doing?

We have tried several ways. Taylor keeps a record book, a loose-leaf notebook with a page for each student. A notation is entered here of the results of each test and sometimes of other events such as consultations and special arrangements. A picture of the whole class's status is available from a wall chart showing when each student passed each unit. In 8.02x we once used a computer for record keeping, which made it possible to print out a variety of graphs and summary statements. We have since settled for just a wall chart and a status graph for each student.

In all of our x courses, we keep a file folder for each student, which contains his completed unit tests. These tests are raw data for any analysis we choose to make.

What can you do for students who procrastinate?

This is a little complex. Keller advocates ignoring them, on the ground that surely they already know what is expected of them. If they choose not to work, that is their privilege. Certainly if someone has been prodded to work all

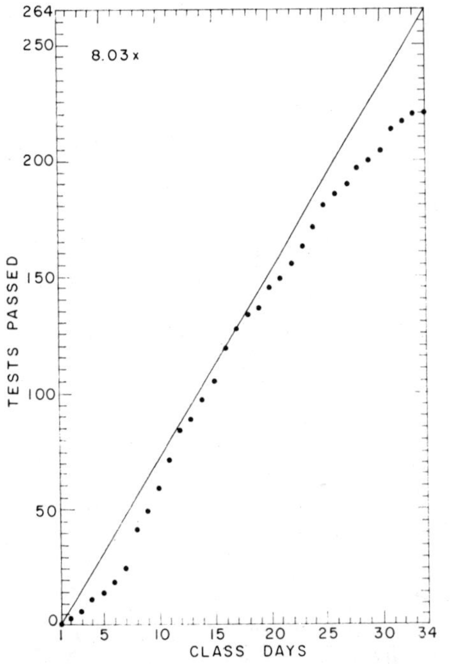

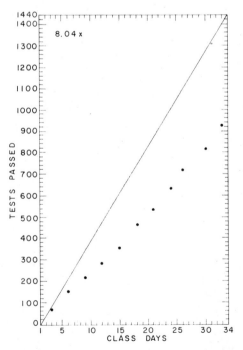

FIG. 2. Total tests passed by class in subject 8.03x vs class days, fall 1970. The students were sophomores.

FIG. 3. Total tests passed by class in subject 8.04x vs class days, fall 1970. The students were sophomores.

his life, it may take him some time to learn to work without the prod. If we prod him some more, he will never have a chance to learn self-motivation. In our experience, this policy is very hard on the instructor. He wants his group to do well not just for their sakes, but for the sake of the experiment. This puts a pressure on him to get in touch with slow students and to bully them on. Our best results in avoiding large-scale procrastination without nagging have been gotten by offering short-term rewards for passing units (admittance to fun lectures), long-term rewards (admittance to early final exams), having a clearly announced policy that I's are hard to get, and giving guidance in setting paces (calendars).

What about students who finish all the work early?

We stand ready to suggest further reading, etc., but we are perfectly content to see them play tennis or watch girls. They have mastered the content of the course, and if further work is not attractive to them, they should not be penalized for their speed. We have recently allowed students in 8.01x and 8.02x to take the final examination early, although some prefer to wait for the regularly scheduled time.

How are grades determined?

We have tried various ways to assign course grades. (Unit test grades are always pass/fail, of course.) In freshman courses, we have set the grade according to mid-term and final examination scores only. This has several theoretical advantages: it takes cheating pressure off the unit tests, it takes the tutors out of the judging business and leaves them purely as coaches, which improves the student–tutor interaction. On the other hand, it puts a great burden on only two examinations. The courses are graded P–F (for freshmen), however, and experience has shown that students who pass the unit tests always pass the final exam. The student who freezes on the final in spite of knowing the material is apparently rarer in our self-paced courses than in others. In sophomore course 8.04x, there is no final and grades are given according to the fraction of the term's work completed. This works well in practice and it seems to give the students a feeling of being above such "childish matters" as final exams. And there are no finals to grade!

What about cheating on the unit tests?

Each unit has four test forms. It would be possible to give a student any one of these at random as a first test. Thus to cheat he would have to have advance information on all four forms of the test. But we don't do this. We just give form 1 first, form 2 (if necessary), etc. In the freshman courses, the unit tests do not count toward a grade, so there is no motive for cheating. There has been no evidence of efforts to cheat in the sophomore courses either.

What goes into a good study guide?

A study guide should tell the student what the unit's objectives are and how to accomplish them. This could be as brief as

Objective: Know what is in Chapter 13,
Procedure: Read it,

but one can do better than that. We like to state the objectives for a week's work in about half a page, single-spaced.

A good procedure is the product of trial and error by the instructor. He must guess what reading is required, what is the minimum set of problems a student needs to work, what outside reading would help, and he must write programmed or other explanatory material to patch over the weak places in the text. Then he must listen to students who try out his procedure and modify it in the light of their experience until finally it works—works for enough students that he is willing to teach the rest by hand.

A seduction to be avoided is to test on juicy items you cover in the procedure which are not also covered by the objectives. Remember, a student should not have to go through your procedure. He may know the material already, and he should be able to judge this by reading the objectives only. Once you discover that you have sinned (you get an irate complaint from a student who skipped the procedure legitimately) you must decide whether you really want everybody to learn the cute item in the procedure (and must say so in the objectives) or you didn't really mean it (and must take it off the test).

How do you handle a laboratory under the Keller plan?

Unfortunately, MIT does not have a full-scale laboratory for the introductory physics sequence, so we cannot answer from personal experience. However, Keller's original course in psychology did have a laboratory, as do several of the physics courses described below. One simply keeps the laboratory open for some scheduled hours and lets anyone come in who wants to work. There is no reason why unit tests should not cover things learnable only from laboratory experience. Swartz (Stony Brook, see below) frequently specifies performance tests using actual equipment. Postlethwaite's botany course at Purdue, which is nearly self-paced, is also centered around laboratory experience.

What kind of student does best under a self-paced regime?

This is a research question we cannot answer well as yet. We hope to develop a test which can predict success under this mode of work. There are, at least, some common-sense things to ask. Does the student have a record of putting things off? Has he succeeded at some kind of independent study? Does he have a clear idea of why he is taking the course?

It may not be worthwhile to try to answer this question. In courses where the students had no alternative to the self-paced version (Arizona State, Portland), they seem to do as well as if they were all volunteers (MIT). It might be that volunteers are self-selected because of the opportunity to procrastinate!

How do you recruit tutors?

So far it has been sufficient just to announce the opportunity to serve by means of bulletin boards and some class announcements.

But what happens if half the courses in the school go Keller-style? Are there enough tutors?

An interesting possibility has been explored by Sherman of Georgetown University. Sherman served as tutor for the first 10 students to finish the first unit. They all accept an invitation to become tutors for the rest of the class! There was no pay and no extra credit, but they all served cheerfully and faithfully.

How does the Keller plan compare on cost of operation?

This depends, of course, on what you compare it to. To teach 100 students, we believe one should provide one instructor (faculty) and one course manager (teaching assistant), both paid. There should be about 10 tutors, who are paid in academic credit in most of our courses. If the course has not been given before, the instructor must spend some time preparing study guides and tests; if he is happy with some particular textbook he can prepare skeleton study guides rather easily. This time is a one-time cost incurred whenever the course is materially altered. Space is a bit of a problem. A collection of three or four rooms totaling about 2400 square feet

would serve 700 students if it were available 42 h per week. (Add 600 more square feet for a labroatory room.) Compared to a 1000-man lecture section with no recitation leaders or laboratory instructors of faculty rank, a Keller-plan course is expensive. But compared to 25-man faculty-led sections, it is very cheap. (Should one count the saving of student time and effort?!)

More on earning the right to attend lectures.

It is interesting that almost everyone who has tried some form of self-pacing in university courses has eventually instituted some deadlines. As Bill Moore puts it,[7]

> We need to differentiate between self-pacing and individual pacing. That is, we need to maintain the notion of individualized instruction, but at the same time provide some means of controlling the pacing in a way which is best for the individual. A purely self-pacing procedure tends to nurture procrastination in some students.

A generous minimum pace requirement exerts pressure only on the dilatory student, however, so a sense of freedom remains for the majority. The Summerhill alternative (wait indefinitely for the student to act) causes too much administrative bother.

Yet it is possible to get an adequate rate of work from a class without *punitive* deadlines.

I have already mentioned the tricks we introduced in order to combat procrastination in our latest trial of 8.01x and 8.03x: the calendar of dates for passing units in order to keep on the minimum or the accelerated pace (not required, however), the early final exams, the no-Incomplete grade policy, and the restricted admittance to lectures. This last one deserves more comment.

In the fall term of 1970, I finally amassed the courage to try Keller's idea of requiring a certain amount of work from a student before admitting him to lectures. In 8.03x, for example, one must have passed Unit 6 in order to be invited to the second lecture of the course. This strikes many people as very odd, if not illegal! What saves my conscience is that the material covered in the lecture is definitely not essential, or even helpful, to mastery of the required course content. Once I had a guest lecturer talk on the physical basis of perception in a course on waves and vibrations! Those who came had a treat, but those who could not were not directly penalized.

Will students actually work to be able to attend a lecture?

We missed a chance to prove that they will. The data of Fig. 2 for 8.03x shows a jump in rate of test passing on the ninth day of the course, which is the day just before the first lecture. However, that is also the day after each student was given the schedules referred to above. Some students have volunteered comments such as "I want to pass two units today so that I can go to the lecture."

Why do students come to lectures at all?

They come for fun, to see a professional in action, and because they still can't believe they don't have to. (If half of the class attends, that's doing pretty well.)

How can you keep out students who are not qualified?

We do not stand at the door and turn people away. We just tell the location of the lecture only to the qualified students. I doubt that even this subterfuge is necessary, however.

Doesn't grading only on mastery degrade grades? Shouldn't a man who learns quickly get a higher grade than one who takes three times as long?

This is a matter of personal philosophy which is widely debated. I take the position that so long as you make yourself clear, you can make the grade mean what you want it to. I choose my dentist by how well he works, not how fast he learned. Why not apply the same standard to physics students?

How can a sophomore possibly be wise enough to be a tutor?

Two factors: (1) The sophomore need not know everything just to grade a specified set of tests. He works from a limited agenda. (2) Sophomores turn out to be better tutors than graduate students in general, perhaps because they are fresher from the tribulations of learning the material at hand. Also, the tutor's work is subject to review, appeal, and reversal by the instructor although appeal is seldom necessary.

Don't students rebel at taking so many tests?

Not at all. Students have passed tests and returned asking to take another test on the same unit. Tests in the context of a Keller-style course are an opportunity to show off what one can do. The penalty for failure is mostly internal disappointment, not external punishment. And one always has another chance.

Why can't you teach 1000 students as easily as 100 in a Keller-style course?

The limit is due to two factors: (1) The instructor must handle situations which the tutors cannot. He is a court of appeal, and must not be overloaded. (2) He must also oversee the tutors. A tutors meeting with 100 tutors is absurd. One must be able to discuss individual students at meetings and must help tutors individually with difficulties in the material. With adequate supporting faculty, of course, one can expand.

OK, it works at MIT, but will it work anywhere else?

How about Stony Brook, Bucknell, Portland State, University of Texas, Georgetown, Arizona State, C. W. Post College, Florissant Valley Community College, and Western Michigan.[8]

OTHER EXPERIENCE WITH SELF-PACED STUDY

The Keller plan has spread in a few years from its beginnings in one psychology course at Arizona State University to other schools and other subjects (although the published accounts of such courses are not yet numerous). Since we are physics teachers, I would like to describe some other instructional systems now being used in physics teaching at several universities—systems which share two features of the Keller plan: self-pacing and mastery as a criterion for advancement.

Bucknell University

Bucknell has had support from the Carnegie Foundation for several years to experiment with a "Continuous Progress Program," which has been implemented in the departments of physics, biology, psychology, philosophy, and religion. Students work at their own paces on units of about two week's work. There is a laboratory open for students whenever they want to use it. Unit tests are available when a student is ready for them. Tests are composed by computer, randomly sampling a bank of test items and are graded by machine, the results being communicated to the student within a week of his taking it. The instructor handles all tutoring. The physics program is directed by Owen Anderson.

A report on the Continuous Progress course in biology, philosophy, and psychology has been published by Moore, chairman of Bucknell's department of education, and his co-workers.[9] They found that students in the experimental course compare favorably with those in regular recitation sections both in terms of accomplishment and attitude. They also see great value in having sequences of several courses available in this form to permit students to complete more than one course per semester (whence the name "Continuous Progress").

University of North Carolina

The quickest entry into self-paced study I know of was made by Marvin Silver, who divided 16 chapters of *Halliday and Resnick* into eight two-chapter units and made up a set of 50-min four-problem exams from the problems at the end of the relevant chapters. He required perfect solutions to at least three problems on an exam for a pass. He acted as tutor for all students and also gave optional lectures on "the Physicist's World" and sometimes presented his colleagues as guest speakers. Silver reports that student morale was high, that he enjoyed the course greatly, and that he won three new majors away from chemistry! Grades were determined by total number of tests passed with an option to raise one's grade by a final examination. He gave 27 A's and 9 B's in a group of 45 students. This success has led others at UNC to try the same technique.

The State University of New York at Stony Brook

A plan very similar to Keller's was designed by Clifford Swartz for an introductory course. Physics 161, a text and lab course for nonmajors, has a large room open continuously in which students get help, take tests, and do experiments. Participating faculty tutors keep scheduled tutoring hours in their offices, and graduate-assistant tutors man the course headquarters. Course objectives are detailed in handouts. Tutors give tests, written and oral, on the spot and sometimes include a requirement to demonstrate competency with equipment. Grades are given for effort, achievement, or whatever the tutor thinks best, but are accompanied by a paragraph on what the student accomplished. (The registrar was persuaded to establish suitable files for this purpose.) While detailed results on this new program are not yet available, the plan seems to be enjoyed by both students and faculty.

Portland State University

After Phil Pennington heard Keller describe his "personalized system" at the fall 1968 meeting of the Pacific Northwest Association for College Physics, he decided to try it out with 34 students in the physics segment of a Basic Science course sequence which covers biology, chemistry and physics in a two-year program. Most of the students were freshmen interested in the health sciences.

Pennington writes:

> The most notable reaction was in attitude toward physics of most of the students. Previously, physics had been something to get over, like a bad cold. Now there was considerable hallway discussion of physics; my office hours became jammed with students asking about physics; and my library of related books—Gamow's *One, Two, Three, Infinity*, Steinhaus' *Mathematical Snapshots*, Schrodinger's *What Is Life*, for example— became much in demand. (I allowed the students to check them out.) Even several issues of *Science* were checked out. This activity did not abate even after students had completed the units, and it was going strong after the final exam (several of my books were checked out for the summer).

THE KELLER COURSE AS TEST BED

Once you have a Keller-style course in operation, you suddenly find yourself equipped with an educational laboratory. The course is a culture medium for new teaching ideas. You can try something new with a single unit, give it to the first few students who come to that unit, get their reactions (including test performance and personal impressions) and then change the thing in time for the next wave of students one week later. This is a very fast feed-back cycle compared to the typical semester-long course.

It is very appropriate that the fast students hit you first, since they will find the most serious flaws in your material. The minor things will not stop them. Then the second wave will be protected against overwhelming obstacles and can report to you the next less serious problems.

A SUBVERSIVE FEATURE AND AN INHERENT LIMITATION

The Keller plan is destined not to spread quickly. If one lays out in study guides exactly what one expects of students and how they are to accomplish these goals, then one has specified the course in much greater detail than one usually does even in a syllabus. This has two important effects.

First, one's teaching becomes subject to audit. How often has it been asked how one can evaluate good teaching when teaching is such a private act between teacher and student! But when most of the teaching goes on in the medium of print, the teacher's privacy is gone (though the student's privacy is enhanced). The teacher is now open to detailed criticism. The result can be a little frightening. Keller says he feels practically naked when he gives his materials to a colleague.

The hope is, of course, that good teaching will be recognized by one's colleagues. If differences of opinion on specific pedagogical techniques arise, they can, in principle, be settled by a comparison experiment. For the long run, the more the teaching process is captured in observable form, the easier it is for the teacher to grow in knowledge and skill.

The second effect is that it becomes very hard for anyone other than the author to use a given set of materials. In the standard course, an instructor can use a textbook flexibly, leaving out sections and introducing other material. Through his lectures a teacher can also introduce topics in his own style and thus make the course his own. This is harder to do when lectures are no longer the main channel of communication and the approach to each topic is enshrined in print. The result can be that the instructor no longer feels sufficiently involved with the course—it's no longer his baby. If the adopted-child effect cannot be avoided, you cannot publish good study guides successfully.

There may be some ways to avoid this difficulty. One is the "Chinese restaurant" approach: You write study guides like a catalog from which the instructor can pick the objectives he judges important for his students. With each objective is listed the suggested procedure for accomplishing it. The instructor composes his own study guides by taking one objective from column A and so forth. Unfortunately, what is left out in Unit 3 may be required in Unit 7. Another alternative (due to Ed Taylor) is the "add-the-eggs" approach: the study guides are written with a little bit missing, which the instructor adds.

The barrier to proliferation still must be overcome, but I do not have the answer at hand.

CONCLUDING REMARKS

The Keller system of instruction is far from ideal. It accepts a dogma now under attack in higher education: The teacher should select for the student what he is to learn once he is enrolled in the course. It denies that having the student bathe in the aura of the charismatic teacher is the most effective means of having him learn physics. There are subjects in which the precise content of the syllabus is not as important as the influence an outstanding personality can have in a seminarlike encounter. The Keller plan is not a good candidate for such subjects, in my opinion. But if there are specific things to be learned, the Keller plan will do the job effectively and most students will enjoy it. A statistic which measures quantitatively how much our students enjoy it is that 90% of those who have taken on Keller course have applied to enroll in another.

Note added in proof: To receive a newsletter about Keller-plan courses, address J. G. Sherman, Psychology Dept., Georgetown Univ., Washington, D.C. 20007. For information about a conference on this topic 16–17 Oct. in Cambridge, write the author. Invited and contributed papers will be presented.

* This research supported in part by the National Science Foundation.

[1] B. F. Skinner, *The Technology of Teaching* (Appleton–Century–Crofts, New York, 1968), p. 8.

[2] F. S. Keller, J. Appl. Behavior Anal. **1,** 78 (1968); reprinted in Ref. 4. [Article 1]

[3] A. P. French, *Special Relativity* (Norton, New York, 1968); E. M. Purcell, *Electricity and Magnetism* (McGraw–Hill, New York, 1965); B. A. Green, *Vector Calculus* (Appleton–Century–Crofts, New York, 1967).

[4] An early report on 8.02x, "A Self-Paced Course in Freshman Physics", B. A. Green, is available as Occasional Paper No. 2, Education Research Center, Room 20C-228, M.I.T., Cambridge, Mass. 02139.

[5] B. V. Koen, Eng. Ed. **60,** 735 (1970). [Article 13]

[6] J. S. McMichael and J. R. Corey, J. Appl. Behavior Anal. **2,** 79 (1969). [Article 2]

[7] Private communication. See discussion of the Bucknell University program described below.

[8] Six of these institutions have given Keller-style courses; the others have given courses similar in spirit, some of which are described below.

[9] J. W. Moore, J. M. Mahan, and C. A. Ritts, Psych. Rept. **25,** 887 (1969).

12

STUDENT PERFORMANCE IN A KELLER-PLAN COURSE IN INTRODUCTORY ELECTRICITY AND MAGNETISM*

Sam M. Austin and K. E. Gilbert

A group of 25 students chosen at random from a larger class was taught in a Keller-plan (self-paced) format following the method of Green. The performance of these students was compared with that of the students in the lecture-recitation section through a common final examination and through a retest taken approximately two months after the end of the course. In each case the Keller-plan students did substantially better. Suggestions are made for improvements in the usual Keller-plan format.

I. INTRODUCTION

During the past few years experimental physics courses using the Keller plan (KP)[1] have been taught at a number of colleges and universities.[2-6] Rather than attending lectures or recitations, the student in such a course studies the material on his own with the assistance of a text and study guides. Within limits he works at his own pace. The course material is divided into units, typically one to two per week of the course, and the student must demonstrate his mastery of the subject matter by passing a unit test in order to proceed from one unit to the next. Undergraduate tutors are typically available to provide assistance and to grade the unit examinations.

While no controlled studies of student performance in Keller-plan physics courses have been published, information from uncontrolled situations[3-6] suggests that performance in such courses is usually about the same as in the standard lecture-recitation format.[7] This result is somewhat surprising in view of the infamous "Hawthorne effect"—one would expect students to do better in any new or experimental course. It also contrasts strongly with experience in the soft sciences where dramatic improvements in performance have been reported.[1]

In view of the above, it appears that controlled studies of the achievement of students in KP courses would be useful both in deciding whether such courses should become a permanent feature of the educational scene in physics and in suggesting improvements in these courses. In this paper we describe a comparison of the performance of a group of students taking introductory physics taught using a KP format with that of the larger group of students in the same course who were taught by the standard lecture-recitation (LR) method.

II. COURSE DESCRIPTION

The course to be described here, Physics 292, is the second in a five-quarter sequence of courses for students of high ability, primarily majors in physics, mathematics, or the other sciences. It is taught to first quarter sophomores from the text *Electricity and Magnetism* by Purcell[8] and usually covers the first seven chapters of this book. These deal with electric and magnetic fields in vacuum.

A. Students and Staff

Selection of a random group of students for the KP section was complicated by the fact that Physics 292 is taught in the fall term and registration takes place during summer vacation. Thus, the selection could not be made after arrival in the fall because the two sections met at different hours and conflicts would be inevitable. We proceeded as follows: (1) students in the preceding course in the series, Physics 291, were polled as to whether they were planning to take 292 and whether they would prefer to be taught by the Keller plan. Of the 76 students planning to continue in physics, 83% preferred the KP section. From this group we randomly picked 34 who were asked to register for this section. Of the group, 30 actually registered and 28 showed up for the class in the fall. An examination of the seven students who could have registered for the KP section but did not, shows that four dropped out of the physics sequence altogether and three enrolled

From *American Journal of Physics*, Vol. 41, No. 1, January 1973.

in the regular section. Two of these three were above average students in Physics 291, the third below average.

In addition to the instructor, three tutors were involved in the course. Two of them were undergraduates who had taken Physics 292 the previous year and the third was a graduate student. Nine or ten students were assigned to each tutor; students were told that they could change tutors if they wished but there were no such requests. There were no lectures, but the entire staff was available during three two-hour periods each week. Assisting students with problems and grading tests occupied essentially all of each tutor's time. The instructor was available to handle any difficulties or misunderstandings, to provide assistance or test grading if the tutors were busy, and, probably most important, to speak with students about physics or any other subject.

B. Procedures

The present course was taught following the methods of Green.[2] The subject matter of the course was divided into fourteen units, one of which was a review unit. For each unit a study guide was prepared which described briefly the material to be covered in the unit, stated the objectives of the unit and outlined the way the student was to demonstrate his mastery of these objectives. The study guide also included a procedure, with recommended reading, problems, and occasionally, additional textual material, which the student could follow to achieve the stated objectives. An additional, introductory, unit outlined the policies and procedures of the course in order to avoid any misunderstanding of these procedures and of the grading system.

When a student felt he had mastered the material of a unit he obtained a unit test from his tutor, took the test (with no time limit) and returned it to his tutor for immediate grading. An essentially perfect performance was required to pass. If the student passed he was allowed to proceed to the next unit; if he did not pass, he was required to study the material and take a test on the same unit during the next period. There was no other penalty attached to failing the unit examination. The unit tests were constructed so as to cover every point in the objectives. Except for the fact that derivations were more heavily stressed, the difficulty of the unit tests was about the same as that of exams in the lecture-recitation versions of the course taught in previous years.

Three tests were written for each unit and these were given in random order.

The major problem one encounters in Keller-plan courses is procrastination. Formal incentives of four types were provided. (1) The grading schedule shown in Table I was passed out at the beginning of the course. This schedule is highly nonlinear and strongly encourages the completion of as many units as possible. (2) Students were told that if they did not pass four units by a deadline they would be asked to drop the course. (3) It was stated that incompletes would be hard to get. (4) Schedules were provided which led to completion of the course either on time or three weeks early. Perhaps more effective than any of these, however, was the social pressure provided by the tutors.

III. ASSESSMENT OF STUDENT PERFORMANCE

A. Progress Through the Course

Of the 28 students who began the KP section, 25 stayed with the course for the quarter, one could not tolerate the testing procedure and transferred to the LR section, and two others dropped. The drop rate, 2 out of 28, was essentially the same as the 4 out of 58 that dropped from the LR section and is lower than usual for a KP course.

The number of units passed as a function of time is shown in Fig. 1. There is an obvious surge of test passing at the end of the quarter, with the average student passing 13.2 units. Of the 25 students, 20 completed all 14 units and one student each completed 13, 12, 11, 8 and 6 units.

B. Examinations

Student performance in the Keller-plan section was compared with that in the lecture-recitation section in two ways. First, both groups of students

TABLE I. Grading scale for KP section of Physics 292.

Score[a]	Grade	Score	Grade
>450	4.0	250–324	2.0
425–449	3.5	175–249	1.5
375–424	3.0	125–174	1.0
325–374	2.5	<125	0.5

[a] Each unit passed was worth 25 points for a total of $14 \times 25 = 350$ points. The final exam was worth 125 points, maximum, yielding a total possible score of 475 points.

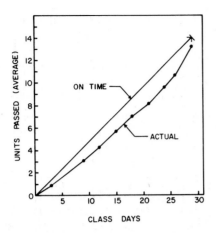

FIG. 1. The average number of units passed by a given class day. The straight line labeled "on time" is the progress of a student who works at a uniform rate throughout the term, finishing the last unit on the last day of class. The connected points are the actual average progress of the class.

were given a common final examination. The final exam grade was 40% of the course grade for the LR section, while in the KP section the weighting was variable as shown in Table I. After course grades had been assigned students were queried as to how long they had studied for the final. The averages were: KP, 7 h; LR, 6 h, the difference being about one standard deviation.

The exam was jointly prepared and graded by the staff of the LR and KP sections; it consisted primarily of problems. The KP section had covered about 10% more material than the LR section; none of this material appeared on the examination.

The results are shown as a histogram in Fig. 2. Also shown in this figure are the performances of the two sections on two measures of intrinsic

ability: the overall grade point average and the final examination grade in Physics 291, the previous course in the sequence. Although the two groups have very similar distributions on these two measures, their scores on the Physics 292 final exam are quite different. The message of these graphs is that the KP section had an average score about 14% higher than the LR section, and that the better performance is due to an improvement in the performance of the lower ability students. There is no tail toward low grades in the KP section.

The second comparison was a retest (RT) given approximately two months after the end of the course. Former students in both the KP and the LR sections were paid to take a test on the subject matter of the course. They were asked *not* to study for this test. The test was meant to be relatively straightforward and consisted of 10 problems. The result of the comparison was approximately the same as that obtained for the final examination and is shown in Fig. 3.

C. Examination Scores

Although an attempt was made to divide the groups randomly, there is still the possibility of differences in average ability arising from the small sample size. The overall grade point average (GPA) of the LR section was slightly higher than that of the KP section. However, on the other measures of ability, the SAT math test and the final exam in the preceding course (Physics 291), the KP section had a slightly higher average score than the LR section. The difference was roughly one standard deviation in all these cases.

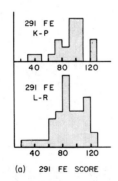
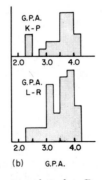
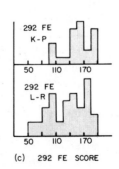

FIG. 2. Histograms of student performance on several tasks. Results for students in the KP and LR sections are plotted separately. (a) Grades in the final exam in the preceding course, Physics 291. If students were chosen randomly and statistical fluctuations could be neglected, these distributions would be identical. (b) Overall grade point averages. The scale is nominally 0.0 to 4.0, but until recently it was possible to give a grade of 4.5 to the top 1 or 2% in a class. (c) Grades in the final examination of Physics 292, the course described herein.

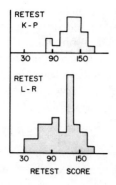

FIG. 3. Histogram of student performance on a retest given two months after the end of the course described herein. Results for students in the KP and LR sections are plotted separately.

One can correct the test grades obtained for differences in average ability if one can find a measure of ability which correlates strongly with these grades. The measure which was intuitively most appealing was the grade on the Physics 291 final exam (291 FE). This grade was found to have an average linear correlation coefficient[9] with the grades on the Physics 292 final exam (292 FE) and retest (RT) of 0.61 which was slightly larger than that for the overall GPA (0.56) and substantially larger than that for the score on the SAT math test (0.33).

A scatter plot of the 292 FE grade versus the 291 FE grade is shown in Fig. 4, with the KP and LR sections plotted separately. The lines shown are linear least square fits (with equally weighted points) of the 292 FE grade as a function of the

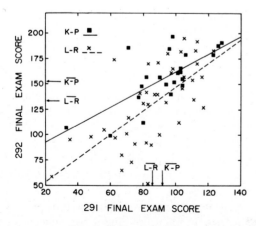

FIG. 4. Scatter plot of grades in the final exam of Physics 292 vs those in Physics 291. Results for the KP and LR sections are plotted separately. The straight lines are linear least square fits of the 292 grades as a function of grades in 291, done separately for the two sections. The mean scores of the two sections are noted by arrows on the axes.

291 FE grade. The difference between these lines at a given abscissa is the improvement in performance expected of a student in the KP section. One sees in this figure a reflection of the point made in discussing Fig. 2, namely, that the high ability students benefit less from the KP format than do low ability students.

Using the slopes of the lines on Fig. 4 we have corrected the Physics 292 final exam scores to account for the different mean scores on the Physics 291 final exam. A similar correction was made for the scores on the retest. The results are shown in Table II. The raw scores are shown in the first line while the scores in the second line include the correction outlined above. This correction decreases the difference between the two sections. On the other hand, if one makes the correction using the least squares fit of 292 FE as a function of GPA (i.e., by using the correlation of the 292 FE with GPA) the difference increases and one obtains the results shown in line three.

One can summarize these results by stating that students in the Keller-plan section did 10–15% better than those in the lecture-recitation section, as measured by performance on the common final examination. On the retest, the KP students did 15–20% better (see Table II).

TABLE II. Mean scores on Physics 292 final exam and retest.

Method of correction[a]	Score on 292 FE		Score on retest	
	LR	KP	LR	KP
Raw score	133±6	152±6	109±6	129±6
Corrected (291 FE)	133±6	147±6	109±6	125±6
Corrected (GPA)	133±6	154±6	109±6	130±6

[a] The KP section mean scores were adjusted as discussed in the text to account for the difference in the mean performance of the two sections on the Physics 291 final exam (row 2) *or* the overall grade point average (row 3).

D. Student Comments

As part of the course evaluation procedure, students were asked whether they would take the next course in the series in the Keller-plan format if that option were offered. Of the twenty students answering the questionnaire, eighteen answered yes, one answered no and one was not taking physics. The students were also asked to state the main reason for their answer. These reasons are summarized in the following list (with number of students giving that reason): learn the material better and in more depth (10); self-pacing, primarily because it avoids conflict with other interests (6); availability of individual help (4); better student-professor relationships (2). The one student who did not prefer the KP option felt that it was too rigid and not really very self-paced.

It is clear from these replies that the main advantage of the KP format as seen by these students is the possibility of learning the material better and not the self-pacing feature. Of course, these answers are from a relatively highly motivated group of science majors and the answers of a less select group might be quite different.

E. Instructor's Impressions

The most striking thing one notices in a KP class is the relaxed, informal atmosphere in the classroom and the easy relationship which develops among the students and the staff. The students appear to work harder than usual with less than the usual preoccupation with grades. We were also surprised at the amount of individual assistance some of the lower ability students required in order to master the material. The possibility of giving this assistance was presumably responsible for the better performance of these students in the KP section.

The instructor in the present course felt certain that the average student in the KP section understood the course material much better than the students he had taught the previous year in the same course using a lecture-recitation format. We were then quite disappointed that the performance of the KP section was only 10–20% better than that of the LR students, although the performance of the lower ability students was gratifying. Several explanations for this discrepancy suggest themselves: (1) KP students perceived that the final exam was not likely to affect their final grade very much (this possibility should not apply to the retest) (2) KP students were not used to the type of exam given and the fact that the time was limited (there was no time limit on mastery tests in the KP section). (3) The KP students were not accustomed to correlating information from a wide range of subject matter, since each of the mastery tests covered only a limited amount of material, the content of a particular unit (except for one review unit over the first half of the course). (4) The better students did not study as much as in the LR format course. This is perhaps to be expected since the objectives of the course were clearly laid out and it was not necessary to overstudy to be sure of passing a unit. (5) The Keller-plan format, as presently used, is only slightly superior to the lecture-recitation format for above average students. We suspect that the main reasons are (3) and (4), though we have only anecdotal evidence to confirm these suspicions.

IV. POSSIBLE IMPROVEMENTS

The major difficulty we encountered in teaching the KP course was that a few students did not finish the material. This was sometimes because they had trouble with the material, even after substantial tutoring, and could not finish in time and sometimes because of procrastination. Of course, some students do not finish the material in LR courses either, but in the KP format it is much more apparent to the student that he has never seen material he will need in the following course, with subsequent bad effects on his morale. There is a simple remedy for this problem which we would certainly incorporate into any future course taught using the Keller plan. It is to have units of two levels of difficulty. The simpler units, one-half to two-thirds of the total number, would come first and would cover the most important material, especially that required for the following course. Students would have to finish all these units to obtain a passing grade in the course, a C or C+. To receive a higher grade it would be necessary to finish a number of supplementary units which would be written at a higher level and would enlarge upon the material in the basic units. For example, in the present course there is a substantial amount of material on the transformation properties of the electric and magnetic fields which is difficult for C students. This material would clearly be part of a supplementary unit. Breaking the units into two categories offers a secondary benefit in that the supplementary units can be used to provide options for students with particular interests and to provide additional material for students of high ability. A similar procedure has been used successfully in a course taught by J. S. Kovacs and P. Signell at Michigan State University.[4]

A second change would be to add at least two more review units, making a total of three. The purpose of these units would be to help the students understand the correlations between important concepts and to provide practice in problem solving when the applicable methods are less obvious, i.e., are not those learned in a single unit.

V. SUMMARY AND CONCLUSIONS

We have taught a Keller-plan course in introductory electricity and magnetism to a group of 25 students selected essentially at random from a larger class taught using a traditional lecture-recitation format. A comparison of the performance of the students in the two sections showed that the Keller-plan students did 10–20% better, both on a common final examination and on a retest given two months after the end of the course. The improvement in the performance of lower ability students was especially striking.

The question of how one assigns grades in a Keller-plan course is a difficult one, and in our experience, arouses more criticism than any other point. The problem is that the performance required of the Keller-plan student to pass a unit mastery test would earn an A if exhibited on the final exam of a lecture-recitation course. On the other hand, KP students do not all do A level work on actual final examinations, although few do poorly. Based on our experience, and lacking a control lecture-recitation group, we would probably give fewer than the usual number of C grades in a Keller-plan course, increase the number of B grades and leave the number of A grades about the same.

Up to now we have discussed primarily performance on tests although this is by no means the only reason for adoption of the Keller-plan format. The other advantages, namely, an improved classroom atmosphere, better relationships with students, the opportunity to provide options for the better students, and the instant feedback on a chosen teaching method are the main reasons we would cite for adopting the Keller-plan format.

One should also not ignore the benefits which accrue to the undergraduate tutors. Ours felt that tutoring was an exceptionally rewarding experience, both an opportunity to learn the course material again and an opportunity to see what one kind of teaching is all about.

VI. ACKNOWLEDGMENTS

The authors are grateful to their tutors John Hamann and Shirley Hartline for their unflagging interest and enthusiasm throughout the course and for the contribution they made to its success. We also wish to thank W. H. Kelly for his encouragement and the Educational Development Program at Michigan State University for financial assistance. Finally, S. M. Austin expresses his thanks to B. A. Green for introducing him to the Keller-plan format.

* Research supported in part by the National Science Foundation and by the Educational Development Program at Michigan State University.

1 F. S. Keller, Jour. Appl. Behavior Analysis **1**, 79 (1968). [Article 1]

2 Ben A. Green, Jr., Amer. J. Phys. **39**, 764 (1971). [Article 11]

3 The PSI Newsletter circulated by the Psychology Department of Georgetown University, Washington D.C. 20007, contains lists of institutions, departments, and individuals offering Keller-plan courses.

4 J. S. Kovacs and P. Signell, AAPT Announcer, **1**, 23 (1972); spring meeting of the Michigan section of the AAPT; private communication.

5 D. Winch, spring meeting of the Michigan section of the AAPT.

6 M. Philippas, quoted in Phys. Today, **25**, No. 1, 104 (Jan. 1972).

7 An exception to this conclusion is found in the studies of Ref. 4, where a subset of students (those who had not finished a set number of units) took the same final exam as students in a lecture-recitation section of the course and did about 15% better.

8 E. M. Purcell, *Electricity and Magnetism*, (McGraw-Hill, New York, 1965).

9 P. R. Bevington, *Data Reduction and Error Analysis for the Physical Sciences*, (McGraw-Hill, New York, 1969) Chap. 7.

13

SELF-PACED INSTRUCTION FOR ENGINEERING STUDENTS

Billy V. Koen

Countless experiments in learning theory have produced data applicable to engineering education. Engineering educators can therefore use the best information available to "design" the learning situation for the most effective instruction.

A teaching strategy[1] has been developed in which every element is carefully chosen and interrelated to maximize student learning. This method, often called simply PSI (personalized system of instruction) was used in a senior level nuclear engineering course at the University of Texas with great success, as judged by student learning, motivation, and enjoyment. This article gives an example of the results that may be obtained by using modern learning theory in the classroom.

The PSI Method

To implement the PSI method, course material is divided into units, each containing a reading assignment, study questions, co-lateral references, study problems, and any necessary introductory or explanatory material. The student studies the units sequentially at the rate, time, and place he prefers. When he feels that he has completely mastered the material, a proctor gives him a "readiness test" to see if he may proceed to the next unit. This proctor is a student who has been carefully chosen for his mastery of the course material. On the "readiness test" the student must make a grade of 100, but if the student misses only a few questions, the proctor can probe to see if the questions are ambiguous and can reword the questions if necessary. If the student does not successfully complete the test, he is told to restudy the unit more thoroughly. He receives a different test form each time he comes to be tested. No matter how many times a student is required to retake a unit, his grade is not affected; the only interest is that he ultimately demonstrate his proficiency. All students who complete the course receive a grade of A.

Lectures are given at stated intervals during the course to students who have completed a specified number of units and can therefore understand the material to be covered. The students who qualify for a lecture are not required to attend them; and the lecture material is not covered on any examination.

The basic features of the PSI method are:

1. The go-at-your-own-pace feature, which permits a student to move through the course at a speed commensurate with his ability and other demands upon his time.
2. The unit-perfection requirement for advance, which lets the student go ahead to new material only after demonstrating mastery of that which preceded.
3. The use of lectures as vehicles of motivation, rather than sources of critical information.
4. The related stress upon the written work in teacher-student communication; and, finally:
5. The use of proctors, which permits repeated testing, immediate scoring, almost unavoidable tutoring, and a marked enhancement of the personal-social aspect of the educational process.

Student Response to PSI

A questionnaire prepared by professors in educational psychology at the University of Texas evaluated the attitudinal response of the 20 students in the class to the PSI method. The response to this self-paced course was highly favorable.

Student answers to other questions were as follows: 72% considered the self-paced mode of instruction better than the lecture-discussion method (22% judged both methods equal); 88% considered that their effort was more than that in standard courses; 88% felt that they looked forward to the activities in this course more than to those in all of their other courses. Another significant response is quoted: "For

---

[1] See Keller, F. S., "Good-bye, Teacher . . .," *Journal of Applied Behavior Analysis*, vol. 1, 1968, pp. 79-89. The method developed by Dr. Keller is called a personalized, proctorial, or self-paced system of instruction. [Article 1]

Dr. Koen is assistant professor in the Department of Mechanical Engineering, The University of Texas at Austin. The method described in the article was developed by Dr. Fred S. Keller, who is professor emeritus at Columbia University. The author expresses appreciation to Dr. J. Stice, director of the Bureau of Engineering Teaching, and to Dr. Luiz Natalicio, Department of Educational Psychology at UT Austin for their help in this teaching experiment.

From *Engineering Education,* Vol. 60, No. 7, March 1970, copyright 1970 by the American Society for Engineering Education.

purposes of stimulating new ideas, I consider this course, when compared with other courses I have had ...": (a) one of the best 50%, (b) above average 39%, (c) average 10%, (d) below average 0%, (e) far below average 0%.

Discussion of Results

Using the same instructor and textbook, this nuclear engineering course was taught the preceding year by the conventional lecture-discussion method. Figure 1 compares the grade distributions of the two groups. The extremely "skewed" grade distribution was predicted by Keller (1968), and it exists in spite of the fact that the instruction staff feels that the self-paced students covered 20% more material.

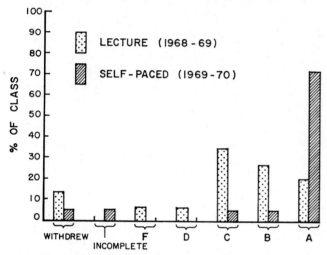

Figure 1. Grade distribution for lecture and self-paced classes.

In figure 2 the number of students working on each unit is given as the distribution appeared two-thirds of the way through the course, showing the wide spread in the students in a typical class. The flexibility of the self-paced course minimizes the effects of quizmanship, illness, the folklore as to the student's ability in the department, etc. It is also next to impossible to cram for this kind of course. The grade of *A* signifies that a certain amount of material has been learned. Figure 2 also points out the difficulty in attempting to prepare a lecture at this juncture in the course that would fit the level of learning of all students. A student who finishes this course early is

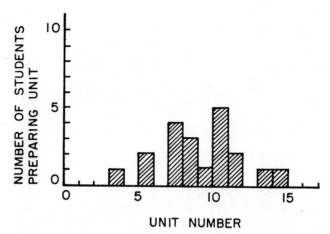

Figure 2. Student distribution with unit number at a point two-thirds through the course.

not required to attend class and is free to study his other courses.

Why PSI Works

PSI is successful because it is built upon well-established principles of learning theory. To illustrate the sophistication of PSI, let us compare it with the usual classroom technique using one elementary principle of psychology—that is, an organism tends to repeat and enjoy behavior for which it is rewarded (i.e., positive reinforcement); it tends to avoid and dislike behavior for which it is punished (i.e., negative reinforcements). The objective of the teacher is to encourage a student to learn and to enjoy learning. PSI has been carefully "designed" so that a student is only *positively* reinforced (he passes units, attends lectures, is not penalized for not passing an exam, has a chance to get an *A* up until the last day of class, etc.); he is never negatively reinforced. Contrast this with a conventional system in which a student wagers one-fourth of his grade at each hour examination—a failure from which there is no reprieve.

Optimum Learning

PSI may not be the best way to teach all courses. The results of this study do suggest that at least in some courses the lecture method is far from optimum. Sound engineering practice requires that the optimum be approached by using the best available data. Engineering students have the right to expect their professors to "engineer" their education. △

14

PERSONALIZED INSTRUCTION IN MECHANICAL ENGINEERING

Lawrence L. Hoberock

A method of instruction based on the Skinnerian principle of positive reinforcement in learning theory and designed by F. S. Keller is known as PSI (Personalized System of Instruction), or simply proctorial or self-paced instruction. Applications of this technique have been made in psychology (Keller, 1968), physics (Green, 1969), and nuclear engineering (Koen, 1970), with success in terms of student learning, motivation, and enjoyment. This article presents and interprets the results of applying this method to a course in mechanical engineering, taught under circumstances somewhat different from other known applications—i.e., the course required a large amount of graphical construction; and the course, normally taught during a 14-week semester, was taught by an inexperienced instructor for the first time in a 6-week summer session.

Applying the PSI Method

The method was applied essentially as outlined by Keller (1968) and Koen (1970). The students worked on assigned units of study, using textual material, supplementary notes, and study questions. Whenever a student wished to be tested over that unit, he requested testing. If he passed the test with a score of 100, he was sent on to the next unit. If he did not make 100, he was asked to go back and study that unit again. He could take as many tests over one unit as he liked with no penalty, as the object was to test only his eventual proficiency. If a student missed only a few questions on a test, he was quizzed by his proctor to ascertain reasons for wrong answers (perhaps ambiguous questions or misunderstanding of the question). If he satisfied the proctor, he was passed. Otherwise, he was sent back to study again, perhaps with emphasis in a certain area.

Dr. Hoberock is assistant professor in the Department of Mechanical Engineering, Univ. of Texas, Austin. He acknowledges the help of Dr. Billy V. Koen, assistant professor of mechanical engineering, and the encouragement of Dr. J. E. Stice, director of the Bureau of Engineering Teaching, in the teaching experiment described in this article.

Design of the Course

Kinematics and Dynamics of Machinery is a required, three-semester-hour course at the junior level in mechanical engineering at The University of Texas at Austin. The decision had been made to offer it for the first time in six weeks when I was assigned to teach it. Obviously, the necessary graphical techniques are more time-consuming than analytical methods. The problem then was how best to conduct an unfamiliar course in six weeks. The solution was to avoid "teaching" and to place the task of learning squarely upon the students. However, it was recognized that unless the experience could be made pleasant, the students would all drop the course within the first few weeks. The PSI method seemed a natural approach.

By constructing the units so as to stay ahead of the most advanced student, the material could be adapted to the students' ability to learn. The unit progress curve, shown in figure 1, was used to estimate the rate at which students were learning. After about the sixth class day, it became apparent that the units were too difficult and that the readiness tests were too long. A

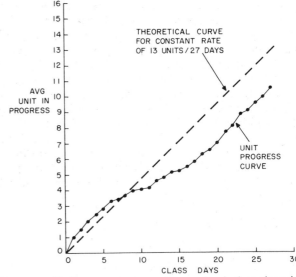

Figure 1. Unit progress curve for mechanical engineering class taught by PSI method, as compared to theoretical curve.

good part of the testing time was taken by the graphical construction required. When it was found that this time could be drastically reduced by reducing the number and complexity of the test questions, the curve began to bend upward again (after about the 15th class day). As the earlier units were not redesigned, the slower students continued to stall on them, and the change did not become noticeable until more than halfway through the course.

One of the prime motivators of PSI is the ability of students to move at their own pace. Figure 2, patterned after Green (1969), indicates that students do take advantage of this factor. The fast students move the bottom of the "wave" out quickly, while the slower students retard the upper portion. As can be seen, only 18% of the students finished the course on or before the class formally ended (27 class days). Because most of the students could have finished if the earlier units had been redesigned, they were given additional time to complete any remaining units, with a final grade of A for all units completed.

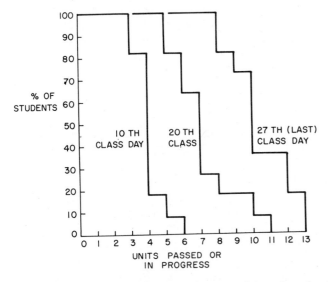

Figure 2. Status of student achievement in number of units passed or in progress for PSI-taught course in mechanical engineering.

The proctors are important in the PSI method. They are responsible for a large amount of "tutoring" as they grade the readiness tests. Hence, they not only must be carefully selected but also must be continually monitored by the instructor and briefed on forthcoming units and readiness tests. Because of time limitations, the single proctor in this course could not be effectively briefed on each unit and test, and many students felt that he was not properly prepared. In spite of this shortcoming, 64% of the students felt that the PSI-taught course was better than the traditional lecture course, and 18% felt that it was equally good.

Evaluation of Teaching Method

The textbook and the material covered were essentially the same as used in previous courses taught by other instructors. The unit perfection requirement, measured by tests that required as thorough a mastery of the material as in earlier courses, supports the view that the students did learn by the PSI method. It was therefore decided to compare the grade distribution with that of a representative previous class to indicate the learning effectiveness. Figure 3 presents this comparison.

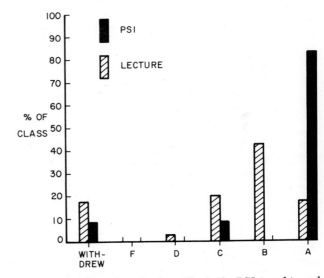

Figure 3. Grade distribution for both PSI-taught and lecture-taught classes in the same mechanical engineering course.

The students' attitude toward the PSI course, as measured by a questionnaire prepared by professors in educational psychology, was very favorable. Comparing this course with others that they had had, 60% looked forward more to the activities of this one and 45% considered it one of the best; 54% put into the course well above average effort; and 45% said that they got more than they had expected from this course. One student said, "This course is great because for the first time in my curriculum I can take the time to really learn the material." Several of the slower students asked whether other required courses would be taught this way, stating that they preferred not having to compete for grades.

Finally, a great deal was discovered about how students learn. The instructor had to formulate his course objectives, and his approach to teaching other courses was definitely affected by his experience with the PSI method. In particular, he realized for the first time that students can learn much more effectively in many cases if teachers "teach" less and motivate more.

References

1. Green, B. A., Jr., "A Self-Paced Course in Freshman Physics," Occasional Paper no. 2 of the Education Research Center, April 24, 1969, Massachusetts Institute of Technology, Cambridge.

2. Keller, F. S., "Engineering Personalized Instruction in the Classroom," *Revista Interamericana de Psicologia*, vol. 1, pp. 189-197, 1967.

3. Keller, F. S., "Good-Bye Teacher . . .," *Journal of Applied Behavior Analysis*, no. 1, 1968, pp. 79-89. [Article 1]

4. Koen, B. V., "Self-Paced Instruction for Engineering Students," *Engineering Education*, vol. 60, no. 7, pp. 735-736, March 1970.   △ [Article 13]

15

TEACHING WITHOUT LECTURES

A. J. Dessler

LECTURING is an uncertain art. The successful lecturer is able to present the course material to the class in a way that is interesting, even entertaining. At the same time he conveys information at a satisfying level and rate. Lecturing may be as much a theatrical performance as it is an intellectual exercise. If we look at lecturing in these terms we at once can understand the paradox of the brilliant scholar who is regarded as a mediocre lecturer and the indifferent scholar who is extremely popular with the students because of his lectures. The stage presence that is so important to the successful lecturer is not a valid measure of scholarly ability. In my opinion, all the faculty at Rice have good command of the material they teach, and most of them work hard preparing their lectures. Yet, outstanding lecturers are rare on this (or any other) campus.

As seen from the students' point of view, the transfer of information during a lecture is a risky thing at best. The lectures are presented at a time and place dictated by a relentless schedule. The lecturers are of uneven quality, and even a good lecturer has bad days. No account is taken of special pressures or distractions from other quarters. The pace through the course is an unyielding lock-step established to fit the mythical "average student." But the average student, too, has his good and bad days, days in which his attention span is shortened by, say, the last-minute effort to prepare for an examination in another course, or even by illness. And, what of the student who has latent ability but who comes into a course with some minor deficiencies in background material? Without special tutoring of some sort, he falls even further behind as the lecturer alludes to and builds on knowledge common to the majority of the class. The student is not apt to know why he is not learning the material. His plight is not usually apparent to the lecturer until the student is in trouble, and that is sometimes too late.

The students, at times, react to the ineffectiveness of the transfer of knowledge by the lecture method in a rather direct manner. A professor, after giving what he thinks is an especially lucid and significant lecture, his eyes sparkling with excitement generated by the beauty of his subject, will be approached by a contingent of students, the spokesman asking something like, "Are we really going to be held responsible for all that stuff?"

I had often felt, more from a sense of frustration than rational thought, that there must be a better way.

Almost two years ago, while spending a year in Washington, D. C., I learned of a better way while attending a symposium on communications. One of the speakers (Professor Charles Ferster of American University in Washington, D. C.) described a new teaching method, generally called the Keller method, that had been developed by Professor Fred S. Keller and a team of psychologists working to apply what they had learned from laboratory studies of "reinforcement theory" to teaching. It all seemed so obvious. I could hardly wait to get back to Rice to try out the new teaching method Ferster had described.

There is no unique description of the Keller method; there seems to be an infinite number of variations in its application. The principal features of the Keller method are (1) self-paced study, (2) personalized or programmed instruction, and (3) concentration on student motivation.

During one brief visit here during my year in Washington, I discussed the Keller method with the late Professor Zevi Salsburg, truly one of the finest teachers on the Rice faculty. He too was intrigued by the teaching technique, and he introduced it during the spring semester of 1970 in his junior-level class in quantum chemistry. In later conversations, he told me he was satisfied that the Keller method was a definite improvement in teaching, but he had encountered some difficulties. He was planning to use the Keller method again this academic year, but with modifications to obviate the problems of last year. Since we had kept in touch, I was aware of Professor Salsburg's plans and have thus been able, to a large extent, to avoid similar problems.

From *Rice University Review,* Spring 1971.

I am presently using the Keller method to teach an introductory astronomy course that is directed primarily toward providing a science elective at the sophomore level for humanities majors. The course is taught at a descriptive, non-mathematical level, which makes it a relatively easy science elective. It should be one of the most interesting subjects a student could study in college. Astronomy, held by some to be the Queen of the Sciences, opens for the student a view of the awesome grandeur and spectacle of the universe, of which our solar system is but a miniscule part.

If one walks into my astronomy class, he will see what on first glance appears to be a state of disorder. There is a general conversational hum in the room, as at a cocktail party. A few students are reading; a few are moving around. There is some traffic in and out of the room. This appearance is quite deceiving, however. As we shall see, the course is highly structured.

The class operates as follows: Each student receives a written study guide that details his reading, problem, and laboratory assignments. The study guide also presents both helpful clarifications of the text material and suppplementary material that is not in the assigned text. If I were to lecture, my lectures would cover much of what was in the text and supplement or highlight certain parts. Now, instead of giving a lecture, I endeavor to write the material into the study guides to add to or comment on important points and to note interesting features.

The subject matter for this course is divided into units, each unit having a separate study guide that covers one chapter of the basic text. There is suppplementary reading assigned from a second book. A third, highly-mathematical text is available for those students who have an adequate background in mathematics and physics and who wish more than the descriptive treatment.

The student, following the study guide, reads the text material and works the assigned problems, usually outside of class hours. The student then lectures (or explains) to one other student on what he learned and how he worked the problems. Thus, the student "lectures," not the professor. These "lectures" (or oral exercises as they are called) may be performed only in the classroom.

The purpose of the oral exercise is to reinforce the reading and to expose weaknesses in understanding. Haven't we all had the experience of starting to explain something to someone, and suddenly we realize that there is a serious flaw in our understanding? Or the converse, we go to someone for help with a problem, and in the very process of explaining what it is that we can't understand, the light dawns. We usually depart thanking the bewildered listener who never did quite understand even what our question was.

Professors are quite aware of this process. Most of them talk glowingly of the intellectual stimulation that comes from teaching. It is often said that if you want to understand a subject, teach it. It has also been argued that it is our use of words, either written or spoken, that unlocks our ability to reason.

The duties of the student who listens to the oral exercise are simply to sit and listen attentively. He is encouraged not to interrupt the "lecturer". The listener may, however, comment after the presentation. His primary function is to provide an "audience" for the lecturer. Few people can talk to themselves with enthusiasm; a listener is usually necessary for us to speak our thoughts. Thus, the student learns by reading, working, and explaining—he learns by doing The passive role he plays when he is the listener is a useful part of the learning process, but commonly it is a relatively minor one.

The class is divided into sections. Each section contains 10 students and has one tutor assigned to it. The tutor is ideally an undergraduate who completed the course satisfactorily the year before. The tutor administers the written exercises, keeps progress records for each student in his section, finds a listener when a student is ready to present an oral exercise, and answers questions that arise from students in his section. Often a student will discover during his lecture that he doesn't quite understand some of the material. Help is immediately available from his tutor. If the tutor has trouble answering the student's questions, either the tutor or the student can come to me for help. I make it a point to be present at nearly all the class meetings, primarily to help the tutors, but also to make personal contact with the students.

After the required oral and laboratory exercises are completed, the student takes a closed-book written exercise with which he can demonstrate his mastery of the unit material. These written exercises differ from the usual tests in several significant ways. Only two scores are possible—Perfect or Incomplete. A score of Perfect is required before the student is allowed to go on to the next unit. An Incomplete means only that more study is required. There is no penalty associated with an Incomplete. Since mastery at a specified level is required, a score of Incomplete serves simply to reveal some weakness. After an analysis of the weakness, the student is sent back to some specific material for more study, after which he may try again on a new written exercise. (There are usually four different written exercises available for each unit.) The written exercises, which are an additional reinforcement of the reading, problem solving, laboratory exercises, and oral exercises, may be administered outside of class hours if arrangements are made with the tutor. They are usually taken during class hours, however.

Each student proceeds at his own pace through the course. His mastery of the material is checked constantly. The average student is tested for mastery of the material approximately twenty times each semester. Some work diligently to finish early. Other students work at a slow steady pace, finishing the last unit on the last day of class. Others work sporadically, getting ahead or falling behind according to the demands on their time from other activities.

An award was presented to the first student to complete the first semester syllabus, and another award to the student who maintained the most steady pace through the units to finish on the last day of classes. Henceforth, these awards will bear the names of their respective first winners: The Stephen G. Dvorak Award and The William R. Coley Award.

Grades are determined by how many units a student completes. The standards of performance are set by the instructor and announced the first time the class meets. Each student's progress is shown graphically on a chart that he sees each time he completes a unit. The individual student knows, therefore, at all times where he stands. The responsibility for learning thus rests with the student. The instructor is responsible for overall course direction, maintenance of standards, and (with his tutors) teaching.

A student who does not earn a semester grade of 1 (or A) will not have read all the material. For example, to earn a 3— (or C—), the student must master slightly more than half the syllabus. In the conventional teaching technique, the student with a grade of 3— might have been exposed to all the material but only learned part of it. In a terminal course such as introductory astronomy, I believe it is a moot point whether there is any advantage to learning some of all the material or all of some of the material. In any case, with this application of the Keller method, it is clear that a 3— student learns all of some of the material.

To avoid the problem of the student who procrastinates unduly, an early deadline is set for completion of Unit 1 to assure that everyone at least gets off to a good start. The only other prod is a one-hour, open-book mid-term examination covering the first few units. The mid-term exam does not count toward the student's final grade but rather serves as a recheck of his mastery of these units. A grade of less than 70% requires that he retake the mid-term after more study and redoing certain of the units. There is no final examination.

The Keller method is probably best applied to the more elementary courses in which some definite knowledge or specific skill is to be taught. Science and mathematics courses are ideal since each element of the subject is often prerequisite for the next step. The complete mastery of each step leads to greater student motivation and interest. It eliminates the possibility of losing a student at some critical point and leaving a gap in his knowledge that will hound him through the discussion of the related material. With the **Keller** method, he must demonstrate mastery of each step before being allowed to proceed. If he is having trouble, he receives personalized instruction from his tutor. He is programmed back for more study in just the areas where he has shown the need for greater strength.

The able students go through the course using little help. The available manpower is automatically concentrated on the student who is trying but is having some difficulty. Special treatment can be afforded students with exceptionally weak or exceptionally strong backgrounds. The fast student is not held back, nor is the slow student left behind. Yet, standards are easily maintained. The lines of responsibility between student and teacher are clearly drawn. Lecturing skill and stage presence are no longer factors in the teaching process.

The Keller method is becoming a relatively popular educational experiment; it is being applied to a variety of courses at several universities throughout the nation. At Rice, Professor G. K. Walters has produced a novel variation of the Keller method for use in his junior-level quantum-physics course. Professors F. R. Brotzen and R. L. Sass are considering use of the Keller method in their physical science course. And, the Keller method is being evaluated for possible use in both freshman physics and freshman chemistry courses. Within a few years, there may well be a significant mix of standard and Keller-method courses offered at Rice.

The Keller method changes the principal role of the teacher from that of the classroom expositor to that of one who makes it possible for students to learn how to teach themselves. This may well be the ultimate goal of the educator. A student who emerges from a Keller method course should feel that he has mastered at least some aspect of a subject. He further should eventually feel confident that he is able to learn any subject that someone else has written down in a book.

With the Keller method, the teacher does not serve as an intermediary in the transmission of knowledge. He becomes more of a scholar-administrator who decides what aspects of a subject the students are to learn, what written material they need to properly employ the text, and what standards of excellence are to be maintained. The teacher who utilizes the Keller method must be prepared to spend additional time on his course. He must organize the course, recruit and supervise his tutors, write both the study guides and written exercises, and evaluate student progress on a student-by-student basis. In addition, he should be in the classroom during the regularly assigned class hours even though he does not lecture. The tutors need assistance or guidance, the students expect to see the instructor and to interact with him occasionally, and the instructor needs the feedback that can come only from firsthand observation.

One might expect that after the first year, when the study guides and written exercises are available from the previous year, the instructor's job would be minimal. Such is not the case. For example, I have learned much from the experiences of this year that will enable me to improve the study guides. Most will be rewritten or modified. New written exercises will have to be prepared regularly to keep the course work current and vital.

The Keller-method instructor can no more be replaced by written material than a lecturer can be replaced by a movie projector and tape recorder. The job of education remains; it is only the emphasis that is changed.

The conventional lecture method, which has reached its present state of refinement after centuries of evolution, is certainly not in any danger of losing its prime position. The Keller method will, for many years to come, be a useful adjunct to the lecture method. The degree of acceptance achieved by the Keller method will, of course, ultimately be determined by its utility and by its effectiveness.

16

PERSONALIZED INSTRUCTION IN A THREE SEMESTER MATHEMATICS AND STATISTICS SERVICE SEQUENCE

Harlley E. McKean, Frederick L. Newman, and Ronald Purtle

As a mathematician concerned about creating an adequate and meaningful service sequence for the social and biological sciences the senior author had been concerned about several facets of the traditional lecture approach to staffing and teaching this service sequence. To begin with, few of the students taking the sequence really like mathematics: they were taking the sequence only because of a college or departmental requirement. Because the student attitude is relatively negative and mathematical aptitudes largely minimal, most faculty members avoid teaching the sequence like the plague. When "trapped" into teaching such a course the presentation was often sterile.

The result was to be expected—the students actively avoided as much work as possible. Performance levels were marginal. This resulted in grading on a curve where 40 to 50 percent correct might well mean a passing grade. We understand that the psychometrician believes such a curve to be desirable; but in view of the fact that we had tried to construct our tests to cover the material essential to the students' future needs, the curve is not appropriate. We could have set an absolute performance cut-off for grades, but the politics of failing 60% of the students would have reverberated over several colleges and many departments, to say nothing of an in-loco-parentis oriented administration!

Because of these factors our three semester service sequence was really not providing effective service. Mathematical and statistical skills transferred out of the course were minimal (and often the subject of snide comments by colleagues in colleges we were supposedly serving). Furthermore, the professor-student interaction was distant at best. The students hated mathematics and moreover, the mathematicians had the distinct impression that the students, and the academic disciplines they represented, were mathematically shoddy.

When Fred Newman suggested some of his ideas, nearly all of the aforementioned objections

were removed; the learning model he proposed was intuitively appealing, and the idea that the system required students to demonstrate near perfect command of the material had a ring of academic integrity.

Let us outline the basic model and assumptions of the sequence as it is now developing. We started by breaking the three-three credit courses into nine one-credit segments. Each of the nine one-credit segments consists of four conceptual units. It is at this level we applied a basic learning model. We viewed the learning process as consisting of three stages:

1. Stimulus-Response Learning
2. Concept Formation and Utilization
3. Consolidation

The model was translated into practice within each segment. For each one of the segments, there would be four units. For example, in the segment dealing with Linear Algebra and Systems of Linear Equations the units are:

Unit 1. Addition, subtraction and multiplication of vectors and matrices.
Unit 2. Linear analytic geometry.
Unit 3. Systems of Linear Equations. I. 2×2 systems
Unit 4. Systems of Linear Equations. II. The Gauss-Jordan method.

The first stage of learning is focused upon a closed-book quiz covering basic definitions and concepts. For the closed-book quiz, students are asked to memorize and otherwise gain a high degree of fluency with the basic vocabulary and simple concepts of the unit. The student may have to take a second form of the closed-book quiz to demonstrate his competence. The decision to take the second form of a quiz is usually a joint decision by the student and his proctor as they review and diagnose the results of the quiz.

The second stage—concept formation and utilization—is realized by an open-book quiz which is essentially the homework assignment or problem set. Under PSI, of course, they are done in the classroom, under the guidance of our student proctors. The open-book quiz is worked until it is perfect. After a student successfully completes the four closed- and open-book quizzes covering the four units of the segment, a closed-book comprehensive is required covering the four units of the segment. This represents the consolidation stage of the learning process. Again, a diagnostic conference between a student and his proctor may result in the student taking a second form of the comprehensive. Once the segment's comprehensive exam is completed to a satisfactory level, the final grade is computed according to a fixed scale, and the student has one credit in the bag. In our opinion, the notion of "immediate reward" in terms of immediate credit and grade is highly motivating to the grade-and-credit oriented students.

In addition to the usual teaching aids of PSI such as availability of student proctors and supple-mentary handouts, we will have started (by fall) to use some of the aspects of the auto-tutorial system popularized by Professor Postlethwait of Purdue's Botony Department. For each unit there will be one or more slide-tape shows. These will be kept on file in the library of the university's Language Laboratory. During several convenient hours of each day (about forty hours per week) a student will have access to these materials. Eventually, we hope to have these slide-tape shows serve as on-demand teaching aids for the course. The Language Laboratory and the Math Department happen to be located in adjacent buildings. This allows our proctors to recommend that the student hop next door and review the unit's slide-tape show before taking the second form of a test, or before proceeding with the open-book quiz.

The results of our efforts over the first two segments of the present semester are given on the bar graph in the handout [Figure 1]. Math 122 A and

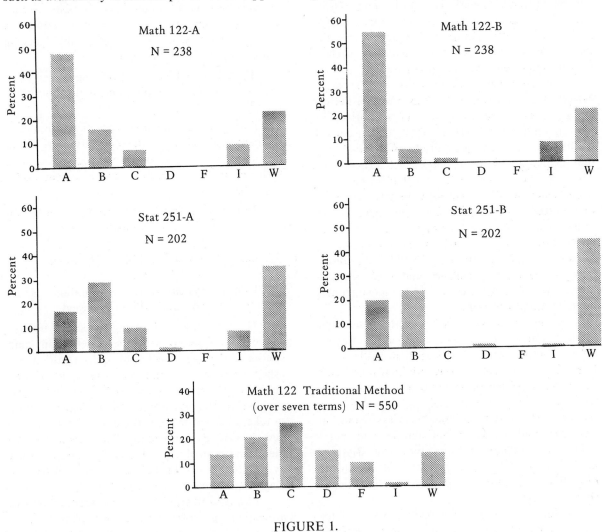

FIGURE 1.

Math 122 B are the fourth and fifth segments in our nine-credit sequence, and Statistics 251 A and 251 B are the seventh and eighth segments. The segments Math 122 C and Statistics 251 C are now in progress. The first three segments are still under development. The bar graph at the bottom of the page is the grade distribution for the seven semesters of Math 122 under the traditional system of lecture-recitation-exam.

Over time, our hopes are to design a collection of seventeen or so one-credit segments for students and their departments to select from. Some of the courses will be prerequisite to others, but the general idea is that, in successive five-week periods throughout the academic year, a student will be able to register for the segments which will benefit him most. In the area of statistics, for example, a student might have six segments to choose from:

A. Descriptive statistics and continuous probability
B. Estimation and tests of hypotheses
C. Regression, correlation, and non-parametrics
D. Analysis of variance
E. Index numbers and time series
F. Games and decisions

We also hope to develop different versions of the open-book quizzes (concept formation and utilization) and slide-tape shows so that the discussion of applications are relevant to a student's field of interest (business, psychology, biology, etc.).

It should be pointed out that we have only presented the data from our most recent efforts, because in the development of the technique we have made a number of logistical and theoretical errors in getting to the present point in time. Let us now list some of the major errors made at both the University of Miami and New Mexico State University so that others can possibly avoid the same pitfalls.

1. At one time we allowed students to pace themselves. Instead of a deadline to finish four units we allowed up to 30 weeks (two semesters) to complete 12 units. Forty-five percent of the students met the requirements of a one-semester course in one semester's time.
2. Letting the proctors and graduate assistants develop their own quiz materials and means of communicating—the result was complete chaos.
3. Early in the game at Miami, Dr. Newman first allowed students to skip a quiz or exam because their overall scores were high enough to get "the grade." The obvious result—islands of ignorance.

From our experience three very important factors must receive careful attention to attain any measure of success with PSI:

1. Unambiguous quiz and handout material. When the goal is a full command of the courses' concepts, ambiguous information and quiz items are counterproductive. Weekly reports by the proctors on the discovery of such ambiguities usually clears up such problems within two or three semesters. As a stop-gap, give the proctors some latitude in grading during the quiz interviews with the student while you are debugging the course material. In fact, *allow* for immaturity and inexactness in the expression of ideas on the part of the student—as long as it is clear that the student *has* the right idea in mind.

2. Careful establishment of the contingencies of work per unit time. This is not an easy task. At first set up a reasonable but arbitrary schedule. Develop a feedback system such that you can recognize *when* you are setting either too stringent or too lenient a standard. Weekly updating of a cumulative record on a student is very useful. Student proctors are useful here, and they seem to enjoy the experience of behavioral analysis involved in such record keeping.

3. Careful training and supervision of student proctors. Before each segment or semester bring the proctors together for a review of all of the quiz material. The theme of discussion should center around the types of misconceptions and methods of explanation. At first, proctors feel very insecure. We recommend that you take advantage of this by encouraging them to depend on each others' strengths and to acknowledge each others' weaknesses. Camaraderie among proctors has a very positive outcome. Encourage mutual respect. Brief weekly written reports and meetings are very important. Encourage them to recommend variations in procedure, but not to act upon their own conjectures until the group has discussed the idea. Overall, impress them with their own value as teachers and administrators of social reinforcement in the realm of contingency management, all the while preserving the teaching concepts underlying the learning model.

17

CHEMISTRY TEACHING BY THE KELLER PLAN

Micah Wei-Ming Leo

The Keller Plan, the personalized system of instruction (PSI)/or the self-paced study, was originated by Dr. Fred Keller and Dr. J. G. Sherman, formerly of Columbia University, eight years ago and has since spread across the States, Canada, and Brazil.

The Keller Plan is self-paced, mastery-oriented, student-tutored for college level instruction with classes of all sizes operating at some 150 to 200 colleges and universities (1). It has also been tested at both the high school level and graduate school level. It has been applied in various subjects. A recent survey (2) has shown that at least twelve disciplines have adopted the Keller Plan in various schools. They are psychology, physics, engineering, mathematics-statistics, chemistry, biology, computer programming, Spanish, English, sociology, speech communication, and office management.

In the Summer of 1971, the writer was granted an NSF fellowship, attended a special course in the Keller Plan at the Education Research Center of M.I.T., and was convinced that the Keller Plan is definitely a better approach for learning than the conventional spoon-feeding method of classroom lectures. In the Fall of 1971, the first Keller Plan course was tried experimentally in the freshman chemistry class at Barrington College on a voluntary basis (Fig. 1). The results were gratifying and rewarding (3). The students who took the Keller Plan did much better in their grades than the conventional group. Similar results were reported from other colleges and universities where the Keller Plan has been adopted. An example of test scores (4) as a function of instructional method and retention interval is given graphically in Figure 2.

With the above positive notes about the new learning process, we are encouraged to further emphasize the Keller Plan in other areas of chemistry, namely, organic chemistry and biochemistry, this school year.

The purpose of this paper is to introduce this new approach of instructional system to educators in chemistry and associated fields who may be interested and benefitted by it. The philosophy and mechanics as well as pertinent information of the Keller Plan applied in chemistry are presented herein.

As Dr. Ben A. Green, Jr. (5) of M.I.T. pointed out

The concept of an instructional system is not useful until we distinguish between teaching and the transmission of information. It is obvious that one does not teach violin playing merely by transmitting information to the student about how to play the violin. The student must do his part, and the teacher must evaluate and respond to the student's efforts. The student is an active element in a process, not merely a receiver of information.

Dr. Green further stated that to design an instructional system is to arrange a sequence of three-step cycles of learning process: presentation, response, and consequence, in such a way as to optimize learning. Between extremes of a programmed instruction and a semester plan of lectures (presentation), final exams (response), and course grades (consequence), the optimal mean, which is psychologically and behaviorally sound, appears to be the

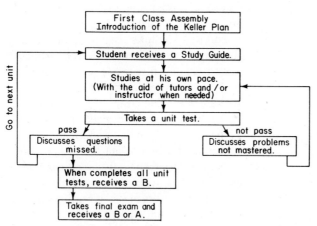

Figure 1. A flow chart of the Keller Plan adopted in chemistry at Barrington College.

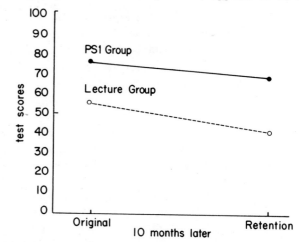

Figure 2. An example of test scores as a function of instructional method and retention level.

From *Journal of Chemical Education*, Vol. 50, No. 1, January 1973.

Keller Plan in which the content of the materials of a course is divided into about 12 to 20 units. The student is expected to study and to master unit by unit at his own pace.

When the Keller Plan was introduced in the chemistry class, students were advised on a self-paced, personalized learning process during the first class and were given detailed instructions on the mechanics of the course in oral and written forms which constituted a "contract" between the students and the instructor.

The student is given a "study guide" which was prepared by the instructor in advance. The study guide gives explicit objectives which the students have to achieve. When the student has achieved the objectives, he will take a unit test. A tutor gives help when needed and administers and reviews each unit test with the student as soon as the test is completed.

One can take as many tests as he wants every week. There is no penalty for the number of failures for these tests as long as he finally learns the materials and passes the tests. If the student passes, he goes back to the instructor for the next unit's study guide. If he fails, he also goes and reports to the instructor, who will note the time. Thirty minutes later, the student is entitled to take a retest on the unit.

The tutor is instructed to grade the test on the basis of what the student wrote, and then to talk with him about his work. The student can then clarify what he meant on the paper. The tutor is also instructed to let the student fix arithmetic errors without taking a retest and the tutor is allowed to cross out the old grade and enter a new one if he thinks the student really understood the point of the problem. The tutor keeps the test paper for review by the instructor at a later time.

Tutors are students who passed the course previously. The most important role a tutor plays is the detection of problems and discussion of errors after the unit tests. Whether a student advances to the next unit or takes a retest, the mistakes are always discussed. This prevents the unfortunate situation of going ahead without mastering the subject matter in each unit. The tutor also keeps records and gives feedback to the instructor.

The role of the instructor is to prepare study guides, to make unit tests, to administer and to review the testing program, to schedule tutorial service, to supervise tutors and laboratory assistants, to conduct special lectures, trips, films and other enrichment activities, and to manage and direct the total Keller Plan as smoothly and efficiently as possible. He also works individually with students who have special interests or problems encountered by the tutor.

Grades are decided by the student's completion of unit tests in combination with his performance on final examinations and laboratory work. Successful completion of all units will ensure a student a B, and will admit the student to the final examination, where he may raise his grade to A with a good score. The grade thus obtained will account for 80 per cent and the lab grade the other 20 per cent. However, unless a student passes his laboratory work, he will not pass the course. For passing less than the whole assigned units, a less-than-B grade will be given. However, a student who wishes to take longer than one semester to finish the course is allowed, provided that (a) he has completed over half of the total number of unit tests by the drop date and is still in the course at the end of the semester, and (b) he talks it over with the instructor and gets his permission and the Dean's approval. On the other hand, by special permission, a student can take the whole school year's course in one semester. This flexibility allows students to achieve what they usually cannot in a course of the conventional approach.

Those who finish unit tests early will be eligible to take their final examination about two weeks early. This gives those students a chance to get the course out of the way so they can concentrate on other subjects.

Because of the built-in nature of the system, the grades of students do not follow a normal curve with a few A and B students, and a majority of C students, but the numbers of A and B students are greatly increased.

Lectures are few and are open only to students who qualify to attend them. This means one will have to have passed a certain unit to be admitted to a certain lecture. Attendance is not required, however, and the materials covered would be relevant, and hopefully interesting and entertaining, but it is not to impart basic course material, but to motivate students and provide an example of professionals at work.

Laboratory experiments are conducted in usual manner, except open lab is also made available to enhance the self-paced approach.

Students' reactions toward the Keller Plan have been most favorable. They are glad that it has done away with the ritual of class attendance, and has motivated their own initiatives. The Keller Plan gives them both the freedom and responsibility they long for in their search for knowledge and truth. The fact that the student newspaper had picked up the news item on the Keller Plan and published it on its front page seems to say that it is a relevant approach to today's students. Local newspapers also published the news of the chemistry teaching by the Keller Plan at Barrington College. Many inquiries about teaching chemistry by the Keller Plan have been received from universities in the States and Canada.

The reactions of colleagues have been influenced by students' attitudes. Many have shown curiosity and interest. Several faculty members are adapting the spirit if not the body of the Keller Plan in biology, geology, ecology, genetics, lower plants, and psychology. The uncertainty and worries of the administration were changed into cooperation and encouragement as good responses from students became evident.

In conclusion, the Keller Plan appears to be an excellent alternative method for teaching chemistry as well as other disciplines of today.

Literature Cited

(1) E.R.C. Conference Studies Innovative Keller Plan. M.I.T. Teck Talk. October 20, 1971.
(2) P.S.I. Newsletter, Issue No. 5, June (1972) Psychology Dept., Georgetown University, Washington, D.C.
(3) Leo, Micah W. M. A preliminary report on teaching chemistry by the Keller Plan at Barrington College. Paper presented at E.R.C. Conference, M.I.T., Fall, 1971.
(4) Corey, J. R., McMichael, J. S., and Tremont, P. T. Long-term effects of personalized instruction in an introductory psychology course. Paper presented at E.P.A., Spring, 1970.
(5) Green, B. A., Jr., *Amer. J. Physics*, 39, 765, (1971).

18

A REPORT ON THE USE OF THE KELLER PLAN IN A GENERAL BIOLOGY COURSE AT LOWELL STATE COLLEGE

Paul Protopapas

STUDENT COMPOSITION AND TEACHING PERSONNEL

The 32 students who enrolled in the general biology course during the fall semester had no prior knowledge that a self-paced method would be used. The teaching personnel included the instructor and 9 tutors. All the tutors were undergraduate biology majors—4 juniors and 5 sophomores. The tutors received neither salary nor semester hour credit.

PROCEDURE

The method of course presentation was based on the self-paced instructional program introduced by Keller. The course material was divided into 14 study units each accompanied by a unit examination. The texts were: *Biology,* Curtis, and *Human Biology,* Asimov. In addition, *Scientific American* offprints were assigned.

The general biology course, two semester hours, is assigned two 50-minute periods per week. The students in the Keller plan were required to arrange an additional hour per week with their tutors. The students used this extra hour for tutoring and for taking examinations. No lectures were given under the Keller plan. The students had access to audio visual material in addition to tutoring. The study units consisted of a brief introduction, a list of objectives, student activities, and study questions.

EXAMINATIONS AND GRADING

Each unit test consisted of ten questions. A student had to score a minimum of 90% in order to receive the next unit. If the score were less than 90% the student was asked to do more studying before he took another examination on the same material. There is no penalty attached to failing a test except that the student is not allowed to progress in the course. When a student completed an examination the tutor graded it. This provided an opportunity for the student to discuss his performance. Seventy-five percent of the final grade was determined by the student's performance on the unit examinations. If a student finished all 14 units his grade would be A; 13 units, B+; 12 units, B; 11 units, C+; 10 units, C; 9 units, D. The final examination comprised 25% of the final grade.

COURSE COMPLETION

Of the 32 students taking the final examination 16 had completed all 14 units, 28 had completed 13 units, 31 had completed 12 units, and all 32 students had completed 11 units. No student withdrew from the course and no student received an incomplete grade. The final examination was one given by another instructor to her lecture section. A comparison of the two classes is shown in Table 1.

TABLE 1.

	% A	B	C	D	F
Keller plan	20	40	40		
Lecture section	4	16	41	16	16

A comparison of the final grades earned in the course between all lecture sections and the Keller plan students is shown in Table 2.

TABLE 2.

	% A	B	C	D	F	I
Keller plan	34.4	50	12.5	1		
Lecture (297 students)	5.4	23.8	41	21.8	7	1

COURSE EVALUATION

Student Evaluation of Proctors.   The tutors play a crucial role in the administration of the Keller plan. Therefore the level of their performance is important. The students rated the tutors in the following categories on a 1–7 scale:

(a) helpful—actively helpful
(b) required independent thinking: never—always
(c) grading: unfair—completely fair
(d) knowledge: none—very knowledgeable

The students evaluated the competence of the tutors very favorably in all categories, thus it would appear that students can receive valuable assistance from other students.

GENERAL COURSE EVALUATION

Only one student replied that he would not recommend the course to others. It is interesting that this student enrolled for the second semester Keller plan and stated that he liked the course because he was not treated as an IBM number. The overall student evaluation was most favorable. The students indicated that the chief factors contributing to the success of the course were (1) being able to proceed at their own pace, (2) being allowed to choose their own time for taking a test, and (3) having the availability of tutors for individualized instruction.

My own feeling is that the Keller plan course was a complete success. I have always enjoyed lecturing and have received positive feedback from the students. However, I am sure that the students learned more and derived greater personal satisfaction from the self-paced course. My colleagues have made inquiries throughout the semester and have asked me to give a seminar based on my first semester's experiences. The coordinator of the general biology program is involved in this semester's Keller plan and is hoping to increase the number of sections involved next fall. The academic dean has asked for a report on our progress. I have received six inquiries by mail and have had two visitors from other institutions.

STUDENT COMMENTS

"The method employed in my Biology Class that meets on Monday and Friday at eleven o'clock, I find very beneficial. I can proceed at my own pace, and since I am not forced to begin a new topic, I can fit the self-teaching methods into my schedule."

"I am delighted with the programmed learning of this rather exacting subject."

"I really like the Keller Plan, because I feel I'm learning a lot more than I would be in lecture. If you don't understand a particular topic that well, you can study it longer. I plan to take this course next semester also."

"I personally am quite pleased to have ended up in this classroom experiment. . . . There is no distasteful competition, and studying is actually enjoyable."

"I think this type of course is good for a smart student, but not so good for a slow, or, at times, lazy student like myself, because it is very easy to fall behind."

"This course appears to be the perfect course for an average student who is more or less forced to take Biology in their freshman year. I hate doing anything in biology, or even attending a class for it, but in the self-study program, I don't mind it all that much. The only problem I have found, is to make sure I don't fall behind."

"I enjoy this class very much. The only thing I am worried about is falling behind. Another thing I am worried about is studying the points I think are important, and then flunking the final, because I didn't study the points you thought were important."

"It's much easier to learn Biology this way. You are able to grasp more, and it doesn't seem to be as much material."

"The independent study course is a very good way to teach Biology. The student learns more because he is doing all his own research."

"I think that this Keller Plan has been the best experience for learning. I prefer this plan over a lecture course anyday."

"I think that the Keller Plan is a great system for college students. I have learned a lot, and wouldn't take lecture class for anything. I plan on taking this course next semester, without any doubts."

"The course is good. You can pace yourself, and with the student helpers, you get answers to all your questions—not just some, but all."

19

SELF-PACED INSTRUCTION FOR LIBRARY SCIENCE STUDENTS

John J. Knightly and John L. Sayre

SEVENTY-FIVE LIBRARY SCIENCE students at the University of Texas have been greeted on the first day of class with an introductory guide beginning "Welcome to an experiment in library education!" The experiment applied the teaching strategy called self-paced or personalized system of instruction (PSI) to two sections of the library school's Basic Reference Course. PSI, as developed by psychologist Fred S. Keller[1] and others, involves a teaching strategy in which every element is carefully chosen and interrelated to maximize student learning. It puts to use the data produced by experimentation in learning theory. As judged by student learning, motivation, and enjoyment, the method is immensely successful for library science students and merits further consideration and application. This article outlines the PSI method, its application to a particular library science course, and suggests the results that may be obtained by using it.

The PSI Method. To implement the PSI method, course material is divided into units, each containing a reading assignment, study questions, collateral references, study problems, and any necessary introductory or explanatory material. The student studies the units sequentially at the rate, time, and place he prefers. When he feels that he has completely mastered the material, a proctor gives him a "readiness test" to see if he may proceed to the next unit. This proctor is a student who has been carefully chosen for his mastery of the course material. On the "readiness test" the student must make a perfect grade or nearly so but, if the student misses only a few questions, the proctor can probe to see if the questions are ambiguous and can reword the questions if necessary. If the student does not successfully complete the test, he is told to restudy the unit more thoroughly. He receives a different test form each time he comes to be tested. No matter how many times a student is required to retake a unit, his grade is not affected; the only interest is that he ultimately demonstrate his proficiency. This proficiency is recognized with a grade of "A" for each unit. All students are expected to take a final examination, in which the entire term's work is

Sayre and Knightly are U.S.O.E. Doctoral Fellows in the Graduate School of Library Science, The University of Texas at Austin. The method described in the article was developed by Fred S. Keller, who is professor emeritus at Columbia University. The authors express appreciation to Billy Koen of the Department of Mechanical Engineering at the University of Texas for his example and inspiration which led to this teaching experiment. Further information may be secured by writing the authors in care of the Graduate School of Library Science, The University of Texas at Austin.

From *Journal of Education for Librarianship,* Vol. 12, No. 3.

represented. This final examination carries a weighting of 25 per cent of the course grade.

Lectures are given at stated intervals during the course to students who have completed a specified number of units and can therefore understand the material to be covered. These students who are eligible to attend a lecture are not required to do so; and the lecture material is not covered on any examination.

Keller has summarized the features of PSI which seem to distinguish it most clearly from conventional teaching procedures. They include the following:

1. The go-at-your own pace feature, which permits a student to move through the course at a speed commensurate with his ability and other demands upon his time.

2. The unit-perfection requirement for advance, which lets the student go ahead to new material only after demonstrating mastery of that which preceded.

3. The use of lectures as vehicles of motivation, rather than sources of critical information.

4. The stress upon the written word in teacher-student communication; and, finally:

5. The use of proctors, which permits repeated testing, immediate scoring, almost unavoidable tutoring, and a marked enhancement of the personal-social aspect of the educational process.

PSI Application to the Basic Reference Course. The self-paced course for Library Science 340, Basic Information Sources, at the University of **Texas** used as its text, *Introduction to Reference Work,* Volumes I and II, by William Katz. Ten units, each with four Readiness Tests, were developed by the authors of this article, utilizing all chapters from Volume I of the text and emphasizing approximately twelve dozen basic reference tools. Reference service ideals and general concepts were developed through eight special lectures, discussion of case studies, sample interviews, and readings assigned in Volume II of the text. Construction of the units and course procedures were based as nearly as possible on the PSI Method decribed above.

The self-paced concept was applied experimentally to two sections of the basic reference course, with classes of 45 students and 30 students. Instructional staff included the two instructors, both U.S.O.E. doctoral fellows in the library school, and five student proctors selected from the library school, each receiving three hours credit for their participation. A desirable instructional staff-to-student ratio of 1:10 was maintained. Two departures were made from the PSI method developed by Keller: (1) Instructors also served as proctors, maintaining closer awareness of the strengths and weaknesses of the readiness tests through the experimental period and (2) Special lectures and other programs were open to all students in the class, not just to those who had completed a specified number of units. Attendance, although voluntary, was high.

An additional feature of the experimental courses, demonstrating the flexibility available under PSI, was optional laboratory sessions, available through the first half of the course. For laboratory sessions, instructional staff were on hand in the regular class room with reference sources from one or more units, facilitating student access and orientation to the sources. Students were encouraged to seek help from the staff or their fellow students.

Student Response to PSI and Student Performance. Students in the self-paced classes commented on the method and their attitudes toward it in a confidential questionnaire completed at the end of the course. The following responses to a number of the key items on the questionnaire indicate the highly favorable student attitudes toward PSI.

"Compared with all the courses I have had, I consider this course: one of the best (39%); above average (54%); about the same (7%); below average (0%); far below average (0%)."

"For purposes of learning new information, I consider this course, when compared with other courses I have had: one of the best (64%); above average (28%); average (5%); below average (2.6%); far below average (0%)."

"Compared with the effort I usually put into a course, my effort in this course was: well above average (23%); above average (44%); average (33%); below average (0%); well below average (0%)."

"In general, I consider the self-paced mode of instruction used in this course to be: better than the lecture-discussion method (100%!)."

"If I had the opportunity to take another course taught by a similar self-pace method, I would do so: Yes (100%)."

"Compared with all courses I have had, I have looked forward to the activities of this course: much more (36%); more (49%); about the same (10%); less or much less (5%)."

It is fair to note that while evaluation at the *end* of the course indicates enthusiastic student endorsement of the method it has been observed that students exposed to the self-paced method for the first time feel some apprehension and confusion at the beginning of the course.

The favorable attitudes toward PSI have been matched by equally high student performance. On the final examination, a one hundred question test based on the reference tools ordinarily taught in the regular lecture-discussion course, the classes produced a median score of 92. One oddity of the PSI method is a definitely "skewed" grade distribution. As predicted by Keller and verified by other self-paced classes,[2] there is a great percentage of high grades. In this reference course, 90 per cent of the students received an "A" for their course grade. Is that too many "A's"? No, indeed, for to receive that grade each student demonstrated better than 90 per cent proficiency on each of the ten units of the course and performed well on the final examination. High grades seem to be a happy consequence of the PSI methodology, which has been carefully designed to produce high performance.

Possibilities. The system of instruction described in this study may not be applicable to all library courses. It is suggested, however, that, at least for some courses, the lecture method is far from optimum and that PSI might be a stimulating and successful substitute. PSI applies to the teaching process what educational theorists have taught us about reinforcement learning. The method has been designed so that a student is only positively reinforced. Successful mastery of each unit of the course is recognized but failure is not penalized. With each unit, the student receives congratulations and the feeling of progress and success. With each unit the student receives individual attention; and in the self-paced aspect of the course individual capacities and circumstances are recognized. PSI provides many of the benefits of computer assisted instruction without the expense of a computer and student consoles.

Library science teachers, as well as their students, are interested in teaching improvements and innovations in teaching methods. The self-paced or PSI method is one of the approaches which merits consideration.

References

1. Keller, F. S.: Good-by, Teacher. . . . *Journal of Applied Behavior Analysis,* 1:79-89, 1968. [Article 1]

2. Koen, B. V.: Self-Paced Instruction in Engineering: A Case Study. (Paper read at the 78th Annual Meeting of the American Society for Engineering Education, Ohio State University, June 23, 1970.)

20

EXPERIMENT IN INDIVIDUALIZED LEARNING AT GEORGIA STATE

Elizabeth Poplin Stanfield

The latest step toward innovative methods in the FL classroom by a department which has pioneered multi-purpose use of the language laboratory and a two-quarter intensive Spanish course for those wishing to complete four quarters of work is now in progress at Georgia State University. It is a three-quarter excursion into individualized instruction in basic Spanish. The sequence, which began in the fall, includes 101, 102, and 201. Upon completion this spring of the experimental phase, the twenty-odd students will enroll in the regular 202 course taught by the Foreign Language Department.

MATERIALS

Materials for the new course have been developed by Individualized Learning Systems Inc. (ILS) of San Rafael, California. Georgia State along with Atlanta University, the University of Southwestern Louisiana, and Florida A & M are a few of the one hundred colleges and universities across the country where the method is being tested. The class at George State is being taught by Mrs. William T. Stanfield. The individualized or "programmed" approach is based on the concept that a student is an individual and that this status gives him independence. The instructional method employed is directed toward qualitative improvement in the results of his study. In other words, studying Spanish *smarter*, not harder!

Consisting of 24 units, the course can be easily divided for semester or quarter utilization. The materials are multi-media oriented. Student materials include guide, texts, and records. Both the Instructor's Guide and the Student's Guide contain the dialogues and monologues for memorization and small scale replicas of the posters to facilitate memorization on an association or image-building basis. Students associate a line of dialogue with a particular picture rather than an equivalent English phrase. Grammar, vocabulary, and reading selections are contained in the twelve pro-

grammed text booklets. Students receive their own series of 5 records (45 rpm) containing the sound system of the Spanish language and the first 16 dialogues.

In addition to the student materials, there are 24 tapes for language laboratory use, and 32 color posters for use in presenting the dialogues and monologues to be memorized. There is an Instructor's Manual showing how to set up an individualized classroom on either of two systems: the "peer-managed" system in which the better students help the others when group work is in progress and the "proctor-managed" system in which graduate assistants or other qualified personnel are utilized as assistant teachers or group leaders and tutors. Mrs. Stanfield is assisted by graduate students Cathy Phelps and Mrs. J. Curtis, candidates for the Master's degree in Spanish.

PROCEDURES

Essentially, ILS has attempted to provide the student material for learning Spanish grammar on his own, freeing the teacher and aides (facilitators or proctors) to concentrate on developing each student's verbal facility in the new tongue. Classroom procedures, therefore, are not teacher-dominated, but stress student interaction in groups of seven or eight. A typical five-day lesson sequence proceeds as follows:

1. The instructor makes the initial presentation of the dialogue to the entire group using all the techniques—listen and repeat, backwards build-up, split-group—familiar to the audio-lingual specialist. After a fifteen-minute presentation, the class breaks into predetermined groups to continue practicing the dialogue (monologue) patterns. As more control over the material is gained, questions based on the dialogue are introduced by the group leader (instructor, aide, or peer). Oral expansion of the dialogue patterns is en-

couraged by the use of synonyms and antonyms as practice continues on the second and third day.

2. The instructor teaches orally whatever grammar structures occur in the dialogue if they are included in the programmed text.

3. Small group oral practice, expansion; dictation of dialogue (monologue) material; grammar, vocabulary.

4. Small group oral practice, expansion; reading selections; oral comprehension test on dialogue or monologue.

5. For devoting extra time to difficult constructions or, a short in class, written composition to assess achievement or a free-expression oral composition both based on one of the series of independent practice posters.

With each new lesson introduced a vocabulary sheet is distributed containing all items mentioned in the dialogue, monologue, and programmed text.

To show mastery of each grammar unit, a student prepares two short compositions. The first appears in sentence fragments at the end of each unit and must be unscrambled and arranged in logical order to form a coherent paragraph. The second is his own original paragraph patterned after the composition accompanying the unit. These are read by the instructor, corrected, commented, graded, and returned to the student with suggestions for further study if indicated. For example, a student may be directed to prepare a series of sentences using *gustar* or to write the conjugation of four Class III radical-changing verbs. The suggestion to make an appointment for tutoring may be indicated. Most students, however, pass systematically from one unit to the next demonstrating their competence in the materials by submitting acceptable—at times, exceptional—compositions.

Learning options unique to this program clude admission to the language laboratory at any half-hour interval from 8 a.m. to mid-afternoon and access to tri-weekly small group or individual tutoring sessions, conducted by the graduate assistants. During these sessions, individual problems arising from the programmed texts can be attacked.

TESTING

A four-fold testing system measures oral comprehension, speaking fluency, sight reading ability, and grammar mastery. The student's final grade is based on a numerical average in these areas. Ideally, the evaluation of student progress would be an individual session between the instructor and a single student, but even experimental courses must bow to the realities of the academic world and, at this moment, final examinations and grades sheets for the Registrar's office are included among these inescapable facts of life. In May, the Modern Language Association's Reading Test will be administered to the ILS students along with their counterparts in more traditional classes of Georgia State. As a growing number of instructors have already discovered, Mrs. Stanfield hopes to find that individualized instruction enables students to learn more—with better comprehension and better retention[1]—than other methods. The "bonus" quality of the program is that students enjoy learning the language.

---

[1] Figures gathered by Donald R. Leisyak, a "write-in" candidate for Lieutenant Governor of Ohio in the last election, and quoted over WCKY in Cincinatti, propose to show that retention in programmed instruction is 90% as contrasted to 33% in traditional instruction.

21

THE KELLER METHOD IN INTRODUCTORY PHILOSOPHY COURSES: A PRELIMINARY REPORT

George D. W. Berry

During the summer of 1971 I gave a course at Boston University in introductory philosophy, using a version of the Keller plan.[1] The course proved in some ways strikingly successful. While the number of students, thirty-one, was too small to carry much statistical weight, my experiences with the course nonetheless appear to me worth passing on to you—if for no other reason, simply because Keller's methods seem seldom to have been applied in teaching subjects outside the sciences. I shall confine myself as closely as possible to a purely descriptive account of what happened.

The course was entitled "Problems of Philosophy." The selection of problems, which for the most part I inherited with the course, comprised the main traditional philosophic questions associated with three gigantic topics: (1) our perception of external reality; (2) the mind and its place in nature; (3) God and his relation to the world. The students were mostly college sophomores, with a scattering of freshmen, juniors and others. Only one had taken a previous course in philosophy; the rest had, at best, only a casual conversation contact with the subject.

The plan of the course was based not directly on the original Keller method as described in the 1967 "Neglected Rewards" paper[2] but on a variant of it proposed in 1968 by Ferster and Perrott in their book *Behavior Principles*.[3] In this variant, Ferster and Perrott dispensed with Keller's elaborate structure of proctors, individual written quizzes, lectures and group final written examinations, in favor of a simple succession of oral interviews in each of which one student is tested on his knowledge of a given unit of reading by the instructor or an assistant or by another student who has already "passed" his oral interview on the unit. No student is permitted to *be* interviewed on a unit *n* until he has both "passed" his own interview on unit *n-1* and has interviewed another student on unit *n-1*. All this requires considerable book-keeping—I used a small card file—but it is not wasted effort, for it ensures that the student will cover each unit pretty thoroughly three times: first, when he studies the unit on his own; second, when he is interviewed on it; third, when he interviews someone else on it.

I had already decided to restrict, if humanly possible, the assigned reading exclusively to primary sources—to selections, that is, from the actual works of famous past philosophers and distinguished contemporary ones. Since such works are, of course, written primarily for colleagues rather than students, students tend to find them harder reading than, say, the ordinary text book. This, plus the students' lack of philosophic background, led me to make two initial decisions: (1) I would assign a *smaller* sum-total of pages than I should ordinarily be inclined to, and (2) I would liberalize the Ferster-Perrott or pure-interview program to the extent of lecturing regularly one out of every five class hours, with the aim both of explaining to the student the more difficult passages in the reading and of furnishing him continuous orientation with respect to the topics being discussed. The lectures enabled me to dispense altogether with study-questions, unit outlines, and the like.

By a great stroke of luck, suitable reading selections were found already assembled in one spot, namely, in Alston and Brandt's *Problems of Philosophy: Introductory Readings*.[4] This book is admirably suited to a course of this kind. It comprises sixty-one essays, judiciously chosen from

---

[1] I was encouraged to do this by three of my colleagues in Boston University's philosophy department—Professor Paul Sagal and Professor and Mrs. Judson Webb—who had had some experience with the plan and first introduced me to it. The course owed much of its success to their suggestions and advice.

[2] Dr. Fred S. Keller: "Neglected Rewards in the Educational Process." This paper was read at the 23rd annual meeting of the American Conference of Academic Deans, in Los Angeles, California, on January 16, 1967.

[3] Appleton-Century-Crofts, 1968.

[4] Allyn and Bacon, Boston, 1967.

well-known books and monographs, organized by topic and progressively arranged with relation to each other, representing a spectrum that ranges in time from Aristotle to the present and in divergent opinions from St. Anselm to Bertrand Russell. It was no trick at all to choose about three hundred pages (less than half the book) directed to the course's three gigantic topics, divide these pages into fifteen units averaging just under twenty pages apiece, and assign them in a temporal order roughly corresponding, one hoped, to the students' developing interest and expertise.

At the beginning of the course I was seized with qualms about quality-control. It seemed to me that the opportunities for cheating were little, if any, larger than in the conventional course. But, cheating aside, what if many students with the best will in the world simply didn't know a bad interview from a good one and so repeatedly passed their undeserving fellows on to botch another unit of reading? To minimize the frequency of this sort of thing, I took two steps: first, I resolved to sit in on, and where necessary take an active part in, many student-to-student interviews; second, I announced that each student would be required to interview himself on the last two units, write up these two interviews, and turn them in to me at the end of the course for grading.

How did all this work out?

Early in the game certain pedagogic problems began to emerge. Some of these were connected with space and time, or more precisely with the lack of them. Several oral interviews can be conducted simultaneously in a middle-sized classroom. But eight or ten simultaneous interviews strain the capacities of even a fairly *large* classroom. We soon realized the interviews need not be confined to the classroom or even to neighboring empty classrooms or even to the building, but may be held outside on the grass or the banks of the Charles or even over lunch in the dining room. Some sort of upper limit in flexibility was reached when a few students began interviewing each other by telephone. (I always felt something *wrong* with this but could never put my finger on exactly *what* it was, so I permitted it but without enthusiasm.) At any rate, the space problem dwindled away early in the course. Indeed, its flexibility with respect to spatial arrangement might well prove one of the interview method's strongest points, especially where facilities are crowded.

The time problems proved more persistent. This fact stemmed in part from the brevity of the course itself, whose allotted span was a mere six

weeks. But it also arose from the students' difficulties in understanding the reading. An awareness of these two factors prompted me to begin each unit, not merely with the *one*, possibly brief, interview that the method requires, but with several rather long interviews. This speeded things up by initiating each unit with several simultaneous interview chains instead of one. It also assured the first student link in each chain of a good understanding of the unit in question. But it left *me* with little time to sit in on student-to-student interviews and thus one of my two main quality controls largely went by the boards. The realization that I could save time by interviewing several students at once—a solution so simple as to appear in retrospect inevitable—came to me too late in the course to be of much help.

My interviewing several students per unit, whether simultaneously or in succession, also served to exaccerbate a difficulty already present, namely the "last man problem." When on a given unit the teacher interviews eactly one student, and each student in turn interviews exactly one uninterviewed student, the last man to be interviewed finds himself with no uninterviewed student to interview. He thus stands in danger of not being permitted to advance to the next unit. He can solve his problem—the "last man problem"—in only two ways. He can either interview the teacher or he can interview some student who has already been interviewed. Of these solutions, the second—though poor—is probably preferable. But the problem is augmented wherever the teacher, or anyone for that matter, interviews *more* than one student per unit. The last *man* problem then becomes the last *men* problem. In time we discovered that the last *men* problem could always be reduced to the last *man* problem by allowing several students to interview simultaneously one student.

The students' spatial dispersion combined with the proliferation of allowed interview-types generated minor communication problems. In resolving these I found helpful a handful of technical terms that I borrowed—modifying their meanings slightly—from the logic of relations. Thus, we used the expression "teacher-student interview" for an interview in which a teacher interviewed a student. Analogously "student-student interview" for one in which a student interviewed a student. An interview in which exactly one person interviewed one person was called a "one-one interview." When one person interviewed two or more people simultaneously, the result was termed a "one-many interview" and the converse—

with several interviewers and one interviewee—was called a "many-one interview." Finally, an interview in which the interviewer interviewed himself was termed "reflexive."

One problem proved insoluable. A few students—four of the thirty-one—simply found the whole interview method repugnant to them. Whether because of illness or personal problems or personality type, these four found this repeated direct, personal contact a heavy burden. Each completed less than sixteen interviews. These people the course never really reached. They were the ones who ended by getting the poor grades—C and lower.

The remaining twenty-seven students fared otherwise. Of these twenty-four completed all twenty-eight interviews successfully, and of the other three, none *failed* to complete more than four interviews. The final boxscore was twenty-four A's and A-'s, three B's, two C's, one D and one F. Graphed, this resembles the upper half of a normal curve *inverted*. Representing as they do my own personal judgment of the quality of each student's performance, these grades doubtless reflect subjective factors. In particular, the entire curve was without any doubt boosted upward by the feelings which the final, written reflexive interviews engendered in me. These papers, though frequently lacking in polish and other minor virtues, displayed as a body and almost without exception an unmistakable understanding and a vivid appreciation of basic philosophic issues—an understanding and appreciation matched in my previous experience of introductory courses only by the few, best students. Above all, these final interviews answered a question that had plagued me from the onset, namely: Can a course in which most of the teaching is done by amateurs develop in these amateurs the genuine critical standards and the genuinely critical attitudes that characterize the professional expert? The answer was: "Within the limits to be expected of *any* introductory course, yes." The interviews showed in varying degrees but with remarkable unanimity a clear recognition of the differences between reasoning and mere statement. They displayed a satisfying sense of the difference between a good argument and a bad one. They showed a pretty pervasive awareness not only of the reasons that had led, or might lead, an author to adopt given views but also of the reasons that would lead someone else, usually the student himself, to reject these views. Much of this criticism was not as thoroughly thought through nor as well organized nor as well expressed as it might have been. But it

was always *there*, and with the exception of one paper never perfunctory or slipshod.

Perhaps I should not have been so relieved and surprised by this as I was. Because I *had* been troubled by the question of critical standards from the beginning, I had both emphasized and tried to exemplify the role of criticism in philosophy repeatedly throughout the course—in my initial descriptions of the good interview, in my lectures, and in the interviews I myself conducted.

How much of the course's success should be attributed to the Keller plan and how much to a lucky run of students or to more deeply hidden variables? These are hard questions. But there is one effect that I unhesitatingly credit to the Keller plan: I mean the pleasure which the students derived from the course. After an initial period of timid distrust, they took to the interview method like ducks to water. They started interviewing before class and continued it after class. By the end of the second week I knew all my students by name and almost all of them knew each other. What most of them doubtless expected to be a succession of cold, impersonal, largely passive classroom sessions became instead—for most of them—a series of warm, personal, active social occasions, in which they learned both by being taught and by teaching. That more often than not interviewer and interviewee were of different sexes can hardly have decreased their interest in the subject or their acceptance of the method. Such appraisals of the course as I could get, obtained in part through personal conversation and in part from anonymous course-evaluation forms, proved invariably favorable and almost always enthusiastic. Most students obviously enjoyed the course. I did too.

It seems to me that the techniques used in our course could be applied with equal or greater success in courses which introduce the students to philosophy by surveying its history or by sampling its types. Not long ago almost any introduction to philosophy would have followed one of these three—the problems, the types, the history—approaches. More and more often recently, however, students are being introduced to philosophy by courses in logic, particularly symbolic logic. I foresee difficulties in applying the Ferster-Perrott approach to such courses. In logic the student is commonly required to do many problems or exercises. These must also be very carefully examined and corrected. In a subject in which absolute accuracy is of the essence, such correction might well lie beyond the competence of the average beginning student. Perhaps what is called for here is a reversion from the student-interview-dominated approach of Ferster and Perrott to an approach which, as in Keller's original Brazilia experiment,[5] makes extensive use of professional or

[5] See the "Neglected Rewards" paper previously cited.

quasi-professional proctors. More broadly speaking, whatever variant of the Keller method proves most successful in teaching mathematics and the natural sciences should, with minimal adaptations, serve equally well in teaching logic.

Section III

Problems

The tenor of the papers presented thus far border on unrestrained (but hopefully not uncritical) enthusiasm. The previous section suggested one kind of problem: PSI is probably not appropriate, possible, or desirable for a significant part of the curriculum. Furthermore, it would be a loss if the few truly great teachers left the lecturn. Finally, there are conditions where the method just will not work.

Articles 22 and 23 suggest situations where PSI should be avoided. Article 24 is an informal account from a physics professor who reports a failure. It would be comforting if the faults in that course were obvious. They are not, but his paper serves to point out that success is not automatic. There can be little future for any innovation if its failures are not laid bare. A better system cannot develop as long as the results of defective contingencies are hidden, dismissed as bad measurements, or tolerated as inevitable. Here is an account of what can go wrong and some clues as to why. It is the failures presented in this section, not the plaudits in Section II, that the first-time user should review before he begins.

Articles 25, 26, 27, and 28 concentrate less on problems and arguments concerning PSI and more on specific aspects of the system that give rise to difficulties. Procrastination, the drop rate, and the grade distribution seem to be the most troublesome. The most frequent complaint of both students and instructors is that PSI courses are more work. The selections in this section discuss these matters in considerable detail.

One aspect of the grade distribution problem is not emphasized. PSI produces a large number of A's. The contention is that the A earned in a PSI course is equivalent to the A earned in other courses. If true, then we face some new problems. Large numbers of students, performing at superior levels, produce very serious dislocations in an educational system geared to a selection model. This is not the place to develop that thought, but neither our schools nor our social structure are prepared to deal with large scale success. If students do learn nearly everything presented, serious questions arise concerning priorities in what we should teach. Others have pointed out that if education were effective it would be dangerous and probably outlawed.

PSI is not so efficient that it will be honored by being made illegal. However, one important advantage of PSI is that it makes failure visible at a time and under conditions where something can be done about it. As Gallup points out in his paper, the reinforcement contingencies can be experimented with. At least on a large scale this is decidedly not true of more conventional teaching. Whatever its faults, the resolving power of the method is its major asset. We have every right to expect that the self-corrective feedback feature will lead to a better system.

22

FIFTEEN REASONS NOT TO USE THE KELLER PLAN[1]

Ben A. Green, Jr.

The title Alex Dessler gave me to speak on was "The spread of the Keller Plan at MIT," and I hope my substitute title does not get interpreted wrongly. (I cannot imagine ever going back to the lecture method in any future teaching I do.) I merely wish to point out some of the obstacles, real or imagined, in the path of one who would try the Keller method for the first time.

This does not mean that I have totally ignored Alex's charge to describe the spread of the method at MIT. "Watching the method spread" is an accurate description of my role and that of my colleagues in the Education Research Center. We merely gave a few courses in physics for a few hundred students; these students told other students what the method was; and soon students were asking teachers to use it. One slightly more active thing we did was to ask a few colleagues from the physics department to act as tutors during a one-month intensive course in which we served students taking any one of the four semesters of introductory physics. All four courses were taught simultaneously out of one room by the same staff. One of the "tutors" enjoyed the process so much that he Kellerized his own course within a few weeks and gave it successfully to seventy-five students!

I was not always so optimistic about the prospects of the method at MIT. I started out in 1968 with a proposal to the Physics Department that we try the method in the spring of 1969 with a small group of volunteer students. If it were to work well enough, we would revise the materials on the basis of that experience, and then demonstrate the final product by teaching the course to 100 students. Our job then would have been finished. We would have proved that the method was sound and beneficial, the Physics Department would instantly adopt it, and everybody would be very happy.

Well, it didn't work that way at all. After the 100-student trial I wrote a cheery report about the project and submitted it to the people in the department who decide who will teach what in the introductory sequence, how and when. They thought the experiment was very interesting, but they didn't really know who was going to teach second-term physics next term and the decision probably wouldn't even be made until the week before classes begin. So it would be impossible to pick up the method as projected in the original proposal. Besides who ever heard of giving a course without lectures!

Discouraging as it was, this reception could have been predicted. It takes time for people to think through all of the aspects of changing a teaching style; it takes time for student opinion to get spread; it takes time for enough students to experience the method so that there is some base of student opinion. It turned out, two years later, that a large physics course of 500 students given last fall was given at MIT by the method. It was done by my "tutor"-colleague, in fact. Thus I have been taught patience.

On a national scale, the Keller Plan has spread rapidly in the last few years. A newsletter for users and interested bystanders has published three issues by now and the mailing list for each issue has grown from 400 to 900 to 1400. A poorly advertised conference on the Plan at MIT last October attracted 350 college teachers. There have been 1300 inquiries this year about a short MIT course in the Plan to be held in July, 1972, which can accept twenty teachers. There will be at least six conferences or workshops on the Plan within the first half of 1972.

Part of the reason for this rapid spread is that individualized instruction is "in the air" nowadays. Postlethwaite's Audio-Tutorial method, which anticipated some features of the Keller Plan, has been widely adopted. The deficiencies of the traditional methods of college teaching are often discussed. Institutions with open admissions policies

[1] Adapted from a paper delivered at the Keller Method Workshop Conference, March 18, 1972, Rice University, Houston, Texas.

are discovering problems which teaching by lecture cannot solve. It is natural in this atmosphere to grasp a new method which in the hands of its inventor and the first wave of enthusiastic users seems to answer some instructional problems.

The purpose of the rest of this paper is to present fifteen possible objections or reasons not to use the plan. Some are meant seriously; some are not. The Keller Plan cannot solve all of a teacher's problems. There are circumstances under which it would be neither possible nor desirable to use the method. There are physical and political environments in which the method would probably fail and probably should not be attempted. For the Keller Plan can fail and fail hard.

On the other hand, there are many talented teachers in good positions from which to launch a course using the method who shrink from it for fear of phantom difficulties. These objections, too, are discussed below.

1. Mastery is not the object of your course.   There are courses whose object is to provide an experience, not to master a subject matter. Such a course can have great value in promoting the personal growth of a student through seminar-like encounters with other students and a wise instructor. Science courses in which students hear how it was to discover a new element or find a new effect or influence a governmental policy have no concept of mastery as a goal. Grades and examinations seem irrelevant to such courses, and we see no possibility of or motive for using the Keller Plan to teach them.

2. There is not adequate text for your course.   The labor involved in creating study guides and tests for a Keller Plan course are great enough that one should not have to write substantial amounts of corrective or supplementary material to piece out an inadequate text. Sometimes several texts can supplement each other, but writing a new textbook is too much to attempt while trying a new teaching style for the first time.

3. Your subject changes too fast.   If your course's content cannot be predicted five months in advance, then it is impossible for you to plan a coherent course and prepare good study guides.

4. You have 500 students, no help, and no time off to prepare materials.   Clearly a contraindication. We advise people to start with a class of twenty, recruit two tutors, and allow a month to prepare materials. Later one can be more ambitious, but probably never can 500 students be adequately taught by one man.

5. Your students can't read, at least not well enough to do without lectures.   In extreme cases, this might be overcome by use of audio tape or by programmed material written at the proper level. But a standard feature of Keller Plan courses in highly verbal subjects (as opposed to problem-oriented subjects) is a list of study questions in each unit's study guide. The study questions improve the reading performance of most students.

6. You are legislatively required to lecture for a large number of hours.   Even if this requirement is not actually a matter of law, colleagues, parents, and administrators sometimes do not understand what the teacher is doing to earn his salary if he is not giving lectures. Eventually they will come around, of course. The teacher's work may be less visible, but after a semester or two it should be obvious that he has become more "productive" in some sense by the use of the new method.

7. You don't have the energy to try something new at this time.   If you have been sick, put off your experiment! The first time you try it, it will require extra effort and it would be foolish to attempt it without good health.

8. Good teaching isn't rewarded at your school.   Since it will take extra effort the first time you try the Keller Plan, your research will probably suffer. If your position is not secure and will not be made more secure by improving your teaching, better bide your time.

9. You can't get undergraduate tutors for love, credit, or money.   This can usually be overcome. Sherman has shown, in fact, how one can recruit tutors from the very class being taught, provided they are not asked to volunteer too large a fraction of their time. In four-year colleges we have never heard of difficulty in finding enough tutors for the first run of a lower division Keller Plan course. But if one cannot get the tutors, it is a mistake to attempt a course without them unless the class is very small—say under fifteen.

10. One undergraduate cannot judge proficiency in your subject on the part of another undergraduate. This is often said, but it is rarely true. The reasons have been discussed in the literature. But there may be cases in which the objection is valid. Pronunciation in a foreign language, portrait painting, creative writing—these may be examples. In these cases, undergraduate tutors cannot be used to personalize the course, and the Keller Plan is inappropriate.

11. Your administration will not tolerate a large fraction of A's. If this is because you are inflating the market for academic credit, they have a good point. If they don't believe your A is as good as another teacher's A, you must be prepared to defend your grade assignment. Comparative examination grades have been used for this purpose with good effect. The objection usually doesn't occur until the end of your experimental term, but one should be prepared for it.

12. You object on principle to specifying detailed objectives in your course. It is wrong to "teach the test" if the test is only a sample of the behavior you expect to teach. But objectives can usually be stated at a level of abstraction low enough to guide the student's work yet high enough to cover the entire range of the subject matter. The objective can define an infinite class of problems from which one is selected for the test. In verbally-oriented courses, the objectives take the form of study questions, which must be rather numerous to cover the desired ground. In problem-oriented courses, objectives can be stated more compactly.

13. You cannot specify objectives in your course. It isn't always easy. But if you give examinations and grades on any rational basis, you should be able to state objectives. If the student is supposed to "have a feel for" the political situation in 1770, what would you take as evidence that he has this feel? One can often tease out his own objectives by such self-questioning.

14. You are too soft-hearted to withhold a privilege from a student who has not earned it. This will give rise to procrastination problems in most cases. For when one gives the student responsibility for setting his own pace and does not provide him incentives for keeping up an acceptable pace, he often chooses to work on more threatening courses no matter how interesting your subject matter is made. Intrinsic motivation is the ideal, but extrinsic motivation is better than punitive deadlines. It is highly desirable to establish special events, lectures, demonstrations, field trips, seminars in your home, which can be "awarded" as enrichment to students who do work hard on your course. This implies that you do not admit to these events students who do not work on your course. Hence the need for a slightly hard heart.

15. You are satisfied with your present methods. This is the best reason not to try the Keller Plan. You are probably doing a fine job with a method you feel comfortable in. Do not let anyone force you to try the Keller Plan, because without your enthusiastic desire to make it work, it probably won't.

23

PSI: SOME NOTABLE FAILURES [1]

J. Gilmour Sherman

When Dr. Dessler first invited me to this conference I accepted with pleasure. Even before examining the invitation, I immediately started to sort through the advantages, the glories and conquests of PSI to find some fresh new positive attributes of the system that I had not spoken of before. There is a rich list—one adapts quickly to the role of salesman. Fred Keller has characterized himself as being first hooked and now a pusher. I begin to understand the ad agency's delight with a new model car. Larger, smaller, or exactly the same as last year's model, makes little difference; all can become an advantage and all are a challenge to the ingenuity of the clever "marketing engineer."

Perhaps knowing of my past excesses, Alex has made an honest man of me by assigning as a topic "Some Notable Failures of PSI." I assume he did not think the failures sufficient to discredit the system, as he is holding this conference in an atmosphere that does not suggest a wake, and he generously programmed my comments under the schedule-rubric of "Brief Remarks." For my own reasons I am pleased to say this will be a slim report. As one of the group that originated PSI, it is gracious of Alex to provide the occasion for one of that group to cast the first stone.

That said, I would like to take the assignment seriously. None of us involved in developing PSI conceived of it as an answer to all of education's ills. It has out-performed all our expectations; but there are some problems, and I would like to explore them with you. My guess is that when Alex set the title of my talk he had in mind some colossal failures where the students revolted, the system collapsed, and the professors involved were fired— preferably after a lengthy and messy exchange with the rank and tenure committee. The subtle political bickerings of such intrigues are delicious and remind me of the delight with which introductory psychology students, after plowing through chapters of sterile data on learning, memory, and characteristics of the nervous system, finally reach the chapter on abnormal psychology. There, at last, are the lush clinical case-history descriptions of sexual deviations—an account that can only appeal to purient interests. I have such a case history to report as a "goody" (may I say as a "reinforcement") at the end. But there are some serious problems for PSI to face and I would like to air them.

As I see it the problems fall into three groups: (1) problems inherent in the system—real or imagined, (2) problems created by *modifications* of the basic pattern and (3) problems created by the fact that while the world of PSI is totally good, the evil world out there does not know our virtues, and there are some problems of communication.

Let me take up the problem of modifications first. This has been nicely treated in Ben Green's editorial entitled "Something Like It" in the second issue of the PSI Newsletter. His account is similar to an incident last fall when I was treated to a series of long distance phone calls from a lady sociologist teaching in the south. She had purchased a commercially available set of PSI materials and, my guess is, without proper instruction, thought or preparation, had set out to teach in a way that would bring her all the benefits of being known as an innovator. When she called me, just this side of unrestrained hysteria, it was to report breathlessly, something like the following: she had announced a surprise mid-term, irrespective of how many units students had passed. The students thought it was silly and didn't come, and she had planned to use those test results to devise a series of lectures on difficult points and make comparisons between her group and a traditional lecture course and now she didn't know what to lecture on, or how to set test deadlines that would be respected; the usual orderliness of her courses had fallen apart, it was all my fault and *what was I going to do about it?* With all due respect for her sincerity I think we can label this a modified PSI course and not dwell on why it was not working.

[1] Paper read at the Keller Method Workshop Conference, March 18, 1972. Rice University, Houston, Texas.

Some other modifications are more serious. Let me comment on a few.

One modification is to change the requirement from mastery to perhaps 70% correct. This is more than a slight of hand with numbers or a shift along a continuum of possible criteria. One of the unique advantages of PSI is that, since errors are not counted, we can, almost for the first time, demand excellence without being unreasonable. Not only does settling for less waste one major advantage of the system, it degrades the spirit of the endeavor. Keller has spoken of this as the Truman theory, that the job makes the man. The usual treatment of students that implies they are probably only worth a C is an insult. The expectation of excellence, no matter how long it takes, is a compliment; a challenge in response to which students do act in a new way. This is lost when we return to something like a 70% criterion.

A second type of modification deals with the temptation to add all sorts of new, ingenious, and additional contingencies. Often these are an attempt to deal with the procrastination problem about which I'll talk more in a moment. I have seen courses with such a complex set of rules you needed an additional course just to learn and understand the regulations. Generally these additional constraints are devised by those without any knowledge of the subtle operations of contingencies, the law of effect, or basic information concerning reinforcement principles. The proliferation of capricious "do's and don't's" is dangerous and I think to be avoided. I have said before that there is nothing sacred about the *form* of PSI but there are some *functions* built into PSI that are so integral to the process of learning that they are not suitable places to tinker with the system. It is probably wise to embellish with caution—and not until your second try.

A third modification, or at least corruption of PSI, is produced by poor material. Perhaps the majority of programs, study guides, study questions, exams, etc., that I have seen are written by people who have just finished reading some excellent book on "how to write behavioral objectives." With these rules freshly in mind the programs are written with all the grace of the young dancing student waltzing around the room mumbling "1, 2, 3,; 1, 2, 3,; left, step, together." That the student should be active rather than passive does not mean that trivial participation of a copying and echoic kind will do. By using challenging problems, requiring the students to make decisions, to guess, and by showing them how often they are correct you can make each step

during learning an *intrinsically* rewarding one. Much of the current material continues to view the student as a sponge—we don't teach, we "tell"—now on paper rather than in a lecture, which is an improvement, but not sufficient. We should make every effort to engage the student in searching, discovering and verifying. Several ways have been suggested to avoid "telling" and promote real learning. It is as cruel to bore students as to punish them. I suggest many of those writing PSI materials should hunt up Speeth and Margulies' article "Techniques for maintaining student motivation."[2] It gives a hint at how we might go about writing better materials—materials that themselves might decrease the procrastination problem.

One final modification is the notion that, once programmed successfully, the professor has freed himself from the course and can walk away. I know of one disaster, closer to what Alex expected me to talk about, that resulted from exactly this sort of thing. Unfortunately it was at my own university, Georgetown, and we have not outlived it yet. I can assure you a failure is costly and difficult to overcome at the higher levels of Deans and Vice Presidents. In this particular case the professor was absent because of ill health, but unrestrained by a guiding hand the proctors took over, tests were for sale on every corner, and an A was a mark of easy virtue.

PSI was never intended as the educational answer to the San Francisco wharf's walk-away crab cocktail. While most of us have stood in the midst of such a course feeling quite useless, the system has a function for the professor. This is not a correspondence course. That he becomes a manager is clear. That he is writing a program for learning should be clear. But he has another function—one that I personally feel makes PSI superior to Computer Aided Instruction. He is available not only to oversee but to answer questions, treat the unique, add the artistry that can't be predicted, programmed and can't be passed on to those lower in the system. The system frees him from treating the mundane and repetitious, *precisely* so he can have the time to deal with the creative. If the professor walks away, the magic is gone, a great course turns into a bureaucracy.

In short most modifications if not failures, or notable, have at least not been too successful. The modifications I have mentioned have all caused problems.

---

[2] National Society for Programmed Instruction Journal, 1969, vol. vii, pages 24-27.

Now let me quickly mention some failures, problems, or shortcomings inherent in the system.

1. *The professor works harder than ever.* This is true and if he isn't, he's not doing it right. The man too pressed by other duties to increase dramatically the time he devotes to teaching, is one of those on Ben Green's list of "who should not use PSI."

2. *The students work harder than ever.* This is an almost universal report. It may set a limit to the percentage of the total curriculum that can be programmed without running the student to exhaustion. Joel Greenspoon says it isn't a problem or a limit. Personally I suspect that on a totally PSI campus, a man could make quite a reputation for himself by giving a lecture.

3. *There is a substantial logistic and administrative load created by the system* which, as Pooh Bear would say, is "a bother." This is also true and the person who neglects it is headed for a failure. Long waiting lines, poor records, and the difficulties of communicating with a group that never meets are only some of the logistic aspects requiring careful attention. These small details can make or break the course.

4. *Then the staff to run a PSI course becomes expensive.* While there are probably other equally good solutions, my system of using proctors chosen from students in the course solves this problem.

5. *But the staff size and logistical problems set a limit to class size.* This is probably true and sets a real limitation. I think PSI fails to answer the problems posed by courses in the 1,000's. My guess is that a manageable personalized staff, with some student-professor interaction avoiding the walk-away cocktail problem, sets an upper limit in the ballpark of 150 to 200 students. The system can be rigged for more, but again it becomes a bureaucracy, not a *personalized system* of instruction.

6. *The production time for materials is almost prohibitive.* This is a failure that may kill us. PSI materials are extensive and must be written with the greatest care since they *will* be put to a test. They must be in a flexible form responsive to what the jargon calls "formative evaluation." Some commercial materials are available, a better communication exchange for materials already developed is being organized, but the record of those who have adopted, wholesale, the materials of others, if not a record of failure is, at least, not a totally happy story. Hopefully a better information exchange will decrease the magnitude of this problem, but my guess is material production time will continue to be a burden.

7. The final inherent problem I want to mention is that created by *students falling behind, procrastinating, requiring incompletes* which may create difficulties with the administration (my last category). *We have chosen to hold quality constant and let time vary. It does not seem possible to have it both ways.* Students do fall behind; many never finish. These are personal failures that worry many of us. Some students dislike the system, stating clearly it is because they don't have the self-control to deal with it. Now it is possible to take the position students have to learn self control in the real world, so this is a little test of that; let them get started. This sounds a little like the educational philosophy of holding them responsible, sink or swim—the attitudes we are trying to get away from. Certainly speed is subject to reinforcement. If we choose to program speed it should not involve punishment. It should not produce a fast rate to the point where quality suffers, and very complex contingencies, as I mentioned before, should be avoided. I am not sure exactly how it fits, but I think many of us who have not found a final answer in this area could profitably read Lloyd Homme's book *How to Use Contingency Contracting in the Classroom.* His chapter on "Shifting to Self-contracting" may give us some hints

There are some other problems but I have gone on too long already. Let me mention the last category of "the evil world out there"—deans, registrars, *colleagues* who don't understand or like our grade distribution, the lack of lectures, or other aspects of the system. This is the area where juicy political failures *have* been reported. Rather than go through all the problems thoroughly, let me merely refer you to a paper "Tactics for Change" written by Dr. Ed Taylor, one of Ben Green's colleagues at M.I.T. His paper is not only insightful and helpful in this whole area[3] of how to deal with the hostile world, it is written with delightful humor—a rare combination of wit and wisdom.

Let me close then by reading excerpts from a letter that does report one failure of grand proportions. In its entirety it would bring tears to your eyes. I'll just read excerpts, but *all* the problems are there.

In the spring of 1968, a colleague, let's call him Bob, and myself were interested in trying some modification of Keller's PSI in our Introductory Psychology courses at the University of Winnipeg in Canada. We had received a copy of Keller's PSI presentation at RMPA and were impressed. At a departmental meeting, I proposed a comparison of three teaching procedures to be employed during our summer session. Everyone agreed it would be a fine thing to try. Two of the four introductory courses were run using a lecture format with four 80-point multiple-choice exams interspersed throughout the term. Bob's students were: (a) required to take a 10-question multiple-choice quiz after each chapter, (b) allowed to take exams when they wanted, (c) required to master each chapter (get at least 80%) before they could advance to the next chapter, (d) given up to three tries on each chapter. My course was the same as Bob's except: (a) students had to pass an oral exam on each chapter before they could take the 10-question quiz, (b) could attend optional lectures over the course material. I employed eight seniors to give the oral interviews to all of the students. The final exam for all four classes consisted of 140 multiple-choice questions selected by all four instructors from the test file supplied by Hilgard and Atkinson. Everyone agreed prior to the onset of the course not to use the selected questions. Seeing it was summer, students were required to attend class two hours every school day of the week.

At the beginning of the course a large handout was given explaining the course procedures. Most of the students appeared bewildered at the course procedures, but we had no great number of drops. After the course had been running for about two weeks, I received information via the faculty-secretary grapevine that some students had been complaining to

the administration that the course had way too high a grade criterion. (Students were told in the outline if they completed all the chapters at an 80% criterion they automatically had a B for the course. They could get an A by taking the mandatory final and scoring 90% or better.) The department head informed me "unofficially" that the administration felt my criterion was too high and suggested it be lowered. He also stated "they" believed the students would be evaluated much more effectively on a curve. Up to this time the course hadn't been running as smoothly as I would have liked; the testing room (30 ft × 45 ft—containing 10 tables at which to give orals) seemed quite congested. Only having eight proctors for 90 students was a real problem. The following evening I was in my office when about 15 of my students came to see me. They were extremely upset with the course; almost militant. We adjourned to the faculty lounge to discuss the merits of the course. After 30 minutes of discussion it became evident that the problem was not with the difficulty of the material nor the criterion of the course, but the procedures. In the discussion it became apparent that the problem was getting the orals taken care of. Students had to come in and try to catch one of the proctors as soon as he was done with a previous student. Students were, in many cases, wasting an hour of class time waiting to be proctored, and not being able to go study for fear of losing their place in the line to be proctored. One of the students then proposed we have sign up sheets for orals. The group felt that would solve the problem so we adopted the proposal. Sheets listing six 10-minute time slots per hour per proctor were posted weekly so a student could sign up in advance and simply show up at the designated time for the oral. This seemingly minor variable change made a tremendous difference in the course. The lines ceased, the proctors were more efficient with their time, student anxiety disappeared within a week, and the students began moving through the chapters much faster. The testing room was adjacent to a large study hall. Most students began using the study hall during the class period. Prior to the change, about 20% of the students were observed to be using the hall during class. After the change, this rose to almost 85%. The whole class seemed to unite; they began studying together and discussing the course mate-

---

[3]Dr. Edwin F. Taylor, M.I.T. 200-228, Cambridge, Mass.

rial amongst themselves. I believe that night discussion influenced the students' attitudes; especially when I told them they could help each other in this system rather than compete against each other as on a curve criterion.

As the course neared the end it became apparent 86 of the 90 students were going to finish all the chapters. I heard through the grapevine that the administration was aware of the students' progress and now felt that the course was obviously too easy. No faculty member had ever come to the class or asked me about it, so I wondered where they received their information. Upon questioning some of my students, they told me various staff members had cornered them in the hall and quizzed them about what went on in the course. I then went to the department head and told him I had heard rumors saying the course was too easy. I took him to the testing room, told him to select any students he wished, ask them which chapters they had completed, and quiz them orally over the material. He quizzed about 8 of the 14 students that were in the room while he was there. Their responses were so good it sounded as though I had primed them specifically for the questions he asked. When we left, I asked him what he thought. He said he felt they did very well, but I could tell he had made up his mind and was not going to be influenced by data which did not support his opinion.

At the end of the term, Bob and I were informed that the administration felt too many high grades were going to be given; and seeing we would have no way to "really" discriminate between our students except by the final exam, the students would be graded on the curve using only the final exam as the means of comparison. Bob and I objected strongly. We were then informed that the administration, not the instructors, had the final say on grades and the "role" of the instructor was only to "suggest" what grade a student should receive.

After grades were given out, all hell broke loose. Students came into my office enraged over their grades. I called a lot of them together and explained what had taken place. Most didn't believe me. Within a few weeks, however, the facts got around and the students were not so mad at me. Those few weeks, however, were quite aversive. I literally "snuck" through the halls and hid in my office. I finished out my contract time and returned to teach in the U.S.

By the way, when we compared the four class means on the final exam, there was no significant difference. All averaged near 107 out of 140. This was quite concerning to us for we knew the behavior of the students was much better than our previous classes which averaged around 89 out of 140 during prior terms. Later on, I became good friends with three students who had been in the lecture groups and they confided that they had seen many of the final exam questions during the course in a "slightly modified" form. I had previously felt the instructors of the lecture groups appeared somewhat threatened with the comparison, though they did not voice it at the onset of the study.

The man who wrote that letter did return to the U.S. and reports he is in a happier surrounding —and teaching his courses using PSI. I hope that at least one thing I have said may avoid for one person here today a disaster of such proportions.

24

RESULTS OF A ONE-SEMESTER SELF-PACED PHYSICS COURSE AT THE STATE UNIVERSITY COLLEGE, PLATTSBURGH, NEW YORK

P. P. Szydlik

Introduction to Physics (Physics 101) a one-semester, 4-credit hour course with laboratory for non-majors was conducted using the Keller plan during the fall semester, 1971. Since the clientele of the course consisted primarily of majors in biology, nursing and mathematics, the course was designed to be somewhat technical requiring the use of algebra and trigonometry. It was intended that the student should acquire physical principles sufficient to enable him to apply physics to problems in his major field should the need arise.

There were 28 students registered in the course during the first semester with majors in biology and nursing predominating (more than 75% of the total). There was one major in psychology and one in art (who later withdrew). Registrants in the course provided one indication of the flexibility of the method. One student was a nurse (some 10 years older than the average college student) with family obligations necessitating her return to college to obtain a degree. Another was an airman from Plattsburgh Air Force Base whose work schedule and temporary duty assignments periodically interrupted his progress. It would have been impossible for students such as these to take physics under the regular scheme and they received quite legitimate incompletes at the end of the semester. In addition to the 26 original registrants, two entered the course at mid-semester. One of these was notified at that time that she needed to improve her physics grade in order to be accepted into the final year of the medical technology program at a university medical center. The second discovered quite belatedly that he had been advised into the wrong physics course. Valuable time could be saved in these cases by not having to adhere to the rigid semester lockstep.

Three undergraduate students (two physics majors and a chemistry major) assisted as tutors in the regular or text-related portion of the course. Two additional students (a physics major and a medical technology student) were laboratory tutors. Tutors were awarded 4 semester hours of credit in

physics. In addition to aiding the students to learn the course material, the tutors were expected to compose a study guide and, more importantly, to write their evaluation of the self-paced physics course, its content, methods and results.

For developing the study materials and laboratory this instructor was credited with 9 contact hours, the normal teaching load for a faculty member who is also expected to actively engage in research. At my own choice I also taught an additional three-hour course in numerical methods for computers.

Three students completed 21 units and received A grades. This percentage of A's is slightly better than usual for this course, when offered in the conventional manner. One student, unable to endure the trauma of not passing unit tests, withdrew after three weeks. Two other students (with virtually zero attendance records) were advised to withdraw since one had completed only one unit and another zero units at mid-semester, the final time for withdrawal without penalty. With the permission of the Dean of Science and Mathematics, incomplete grades were given automatically to the other students with the usual condition that the incompletes be discharged by the following semester. To stimulate delinquent students to action each received notice in writing of my further stipulation that the deadline for completion was March 29, 1972 (the beginning of the spring holiday and more than $2\frac{1}{2}$ months into the second semester). Five students (averaging the completion of 3 units) made personal pleas for incomplete grades, though the policy on incompletes had been posted on the course bulletin board three weeks prior to the end of the semester! Of the twenty students receiving *I* grades (excluding the two who entered the course near mid-semester) one quickly completed the single additional unit necessary for a C and bailed out very early in the second semester. Of the remaining 19 only 10 can be considered to have taken tests or to have attended tutoring sessions with anything approaching normal regularity.

These 10 can be divided on the basis of performance into 5 who completed a total of 58 units (an average of almost 12 units) and 5 who completed only 30 units (an average of 6). Of the 9 who attended sporadically (completing a total of 36 units) one stopped attending in September, one in October, and six in November. Attendance fell off drastically in December even among those students who attended regularly, as end-of-semester (December 22) pressures mounted in other courses.

Indications were that the general aptitude of students electing the self-paced course was less than that of students in the regular course; for some the self-paced course was a last ditch effort to fulfill a physics requirement; others did not allow sufficient time in their own schedules to avail themselves of quite liberal tutoring and laboratory hours. Quantitative data to substantiate these feelings must await the results of a questionnaire to be distributed to the students upon their completion of the course (or March 29, whichever is sooner).

While a great deal of effort has been expended in obtaining and guiding tutors, in preparing and publishing study guides, laboratory experiments and other written materials it is readily apparent that the self-paced course has as yet not succeeded in improving substantially either student achievement in physics or student attitude toward the subject. Some reasons can be proffered for this lack of success and no apologies will be made for the subjectivity of the assessment. The seeds of defeat directly planted by the instructor are not evident to him. An external objective, perceptive and courageous critic will be required to bring such deficiencies to his attention.

The figure of attainment for a satisfactory grade in the course, as determined from a combination of course level, degree of mastery required and amount of material to be covered may have been too high. In a regular course if the instructor errs in choosing the amount of material he merely truncates or adds material as the length of the school term dictates. The "curve" can always bury other errors in choosing the figure of attainment much as an undertaker buries the doctor's mistakes. In the self-paced course the amount of material to be "mastered" for a particular grade is most often specified in writing in advance as it was in this course.

Voluntary feedback from the tutors was sparse. Meetings with the tutors were not fruitful in pointing out substantial course defects although lesser problems were exposed in these meetings and

remedies sought. Some tutors did not stay current with the course material, not even to the point of complying with the suggestion of completing unit tests as a relatively painless method of keeping up. In order to obtain academic credit the tutors were required to submit written evaluations of the self-paced physics course. It is significant that three of the five tutors themselves received incomplete grades, failing to complete their reports until pressured to do so one and one-half months after the semester's end. Two of these were not permitted by their advisors to continue their tutoring activities in the second semester because of other academic deficiencies. The third, whom I would not regard as an effective tutor having adopted an "of-the-cuff" approach in the laboratory, did not choose to tutor in the succeeding semester. One of the reports could be characterized more as narrative history than critique. A second stated at the outset that attempting a self-paced approach in this particular physics course was folly akin to believe in Utopia. Most reports had useful suggestions for improving course content and study guides but did not address themselves directly to improving student attitudes or performance.

Some students are reluctant to learn the material as thoroughly as is necessary to progress and are perturbed when their deficiencies are exposed by poor performance on the unit test. Too often students had not completed the suggested exercises, sometimes had not even read the study guide and were reluctant to be "recycled" when they failed unit tests. Apparently some of these students would be content with less than an A grade, providing test evaluations were less rigorous allowing them to proceed at a more rapid pace. Such an attitude may be a carry over from regular courses where failed material often need not be faced again.

With twenty incompletes from the first semester, difficulty in obtaining student tutors and departmental consensus unfavorable toward furthur expansion of the self-paced course, only ten new students were enrolled in the second semester. Poor students carried over from the first semester have not improved their attendance records nor their resultant performance. Progress to date for the new students is quite encouraging—about 70% faster on the average than the first semester's results. Of two students who did very poorly in the regular course the first semester, one is almost certain to receive an A; the second has an excellent chance of also attaining this grade. It is hoped that a faculty member who has become an associate instructor and a tutor in the self-paced course will provide some necessary constructive criticism. It is unfortunate that both he and a new student tutor believe firmly that the mini-lecture is the best tutoring method, particularly to circumvent the fact that a significant percentage of students are not following the suggestions of the study guides.

The Keller plan workshop at MIT should focus more on such questions as the type and level of the course to be offered in view of the anticipated clientele, materials to be used, a working definition of "mastery," and the amount of material to be mastered for a particular grade in view of the time available for the course and noting that the student has conventional courses in addition to the Keller plan course. These considerations are not peculiar to a Keller plan course. Decisions on these points are critical even if only from the crass consideration of obtaining an acceptable final grade distribution if they are to be specified in advance. It may be a laudable goal to generate as many study guides as possible during the workshop. Certainly a potential instructor for a Keller plan course needs to develop skills in composing study guides and associated written materials. Moreover, pressures which may occur during operation of the course are relieved substantially by preparing material in advance. But an adequate (whatever that may be) amount of time should be devoted to pondering "big-picture" questions enumerated above. The remainder of the workshop could then be devoted to developing the techniques of writing study guides and actually producing a number of study guides sufficient to obtain a feeling of accomplishment and sufficient to generate the positive inertia necessary to continue this creative process after the workshop has concluded but before the course commences.

Course results, student attitudes, the (not entirely unjustified) skepticism of colleagues and the contrast of self-paced physics with a similarly conducted psychology course which is progressing swimmingly have damaged significantly the psyche of this instructor. The interest and support of the Dean and Department Chairman, the interest demonstrated by others at this college, the interest shown by physics faculty from outside this college have provided a necessary, but alas, insufficient impetus for continuing with self-paced physics. The added ingredients to produce sufficiency must come ultimately from an inherent hard-headed belief that in spite of current personal experience that learning must be facilitated by as personalized a system as possible; that the student must be given some freedom to choose what he wishes to learn in a particular course; that his rate of progress and amount of material mastered must not be controlled by the semester lockstep; that what is told in a lecture is always greater than what is learned; that the self-paced course has not so much caused problems as it has unearthed problems which could not surface above the sea of students in the large lectures. Presenting the Keller plan course has provided an insight into my methods of instruction and the student learning process which could never have been provided using the lecture approach. An innate stubbornness further reinforces my conviction that the apparent problems of this Keller plan course are just an exposé of the problems of teaching science. To our alleged concern with the cognitive aspects of teaching science must be added the affective. Attention must be focused not just on what is to be learned but on student attitudes as well—not merely his attitudes towards physics or science itself but to the entire educational process in the sciences.

25

PROBLEMS IN THE IMPLEMENTATION OF A COURSE IN PERSONALIZED INSTRUCTION [1]

Howard F. Gallup

The Chairman of this symposium began his remarks by saying that "Lectures are used primarily to arouse . . . interest rather than to transmit information." In keeping with this policy, which I think forms an essential aspect of personalized instruction, let me refer you for information to the handouts which are available [see p. 000]. On these handouts you will find, in outline form, a list of and set of brief comments about the various problems which I have either encountered or circumvented, or which others have mentioned in talking or writing about personalized instruction.

Please note that some of these problems would be relevant only for personalized courses; others of these problems would be relevant for any attempt at innovation in college teaching, the severity of the problems increasing directly with the success of the innovation.

As I proceed to run through the problems and to make a few comments about them, you may follow with me on the handouts. As you do, let me call your attention especially to the references at the end. You will find David Born's two manuals most useful if you are planning to organize your first course in personalized instruction. I think he has anticipated most of the practical problems you are likely to encounter as you organize and operate your course. Johnston and Pennypacker deal with problems in a different way, as do Ferster, Malott, McMichael and Corey, Witters and Kent, and myself. The forthcoming Keller-Sherman collaboration which is referred to in Issue #1 of the PSI Newsletter ought to provide an invaluable service for all of us in this field.

The more general problems of innovation cannot be anticipated quite so specifically, even though most of the papers, written or delivered, have alluded to them in one way or another. Perhaps the best single source on such problems is *Resistance to*

Innovation in Higher Education by Richard Evans which deals explicitly with the topic; but Algo Henderson's *The Innovative Spirit* gets at the same kinds of problems also.

I. Problems arising prior to the actual conduct of the course. "Permission" may not be the appropriate word in many cases. Academic freedom seems to vary in details from institution to institution. At Lafayette, "permission" was tied only to financial aspects of converting our introductory course into a personalized one; and, in our case, this meant using our student aid budget to pay proctors. The decision to convert did involve the entire psychology department, as well as a faculty committee and the college administration, but I do not think the word "permission" is proper in our case.

Although I had read what was available at that time (summer, 1968) and had spent several hours pumping Fred Keller on details, I know now that I did not then appreciate fully the impact our personalized course would soon have on the entire campus. If I were faced today with a request for advice in this matter, I would have to caution those involved; I would have to alert them to the problems we will discuss in a few moments, and perhaps "permission" would be a more appropriate term. After all, it is one thing to have academic freedom, to conduct one's courses in any way deemed most desirable; but it is quite another matter to be successful, for example, to be in charge of a course and thus responsible for assigning perhaps 80% A's and almost no failures in an environment where grading on a curve has been practiced. This is not to say that I have turned chicken or that I am no longer in favor of shaking loose the cobwebs of antiquity; but I do think one's colleagues, students, and administrators have a right to prepare themselves for the consequences.

The organization of a personalized course cannot be postponed and procrastinated as can other courses. In my opinion, before the first day of

[1] Paper presented at "Personalized Instruction: a symposium in honor of Fred Keller," American Psychological Association Meeting, September 6, 1971.

classes (preferably several weeks before, if possible, so that proctors can get ahead of students) the entire course must be planned down to last details. Behavioral objectives should be stated in writing, as well as the assessment devices for determining when the students have reached those objectives. (Please note that I said "when" the objectives have been reached, not "if.") Textbooks and other written materials must be selected, and with more than the usual care, since you will have very little opportunity to straighten out misconceptions by means of lectures; worse, your students will learn their textbooks better than usual, including the misconceptions. The objectives must be spaced out over a series of units; readiness testing must be prepared for each unit, with equivalent alternate tests. Schedules of events, such as testing hours, films, lectures, or demonstrations must all be prepared in writing. If you run your course as I have, there are no required class meetings after the first one; you may literally never see the entire group again together in one place.

The selection of proctors and their utilization is a problem which needs some research. After the first year of operation, proctors can be obtained quite readily from alumni of your course; for the first year, selection criteria are much vaguer. You can look for good students, warm students, interested students, those who can relate to their peers; and I might add, honest students, since we had what I hope was our first and last case this past year of a proctor selling readiness tests to students in the course. Once proctors have been selected, especially in the first year of operation, training is essential. Proctors must be thoroughly familiar with the texts and other written materials, and they must be informed on the usage and desirability of positive reinforcing techniques; they must know when to reinforce and when not to, as well as how to reinforce: in short, they must be ideal teachers in a one-to-one situation.

We need so desperately to find solutions to many problems facing higher education today that I would hope anyone involved in some innovation would plan to let the world learn from it. Good research requires planning; therefore, an evaluation of personalized courses should be planned for at the outset. I will make no attempt here to discuss such an evaluation: my references can supply you with several examples of such research, as will the other papers presented here today. I will add, however, that there may be survival value in your evaluative research. Dull lectures can follow dull lectures like dominoes; grading on a curve can

occur *ad infinitum;* students can be bored in a lock-step system; all manner of inefficient and perhaps harmful teaching can take place. And if such teaching is part of the *status quo* it goes unchallenged, except perhaps by a few alienated students. The innovator does not go unchallenged. Let me alert you to the possibility that your conceptions of learning and education, grading and teaching may all be subjected to pointed analysis by your colleagues and your administrators; you may even find that you will challenge your own assumptions before long.

II. As a personalized course gets under way, different kinds of problems will begin to arise. Most of the eight types of problems listed on the outline have been well covered by Born and by Keller. Many of them will be peculiar to your own situation.

Some workers in this area have assigned a proctor to certain students; I have preferred to make proctors available at certain hours and to permit students to choose any proctor on duty at the time a test is to be taken and scored. There are no doubt advantages and disadvantages to both techniques, which some good research could help identify. At this time, I think my technique provides more flexibility for the students.

You will probably find, unless you are better than I at constructing test items, that you can improve your tests. As in programmed instruction, your students will be the main source of information as to which items need revision. This becomes a practical problem: for example, in Psychology 1, I had 20 units with 4 "equivalent" tests per unit. These were put on stencils and several copies run off. There were thus 20 units times 4 tests each times 5 copies per test, or about 400 test pages needed for Psychology 1. To revise a test item might mean to cut a new stencil and duplicate it; it might mean upsetting equality among tests on a given unit; it would certainly mean that students coming along later in the semester would have a different test from those who came earlier. This is one of the prices to be paid for arranging contingencies for better learning.

Record keeping is essential, not only to keep on top of the progress of each of your students, but to keep yourself informed on the entire course, and to provide the basis for defense and evaluation of your new course. We have found that our computer is most valuable in this tedious aspect of the course administration.

I have listed films, demonstrations, lectures, and discussions among the problems. Actually, with optional attendance and well-prepared audiences, these events are good times. The problem comes in the scheduling of these. For example, all my lectures began with the assumption that everyone in the audience has passed a certain unit and that I can begin my talk at a given level of sophistication. (This coming semester I will be offering an advanced seminar on "Aggression and Nonviolence"—admission to the discussion sessions will only be given contingent upon proven competency with the assigned readings.) In a larger course, as in our introductory one with almost 300 students, scheduling events contingent upon a certain proportion of these students being prepared to attend, requires that you know where all the students are at any time; in fact, one must predict where they are apt to be a week or two hence to allow for publicity for events.

One of the saddest problems I have faced is that of procrastination on the part of students. In an over-all system where students are taking several courses; where aversive controls are used to insure that students keep up with their work; where class attendance, hour examinations, term papers may be required; in short, when your course is the only one in which a student can proceed at his own pace, he may be forced by other contingencies to let up on your readiness tests for a week or more. Unfortunately, this will probably create a dilemma. In an educational system where semesters end, examination periods are scheduled, students take several courses, and so on, you may find large segments, even majorities of your students waiting until the last week or two to take your entire course—or trying to. And why not? If you really mean: go at your own pace. Logistically, we could not permit this.

One possible solution is to provide for a "doomsday contingency"—finish by such and such a date, or else. Another solution is to provide for higher rewards for work completed early in a semester rather than later. A third solution, and the one we have adopted at Lafayette, is to place an upper limit on the number of units which can be passed in the later weeks of a semester, with no limits on those passed earlier. Perhaps you will be able to permit complete freedom, thus eliminating one problem.

A final problem in this section has to do with those few students who do not earn A's. Some PSI courses reported recently have permitted students to contract for a certain grade. Why anyone would

permit, much less encourage students to contract for C's eludes me, although such a system obviously challenges the *status quo* to a lesser degree. If a basic course serves as a prerequisite for advanced courses, should a student who completes only 16 of my 20 units be permitted to move on with a grade of B? Should he receive an Incomplete until he has completed all 20 units? Bookkeeping and registrar policies at the college level may dictate your decision in this matter; if not, I would prefer the use of Incompletes and A's, with no inbetweens. Even more, I would prefer the use of Incompletes or Passes, where pass means an A. I have a standing offer to my college to offer Psychology 1, 2 on a Pass-Fail option only, with perfection on all readiness testing required for a Pass. Perhaps that would not be fair to the students; I am not sure. But I do not think that is the reason the offer is still standing unaccepted.

III.   As a personalized course proceeds, it does so in a sociological framework, not in a vacuum. Very rapidly, at least in our small liberal arts college, rumors begin to fly. As with all rumors, there may be a basis in fact, but leveling and sharpening, and selective perception and retention, and prejudices all go to work in short order. There is evidently something very exciting about the personalized course for those involved in it—and that includes students, proctors and faculty. As those involved begin to share their experiences with friends, bits and pieces are disseminated. Students not in the course may try to enroll late; other faculty members are curious to learn about what you do if you are not teaching—that is, in front of a class. Frictions are born of such rumors, part information, and excitement.

One of the strongest challenges comes in the meaning of grades. The immediate and almost universal judgment about my course has been that it must be easy since so many A's were given out. (It was one of the recurring questions from the floor when I talked about this topic at a symposium during the Eastern Psychological Association meetings last year, presumably to psychologists who should appreciate the power of the reinforcement contingencies involved.) It has not been possible for me to dispel this attitude, despite evidence from students that they worked harder in my course; despite evidence that they passed a tougher final examination than given by me in previous years; despite such data as Corey and McMichael's 19 week retention test showing superior performance by PSI students to those in a standard lecture course. Even the students themselves, who say they work harder than in any other course ever taken at the college, say it is easy. But the word "easy" obviously has two meanings: the students mean a lack of aversive controls and pressures; other faculty members imply a lowering of standards. It has been difficult for me, and I have not been successful, in convincing my colleagues that *good* learning can take place in the absence of pain—not to mention *better* learning. I had difficulty with myself the first year: despite the fact that reading assignments were longer than in previous years, grading was stiffer, no one passed a unit without perfection, and so on—my first tendency as students completed the course long before the end of the semester, was to think how I should make it tougher to earn A's. I think I have resolved this for myself now; I urge you to think carefully about this before you proceed. The contingencies you supply in a personalized course are far more powerful than those supplied in a standard course. If you guarantee an A to anyone who meets your stated objectives, a vast proportion of your students will work to meet those objectives. And if you stiffen those requirements, they may continue to work even harder, perhaps at some expense to their health or to other courses.

As students finish your course, perhaps well before the end of a semester, you may be tempted to provide further work for them; or they may come to you for further readings. They will be better prepared for advanced courses, perhaps even eliminating the need to start such courses by reviewing basic materials. They will have been satisfied with the freedoms of your personalized course and may ask for some of these in advanced courses. Enrollments in your personalized course will increase in subsequent years. At Lafayette we will enroll about 270 this coming semester, having turned away a large number for lack of laboratory facilities. Higher enrollments in the basic course means higher enrollments in advanced courses, perhaps an increase in the number of majors in the department. While there is certainly confounding of causal agents, I am sure that our personalized course has been partly responsible for tripling the number of psychology majors in the last two years. This creates further problems of staffing, course sizes, availability of facilities, as well as lower enrollments in courses from other departments.

I interpret most of the inquiries by other faculty members as showing a genuine interest in a new teaching technique. This has not been without skepticism, especially about the transferability of the system to other disciplines. I have found that I spend a great deal of time talking about the personalized course, both socially and more formally. It is a real challenge to try to explain contingency management to an Elizabethan scholar, a language professor trained in the European tradition, or a history professor who has read *Walden Two* and knows Frazier's opinions on history. The challenge also entails finding the time to share with one's colleagues, both at home and in other institutions. This leads me to the last section of my paper.

IV. Problems of education perhaps solvable by behavioral analysis.

I detect in my reading and in my contacts, a climate for change in higher education. It can be seen in the Hampshire and Evergreen State Colleges; it can be seen in the restlessness among students, with sit-ins and the lean towards humanism and existentialism; it can be seen in the rapidity with which personalized instruction has captured the imagination of a large number of teachers and students.

When I first converted my introductory course, in the summer of 1968, it was one of the first 5–6 or so in the world; I think it was the only one with a survey content, as opposed to a course in behavioral analysis. Since that time, several hundred courses have been run as personalized courses, with enrollments from 30 to 1000; not all of these have been psychology—engineering, physics, biology, astronomy, economics, and mathematics have been converted; this year German 1–2 at Lafayette will be personalized; and not all have been introductory courses. I have corresponded with over 800 persons interested in the system, some of them seriously. According to the PSI Newsletter, about half the courses at Temple Buell College in Denver "are being taught on an individual rate basis;" Eastern Mennonite College is planning to convert all its psychology courses to PSI; and subsequent to the publication of the Newsletter, I have learned that a high school in Ontario plans to convert a course and the Dean of a large university is looking for help on an institution-wide project.

With such a widespread and important foothold in higher education must go some responsibilities. I will touch upon two of these, related to each other, and certainly not exhaustive. In the handouts they are referred to as (a) helping students learn for the future, and (b) weaning students from control by grades. These are not new problems, nor is psychology unique in its concern with them. All of us teachers are deeply involved with both of them, implicitly or explicitly, as long as we are teachers. Which is not to say they have been resolved, which they have not, or that they are being professionally ignored, because they are not. However, the idea of applied behavioral analysis suggests a contribution we could make to each problem. If the Keller system provides a means for better learning on the part of students, then those of us who use the system should also be concerned with what the students are learning, which means the goals of education. And, with our knowledge of conditioned reinforcers, we should be able to poke our noses into changing the schedules by which grades are maintained as conditioned reinforcers, perhaps with a view towards extinguishing their reinforcing powers.

It is a truism to observe that the world is currently faced with many complex problems whose solutions and modes of resolution remain to be discovered. It is almost a truism to observe that current educational institutions, from kindergarten through graduate schools, are less than perfect. Most of us are still teaching content to our students, in an era when content becomes obsolete in less than a decade; most of us are still teaching that content (perhaps fortunately so) with techniques adopted prior to the invention of the printing press.

In operational terms, we should be teaching our students today how to learn, how to perceive, how to think, how to be creative. That is not quite correct: since the problems of the future will be different from those we face today, we should be teaching our students how to learn how to learn; how to learn how to perceive; how to learn how to think about and solve those to-be-formulated problems; we should be teaching flexibility and variability and creativity.

This may sound to some of you as a contradiction in terms, but I do not think so. I think creativity can be taught; I think creativity is behavior; thus, I think that behavioral analysis could provide one means for increasing the creativity in the world. This is a responsibility which goes with our new and important foothold in higher education. Why not design some personalized courses to increase the creativity of college students? This could be one contribution towards helping students learn for the future. Now for the second educational problem.

Large numbers of faculty members, students, and administrators have bemoaned grading systems for decades. I will not try to analyze the

evils of grades or to provide a detailed plan for eliminating them. Let me simply state categorically that I think grades are an evil, as they are used today; and let me state that I do not think they are a necessary evil. By grades, I am referring to letter grades or numerical ones, assigned from A's or 100's down to F's or 55's, usually arbitrarily, almost always unreliably, and too often assuming incorrectly some underlying distribution, such as a normal one.

Grades are externally supplied reinforcers which have both positive and negative reinforcing power. Originally, they were extrinsic to the learning situation; through a history of conditioning, they have acquired their reinforcing power. In fact, they have become intrinsic to the learning processes of young people, at least in the formal academic situations. Even further, they have become more important to young people than what is learned. (They have become more important to some teachers than what is being learned.) Such grades, however, lose their reinforcing power very rapidly upon completion of the educational level which is the highest one the person wants to complete. That is, as soon as someone has earned his bachelor's degree and has secured the necessary recommendations for employment, grades no longer control his behavior. If he has been learning for 16 years in order to earn grades, he may stop learning at this point; he may even stop reading.

It seems imperative to me for experts in behavioral analysis to go to work on this problem. If the aversive properties of grades were eliminated and positive reinforcing aspects stressed, we might expect that, through stimulus generalization and abstraction, the effects of grades could be made to carry over after degree completion and continue to control behavior for a longer time. More useful would be a program, to operate within the educational framework, for the acquisition of a conditioned emotional response—a positive one, which would be elicited by grades. Such a conditioning procedure could be taken further by means of intermittent scheduling, so that fewer and less frequent grades would be needed to maintain the conditioned emotional response; perhaps one could eventually eliminate the middle-man: the learning process itself could elicit directly the positive conditioned emotional response and students would be weaned from grades. Such a positive conditioned and emotional response, elicited directly by the learning process, could only be referred to as a love for learning.

I suggest here that personalized courses are in a very powerful position to try such an experiment. Most courses supply reinforcements very infrequently—such as occasioned by a mid-term or final examination; and very inefficiently—since most examinations are either not returned at all or are returned after weeks of delay in reinforcement (or punishment). Classroom situations provide the opportunity for some reinforcement, but this is poor when the ratio is 25 or 30 students to one reinforcing teacher. Mathematics and language courses provide more opportunities with their daily quizzes and homework assignments, but aversive control is more apt to be involved. Personalized courses provide frequent and immediate instances of positive reinforcement. Could we not train our proctors to serve in such a way that, as they graded tests and talked with students, they also provided the occasion for building up a conditioned emotional response which might someday turn into a love for learning?

It is sad to have to talk about this as a remedial process necessitated by the current system. I think children find learning intrinsically reinforcing, until their parents and teachers begin to make externally supplied reinforcers an intrinsic part of the learning process. But we cannot solve all the problems of education; we cannot even hope to wean students from grades in any mass action in the near future. But neither can we ignore our responsibility to try.

Summary.   I have talked with you about problems in implementing a course in personalized instruction. Some problems are unique with the system itself, but some problems are generated whenever innovation is involved. Problems may come before, during, as well as after the operation of the course in personalized instruction. You can find in my bibliography sources for much help in anticipating and meeting many of these problems. I have also suggested, however, that educational problems still exist which behavioral analysis might tackle. Perhaps some personalized course in the near future will be designed to provide data on the two problems I have discussed; it is only within such personalized courses that reinforcement contingencies can be experimented with, thus placing the responsibility clearly upon our shoulders. I know I am grateful to Fred Keller for awakening in me a feeling of responsibility to provide better learning situations for my students than those I had been supplying, even though that feeling of responsibility led to a personalized course with all the problems thereupon contingent. Best wishes to you, you who choose to join the ranks of people involved in the problems of personalized instruction.

OUTLINE AND BIBLIOGRAPHY DEALING WITH PROBLEMS

I.   *PROBLEMS ARISING PRIOR TO THE ACTUAL CONDUCT OF THE COURSE*

A.   Obtaining permission: this may be from department heads, deans, faculty committees, colleagues. The permission may be simply to try something new, to cancel the usual meeting of classes, to hire proctors, to "run an experiment in education." Such permission may hinge on the understanding of the power structures: lack of knowledge of psychological processes in general, and operant analysis in particular, may make it even more difficult. You may have to teach behavioral principles to faculty and administration.

B.   Financial: large lectures are the cheapest form of education; personalized instruction will cost more, in the form of assistants, lower student-faculty ratio, paid proctors, even paper duplication and record keeping.

C.   Organization of the course proper: most of us do not take the care and pains necessary for a personalized course, such as stating behavioral objectives, writing a description of the course for students, preparing large numbers of unit tests, reading lists and schedules of events —and all prior to the opening class session. If you run your course as I do, the first class may be the last time you see all the students in the same place at the same time.

D.   Selection and training of student proctors: certainly one of the most crucial aspects of your course. No one to my knowledge has been able to specify the characteristics of a good proctor, especially in terms of identifying one prior to actual operation. Once selected, proctors must be trained, provided with course materials, given practice; as well as scheduled for testing hours, with substitutes.

E.   Evaluative research: aside from the desirable aspects of such research for science and the teaching profession, there may be survival value in the research. No one operating within the system is challenged to justify his teaching, his testing, his grading, or whatnot, the way an innovator is challenged. Some kinds of research (such as with the use of control groups) had best be done the first time, since getting control subjects may be difficult after your success has become known.

II. PROBLEMS ARISING AS THE COURSE BECOMES OPERATIVE

A. *Logistics:* this will vary with the size of course. With 200-300 students, as we have had, scheduling of testing hours, use of rooms, administration of tests, waiting for tests or for proctoring all create logistic problems. Tests must be maintained, perhaps replaced; answer sheets must be available; scoring pens or pencils; etc.

B. *Oversight of personnel:* a fleet of 25-30 proctors must be organized and scheduled; absences must be covered; poor proctors improved or replaced; disputes moderated. Any other assistants may require some supervision.

C. *Test revisions:* item analyses should be performed, including both right-wrong analyses and comments from students and proctors about test items. Students and proctors both will know the material more thoroughly than you will expect, and poor items will be discovered more efficiently.

D. *Record keeping:* in Psychology 1 at Lafayette, we had 20 units, with 4 alternate forms of tests for each unit; with 250 students, taking from 1 to 4 tests to pass a unit, record keeping becomes a full-time job for someone. We keep complete records on who takes which form of which test at what time on what day, who graded it, etc. We have computerized this job.

E. *Record keeping:* for the course, as opposed to individual students. It is necessary to know at any time how many students are working on which units so as to be able to plan on more or fewer proctors, jam-ups, etc. We have computerized this job.

F. *Other events:* films, demonstrations, lectures, discussions must be scheduled and prepared. This should be done in conjunction with the pace of readiness testing.

G. *Changes in plans:* students are probably taking 3-4 other courses plus yours; with an absence of aversive control and with essential freedom to proceed at their own pace, students may procrastinate during given portions of a semester (mid-term exam days in other courses); catching up later may strain facilities and personnel; limits may have to be imposed.

H. *Decisions must be made on grades:* should a student who has completed only Unit 13 be allowed to pass the course with a grade of D, given a full exam, given an Incomplete?

III. PROBLEMS ARISING AS THE COURSE BECOMES KNOWN

A. *On campus:* rumors spread, often with misinformation, usually with positive tone about your course, and invidious comparisons with other courses, if rumors are spread by students. Faculty rumors reverse the tone. People wonder what you are doing if you are not "teaching;" they wonder what the students are doing if you are not teaching them.

B. *Grades:* the meaning of grades is different from most other courses. Since the students know they can contract for an A by completing all units, most of them (85%-95%) work for and earn A's. The resulting negatively skewed curve threatens other instructors and will begin to concern your colleagues and your administration. It also tends to lead to further selective perception by other faculty and students. The course becomes known as "easy," despite the almost 100% admission by students that they work harder in your course than in any other college course.

C. *Upper-level courses:* preparation by students in the introductory course may be superior to previous occasions, necessitating revision of these courses.

D. *Students:* not only better prepared, but charmed with the trust and freedom in the PSI course, they demand such treatment in upper courses.

E. *Enrollments:* the success of the course may lead to higher enrollments in the following year, in the course itself, as well as in other courses, and the major. This leads to problems of departmental expansion, cutting-off enrollments, or heavier work-loads.

F. *Explanations:* administration and faculty committees may request explanation, defense, and justification of the innovation. This may require written documentation and/or verbal contact, both of which take time. Once again, you may have the problem of explaining behavioral analysis and contingency management to non-sophisticated audiences.

G.   *Advice:*   some other faculty, from outside departments, may become interested in trying PSI. This will take time to explain even more carefully the principles involved, help adapt the system to other content material, etc.

H.   *Off campus:*   with publications, presented papers, and now a Newsletter, requests for copies of papers and for help may come parts unknown. Most of this is typical "reprint" requests; but a sufficiently large number is for real help. Giving advice at a distance is even more difficult than at home; for example,

recent request to help write grant proposals to convert large portions of an entire campus to PSI.

IV.   *PROBLEMS IN EDUCATION PERHAPS SOLVABLE BY BEHAVIORAL ANALYSIS*

A.   *Helping students learn for the future:* learning how to learn how to learn, to perceive, to think, to be creative.

B.   *Weaning students from control by grades:* conditioning a love of learning.

BIBLIOGRAPHY

Born, D. G., *Instructor Manual for Development of a Personalized Instruction Course,* Center to Improve Learning and Instruction, Univ. of Utah, Nov., 1970; Rev. April, 1971.

Born, D. G., *Proctor Manual,* Center to Improve Learning and Instruction, Univ. of Utah, Nov., 1970; Rev. April, 1971.

Evans, Richard I., *Resistance to Innovation in Higher Education.* Jossey-Bass: 1968.

Ferster, C. B., "Individualized instruction in a large introductory psychology course." *Psychol. Rec.,* 1968, *18,* 521–532. [Article 34]

Gallup, H. F., "The introductory psychology course at Lafayette College, Easton, Pennsylvania: a description and tentative evaluation." Paper presented at MPA, 1969.

Gallup, H. F., "Individualized Instruction in Introductory Psychology"; Chapter VI, in Sheppard, W. C. (Ed.), *Proceedings of the Conference on Instructional Innovations in Undergraduate Education,* Univ. of Oregon, Eugene, 1969.

Gallup, H. F., Report on Psychology 1, 2 to the Curriculum Committee, Lafayette College, Feb., 1970.

Gallup, H. F., Individualized Instruction in an Introductory Psychology Course; paper presented at EPA, April, 1970.

Henderson, Algo D., *The Innovative Spirit.* Jossey-Bass: 1970.

Johnston, J. M. and Pennypacker, H. S., "A Behavioral Approach to College Teaching," *American Psychologist,* 1971, *26,* 219–244.

Keller, Fred S., "Good-bye teacher . . ." *J. of App. Beh. Anal.,* 1968, *1,* 79–89. [Article 1]

Keller, Fred S., A programmed system of instruction, *Educational Technology Monographs,* 1969, *2,* 1–26.

Malott, R. W., and Svinicki, J. G., "Contingency management in an introductory psychology course for one thousand students," *Psychol. Rec.,* 1969, *19,* 545–556.

McMichael, J. S. and Corey, J. R., "Contingency management in an introductory psychology course produces better learning," *J. of App. Beh. Analysis,* 1969, *2,* 79–83. [Article 2]

PSI Newsletter; Issue No. 1; June, 1971 (J. G. Sherman, Georgetown Univ.)

Witters, D. R. and Kent, G. W., "An experimental evaluation of programming student study behavior in undergraduate courses." Bridgewater College, 1970.

26

KELLER PLAN INSTRUCTION: IMPLEMENTATION PROBLEMS [1]

John H. Hess, Jr.

Since Fred S. Keller first introduced the systematic application of operant principles to the teaching of college courses in 1964, several careful comparative studies have demonstrated that the Keller Plan produces greater mastery of academic material (Keller, 1968 [Article 1]; McMichael and Corey, 1969 [Article 2]; Sheppard and MacDermot, 1970 [Article 9]; and Born, Gledhill, and Davis, 1971 [Aarticle 10]), better retention (Corey, McMichael, and Tremont, 1970 [Article 3]), and more favorable student attitudes toward a course (Gallup, 1969; and Koen, 1970 [Article 13]) than does traditional instruction.

Manuals have been prepared to explicate both a rationale and an implementing methodology for instructors and proctors using the Keller Plan (Born, 1970a and 1970b; and McMichael and Corey, 1970). Individual Learning Systems of San Rafael, California is currently marketing thirteen commercially prepared college-level courses in the Keller format. At least 300 courses in the United States and abroad are being offered *a la* Keller (Green, 1971). During August of 1971, the initial issue of the Personalized System of Instruction Newsletter edited by Gil Sherman appeared and in October, this state-of-the-art conference was convened at M.I.T.

Because of the increased visibility of personalized instruction, this report does not contain an extensive description of Keller Plan mechanics or a comparison of Keller and traditional modes of instruction. All of this activity has turned the data reported in the first six pages of this paper into a kind of "so what phenomenon." That is, for many of us this embarrassingly good mastery and attitudinal data can be summarized by saying, "we tried it and it worked for us, too!" I call the data embarrassingly good because for those of us who thought we were educators or psychologists, it is startling to discover that the same principles we

have been preaching at students in courses about learning, work so well when actually used in those same classes. Data reported herein are used primarily as a foil to permit discussion of the difficulties encountered when the Keller Plan was introduced in a General Psychology course at Eastern Mennonite College during the winter term of 1970-71.

Data presented in Table 1 were obtained from each student's cumulative record which was maintained by the proctor to whom he was assigned. Pretest scores are the number of items correctly answered from a test of 100 items (covering the entire course) given to each student during the first class period. Post-test scores were calculated similarly for 100 items (in a comparable form) given as a final test. Gain scores are calculated by obtaining the ratio of actual gains made through the course by each student, to the maximum gain possible for him:

$$\frac{\text{Post—Pretest}}{\text{Total—Pretest}}$$

The mean gain for students in our course was .84.

Not all of our students mastered all units before taking the final test. Some stopped taking unit tests and simply read the narrative sections of the ILS materials before taking the final. A significant correlation was obtained between the number of units mastered (before the final) and gain scores (rho = .52, z = 3.28, p < .002). The correlation of mean errors per unit test with gain scores was not significant (rho = -.26, z = 1.64, p > .05). It is to be expected that an effective individualized program of study would yield terminal scores not highly related to the number of errors committed during the course, provided that each unit was *mastered* before the student progressed to the next unit.

Final test grades (consequently, final grades) for Psych 202 are presented in Figure 1. The incompletes were later (within six weeks of the end of the term) changed to the earned letter grade and are contained in the A–F categories reported on

[1] Presented at Keller Plan Conference, October 16-17, 1971, Massachusetts Institute of Technology, Cambridge.

TABLE 1. DATA COLLECTED FROM EACH STUDENT'S CUMULATIVE RECORD.

Student	Pretest score	Total units mastered	Mean errors per unit	Post-test score	Gain
1	17	13	1.07	89	.86
2	14	12	1.08	88	.86
3	20	3	1.67	83	.78
4	18	11	1.25	95	.93
5	16	8	2.59	88	.85
6	28	5	1.00	90	.86
7	23	13	.85	92	.90
8	13	6	2.13	68	.63
9	19	10	.70	89	.86
10	15	13	1.31	90	.88
11	9	13	.92	91	.90
12	10	13	.76	89	.88
13	29	2	2.50	—	Drop–F
14	20	13	1.42	95	.94
15	14	1	2.00	—	Drop–F
16	16	11	.50	94	.92
17	19	4	8.00	65	.57
18	10	13	1.71	88	.86
19	12	9	.88	88	.86
20	20	13	.84	92	.90
21	26	13	.78	94	.91
22	19	13	2.11	98	.97
23	10	7	1.50	80	.77
24	12	13	.92	91	.89
25	21	11	1.46	86	.82
26	12	10	1.58	87	.85
27	15	13	.92	86	.83
28	11	12	2.30	94	.93
29	18	6	1.83	80	.75
30	23	12	1.25	90	.87
31	15	12	1.69	93	.91
32	7	11	1.09	94	.93
33	22	1	1.00	80	.74
34	23	13	1.61	96	.95
35	22	13	.61	85	.80
36	23	13	.69	91	.88
37	12	13	1.30	84	.82
38	16	12	1.25	89	.86
39	18	6	2.21	—	Drop–F
40	22	7	2.28	81	.75
41	20	8	.25	94	.90
42	14	10	1.30	81	.77
43	25	13	.50	97	.96
44	7	13	1.15	86	.84
45	28	1	2.45	—	Drop–F
$\overline{X}$	17.36	9.82	1.49	87.79	.84

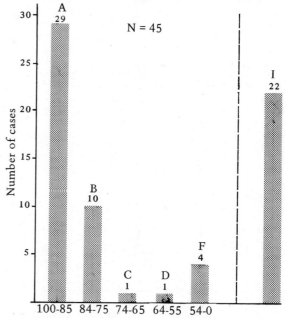

FIGURE 1. Distribution of grades on comprehensive final tests in General Psychology on the Keller Plan.

the left portion of the figure. The criterion of mastery for each unit test was 90%. For the final test we used a less stringent criterion of 85% to indicate mastery of the course. Determination of an appropriate mastery criterion is somewhat arbitrary. We used a rather liberal criterion since the validation edition of the ILS General Psychology package was saturated with errors. As individual instruction materials are successively refined, it is possible to use a 100% mastery criterion on unit tests without unduly penalizing students (Born, 1971).

A comparison of grade distributions for the 1970–71 General Psychology course (Keller Plan) and the 1969–70 General Psychology course (Traditional-Lecture) is presented in Figure 2. Using the same percentage categories, 86% of the students in the Keller version of the course scored above 80% on the final, whereas 83% of the students in the traditional course scored below 70% on the final. While these data are not derived from a controlled comparison of Keller and traditional modes of instruction, it is the writer's judgment that the two courses were sufficiently similar in content and the populations sufficiently comparable in composition to make a difference of this magnitude attributable to use of the Keller Plan.

Three major problems which arose during the course necessitate extended discussion: excessive

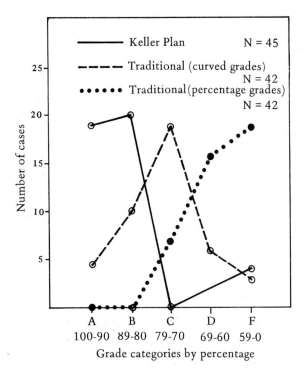

FIGURE 2. Comparison of grade distributions from a Keller Plan and Traditional General Psychology course.

incompletes, poor attendance at enrichment sessions, and determination of a final grade.

I.   EXCESSIVE INCOMPLETES AND PROCRASTINATION

Ideally a personalized instruction course should be open-entry and open-exit, i.e., a student should be able to start and finish any particular course when he wishes. To make this possible, enough personalized courses must be available within a college, or at least within a department, to enable a student to pick a new course at any time he finishes a previously selected course. Temple Buell College in Denver, Colorado, has a program in which 50% of the course offerings are available in a modified Keller format (Greenspoon, 1971). A student carries the usual number of courses but the Keller courses are not tied to semester time periods. Credit is entered when the course is mastered and if the course is not mastered, nothing is entered on the student's record. If the student lags in his studies or fails to complete the course, he is penalized only in terms of the time and money he has invested.

It is unlikely that most colleges or departments will have the luxury of beginning a personalized instruction program with a sufficient number of offerings to permit an open-entry/open-exit option, since preparation of the materials initially is very time-consuming. (This will change as more materials are commercially prepared and distributed.) For the present, many Keller courses will be offered in programs having most courses available only on the traditional semester or quarter basis.

If you permit students an unlimited amount of time for the Keller course while other courses are tied to the semester system, it is not uncommon for as many as 30–40% of the enrolled students to carry the Keller course into the next term if incompletes are permitted (Born, 1971; Keller, 1971). Students put their effort where the pressure is greatest, i.e., into non-Keller courses. If another Keller course is not available when the first is completed, the student ends up carrying an overload or a light load in the new term. Registrars are unhappy with this situation as they need to make changes in their computer processed information base when the incompletes are eventually removed, deans are unhappy with load deviations, and accountants are worried about irregular billing. When Keller courses are initially being introduced, the problem of incompletes is compounded by the fact that many students are inexperienced in handling the freedom inherent in personalized instruction.

Most of the incompletes do not arise because of students' inability to master course units, but due to late entry into the course materials. As in traditional courses, students underestimate the amount of work remaining and overestimate the amount of time remaining. Consequently, if no deadline for completion of the course is set, many incompletes occur.

To simply set a deadline for course completion generates another problem. Low GPA students, who benefit most from Keller courses (Born, 1971; Witters and Kent, 1970), selectively withdraw from those courses even though they are mastering the units satisfactorily, but at a rate too slow to finish the course work in the fixed amount of time available in a term (Born, 1971).

One possible interpretation of these results is that low GPA students if given a choice between a non-mastery course section graded on the curve and one requiring mastery, will choose the section yielding a lower grade for less work within a fixed period of time.

To solve this problem, the course needs to be severed from the term structure as in the Temple

Buell program, or course content must be limited to an amount that most students will be able to master within a term. This amount will be determined in part by the amount of time theoretically available for work in a particular course (about 130 hours total at two hours out of class for every term hour spent in class). We need reliable study time data showing the range of individual study times required for all class members to complete the mastery requirements of a particular course. A decision could then be made as to the quantity of course material which constitutes a reasonable amount for a particular course. It would be acceptable for a predetermined percentage of students to exceed the theoretical amount of time to be devoted to that course. Slow students are, of course, identified early in personalized instruction and receive intensive aid from proctors and the instructor. For the bright student who finishes the course early, several options exist. The student may:

1. *goof-off:* In Keller courses this tends to be concentrated into the part of the term after course completion rather than throughout the course as is the case when a bright student is unable to accelerate his progress in a traditional lock-step format.
2. distribute the time gained among other non-Keller courses.
3. pursue independent study related to the course just completed.

If a Keller course is offered within a fixed time period and incompletes are not permitted other than for the traditional reasons (death in family, student illness, etc.) the problem of procrastination within that time period remains. Some instructors have handled this problem by instituting deadlines for the mastery of each unit so that students may progress at their own rate *only if they exceed a predetermined minimum rate of progress.* In addition to this guideline, some instructors use a "doomsday contingency" which causes a student to be dropped from the course if he falls behind the expected rate of progress by a specified amount. Not only are these strategies coercive, but they also violate the letter and spirit of the concept of mastery learning.

We believe that the following strategies are effective in curbing the problem of procrastination.

1. Use of a cumulative record by both the student and his proctor to plot the student's progress through the course. As the student masters each unit, his proctor plots his progress on the chart in his presence, in this way making visible to the student the relationship between remaining work and remaining time.
2. Use of an early one-shot time contingency in the course. We asked that students complete one-fourth of the course units by the end of four weeks, which is approximately one-third of our term. Students were informed that if they did not meet this guideline, they would be asked to counsel with the instructor about remaining in the course. Our objective was not to coerce student performance, but to discuss with the student the consequences of his low rate of progress, i.e., loss of time, effort, money and credit. We wanted only to encourage students to enter the materials early in the course. Once a student has entered the materials he usually works at a steady rate until all the materials have been mastered (Lloyd and Knutzen, 1969).
3. Proctors were instructed to contact persons falling more than one week behind the rate of progress needed to complete the course. The proctor simply told his student that he had noticed the student's declining rate of progress, asked the student's plans for increasing his rate of progress, and offered assistance to the student.
4. The final examination was scheduled at three discrete times: four weeks, two weeks, and two days before the end of the term.

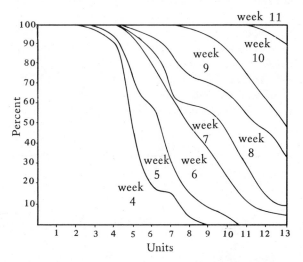

FIGURE 3. Cumulative unit master—First term 1971-72 Keller Plan General Psychology course.

That these strategies produced early entrance into course materials, reduced procrastination, and eliminated the problem of excessive incompletes is indicated by data in Figure 3. Ninety-one percent of the students met the four week guideline, forty-eight percent were finished with the course two weeks before the end of the term, and no one failed to complete the course within the term. These data were particularly interesting to us since the 1971–72 course had more students, more hetergeneous students, and required approximately 40 more hours of work than did the 1970–71 course.

One of our educational objectives is to teach students to manage their own academic behavior. For that reason we find these tactics more attractive than a series of coercive deadlines.

II. POOR ATTENDANCE AT ENRICHMENT SESSIONS

One of the prominent features of the Keller Plan is that critical information should be presented primarily in narrative form with study guide questions and progress checks rather than in a one-shot form such as lecture presentation. There are, however, educational activities which do not provide critical information but do enrich by illustrating critical information through application as in demonstrations, experiments, discussions, field trips, films, or problem solving exercises. It is also desirable to embed critical information in a variety of contexts (especially social contexts) to increase the student's ability to generalize applications beyond the classroom.

The problem arises through a paradox: students demand enrichment activities of this kind but then such sessions are free (unevaluated), they do not attend even though they evaluate the enrichment activities as excellent (based on the few times they do come). It is not uncommon to find 50% attendance at enrichment sessions early in the term decreasing to 5–10% at enrichment sessions at the end of the term (Born, 1971; Keller, 1971). This may simply be another indication that the reinforcers inherent in the educational process are weaker than those available to a student via his girl, the student union, and the gym!

Possible solutions to this problem include:

1. Dispense with the enrichment activities entirely—which reduces the educational process to the absorption of information.
2. Require attendance—which produces a lot of warm bodies, which may be engaged in many things other than attending to the enrichment activity.
3. Let enrichment activities be free despite low attendance—in which case a great deal of effort is expended for the benefit of very few people.
4. Arrange a contingency producing *attendance and attention.*

We specified a pool of points for various enrichment activities as indicated in Table 2. In addition to mastering the course materials, a student needed to obtain a fixed number of points from out of the pool in order to receive an A, B, or C. To receive a C in the course, the student had to obtain 10 enrichment points, to receive a B—20 enrichment points, to receive an A—30 enrichment points. Any student was free to participate in any activity even though he did not wish to receive points for it. To obtain points which count toward the required number for a given grade, a student must pass a low criterion quiz covering each film and lecture. The criterion for obtaining points was deliberately set low in keeping with the rationale that these activities were enrichment rather than critical information. For the reprints, students were asked to prepare a critique and for experiments they were asked to complete a standard laboratory report form. By setting the minimum and maximum points to be obtained for each enrichment activity we ensured student participation in each kind of activity but gave him the freedom to accumulate most of his points in the categories of his choice.

TABLE 2. ENRICHMENT ACTIVITIES

Point worth	Activity	Number available	Minimun points	Maximum points
2	Experiment	18	2	12
1	Reprint	20	2	10
1	Test item	—	2	10
1	Discussion	10	2	10
1	Film	10	2	10

TABLE 3.   CLASS ATTENDANCE

	#1	#2	#3	#4	#5	#6	#7	#8	#9
Lectures	95%	70%	70%	56%	38%	53%	67%	42%	34%
Films	94%	81%	72%	73%	75%	31%	22%	36%	72%
Demonstrations	41%	33%	24%	16%					

Films and lecture/discussion were time-dependent, but students could choose the timing of other enrichment activities. Attendance at lecture/discussions, films, and demonstrations is recorded in Table 3. Demonstrations were free and unevaluated, consequently attendance was curtailed rapidly and we discontinued them. That students learn a great deal in the process of meeting the low criterion on the quiz after lectures and films is indicated by the point distributions in Figure 4. We have recently decided to raise the criterion and change the quiz to an exercise to be completed with the aid of the student's notes since we are more interested in his attention and response to the activity than in creating a hurdle for him.

Dave Born's Cumulative Record of Student Performance, altered to indicate a student's progress in the acquisition of enrichment points in addition to unit mastery programs is shown in Figure 5.

III.   DETERMINATION OF THE COURSE GRADE

Several end-of-course strategies with their associated advantages and disadvantages are as follows:

1. Final grade is determined by the percentage scored on the final test *whether or not all units in the course have been mastered*. This procedure permits a student to receive credit for partial mastery of a course by determination of percentage criteria for the comprehensive final appropriate for an A, B, or C. (A variation of this strategy would permit credit for partial mastery in terms of the ratio of mastered units to total possible units.) Since there is no contingency placed upon mastery of all units before the final is taken, students who are pressed for time only read the last few units rather than take the mastery tests. Consequently they achieve lower gain scores as indicated earlier in this report.

2. Specify that all units must be mastered before the final will be made available and use the same criteria as in item 1. Only one of the seventeen students, who finished all the units in our course received a B, the rest received A's.

3. Allow a student who achieves a 95% criterion on all individual units to skip the final (based on the assumption that he probably would have met a 90% criterion on the final anyway). This is a viable op-

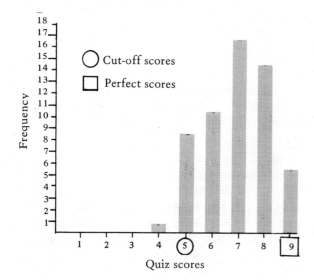

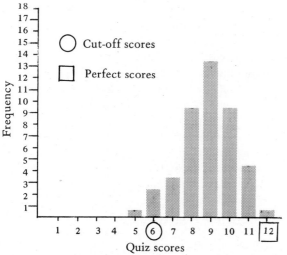

FIGURE 4.   Enrichment point quiz scores (films).

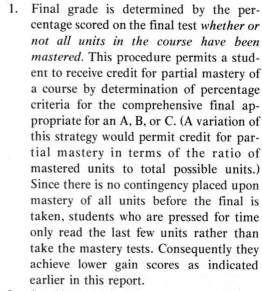

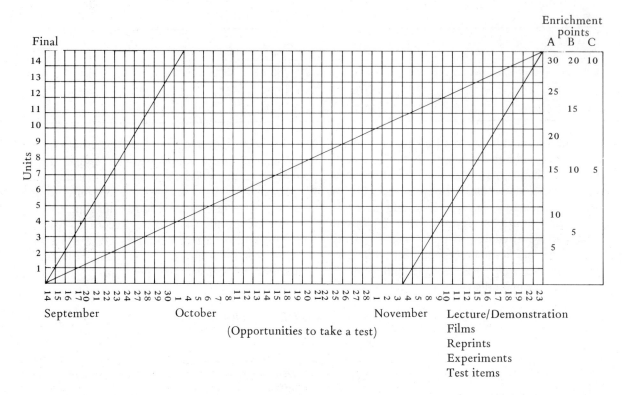

FIGURE 5.   Cumulative record of mastery (cumulative student performance).

tion only if occasional review units are built into the course materials and if security on the unit tests is adequate.

4. Dispense with the final test entirely and specify only that all units be mastered at some high percentage criterion. While this strategy may be intuitively appealing to both instructor and students, several difficulties arise:

a. The final is necessary to produce comparative data on the overall effectiveness of a particular course relative to other versions of the course. (It is possible to argue that this evaluative function could be adequately performed at the level of individual units.)

b. Final test data are useful in holding off the Calvinists, i.e., those colleagues who insist that anything learned so easily and completely must be of lesser quantity or quality.

Final tests in Keller courses differ from those in non-mastery courses in that they are truly comprehensive and are composed of items related to concepts which have all been previously mastered by the student. In this case the final test simply verifies a student's performance in the course. Despite this rationale, some students react unfavorably to a grade based entirely or primarily upon performance on a comprehensive final test. It may be desirable to give a test after half of the course units have been completed and to average these scores with those obtained on the comprehensive final. A mid-course test tied to a review unit would aid the student's integration of the first half of the course and would indicate concepts requiring further remedial study.

The writer's preference would be to simply record "Credit" on the student's permanent record when he masters a course at 85% or better on the final. Specific comments could be added in recognition of "honors" quality work. This preference is based on the assumption that mastery is now the standard rather than the exception.

The remainder of this report consists of an extensive student evaluation of the course. Responses to several of the items require the interpretive comments which follow.

A. *Item 6:* Although students say they worked harder in this course than in others, the actual amount of time they report spending on this course is only half the theoretical amount they should be spending. (Perhaps, students are studying even less than we think they are.)

B. *Item 7:* The pressure mentioned here was not identified as aversive by anyone. It seems probable that consistently paced study may be seen as producing more pressure than the larger but less frequent sieges of anxiety occasioned by midterm and final tests in the traditional format. A small amount of anxiety might be conducive to learning, while sieges of anxiety and activity accompanying them are not.

C. *Item 14:* This one is tricky! In the writer's judgment, the test items used in this course were superior to those used in most of his other courses, i.e., they called for less memorization and more application and analysis. What students may be reporting in this item is that they are aware of knowing more than they usually do in an unpaced course!

D. *Item 17:* Many spontaneous comments were made during the course to the effect that study habits learned in this course

were helping the student in his other courses as well.

E. *Items 28, 29, 30:* The responses to these items would be encouraging to any instructor whether he was a raving humanist or a strict behaviorist. For item 30, only 43% of the students in the 1969–70 General Psychology course rated that course as "Excellent" (although ratings of instructor were the same).

F. *Items 31–38:* The extremely favorable reaction to the proctors is very interesting since many persons express doubt that undergraduates should teach undergraduates. It is helpful to remember that proctors are not sources of critical information, rather, they are monitors of fellow student's progress through the same material they have previously mastered. There is some evidence that the more advanced the proctor, the less effective he is. He gives too much extra information to the student at the expense of his work on the student's mastery of the course materials (Born, 1971; Keller, 1971).

STUDENT EVALUATION OF 1970–71 PERSONALIZED GENERAL PSYCHOLOGY COURSE

1. Are the objectives of the course clear?

    71% A   19% B   10% C   0% D   0% E
       clear   *unclear*

2. Are the tests fair?

    81% A   16% B   3% C   0% D   0% E
       fair   *unfair*

3. Are the grades assigned fairly?

    94% A   6% B   0% C   0% D   0% E
       fair   *unfair*

4. How would you rate the contribution of the textbook to the course?

    71% A   26% B   0% C   3% D   0% E
       excellent   *poor*

5. Papers, examinations and quizzes have been returned in a reasonable amount of time.

    93% A   3% B   3% C   0% D   0% E
       reasonable   *very late*

6. In comparison with group instruction courses, I think that the amount of work required by this course is:

    6% A. much greater   10% D. less
    39% B. greater   0% E. much less
    45% C. about the same

7. In comparison with group instruction courses, the degree of pressure on me to do the work of this course was:

    10% A. much greater   *39% D. less*
    29% B. greater   10% E. much less
    13% C. about the same

8. In comparison with group instruction courses, the percentage of my mastery of the assignments in this course was:
    42%   A.   much greater   0%   D.   less
    42% B.   greater   0%   E.   much less
    16%   C.   about the same

9. In comparison with group instruction courses, the feeling of achievement generated by passing tests in this one was:
    32%   A.   much greater   4%   D.   less
    32% B.   greater   0%   E.   much less
    32%   C.   about the same

10. In comparison with group instruction courses generally, my enjoyment of this one was:
    42% A.   much greater   7%   D.   less
    35%   B.   greater   0%   E.   much less
    16%   C.   about the same

11. In comparison with group instruction courses generally, the likelihood of cheating was:
    0%   A.   much greater   *42% D.*   less
    3%   B.   greater   19%   E.   much less
    36%   C.   about the same

12. In comparison with group instruction courses generally, the temptation to cheat was:
    0%   A.   much greater   *42% D.*   less
    3%   B.   greater   23%   E.   much less
    32%   C.   about the same

13. In comparison with other courses generally, my understanding of basic concepts and principles in this course was:
    29%   A.   much greater   0%   D.   less
    58% B.   greater   0%   E.   much less
    13%   C.   about the same

14. In comparison with group instruction courses generally, my tendency to memorize details in this course was:
    26%   A.   much greater   6%   D.   less
    45% B.   greater   4%   E.   much less
    19%   C.   about the same

15. In comparison with group instruction courses generally, the influence of the instructor on me in this course was:
    3%   A.   much greater   *60% D.*   less
    17%   B.   greater   13%   E.   much less
    7%   C.   about the same

16 In comparison with group instruction courses generally, the recognition of me as an individual in this course was:
    42%   A.   much greater   3%   D.   less
    42% B.   greater   0%   E.   much less
    13%   C.   about the same

17. As the term went on, I found that my study habits in this course were:
    26%   A.   greatly improved   3%   D.   harmed
    55% B.   improved   0%   E.   greatly harmed
    16%   C.   unaffected

18. As the term went on, confidence in my ability to master the modules:
    23%   A.   increased greatly   0%   D.   decreased
    68% B.   increased   0%   E.   decreased greatly
    10%   C.   was unchanged

19. The size of the modules in this course was:
   0% A. much too great   6% D. too small
   6% B. too great   0% E. much too small
   87% *C.* about right

20. As the term went on, my worry about my final standing in the course:
   3% A. increased greatly   *45%* *D.* decreased
   13% B. increased   13% E. decreased greatly
   26% C. remained about the same

21. As the term went on, my desire to hear lectures:
   0% A. became much greater   19% D. became less
   19% B. became greater   3% E. became much less
   58% *C.* remained about the same

22. Of your total study time per week, approximately what percentage of this time do you devote to studying material in this course?
   3% A. 0-15%   30% D. 45-60%
   17% B. 15-30%   13% E. more than 60% of the total study time
   36% *C.* 30-45%

23. Approximately what percentage of class periods did you attend in this course?
   45% *A.* 0-15%   10% D. 45-60%
   16% B. 15-30%   16% E. more than 60% of the total class periods
   13% C. 30-45%

24. Where do you study?
   71% *A.* my own room   16% D. library
   6% B. dorm lounges   7% E. other
   0% C. Wyse Owl

25. Under what conditions do you study?
   77% *A.* in silence
   17% B. usually with a record player, or radio
   7% C. other

26. Do you frequently study the course material with someone else?
   94% *A.* no   0% D. yes, with 3 other persons
   6% B. yes, with 1 other person   0% E. yes, with 4 other persons
   0% C. yes, with 2 other persons

27. What was the most interesting aspect of this class?
   76% *A.* text materials   0% D. small group discussions
   7% B. films and demonstrations   17% E. interaction with proctors
   0% C. lectures

28. Would you recommend the subject matter of the course to any of your good friends?
   0% A. definitely not   *84%* *D.* yes
   3% B. maybe   0% E. no opinion
   13% C. probably

29. Would you recommend this type of instruction if some features of the course were altered?
   0% A. definitely not   *71%* *D.* yes
   0% B. maybe   6% E. no opinion
   23% C. probably

30. Considering all of the above qualities which are applicable, how would you rate this course?
   71% *A*   23% B   6% C   0% D   0% E
      excellent   *very bad*

STUDENT EVALUATION OF PROCTOR

31. My proctor was:
     A. Pat Armstrong   C. Dave Glanzer
     B. Roger Rhineheimer   D. Cherly Lyon

32. Was your proctor helpful when you had difficulty?
     55% *A*   45% B   0% C   0% D   0% E
     actively helpful   *not helpful*

33. Did he appear sensitive to your feelings and problems?
     55% *A*   35% B   6% C   3% D   0% E
     responsive   *unaware*

34. Was he flexible?
     55% *A*   42% B   3% C   0% D   0% E
     flexible   *rigid*

35. Did he make you feel free to ask questions, disagree, express their ideas, etc.?
     68% *A*   29% B   3% C   0% D   0% E
     encourages student ideas   *intolerant*

36. Was he fair and impartial in his dealings with you?
     77% *A*   23% B   0% C   0% D   0% E
     fair   *favors some*

37. Did he tell you when you had done particularly well?
     65% *A*   23% B   10% C   3% D   0% E
     always   *never*

38. Considering all of the above qualities which are applicable, how would you rate this proctor?
     61% *A*   35% B   3% C   0% D   0% E
     excellent   *very bad*

STUDENT EVALUATION OF TEACHER

39. Was your teacher helpful when you had difficulty?
     43% *A*   40% B   13% C   4% D   0% E
     actively helpful   *not helpful*

40. Did he appear sensitive to your feelings and problems?
     50% *A*   36% B   11% C   4% D   0% E
     responsive   *unaware*

41. Was he flexible?
     48% *A*   34% B   17% C   0% D   0% E
     flexible   *rigid*

42. Did he make you feel free to ask questions, disagree, express your ideas, etc.?
     55% *A*   38% B   3% C   0% D   4% E
     encourages student ideas   *intolerant*

43. Was he fair and impartial in his dealings with you?
     79% *A*   14% B   7% C   0% D   0% E
     fair   *favors some*

44. Is his speech adequate for teaching?
     77% *A*   23% B   0% C   0% D   0% E
     good   *unintelligible*

45. Did he tell you when you had done particularly well?
     18% A   46% *B*   32% C   0% D   4% E
     always   *never*

46. Does he dwell upon the obvious?
     59% *A*   34% B   7% C   0% D   0% E
     introduces interesting ideas   *dwells on obvious*

47. Is he interested in the subject?

83% A   17% B   0% C   0% D   0% E

seems interested   *seems uninterested*

48. Does he use enough examples or illustrations to clarify the material?

50% A   40% B   10% C   0% D   0% E

many   *none*

49. Does he present material in a well-organized fashion?

50% A   40% B   7% C   3% D   0% E

well organized   *disorganized*

50. Does he stimulate thinking?

60% A   33% B   7% C   0% D   0% E

stimulating   *dull*

51. Does he put his material across in an interesting way?

43% A   *50%* B   7% C   0% D   0% E

very interesting   *dull*

52. Are helpful comments and criticisms made on returned papers?

17% A   17% B   *57%* C   4% D   4% E

helpful comments   *scanty*

53. Considering all of the above qualities which are applicable, how would you rate this teacher?

47% A   *47%* B   7% C   0% D   0% E

excellent   *very bad*

54. Please indicate the following on the back of this card:
    1. Main advantages
    2. Main disadvantages
    3. Suggestions for improvements

You may also add any comments not elicited by this questionnaire.

BIBLIOGRAPHY

Born, David G., *Instructor Manual for Development of a Personalized Instruction Course.* Center to Improve Learning and Instruction, University of Utah, Salt Lake City, Utah, 1970a.

Born, David G. *Proctor Manual.* Center to Improve Learning and Instruction. University of Utah, Salt Lake City, Utah, 1970b.

Born, David G., University of Utah. Personal communication, 1971.

Born, D. G., Gledhill, S. M., and Davis, M. L., "Examination performance and number of student withdrawals in lecture-discussion and personalized instruction courses." Submitted to the *Journal of Applied Behavior Analysis,* 1970. [Article 10]

Corey, J. R. and McMichael, J. S. "Using personalized instruction in college courses." Meredith Corporation, 1970.

Corey, J. R., McMichael, J. S., and Tremont, P. J. "Long-term effects of personalized instruction in an introductory psychology course." Paper presented at the 41st annual meeting of the Eastern Psychological Association, Atlantic City, N.J., 1970.

Gallup, H. F. "Personalized instruction in introductory psychology." Paper presented at the annual meeting of the Midwestern Psychological Association, Chicago, Ill., 1969.

Green, B. A., Jr. Massachusettes Institute of Technology, Cambridge, Mass. Personal communication, 1971.

Greenspoon, Joel, "The New College Program of Temple Buell College." *Educational Technology,* 1971. In press.

Keller, F. S., "Goodbye, teacher . . ."*Journal of Applied Behavior Analysis,* 1968, *1,* 79–89. [Article 1]

Keller, Fred S., Western Michigan University, Kalamazoo, Mich. Personal communication, 1971.

Koen, Billy V. "Self-paced instruction for engineering students." *Engineering Education,* March, 1970, 735–6. [Article 13]

Lloyd, K. E., and Knutzen, J. J., "A self-paced programmed undergraduate course in the experimental analysis of behavior. *Journal of Applied Behavior Analysis,* 1969, *2,* 125–133.

McMichael, J. S., and Corey, J. R., "Contingency management in an introductory psychology course produces better learning." *Journal of Applied Behavior Analysis,* 1969, *2,* 79–83. [Article 2]

Sheppard, W. C., and MacDermott, H. G., "Design and evaluation of a programmed course in introductory psychology," *Journal of Applied Behavior Analysis,* 1970, *3,* 5–11. [Article 9]

27

INITIAL ATTITUDE DIFFERENCES AMONG SUCCESSFUL, PROCRASTINATING AND "WITHDRAWN-FROM-COURSE" STUDENTS IN A PERSONALIZED SYSTEM OF STATISTICS INSTRUCTION [1]

Frederick L. Newman, Dennis L. Young, Stanley E. Ball, Clarence C. Smith, and Ronald B. Purtle

A Personalized System of Instruction (PSI) with a mastery learning component was used to teach introductory statistics to non-mathematics majors at two universities. At the beginning of the semester 250 students were given a mathematics attitude questionnaire (standardized on 938 students) to determine if certain seemingly counter-productive attitudes were characteristic of the students who procrastinate (erratically pace themselves) or those who withdrew course registration. The attitude factor scores of these two groups were contrasted with a Success Group. Initial feelings of anonymity in traditionally taught math courses and a diminutive interest in the acts of doing math problems were consistently counter-productive. Initially perceived difficulty or usefulness of the mathematical subject matter did not differentiate the groups.

Techniques of individualized instruction (White, Indelicato, Jerman and MacPhersen, 1972) and mastery of learning (Block, 1971) have apparent promise for mathematics instruction. These techniques offer particular appeal to those instructors responsible for terminal mathematics and statistics courses designed to service the students in other academic departments. Particularly appealing are the goals of identifying mathematical objectives in terms of specific behaviors and invoking a requirement of mastery.

One individualized technique with a mastery learning component was developed by Professors F. S. Keller and J. G. Sherman and is called Personalized System of Instruction or PSI (Keller, 1968 [Article 1]). Two distinguishing features of PSI are the heavy reliance on the immediacy of feedback (reinforcement) and the use of peer-level tutors, called proctors, as the feedback agents. Under PSI the students are directed through a sequence of units with well-defined objectives. The sequential process is guided by unit tests which must be passed at a level of defined mastery (usually a perfect score). Immediately after a student completes a unit test the student's proctor evaluates the test with the student. The purpose of the evaluation is to determine whether the student should move onto the next defined unit or should restudy the present unit in a fashion prescribed by the proctor.

A number of studies have shown that PSI produces favorable results relative to lecture or discussion techniques. Comparative final exams produce a preponderance of A and B grades for PSI students relative to the normal distribution of grades for the traditional techniques (Keller, 1968; Johnston and Pennypacker, 1971; McKean, Newman and Purtle, 1971 [Article 16]; Born, Gledhill and Davis, 1972). There are some apparent problems, however, with PSI. Several authors have reported increases in the number of students to withdraw from PSI courses (Born, 1971; Sheppard and MacDermot, 1970 [Article 9]). Furthermore, many descriptive statements have been made about the noticeable number of "procrastinating" students who seem to allow the self-paced feature of PSI to result in erratically paced efforts (Keller, 1968; Leidecker, 1972). The procrastinating students often do not finish the course's sequence of units or score low on comprehensive final exams retesting concepts supposedly mastered on the unit tests. The present authors viewed these two groups of students as failures of PSI since our records showed that grade point averages in other courses, including traditionally taught mathematics courses, were not reliable predictors of whether students would (a) successfully master the course objectives, (b) procrastinate, or (c) withdraw their registration from the course.

The present study represents one effort to understand the problem of withdrawals and procrastinators. Interactions with our students and the

[1] This paper was read at the Rocky Mountain Psychological Association Meetings, May, 1972, Albuquerque, New Mexico. The project was partially supported by NSF GY-8304 given to NMSU, Department of Mathematical Sciences and a fellowship awarded to the first author by The Center for Advanced Study in the Behavioral Sciences.

literature (Aitken, 1970) had recommended an assessment of possible attitude differences among three groups of students: successes, procrastinators, and withdrawals. The literature has been consistent in suggesting that initial attitudes toward mathematics could have a counterproductive influence on performance in a mathematics course. The basic assumption under test in the present study was whether the attitudes of students, identified as either procrastinators or withdrawals, were reliably distinguishable from the successful students at the outset.

METHOD

THE ATTITUDE SCALES

Two mathematics attitude scales were developed collaterally with the present study (Ball, 1972; Smith, 1972). Students enrolled in mathematics courses for non-science and non-mathematics majors at two universities (715 students at New Mexico State University and 223 students at University of Texas, El Paso) were asked to give Likert 5-point ratings to items regarding their attitudes toward mathematics, classroom pedagogy, and self-perception of mathematical ability. The factors identified for each scale were:

Scale A. Attitudes toward the subject matter of mathematics.

Factor A-I. Mathematics is perceived as a *difficult* academic topic area.

A-II. Mathematics is an *interesting* area (e.g., math problems are fun and/or interesting to work).

A-III. Mathematics is a *useful* area in daily life.

Scale B. Attitudes toward the traditional methods of teaching mathematics.

Factor B-I. Amount of classtime devoted to student questions (in the Lecture-Discussion type class).

B-II. Class atmosphere (degree of perceived tenseness).

B-III. Amount of individual help desired in the Lecture-Discussion type class.

B-IV. Feelings of anonymity in the Lecture-Discussion type class.

The factor analysis used the varimax rotation criterion (Kaiser, 1958) and two different computer programs (one was Veldman's 1967, program) which agreed to the nearest hundredth. Ball's (1972) analysis of the data showed that these factors

were reliable and generalizable between the two university samples. Furthermore, no infringement upon generality was found when partitioning either by sex, levels of grade-point average, classification in college, colleges within university, or by the number of years out of high school.

SUBJECTS AND IDENTIFICATION OF GROUPS

Students from the introductory statistics course at New Mexico State University (N = 200) and the University of Miami (N = 50) were given the two Math Attitude Scales at the beginning of the semester. The data of 21 students were discarded because of problems such as item response omission. At the end of the semester the profiles of the remaining 229 students were partitioned as follows:

Successes (N = 97)   Students who proceeded to do all of the required work at a consistent rate: One-closed and one-open book quiz for each of the twelve units and three comprehensive exams over the successive thirds of the twelve unit sequence. Cumulative records on these students showed a consistent rate of progress. The Successful students were best categorized by being neither Procrastinators nor Withdrawals, as described below.

Procrastinators (N = 49) Students who characteristically increased their rates of activity as deadlines approached. At NMSU, the students were allowed 25 class days (five weeks) to finish each successive third of the sequence. A procrastinator was defined as a student who started one or more thirds within the last ten days and who would show an increased rate of production up to the close of the last day. A student was not labeled a procrastinator if no increase in rate was found or if he or she finished the four units and the comprehensive prior to the last day. At the University of Miami the course was run for four days a week and deadlines were set at the end of the sixth week and the end of the fifteenth week of the semester for the first two-thirds of the units. The seventh week of the second semester served as the deadline for the last third of the units at Miami. The last deadline was not consistently enforced and, therefore, the first two deadlines were used to distinguish the procrastinators at Miami. In summary, Procrastinators were students who characteristically showed "the last-day spurt of effort."

Withdrawals (N = 83) Those who dropped the course. Since the corresponding proportions of students in the group categories of Successes;

Procrastinators; Withdrawals at the two universities were within five hundredths of each other, the data of the two universities were pooled and comparisons were made with the analysis provided by Ball (1972). The same factors were found in the data assembled in the present study as that found by Ball with only one item shifting in factor identification. The proportions of variance accounted for by the factors were ordinally the same as Ball's, with no evidence of significant differences among the various partitions (e.g., sex, university, and so forth) between the present data and that provided by Ball. Thus, using Ball's interpretation of the factor loadings, the present study proceeded to test for initial attitude differences. Specifically, contrasts of factored attitude measures were partitioned by group and were designed to reflect whether the Procrastinator and Withdrawal Groups had counter-productive attitudes relative to the attitudes of the Success Group. Efforts were made to also assay the possibility of modified attitudes at the end of the semester. This intention was fruitless since few of the Procrastinators and only two Withdrawal students would take the time to fill out the follow-up questionnaires.

RESULTS

The factor scores from each of the two scales within each of the three groups were obtained by a technique Kaiser (1962) had recommended. The

factor scores represent an adjustment of each student's score for items loaded on a particular factor by the factor loadings for the items. The adjustment was such that a zero factor score for a student on a particular factor corresponded to the mid-point of the factor items of the Likert rating scale. The analysis was based upon an Attitude Scale × Factor × Group partitioning of the factor scores. Table 1 summarizes the group means and standard deviations of factor scores from the attitude scale dealing with "The Subject Matter—Math." Table 2 provides a similar summary of factor scores on the attitude scale "Regarding The *Traditional Methods* of Teaching Math." The positive and negative valances of the mean factor scores are defined in the tables by a declaration of what a higher (positive) factor score is assumed to imply (Ball, 1972).

The attitudes toward the subject matter of mathematics had three overall factors: Difficulty, Interest, and Utility (Table 1). Of these three factors, only the Interest factor was shown to load

TABLE 1.   MATH ATTITUDE SCALE A: ATTITUDES REGARDING THE SUBJECT MATTER—"MATH." FACTOR SCORE MEANS AND $\hat{\sigma}$ FOR EACH GROUP.

Factor A-I. Math is Difficult: Higher Scores → More Difficulty

Group	Sample size	Mean	$\hat{\sigma}$
Success	97	−.0928	1.0090
Procrastinators	49	+.0383	.8712
Withdrawals	83	+.0859	.8533

Factor A-II. Math is Interesting: Higher Scores → More Interest

Group	Mean	$\hat{\sigma}$
Success	+.1458	.9523
Procrastinators	−.0692	.9054
Withdrawals	−.1296	.8382

Factor A-III. Math has Utility: Higher Scores → Greater Utility

Group	Mean	$\hat{\sigma}$
Success	−.0378	.9098
Procrastinators	−.0480	.8477
Withdrawals	+.0725	.6982

TABLE 2.   MATH ATTITUDE SCALE B: ATTITUDES REGARDING *TRADITIONAL METHODS* OF TEACHING MATH. FACTOR SCORE MEANS AND σ FOR EACH GROUP

Factor B-I. Class Time Spent on Student Questions: Higher Scores → Too Much Class Time

Group	Sample size	Mean	$\hat{\sigma}$
Success	97	+.0303	.8209
Procrastinators	49	+.0515	.6993
Withdrawals	83	−.0658	.8099

Factor B-II. Class Atmosphere: High Score → Greater Tenseness

Group	Mean	$\hat{\sigma}$
Success	−.0859	1.0011
Procrastinators	+.0015	.8784
Withdrawals	+.0995	.8686

Factor B-III. Amount of Individual Help: High Score → Less Help Desired

Group	Mean	$\hat{\sigma}$
Success	+.0807	.9696
Procrastinators	+.0370	.9299
Withdrawals	−.1161	.8376

Factor B-IV. Anonymity: Higher Score → Less Anonymity

Group	Mean	$\hat{\sigma}$
Success	+.1606	.8157
Procrastinators	−.1548	.7687
Withdrawals	−.0963	.8468

differentially among the three groups. Using Dunnett's *d*, with the Success-students as the reference group, the effect on the Interest factor was found to be between Success and Withdrawal Group means. *d* = 2.110, (3 means, *df* = 226, *p* < .05).[2] Essentially, the Withdrawal Group was reliably less interested than the Success Group in working mathematical problems. Examples of some of the heavily loaded items in the Interest category were:

> Working with math is fun.
> Math turns me on.
> Finding answers to math problems is exciting.
> Math is very interesting.

No reliable differences among the three groups were discernable on either the Difficulty or Utility factors. The *a priori* conjectures had predicted the Difficulty items to be the most discriminating factor for the present group partitioning. Instead, the Difficulty factor scores were closely clustered about zero and each other on heavily loaded Difficulty items such as:

> Math is frightening.
> I wish I was not so discouraged with my math work.
> My mind goes blank when I have to think how to work a problem.
> I am surprised when I get a right answer.

A similar lack of discriminability among the three groups and clustering about zero was found on the Utility items, e.g.:

> Math is needed in daily life.
> Math is useful in the home.
> My mathematics helps me in other courses.
> It is important to know math to get a job.

The items which sought to measure attitudes toward the traditional methods of teaching mathematics had four factors: Class Time Spent on Student Questions; Class Atmosphere; Amount of Individual Help Desired; and Anonymity. Here only one factor was found to discriminate significantly among the three groups: Anonymity. The contrasts of the Success Group with both the Procrastinator, *d* =2.081, and the Withdrawal Groups, *d* = 2.948, were significant (3 means, *df* = 226, *p* < .05). The direction of difference in factor means

indicated that the Successes thought the *Traditionally* taught mathematics courses as involving less anonymity than did either the Procrastinator or the Withdrawal Groups. Both the Procrastinators and the Withdrawals showed a reliable tendency to agree with the following items more than the Success Group did:

> I never get to know anyone in my math classes.
> No one knows my name in my math classes.
> I am just a social security number in my math classes.

The remaining attitude factors (on methods of teaching) were not differentiating the three groups. For the two most heavily loaded factors (Class Time on Student Questions and Class Atmosphere) the factor means were closely clustered about zero. The factor of Individual Help Desired did have group means aligned in the expected directions, however, the differences among the groups were not reliable.

DISCUSSION

There were three major results of the present study:

(a) Students who withdrew from the introductory statistics courses using PSI had two prevailing counter-productive attitudes at the outset (relative to the Successful Group). These attitudes were a low degree of interest in "doing math problems" and feelings of anonymity in their traditionally taught mathematics courses.

(b) Students characterized by their erratically paced efforts, the Procrastinators, were also characterized at the outset as having the counter-productive attitude of anonymity in their traditionally taught mathematics courses.

(c) The remaining factors (including perceived difficulty and usefulness of the subject matter) did not reliably differentiate the three performance groups (Successes, Procrastinators, and Withdrawals).

The results provide the basis of two recommendations of simplistic appearance: Increase the interest in doing the mathematical problems and reduce the feelings of anonymity. One would think that if we understood the nature of these recommendations, then the situation could be remedied and the ideals of mastery learning (Bloom, 1971) could be realized.

---

[2] While the Dunnett test uses the *t*-statistic, it adjusts the Type I Error probability to cover all possible contrasts between a single reference group mean (the Success Group in the present case) and the other group means in the experiment. The .05 level was used throughout the present study and it represents an error rate for a set of *a priori* contrasts rather than that of a single contrast.

Regarding the interest factor, the present results provide some indication of what may be needed. The interest in doing mathematics problems was not affected by how *useful* or *relevant* the Withdrawal students thought the subject matter of mathematics to be. Furthermore, the results recommend that to increase interest one does not necessarily need to decrease perceived difficulty. One conjecture here may be that interest may be related to the feelings of competency when actually doing the mathematical work and how rewarding the demonstration of such competency is. The often heard cry for more practical mathematical examples may only serve the purpose of enticing students into the act of doing the problems. Such enticing techniques may, in turn, allow the reward system of competency and interest in doing the problems to be established.

The pervasive problem of feelings of anonymity, characteristic of both Withdrawals and Procrastinators, presents a distasteful outlook for PSI since the personalized aspect of PSI has been touted as reducing such feelings. Recall that the measures of anonymity were taken at the beginning of the semester. This provides an important clue to understanding the effects of anonymity as they relate to the acts of procrastination or withdrawing from the course. An important question is whether the personalized aspect of the technique had a chance to operate in the present case. Typically, the first week of a new semester in a PSI course is rather chaotic for a variety of reasons; e.g., students and new proctors learning the nuances of the course's logistical procedures, proctors learning how to teach and not lecture, or learning how to evaluate a student's performance on a quiz and not just score it, and so forth. In short, the technique of personalized instruction can be slow acting, possibly too slow for a certain subset of students.

Another side of the problem is whether the students with such attitudes would allow the technique to have effect. Teaching is quite difficult if a student either does not come in to receive the individualized attention, or only comes in sporatically with the anticipation that he or she will be able to rush through as much material as possible in the shortest amount of time. At the University of Miami, we have even tried personal telephone calls, office conferences, and mailed notes as means of counteracting these tendencies. We may have counteracted the feelings of anonymity but we did not change the overall incidents of procrastination and withdrawals. While one possible avenue would be to put tight time contingencies on those who show the characteristics of procrastination, this approach brings on other problems of logistics and techniques of enforcement (Liedecker, 1972).

If the incidents of procrastination and withdrawals are not affected by any of these more direct and more personalized approaches, then one would suspect that the manifest attitude of Anonymity measured here was not really anonymity. Instead, the items which were manifest as anonymity in the present study were very likely tapping some other variable of effect. We have no recommendations as to what the nature of such a variable may be.

BIBLIOGRAPHY

Kaiser, H. F., The Verimax Criterion for analytic rotation in factor analysis. *Psychometrika*, 1958, *23*, 187–200.

Kaiser, H. F., Formulas for component analysis. *Psychometrika*, 1962, *27*, 85.

Keller, F. S., "Goodbye, teacher . . ." *Journal of Applied Behavioral Analysis*, 1968, *1*, 79–89. [Article 1]

Leidecker, H., The removal of time constraints, in *Proceedings of Keller Method Workshop Conference*. A. J. Dessler Ed., Rice University, Houston, 1972.

McKean, H., Newman, F. L., and Purtle, R. B., A three semester mathematics and statistics service sequence. Paper presented in a symposium on PSI at the Rocky Mountain Psychological Association meetings, Denver, May, 1971. [Article 16]

Sheppard, W. C., and MacDermot, H. G., Design and evaluation of a programmed course in introductory psychology. *Journal of Applied Behavior Analysis*, 1970, *3*, 5–11. [Article 9]

Smith, C. C., *Partner Learning in Mathematics*. An unpublished Ph.D. proposal, New Mexico State University, 1972.

Veldman, D., *Fortran Programming for Behavioral Sciences*. New York: Holt, Rinehart, and Winston, 1967.

White, V. T., Indelicato, A., Jerman, M., and MacPherson, E. D., The forum: Individualization of instruction. *Mathematics Teacher*, 1972, *65*, 394–395 and 448–478.

28

SOME DESCRIPTIVE CHARACTERISTICS OF STUDENT PERFORMANCE IN PSI AND LECTURE COURSES [1]

David G. Born and Paul Whelan

Data are reported showing that the Utah version of PSI used in beginning psychology courses leads to a substantially higher percentage of student withdrawals than occurs typically in comparable lecture courses. Several academic charcteristics of students who withdraw and students who complete PSI courses are reported.

Compared with traditional instructional procedures, the personalized system of instruction (PSI) described by Keller (1968) demands a number of new responses from both students and faculty. Although the impact of the new mixture of contingencies, rewards, punishers, and setting events comprising PSI has not been thoroughly evaluated, several important comparisons of PSI and lecture-type instruction have been made. For example, Born, Gledhill, and Davis (1972), McMichael and Corey (1969), and Sheppard and MacDermot (1970) have all demonstrated superior student mastery of course materials using PSI; Corey, McMichael, and Tremont (1970) have recently reported that in comparison with students taught via lecture, PSI leads to superior student retention of course material over a period of at least one semester. In addition, a number of sources (e.g., Born & Herbert, 1971; Gallup, 1969) have obtained questionnaire data suggesting that PSI courses are very popular among students, even though they seem to require more work.

As one might expect from the fact that superior student performance is generated in PSI courses, the final distribution of letter grades awarded is usually not typical. Often the modal grade is A, with progressively fewer grades of B, C, and D (e.g., Keller, 1968) even though standards from comparable lecture courses are used in determining the PSI letter grades (Born, Gledhill, & Davis, 1972). However, in addition to higher letter grades, there is usually a substantial number of students who withdraw from PSI classes over the course of the academic term. These students are of special interest because in a sense they are persons for whom the PSI program has failed, and an understanding of the conditions leading to their withdrawal may help clarify some of the overall impact of PSI on student behavior.

Do more students withdraw from PSI courses than from lecture courses?

The data shown in Table 1 are from three recent lecture courses and three recent PSI courses in beginning psychology at the University of Utah. The table shows total registration, total number of students withdrawing from each course, and the percentage of students withdrawing from each course. Inspection of these data reveals that the percentage of withdrawals in the PSI courses is about three to five times greater than that in more traditionally taught courses. Thus the very substantial

---

[1] Some of the data contained in this paper have been previously reported by the senior author in a symposium presented at the Rocky Mountain Psychological Association, Denver, May, 1971, and at the M.I.T. Conference on the Keller Plan, Cambridge, October, 1971.

From *The Psychological Record, 23,* 1973.

TABLE 1

Total Student Registration and Withdrawals from Three
Lecture and Three PSI Courses

	Lecture Courses			PSI Courses		
	A	B	C	D	E	F
Number Registered	451	410	527	374	143	100
Number Withdrawals	23	24	26	54	20	25
Percentage Withdrawing	5.1%	5.8%	4.9%	14.4%	14.0%	25.0%

increase in the number of students who "quit" our[2] PSI courses would appear to be an important effect of our PSI system.

Do students who withdraw from PSI courses have histories of being academically "successful" or academically "unsuccessful"?

In a sense PSI courses would seem to be ideally suited to the academically unsuccessful student; poor performance on unit examinations does not result in a poor grade, and the slow student has an opportunity to work through the course largely at his/her own rate. Thus the question of which students were withdrawing from our class became of interest. In an effort to answer this question, the cumulative grade point averages (GPAs) of all students in several sections of our beginning psychology course were obtained. Since these GPAs were based on grades obtained up to the time students enrolled in our course, they were not influenced by grades received in beginning psychology.

Generally speaking, the students who withdraw from our PSI courses were students who had poor academic records; students who were academically successful (i.e., had high GPAs) almost never withdrew. Tables 2 and 3 show a tally of withdrawals for students in two of our recent PSI courses (one of these is Course F in Table 1). Of the 25 students who withdrew from Course F, the median cumulative GPA was 1.9 on a scale from 0.0-4.0, while the median GPA of students completing this course was 2.6. In Course G, taught in the same way, the median GPA of students withdrawing was 1.6, and the median GPA of students completing was 2.2. The statistical reliability of these data was evaluated by tallying students above and below the class median GPA in a fourfold table on the basis of whether they completed the course or withdrew. For Course F the resulting $X^2 = 12.00$, $p < .001$, and for Course G the $X^2 = 4.00$, $p < .05$. Thus it would appear that PSI course withdrawals tend to occur predominantly among students having poorer academic records.

Who withdraws from lecture courses?

The next step was to examine the GPAs of students who withdraw from introductory courses taught with more traditional lecture procedures. In the two lecture courses for which we have these data, the median GPA of students withdrawing has been 2.1 and 1.9. Although the median GPA of students enrolling in these courses is not available, over the past 2 or 3 years the mean GPA of students in lecture sections of beginning psychology has consistently hovered around 2.3 (± 0.1), making them very similar to our PSI sections. Therefore, in view of the similarity of GPAs for course enrollment and student withdrawals, it would appear that it is not just PSI procedures which lead academically "poorer" students to withdraw; students who withdraw from both PSI and lecture courses tend to be from the bottom of the

[2] The reference to "our" PSI courses is deliberate and is intended to emphasize the fact that although our PSI procedures are a fairly close copy of the procedures described by Keller (1968), there are nevertheless some (presumably) minor differences. Since the procedures are slightly different, the impact of those procedures may also be slightly different. The generality of our data to other educational programs described as PSI remains to be established.

GPA distribution. However, while both instructional procedures lead to withdrawals from the same group of students, the reader should note that our PSI procedures have a much greater impact on that group since a substantially greater percentage of those students do not complete our PSI couses (see Table 1).

Intracourse performance of PSI students

Test performance of students who withdraw. One suggestion offered to account for the fact that our PSI system has such a dramatic impact on students with poorer academic records is related to the "perfect" performance criterion for passing unit mastery tests. Presumably, poorer academic records are a result of poorer examination performance. Since

TABLE 2

Total Number of Students Registering and Withdrawing from Two PSI Courses, with Median GPAs and GPA Ranges for Those Who Withdrew and Those Who Completed the Courses.

Class	Total Students Registering	Withdrawals				Completions	
		Total Number Students	Percentage of Class	Median GPA	GPA Range	Median GPA	GPA Range
F	100	25	25.0	1.9	0.0-2.6	2.6	0.0-3.7
G	50	13	26.0	1.6	1.1-2.8	2.2	1.1-4.0

TABLE 3

Frequency Distribution of Entering Grade Point Averages, Student Withdrawals, and Students Taking Early Final Examinations in Two PSI Courses.

GPA	Course F			Course Gb		
	f	Student Withdrawals	Early Final	f	Student Withdrawals	Early Final
4.0-3.9				1		
3.8-3.7	2			1		1
3.6-3.5	3			4		1
3.4-3.3	5		1	4		2
3.2-3.1	10		4	1		
3.0-2.9	7		1	3		
2.8-2.7	5		2	3	2	1
2.6-2.5	13	3	2	2		
2.4-2.3	10	3	1			
2.2-2.1	15	5		8	1	2
2.0-1.9	7	1		7	2	
1.8-1.7	10	6	1	3	1	
1.6-1.5	4	2	1	4	2	
1.4-1.3	3	1		3	2	
1.2-1.1	1			4	3	
1.0-0.9	2	1				
0.8-0.7	1	1				
0.6-0.5	2					
0.4-0.3						
0.2-0.1						
0.0a	3	2				

aStudents who had previously registered for classes but had failed to complete requirements for those courses at the time of registration.

bGPAs not available for two students

"good" and "poor" students alike are asked to write "perfect" examinations in our PSI course, it is possible that poorer students have considerably more difficulty meeting this high criterion, are asked to repeat many examinations, and eventually withdraw from the course after a succession of failures.

In an effort to bring data to bear on the suggestion that withdrawals are precipitated by a series of failures on unit examinations, the pass-fail records were studied for the students withdrawing from Course F and Course G in Table 2. Of the 25 students withdrawing from Course F, 20 of them (80%) successfully passed the last examination they took in the course. Furthermore, although each of these students had taken at least one test, 40% of them had *never* been asked to repeat a unit examination, and only 36% had been asked to repeat more than one examination. In Course G the figures are only slightly different; 77% of the students passed their last test in the course, 31% had never been asked to repeat a test, and only 23% had been asked to repeat more than one examination. Although a few students may become discouraged after a series of test failures, from these data there would appear to be little evidence to support the notion that this factor accounts for the bulk of our withdrawing students.

Tests passed and tests failed by academically "successful" and academically "unsuccessful" students. The preceding finding, that students who withdraw do not typically have a long history of unit test failures even though they tend to come from the set of "poorer" students, suggested the need for a more careful look at the examination records of students in our class who have "good" and "poor" academic records. After obtaining the GPA of each student who registered in Course F and Course G, the upper and lower 25% of these students were selected for each course, and the mean percentage of unit tests successfully passed (i.e., $\frac{\text{Tests passed} \times 100}{\text{Tests taken}}$) during successive quarters of the academic term was calculated. These data are shown in Figure 1a. The reader will note that early in the term students in the top 25% of the class passed a higher percentage of their exams than students from the bottom 25% of the class, as one might expect. However, by the end of the term this difference has virtually disappeared. Further, the more rapid improvement by students from the bottom of the GPA distribution is still evident even when data from students who withdrew is excluded

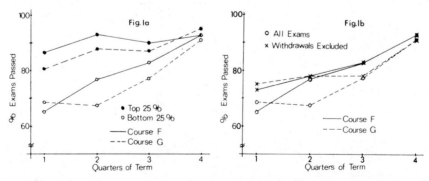

Fig. 1. Percentage of examinations passed in each of the four successive quarters of the academic term by students in two PSI courses at the University of Utah. In Figure 1a the exam performance of students in the top or bottom 25% of the distribution of cumulative grade-point average is shown separately for both classes. Figure 1b shows only the performance of students from the bottom 25% of the two classes; data plotted as open circles are based upon the total number of exams taken by these students in each quarter of the term; those indicated with an "X" are based upon only those students who completed the course.

from consideration (see Fig. 1b). Whether this improvement in test-taking is a result of subtle changes in the proctors' criteria for acceptable answers or whether the quality of answers improves as students gain experience in the course can only be a matter of conjecture at the moment.

Differences in rate of academic progress among academically "successful" and academically "unsuccessful" students

Casual inspection of the records of students who withdrew from our PSI classes revealed that these students often delayed a substantial period of time before attempting their first unit examination, and subsequent test taking was infrequent and sporadic. As a consequence, they fell behind schedule very early in the term. To illustrate, normal progress was defined as having passed at least one fourth of the unit exams by the end of each fourth of the academic term, e.g., 50% of the unit exams had to be passed by midpoint in the term to maintain 'normal' progress. Of the 25 students who withdrew from Course F (Table 2), at the time they last appeared in class to take a unit examination all but one (96%) were *behind* the normal rate of progress necessary to complete course requirements by the end of the academic term.

Having determined that students who withdraw do so at a time when they are progressing at an insufficient rate to complete course requirements by the end of the term, the progress of "good" and "poor" students who completed our PSI course was examined. Table 4 shows the number and percentage of students in the top and bottom 25% of Course F and Course G who completed the course but were behind the normal rate of progress in successive quarters of the academic term. The reader should note that because many of the students in the bottom 25% of the class withdrew during the term, and because data from these students have been excluded from the present comparison, different numbers of students are shown in the top and bottom 25% of the class.

Two things stand out about the data shown in Table 4. First, in both Course F and Course G *all* of the students in the top 25% of the

TABLE 4

Students from Upper and Lower 25% of the Course Completing but behind 'Average' Progress in each of the First Three Quarters.

	No. of Students Completing Course	Quarters of the Academic Term			Number of Students Behind One or More Quarters
Course F		1	2	3	
Top 25% of Class (n=25 students)	25 (100%)	10 (40%)	8 (32%)	11 (45%)	16 (64%)
Bottom 25% of Class (n=25 students)	11 (44%)	10 (91%)	8 (73%)	8 (73%)	10 (91%)
Course G		1	2	3	
Top 25% of Class (n=13 students)	13 (100%)	10 (77%)	6 (46%)	7 (54%)	10 (77%)
Bottom 25% of Class (n=13 students)	5 (38%)	4 (80%)	3 (60%)	3 (60%)	4 (80%)

GPA distribution completed the course, whereas something less than half of the lower 25% completed. Second, among those students completing the course, a consistently greater percentage of students from the bottom 25% of each course is behind 'average' progress at the end of each quarter. Finally, although it cannot be determined from the data shown in Table 4, it is of some interest to note that many of the students who are behind at the end of the first quarter of the term remain behind in subsequent quarters and do not "catch up" to 'average' progress until the fourth and final quarter of the term.

Was an early final taken?

To permit students to complete the course at their own rate, they could elect to take one of (usually) three final examinations, the last of which was given at the time announced in the regular academic calendar and was, therefore, the latest possible opportunity for a student to finish the course requirements. All students were required to take this final examination whether or not they finished the set of unit examinations, but they could not take an early final exam unless the unit tests were satisfactorily completed. The second final examination is typically given 1 week prior to the last week of regular classes, and the first exam is usually given about 2 weeks before the end of the academic term. A tally of students taking early final examinations in Courses F and G is shown in Table 3.

A comparison of the top and bottom 25% of the students with respect to whether they took an early final examination revealed the following information: Of the 25 students in Course F with GPAs of 2.80 or higher, six (24%) took an early final examination; of the 25 students with GPAs of 1.90 or lower, 13 withdrew, and of the 12 remaining only two students (17%) took early final exams (see Table 3). Similarly, of the 25 students at the top of the GPA distribution, all 25 completed all of the readiness tests by the third and last final examination, but among students in the bottom 25% of the GPA distribution, there were four who had not finished all readiness tests; i.e., excluding the 13 students who withdrew, one third of the remaining students had not finished all course requirements at the time the course officially ended.

DISCUSSION

The data described in this paper emphasize the urgent need for empirical evaluation of the effects of PSI procedures on students. For at least two reasons the generality of the present findings might be in question. First, as a public institution with a largely nonresidential student body, it is likely that there are many nonacademic pressures on students at the University of Utah that do not exist on many other campuses. For example, in our most recent PSI beginning psychology course, 55% of the students had at least part-time jobs at the time they registered for the course. To the extent that PSI courses demand additional work (time) from students (e.g., Gallup, 1969) which compete with nonacademic demands on their time, it seems likely that the percentage of students withdrawing will be greater than from educational (instructional) systems that require less work. Second, PSI is a complex educational system, and it seems likely that no one else duplicates precisely the procedures in use at the University of Utah. Different procedures and/or different course material might markedly alter the impact of the system on students. Only additional data will resolve the question of the extent to which the phenomena reported in this paper have generality.

Implicit in the preceding paragraph is the suggestion that student withdrawals are at least partly a function of classroom procedures. Which procedures and how they should be altered to minimize withdrawals is

a matter of conjecture at the moment. However, it would seem extremely
unlikely that by chance we have hit upon the set of procedures which
minimize student withdrawals. Some of the preceding data suggest
that "poorer" students may have difficulty pacing themselves in a self-
paced course and that procedures which promote more careful management of study behavior might have a marked effect on course completion. Conceivably, dividing the same amount of course material into
more study units with correspondingly more frequent testing would
make it easier for students to prepare for each unit and might promote
earlier starts among slower students. Early and successful test taking,
in turn, might serve to maitain higher rates of course progress. On the
other hand, one might argue that as the number of units is increased
for a given academic term, the required study routine becomes increasingly inflexible. Perhaps it is precisely the steady program of study demanded by our PSI which cannot be easily managed by students who
also have substantial commitments to nonacademic agencies (e.g., part-
time work). For them larger units and correspondingly fewer tests might
optimize course completion. Clearly, additional resesarch is required to
make PSI optimally effective for all students.

REFERENCES

BORN, D. G., GLEDHILL, S. M., & DAVIS, M. L. 1972. Examination performance
in lecture-discussion and personalized instruction courses. *Journal of
Applied Behavior Analysis,* 5, 33-43. [Article 10]
BORN, D. G., & HERBERT, E. W. 1971. A further study of Keller's personalized
system of instruction. *Journal of Experimental Education,* 40, 6-11.
COREY, J. R., McMICHAEL, J. S., & TREMONT, P. J. 1970. Long-term effects
of personalized instruction in an introductory psychology course. Paper presented at the 41st Annual Meeting of the Eastern Psychological Associa-
tion, Atlantic City.
GALLUP, H. F. 1969. Personalized instruction in introductory psychology. Paper
presented at the meetings of the Midwestern Psychological Association,
Chicago, May.
KELLER, F. S. 1968. "Goodbye, teacher . . ." *Journal of Applied Behavior Analysis,*
1, 79-89. [Article 1]
McMICHAEL, J. S., & COREY, J. R. 1969. Contingency management in an intro-
ductory psychology course produces better learning. *Journal of Applied
Behavior Analysis,* 2, 79-83. [Article 2]
SHEPPARD, W. C., & MacDERMOT, H. G. 1970. Design and evaluation of a
programmed course in introductory psychology. *Journal of Applied Behavior
Analysis,* 3, 5-11. [Article 9]

Section IV

Extensions and Related Developments

As experience with PSI has accumulated, change and growth have taken three directions. The first was the application of the method to disciplines other than psychology (Section II). The second has been the development of the proctor system. Article 29 describes a proctoring system which many instructors have found advantageous. The third has been the initiation of several PSI courses as part of an experiment in over-all curriculum design. Greenspoon's paper [Article 30] describes a college where the goal is to provide a PSI option for the entire curriculum.

Anyone who has read this far may well feel that there is nothing new about PSI. This is probably true. It is a simple system and a simple idea. That PSI is related to programmed instruction is obvious and acknowledged. Most aspects of the method can be traced back to one or another of the great names in the history of education. The most direct influence is that of B. F. Skinner, as well as Robert Mager whose work has been mentioned many times in these papers. The application of token economies and contingency contracting to education, the development of computer aided instruction, and the English open classroom concept, all contain elements parallel to PSI.

There has been no effort to describe the heritage of broadly related developments. But a few recent reports describe teaching methods which are quite closely akin to PSI. This section contains eight of these.

Olgierd Celinski's paper [Article 31] describes a system, developed independently, which is similar to PSI, without the proctors. Sivasailam Thiagarajan [Article 32] presents a technique developed from a system-analysis point of view which stresses the proctor function. The Morgan and Toy paper [Article 33] describes the successful use of proctors at pre-college levels. Ferster's paper [Article 34] has been discussed earlier (see the introduction to Section I) and grew out of a common collaboration (Section V).

Two other related systems have received wide recognition: the Audio-Tutorial Approach and IPI (Individually Prescribed Instruction). While audio-visual aids, programmed texts, teaching machines and computer terminals could all be used in a PSI course, Postlethwait's method [Article 35] involves a more sophisticated use of media than has been characteristic of PSI teaching to date. The IPI model emphasizes detailed materials, providing for more multi-tracks, branching, and entering assessment than does the typical PSI program. While there are some differences, there are even more similarities between these systems, all attempting to individualize instruction.

29

A PERMUTATION ON AN INNOVATION [1]

J. Gilmour Sherman

In the initial development of PSI several characteristics were built into the system quite deliberately in response to deficiencies, real or imagined, in the traditional teaching situation plus what we knew at the time about learning theory. Many of the features of the system—self-pacing, mastery learning, specified objectives, small step sequenced material, etc.—we share with other recent and clearly related innovative methods. I know of no definitive statement of the characteristics that define the limits and province of PSI or distinguish it clearly from these other methods and techniques. I personally feel some thinking and comments in this vein are needed, but I could be wrong and that is for another time. One characteristic, the proctors, *does* set us apart, and it is some thoughts, developments, and a little data on the proctor aspect of PSI that I would like to share with you today.

I have accused Fred Keller of using a functional illiterate as his first proctor in Brazil. Keller has said "not guilty"—it was our Brazilian colleague Rodolpho Azzi that made this selection. In any case, this proctor was to solve the problem of comparing the student's test with an answer key in a way we would now describe as "matching-to-sample." I may be wrong about Fred's experience but it *was*, at one time, the plan to have the immediate feedback of test results handled by non-professional clerical help. However, the proctor function quickly developed to be more than non-professionals could provide.

At one time or another several of us have taught PSI courses, ourselves serving as test corrector, grader, proctor, tutor. In some ways this works very well, but the time demands on the professor to deal with highly predictable, redundant, repetitious errors and questions, precludes his dealing with the complex, personal and unique questions that only he is equipped to handle. It is a waste of talent to ask the professor to handle what

can be passed on to others, particularly when these tasks prevent him from bringing to his students the special insights, imaginative leaps, even artistry and magic which he alone is *supposedly* prepared to give.

In some PSI courses the proctor role has been handled by graduate students. There is rather general agreement that these professionals-in-training sieze this opportunity to jump into the teacher role, and quickly start to give lectures even though the system has reduced the audience to one. In my own experience, I have overheard graduate students, acting as proctors, fabricate an answer, sometimes ingenious, but wrong. The contingencies operating on these professionals-without-certification are such that we should not be surprised to find them responding under pressure to come up with an answer, especially when faced down by an undergraduate. The face-saving involved suggests distorted facts might occasionally be expected. The graduate student *is* under pressure to demonstrate his *own* mastery. In any case, I know of no one who has taught a PSI course who recommends graduate students as the best occupant of the proctor position.

Most frequently, proctors have been advanced undergraduates, generally chosen for their superior performance in the course during a previous term or year. Typically they have been paid for their services in either of two ways—money or course credit. Money seems to be a very satisfactory reinforcer, but is hard to come by from currently limited budgets. If money is available, it does work well—there is nothing wrong with it and the proctor problem is three-fourths solved. Those teachers with unlimited budgets might well stop reading at this point.

When money is in short supply, course credit is frequently handy. I have nothing against it and in fact I think we were the first to use that solution at Arizona State University, where a course called "seminar in course programming" was created for

---
[1] Paper read at the American Psychological Association, September 6, 1971.

the purpose. Others have used the almost always present "independent study" course designation to award a couple of credits to upperclass majors to enlist their aid.

Again, I have nothing against this solution. Those who are using it successfully probably should be encouraged to continue. However, many colleagues about to initiate PSI courses have said to me, "but I don't think my university, my dean, or my chairman, will allow me to give credit for this activity." My answer has always been, "that's ridiculous, the proctors learn more than anybody." I still feel this way. This is the point where those using this reinforcer successfully might also stop reading.

But there is a message here. In a very early speech that Fred Keller gave to the assembled faculty at ASU he said: "The proctors have also been enthusiastic about the method and its educational value—*for themselves as well as their students.* They claim to have profited greatly from preparing for, and giving tests, talking with students about them, and discussing with the instructor the work to come. The job appears to be especially attractive to those who plan to go on to graduate study and teaching, but its appeal is not limited to them alone." I might add that if Keller was right this certainly seems worthy of course credit.

In a talk I gave to the American Educational Research Association in 1967 I said:

The proctors are another happy story. They receive two points of academic credit for their work and *earn* it several times over. They come early, work late, learn even more than their students, and go on to take the top grades in the advanced courses (as yet traditionally taught). At weekly meetings they plan an important part in program revision, suggesting a unit which is too large, a textbook passage that is unclear or a test question that is ambiguous. The behavior of the students clearly reveals that the proctors provide a kind of reinforcement, however subtle and ill-defined, which has yet to be built into a programmed text. I think they are the key to whatever success we have had.

That was in 1967, but I was not yet listening to my own words. Dr. David Born in his very excellent "Instructor Manual for Development of a Personalized Instruction Course" wrote, "The old saying that 'If you want to learn a subject you should teach it' applies to proctors just as it applies to faculty members." At another point in the same

Manual Dave said, " . . . in preparing for their teaching assignment the proctor staff will learn at least as much about the course material as the students taking the course."

There are other, perhaps better examples, of a theme we were all mouthing. Still we were missing the message. We did notice that a large percentage of our students applied to be proctors the following year—but we never went on to say there must be something about the position that is reinforcing. We did not listen to ourselves say "the proctors learn more than anyone."

In the spring of 1970 I was about to teach a new course in educational psychology. The money had run out; there were no funds to pay proctors as I had done for a different course during the fall semester. My colleagues looked unfavorably on giving course credit. I think they were wrong, but for other reasons I did not want to argue. The system was in ruins and I would probably have gone back to lecturing, if it hadn't been that I had forgotten how.

Out of desperation we decided to make proctors out of some of the students *taking* the course. Here is the way it works. My one assistant and I correct the first few tests for any given unit. The first ten students to pass, on the first try, with a perfect score, can become proctors and take on the function of grading, guiding and interviewing classmates with a very extensive proctor's manual to guide them. They need not accept the job if they do not choose to. Students who miss the chance to become a proctor on Unit One can earn that position by being among the first ten to pass Unit Two—essentially bumping one of the existing proctors, all of whom are working at high rates to retain their position. We essentially have a constantly changing group of ten proctors who are always those students furthest out in front. These ten proctors work with their colleagues on all units up to and including the unit they just passed. My one assistant and I continue correcting the first ten who are prepared to move even further ahead.

Clearly this procedure solves the money problem, and the course credit problem, if anyone is squeamish about that. It also solves the proctor supply problem if someone is moving to a new institution or teaching a new course where already prepared upper class candidates are not available. These advantages are substantial and are essentially the problems the procedure was designed to solve. It turns out there are other more important advantages.

First, there is always the problem of insuring

that upper class proctors who have taken the course a previous year in fact review the material and are reacquainted with it in sufficient detail to guide students who they are now proctoring. Using *this* procedure the proctors have, without question, recently read the material involved. They have recently passed a test on it.

Secondly, the system helps a bit with the procrastination problem. A substantial number of students work to gain the lead—so they don't fall behind. This may introduce some competition for the position (again, the position must be reinforcing) but that competition is not too severe. Those who fall a bit behind at the start have a chance near the end if they keep up. As the leaders finish the course, take the final, and disappear to enjoy or make use of the free time their rapid progress has earned for them, the second string has its chance. A few of the early finishers stay on, reporting enjoyment in the job, but most do not return, making room for those who managed to proceed at a less rapid but still more than acceptable rate. During last spring's term about 40% of the students held the proctor position at some time during the semester. Some students earned the position, but declined it as taking too much time. The number precluded, then, is not large. Some preliminary data show that general class progress is more rapid, and the number of student who fall dangerously behind is less with this procedure.

A third advantage is related to the precision of instruction. The proctors are clearly only a few units ahead of the student being examined and they are not expected to be as wise as the more advanced student. With less reputation to protect, they are less liable to start giving lectures or inventing answers. They find it easier to say "I don't know." This shows up as a greater number of referrals to the instructor. To those of us who have stood around feeling useless in a PSI course, this is pleasing. To the extent that it keeps the instructor from getting bored and leaving the classroom and increases his interactions with individual students, I would also count this as an advantage.

Perhaps a minor point, but important for some of our most important students, the proctor position is especially appealing to the bright student. Those looking for the extra challenge, and sometimes bored in programmed courses, find their "thing" in the proctor role.

While economics, course credit, and proctor recruiting recommend it; while preparedness, precision, and lessened procrastination are secondary benefits, the most important result is what we have been saying all along—the proctors learn more than anyone. It makes more than a little sense to pass this advantage on to those *taking* the course. To indicate that this is the result, let me quickly include just a scrap of data from last fall's course in which about one third of the students worked as proctors. While some students who were *not* proctors received over 90 on the final, no proctor fell below 90. Seven of the 32 proctors scored 100 on the final—a score not attained by *any* student who went through the course without proctoring. This exclusion from the highest rank includes four students who went through the course with a speed equal to the leaders, always qualifying for a proctor position, but declining it as too time consuming. This seems to be a useful procedure for learning—and learning to the point of near perfection at that.

We can again refer to the old saying "you don't learn something until you teach it." "Practice makes perfect" might have led us to predict a happy result from this permutation on an innovation. The data on overlearning, and massed versus spaced practice, might have led us to the same prediction from a more solid data base than an old adage. Alternatively one might say that since the proctors are exposed to nearly every conceivable error, the additional S^{Δ} training leads to more precise discriminations. I am convinced that there is yet another, at least as important, reason that proctoring leads to such effective learning. It is related to the question of arbitrary versus natural reinforcers. This is best illustrated by the not infrequent comment of a student who finds himself unexpectedly in the lead, is asked to be a proctor, and responds by saying "may I wait until tomorrow? I read the material, know that I could answer your test questions, but really feel I need to review it before being ready to explain it to others." This student tells us something important.

The arbitrary reinforcers of grades, points, a "pass" or other instructor-administered reward, even praise, establishes one kind of repertoire, sometimes minimal even at the A level. It maintains the minimal repertoire commensurate with the award. That repertoire can be achieved by a *kind* of study, in almost every way inferior to the behavior of the professional approaching new subject matter for professional or scholarly reasons. We all recognize in our own lives the difference between the perfunctory and patronizing slap on the back and the legitimate recognition of professional competence. Even with the student cry for participation and relevance there is little we can do, particularly at introductory levels, that makes the material in any way useful. Again the gold star is a fake. More important, when the repertoires established by arbitrary versus natural reinforcers are compared in the classroom, the gold star proves to be a defective reinforcer. While hopefully there *are* natural reasons to learn most of the material we teach, beyond merely being able to teach it to others, nonetheless the proctor teaching function does reward learning by making the material learning *immediately* useful in a natural and professional sense. If a student has taken the trouble to learn what we have asked him to learn, it is little enough for us to treat him as professionally qualified with that material. When conferring that deserved, natural, and dignified respect for competence produces the very behavior we want to establish, applaud, and recognize, there appears to be in the proctor function a merit, the limits of which we have hardly begun to explore. What we ask is competence, this is followed by natural appropriate recognition. The many papers on the topic "reinforcers available in the classroom" have suggested so little, we should not throw this one away. The behavior this procedure generates seems to be precisely the behavior we are trying to establish.

30

SHOULD AN ENTIRE COLLEGE CURRICULUM BE TAUGHT BY THE KELLER METHOD

Joel Greenspoon

I have pondered for some time the question of should an entire college curriculum be taught by the Keller plan. I believe that our experience of last year at Temple Buell College would indicate that it is possible to teach an entire college curriculum by the Keller plan. This does not mean that every course at Temple Buell College was taught by the Keller plan. Rather every discipline in the curriculum with one exception offered one or more courses in the Keller plan. The Art Department, for example, offered all courses in art in the Keller plan. Chemistry, on the other hand, offered no courses in the Keller plan. But, to return to the original question, I am going to put forth a tentative yes that the entire college curriculum should be taught by the Keller plan, at least the Temple Buell College version of the plan. I shall describe briefly the way in which the plan functions at Temple Buell College.

Participation by the faculty in what we call our New College Program is voluntary, but well over 50% of the faculty taught one or more courses in the program. Each faculty member was required to develop a set of objectives for each course taught in the program. This set of objectives had to be written out and available for anyone to read. Sets of objectives were subsequently placed in a number of offices at the College. In addition the faculty members were required to describe how the objectives were to be attained and the various materials, books, articles, etc., that would contribute to the attainment of the objectives. The objectives and related materials were available to the student at the time of registration. The student was also informed that she could proceed at her own rate, but the instructor had estimated that the course could be completed in fifteen weeks with reasonable effort. The instructor had complete freedom in the procedures that he could use, provided none of the procedures would limit the rate at which the student could proceed through the course. For example, there are some instructors who apparently derive much reinforcement from giving lectures. The instructor could give lectures but he had to make provisions for a student to get the lecture material in other ways and at other times. Thus, some instructors put the lectures on tapes that were available to the student at any time. Some instructors had materials on videotape, especially materials where it would be beneficial to the student to see as well as hear the material. The student was informed that she could meet the objectives at any time she considered herself to be ready. There were no grades provided for the work turned in by the student. The work was evaluated as acceptable or unacceptable, according to the criteria of acceptability provided by the instructor. If the work was evaluated unacceptable, the instructor was required to spell out the precise bases for the evaluation and inform the student what she would have to do to have the work accepted. Moreover, instructors were required to return any work done by the student within one week after the student turned in the material. This regulation was designed to prevent an instructor from holding up the progress of a student. When the student attained the objectives of the course, the Registrar was notified and the student was awarded credit for the course. There is no time base and the student could complete the course in six weeks or six months. There are no penalties or failures in the system. A student may never get credit for a course, but she cannot get an F in a course. Another feature of the program provided the student, on completing a course, opportunity to add a new course to replace the completed course, to pursue an independent study, or to devote the additional time to other courses.

I have provided you with a very sketchy outline of our program. There are many details that I have omitted. Before proceeding with a discussion of why I answered the original question in the positive, I should like to make one comment in response to a criticism leveled at our program. I have heard it said that there was no reinforcement in our program because no grades were involved. I merely wish to state the density of reinforcement or at least the opportunity for reinforcement was much greater than in a traditional course. I am afraid that some instructors assume that the only possible reinforcement in the academic setting is a grade. I would admit that for some students a grade may have acquired powerful reinforcing properties. However, I believe there are many other kinds of reinforcement, not necessarily associated with school work, that can function as very effective positive reinforcers. Though our program does not include grades there are many opportunities for the instructor to provide immediate, direct reinforcement to the student.

To discuss my reason for responding with a yes to the question, I should like to consider the reasons from the standpoint of the student, the instructor, and the whole matter of behavior acquisition. What are the data from the students? Last spring we conducted a survey among our students to get information on the responses of the students to the New College Program. The program was given a vote of approval by 92% of the respondents and the number of respondents comprised close to 50% of the student body. However, only students who had taken one or more courses in the program were permitted to respond and there were many students who had taken no courses in the program. I would estimate we received responses from about 75–80% of all possible respondents.

There were some other interesting areas covered in the survey that bear on the students' reactions to the programs. About 90% of the respondents said they learned as much or more in their self-paced courses than they did in traditional courses, with about 50% indicating that they learned more. Another interesting result was that the respondents considered the courses in the New College Program to involve less competition with their fellow students. Courses offered in this manner were also considered to be less boring by a large majority of the students. Knowledge of progress in the self-paced courses was considered to be greater by a majority of the respondents. And finally, a large majority of the respondents replied that the New College course was better than the traditionally taught course. Overall I believe the students who took courses in the self-paced program considered the program to be beneficial to the learning of the material.

The reactions of the faculty are not as consistently favorable as the students. Either the individual faculty member said he liked it and thought it was great or else he said he didn't like it and would not consider teaching in it again. There are probably fewer faculty members teaching in the New College Program this year than last year. However, this may be somewhat misleading because some of the more ardent supporters of self-paced instruction resigned and have been replaced by faculty who know little or nothing about the program.

A major complaint of the faculty was that it was too much work. I can attest to the fact that it is more work, but I am not convinced that over a period of several years our self-paced program would require more work than traditional courses. Another complaint of some faculty was that they liked to give grades and grades were not awarded in the program. One faculty member said that he liked to lecture and he didn't think he should lecture in courses taught in this program.

Having digressed a bit with respect to the main theme, I should like to return to the point that the entire college curriculum should be taught by some variation of the Keller plan that may be appropriate to the particular institution. One major factor is the greater variability in the educational histories of students who are entering colleges and universities today. It is a reasonable assumption that with about 60% of the high school graduates entering colleges, there will be much greater variability in their entering behaviors. It is very difficult for a traditional program to take into account these differences, so the instructor attempts to strike a happy medium. As a consequence, he gears his course to the "average" student. In the process he bores to death the better prepared students and loses the less well-prepared students. In addition, the instructor invests a tremendous amount of time evaluating students. Time spent in evaluation is usually taken away from time spent in education. The alternative in traditional programs is to create remedial programs whose effectiveness is questionable. Moreover, remedial courses frequently carry a stigma, a stigma comparable to special education courses in the public schools. They certainly aren't special and are rarely educational. The self-paced program can be geared to the entering behavior of the individual student. The student who has an excellent preparation for a given course is able to move quickly through the material previously learned. The student who has an inadequate preparation may require much longer to complete the course, but once he completes the course he should be able to proceed more rapidly through the next course in the sequence. In a traditional course the student who gets a C or D in the first course in a sequence may be in trouble in the next course. Last June at our college a committee was formed to examine the records of students who had been on academic probation to make some decisions about these students. The one point that stood out very clearly was that a student who got a D in the first course in the sequence was an excellent candidate for an F in the second course. I doubt if this comes as a big surprise to many of you. If knowledge or learning or whatever we want to call it is cumulative and if grades in traditional courses are even a rough estimate of what students have acquired, then it should follow that students who have acquired a below average amount in the first course will be decidedly handicapped in the second course.

Self-paced instruction does place greater demands on the instructor, but not necessarily with respect to time. The greater demands that I am referring to will tend to increase the effectiveness of the instructor. Specifically I am referring to the fact that the instructor must spell out clearly what behavior the student is to acquire in a course. The preparation of a set of objectives stated in behavioral terms is both difficult and time consuming. I am afraid that most of us in the academic world have tended to use some very sophisticated sounding words to describe our objectives but most of these terms or words have no specific behavioral referrants. Such words provide the student with little or no information that he may easily and readily apply to himself. Having struggled over many hours to develop a set of objectives for a number of different courses, I can readily attest to the fact that it is not an easy task. Like many instructors I was always demanding that my students think or analyze something. Of course, I must admit that such verbage allowed or permitted me great latitude in assigning grades. I suspect that it even permitted me to give a lower grade to some obnoxious student or a higher grade to some attractive, well endowed coed. By spelling out the behaviors to be acquired by the student, however, the instructor must be better organized to teach the course because, if for no other reason, the students are in a position to demand that he stick to the subject since they have been provided the means to do so. How often has each of us taught a course and for an entire semester not a question was asked by a student? When asked why they didn't ask any questions, especially in the face of relatively poor examination performances, the students will say they didn't know what to ask. In our version of self-paced instruction the student is always in a position to ask questions since she has been provided with a

set of specific objectives. If worse came to worse the student could always ask a question based on the objectives that have been presented to him at the beginning of the course. There is another aspect to the explicit statement of objectives in behavioral terms. The student is essentially told what the instructor considers to be important. I doubt if there are many textbooks in which each word and each sentence is of earth shaking importance. It may come as a surprise to some instructors to find out that not every word uttered by them falls in the category or class of momentous comments or statements. The statement of the objectives in a clear, unambiguous behavioral language provides the student with direction in her reading or note taking in the case of a lecture.

A frequent criticism against precise specification of the objectives of a course is that it may serve to limit what the student will acquire in a course. This criticism can be applied to any course taught in any way. The precise behavioral specification of an objective does not limit in any way, shape, or form what the student is to acquire in a course. I believe it is possible to demand that a student describe that which has made the great painters great as is to ask them to appreciate the works of the great masters. There is no limit to the behavioral demands that may be made on a student with precise behavioral descriptions. There is much to be gained.

As reflected in our survey the student has more feedback in a self-paced course than in a traditional course. In addition to getting more feedback from the instructor, the student is able to provide more meaningful feedback to herself, since she can continuously evaluate her own progress. The importance of feedback in one form or another in learning has been well established.

Another factor, more difficult to evaluate perhaps, is that the students report much less pressure in such courses. A frequent comment by the student is that they can approach a course much more relaxed because the aversive consequences of failure are not present in the program. Students have also reported to me that they were more inclined to register for "difficult" courses since they believed that they had a chance if the course were offered in the self-paced program. In spite of student views to the contrary I have seen little evidence to support the contention that any subject matter is inherently more difficult than any other. I could ask a question to this group that probably none of you could answer. It would be a very difficult question simply because you had not acquired the behavior that was involved in the answer. I could ask the same question of any student at Temple Buell College and get a correct answer within the range of reaction time. All of us who have served as an advisor to students have encountered the student who refuses to take a particular course because it was reputed to be difficult. In our program we find it much easier to have students register for reputedly difficult courses because they need not be concerned about any aversive consequences accruing to them.

As we move into our second year of operation of our program I hear more and more often from students that they are beginning to learn to manage their time much more effectively. Our records would also indicate that this is correct. The number of students who did not complete a course in the first semester of last year, our first year, was much greater than in the second semester. It is too early to make an assessment for this semester, but if my courses are indicative of a trend, I would have to state that students who took courses in the program last year have indeed learned to manage their time much more effectively. In one freshman course I note that many students have yet to complete a single unit. In my courses that have sophomores or higher classification students I note an increased systematic attack on the course. That is, the students are moving through the course at a rate of one unit of work per unit of time. If the present trend continues every student in my non-freshman courses will complete the courses before or by the end of the semester. I have made no effort to have them move at any prescribed rate. The freshmen, on the other hand, have not learned to manage or budget their time. It is not too surprising since a relatively small number of them have had the opportunity to learn to do this rather difficult task, since most of them have been in academic settings where someone else, teacher or parent, has essentially managed their time for them. I am confident that by the second semester these freshmen will have made much progress in this direction.

I have tried to indicate that I believe there are some important educational reasons to have an entire college curriculum operate under some form of the Keller plan. Now I should like to add some qualifications to this statement. It should be done if and only if the faculty and the students have a clear picture of the demands of such a program. It is very easy to present the position that this type of instructional program is some kind of educational panacea. No instructional program in and of itself is a panacea. The effectiveness of the instructional

program is still dependent on the way in which the faculty carries out the responsibilities of the program. To be honest we did not conduct an adequate training program for both our students and faculty. Many of our students had not been prepared to accept the changed responsibilities that fell on them, primarily because the changed demands of the program were not clearly specified to them. The same is true with some of our faculty. Some of our faculty considered the program to be the means for reducing the amount of work that they would have to do. And they handled their courses accordingly. Our survey among our students indicated clearly that the student who took a self-paced course that was taught according to the principles underlying self-paced instruction rated the course very high. However, students who took a self-paced course that was not so run tended to rate the course as inferior to a traditional course. Similarly students who said they had a clear picture of the demands of self-paced instruction generally rated self-paced instruction well above a traditional course.

A most significant feature of our program is the big increase in the amount of behavior that is emitted by the students. It is almost axiomatic that to shape behavior, it is necessary to have some behavior emitted by the organism. Students in our New College Program have been almost unanimous in saying that courses in the program required them to emit much more behavior than a traditional course. And practically all behaviors emitted by the student are followed by feedback. In a traditional course a student may emit behaviors related to the course two or three times a semester. I am referring to examinations for which feedback may be provided by the instructor, after a reasonably long period of time. In a self-paced course the student emits behavior related to the objectives of the course many, many times over a period of time. As I mentioned previously the density of reinforcement is many times greater in a self-paced course than in a traditional course. There is a greater opportunity for the student to learn to reinforce herself since the probability of reinforcement from the instructor is so much greater.

I believe that a college planning to teach the entire curriculum by the Keller plan should take at least one year to shape up the faculty and students to participate in such an educational experience. There are some very sensitive areas that have to be examined in the process. One very sensitive area may be subsumed within the realm of academic freedom and that is the freedom of the instructor to teach his courses his way. We made participation by the instructors optional, but we also required each participating instructor to prepare a set of objectives of each course to be taught in this manner. However, we had no effective machinery for deciding whether or not the objectives were written in a manner that provided meaningful information to the student. It is not easy to tell an instructor that his objectives are poorly written without suggesting that the content is unsatisfactory. At the same time most instructors simply do not know how to write objectives in behavioral terms. I believe that if a college had a year to prepare, it would be possible to shape instructors to write course objectives in behavioral terms.

This particular issue brings up another related problem. There will be instructors who will contend that they can see how specific objectives can be written in other disciplines but not theirs. This problem can be handled, but it takes time to shape up an existential philosopher to write behavioral objectives for a course in existential philosophy. But it can be done. It has been done.

To approach these problems by fiat or decree will destroy the program before it gets off the ground. But this is the reason that a year's planning is necessary to institute such a program. Numerous workshops should be held where the faculty member can be shaped up to the different demands that this kind of program makes on them. And the demands are different. Both students and faculty members must be shaped up to the different relationships that must evolve from this instructional program if it is going to be successful. The shift from the traditional instructor-student relationship to the colleague relationship requires shaping on the part of students and faculty. It will take some time for some faculty members to step down from the position of the fountainhead to that of the senior colleague. Many instructors find it very difficult to accept the fact that students may learn material from sources other than the instructor. I have been surprised when instructors have said that a student could not hope to pass a course if she did not attend class. There are many aspects of the traditional approach to education that have to be modified if a Keller type plan of instruction is to have a reasonable chance of success. These changes will probably come slowly for some faculty members and some students. We must bear in mind that most high schools have not prepared students to function in this kind of program. Many students have not been prepared to function with so much freedom. The shift of re-

sponsibilities of both student and faculty must be programmed and shaped. And, especially in the case of the private institutions, it is advisable to prepare comprehensible materials describing the program to the parents. Some parents may become a bit disturbed if at the end of a semester the grade report consists of a blank sheet of paper.

There is another issue that should be faced if a college plans to teach the entire curriculum according to some version of the Keller plan that does not have a time base. It may not be possible to have every instructor teach every course in this program which means that a traditional and a self-paced program may be operating in parallel. If this should happen, I believe it would be preferrable to have students take all courses in one program or the other and not mix the two. The year before we initiated our New College Program we had one instructor teach one course in a self-paced, non-time base way. As a consequence, the students in the course were taking three or four other courses in a traditional program. Since the instructor in the time-based courses made specific time demands on the students, the students tended to put off doing anything in the self-paced course to work on the time-based courses. This kind of situation could turn off all but the most devoted faculty members, since it would appear as though this kind of a program could not lead to an education of the student. Since we still have the two programs operating in parallel we still have some of this, but not to the extent we experienced in that one course.

All in all, I believe that instructors must be willing to accept controls and demands that have not been characteristic of college level instructors in the past. Will they accept them? I believe that we are rapidly moving to the point where academic institutions are going to be held legally responsible for what transpires in the hallowed ivy walls. Increasingly we hear the word accountability bandied about at the public school level. The State of Colorado passed a law holding teachers and schools accountable for the performance of the students. The issue of educational malpractice is being raised and there are several educational malpractice suits pending in the courts. The days when a college or university could operate with immunity and impunity are coming to an end. The days when an instructor can dismiss the student who failed his course with a "you just don't have it" responses are coming to an end. I do not believe that curricula taught in the traditional way can cope with these kinds of issues. The good instructor contest as a popularity contest will no longer be sufficient. We must examine carefully and closely the instructional procedures that have dominated the educational scene for so many years. Despite the mass of evidence attending to the inadequacy and ineffectiveness of the lecture method of instruction, we cling to this vestige of yesteryear. The self-paced method with clearly specified objectives open the way to deal with the accountability issue of education in a way that is objective and fair to all. The college can specify clearly what the student is to attain and the evidence for the attainment can be made available to anyone. The tremendous cost of higher education at both state and private institutions is pushing all such institutions to consider what they have to offer. Taxpayers and parents are beginning to ask the frightening, embarrassing question of what is being provided for the money expended. If we went to buy a product as expensive as a college education we would ask for some assurance about the quality of the product. We would probably ask for a guarantee in writing. We may not be too far from that situation in the field of education. To meet this demand we must put our house in order or live with the consequences of non-educators trying to do it for us.

The problems of today and tomorrow demand the best educated, not evaluated, individuals. Self-paced instruction provides one approach to meeting these demands. I must admit that I prefer a self-paced program that has no time base at all. There is nothing magical about a fifteen week semester or a ten week quarter. We are in the education business. Our job is to have students learn. If it takes more than fifteen weeks for a student to attain the objectives of a course, so be it. I would hate to go to a surgeon who had acquired the behaviors necessary to cut me open but had not acquired the behaviors necessary to sew me up be-

cause the semester had ended and the instructor had fallen behind schedule and just couldn't get to that part of the course. He couldn't hold the student responsible so he had to pass him.

I should like to close by commenting on another important aspect of these procedures. Learning or the acquisition of knowledge should be fun. It should be positively reinforcing. There are many behaviors that we acquire for which there may be immediate positive reinforcement. Very often there may be a long delay between the acquisition of knowledge and some terminal reinforcer. There may be much knowledge that we demand students acquire that may have no terminal reinforcement. We would like to believe that a student on graduation from college has been shaped to continue the acquisition of knowledge without the benefits of a formal classroom or an instructor. Yet we find that many graduates of colleges report that they can acquire knowledge only if they return to the classroom. I believe a major factor in their failure is that we have had much knowledge accumulated under aversive control. Acquire a knowledge of Shakespeare to avoid failing the course. We need to adopt instructional procedures that are designed to make the acquisition of knowledge a positively reinforcing state of affairs for the individual student. This in no way denies the efficacy of negative reinforcement. It means instead that I believe that by providing positive reinforcement for the acquisition of knowledge, and the elimination of negative reinforcement and punishment, we can increase the probability that the acquisition of knowledge can acquire positive reinforcing properties that can be maintained once the student leaves college. I believe that our program does just that and for that reason, if no other, I believe it is desirable for an entire college curriculum to be taught by some version of the Keller plan.

31

ANNOUNCED REPETITIVE TESTS

Olgierd Celinski

Conventional teaching is essentially an open-loop operation where the flow of information is from teacher to student.

Flow of information in the reverse direction, i.e., from student to teacher (homework, tests, examinations), is used for grading only. While a certain amount of control is exercised through grading, its effects are delayed and imprecise. This lack of control results in an inefficient use of student material, time, and university facilities, and creates a large number of educational problems.

By reversing the flow of information and adding a feedback loop, the instructor produces a "radical" approach[1] to teaching (Figure 1). The main flow, through written work (Announced Repetitive Tests), is from student to teacher; the other direction is used for guiding the student's activity and for a simple on-off feedback which makes fully controlled teaching possible.

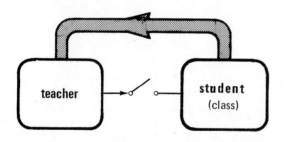

FIGURE 1. Teaching through Announced Repetitive Tests is shown through a quasi closed-loop system with an on-off feedback to control the minimum level of student knowledge. Information is conveyed to the teacher through supervised written work. Each student becomes a well-defined individual in the class.

[1] Olgierd Celinski, *A Radical Approach to Teaching.* Published by the author, 1965. Distributed by the University of Ottawa Book Store, Ottawa 2, Canada.

While in the conventional approach the teacher is a replaceable factor (e.g., by teaching machines or television), here the teacher is an integral component of a control system which makes use of his decision-making abilities rather than of his information-storing abilities.

Control was achieved through the use of Announced Repetitive Tests. The course material was divided into small, logically complete assignments announced to students in advance of the test dates. No restrictions were put on the manner or order of study, sources of information, or the time taken. Each student had to show his command of the material through supervised written work. Satisfactory work was acknowledged without grading, and unsatisfactory work was rejected. In the latter case, the student was required to study the same material, improve its command and repeat the test, with minor variations, until judged satisfactory by the teacher.

This supervised written work provided the workbench on which student weaknesses were eliminated and theory and practice were linked to provide full understanding of the subject and professional command of the material. Thus, a minimum level of student knowledge was being obtained without imposing any upper limit. This work also provided a continuous check on the effectiveness of the teacher's guidance. What was taking place was actually more complex than what is shown in Figure 1.

All these effects together created a situation which offered either a by-pass or a solution to most of the problems of conventional education. Lectures, and the accompanying ceiling on student achievement, have been virtually eliminated by engaging the student in critical and independent studies directly from the information sources. Strong motivation and incentive to work were provided for the student by the necessity of satisfying the teacher's requirements and by the existence of a

From *Engineering Education,* Vol. 58, October 1967; copyright 1967 by the American Society for Engineering Education.

direct intellectual contact with him. The teacher's familiarity with each student's work, and creation of a well-defined minimum store of student knowledge, eliminated the need for examinations, grading, and thus "cramming" practices. Continuous monitoring of student work produced a steady effort resulting in an efficient utilization of time. The ensuing well-founded knowledge of theoretical bases of experiments made it possible for the student to use laboratory facilities with little assistance.

Strong incentive to work, resulting from the student's having the leading role is his own education; intensified interest in the subject, created by the elimination of gaps in student's knowledge; and efficient use of the available time, due to teacher's guidance and control—were all consistently producing a roughly four-fold educational gain. About twice as good command of the material as that in conventional teaching was gained by the student in about half the conventional time.

While this gain in itself should justify the use of this approach, its drawback is the number of students that a single teacher can deal with, which is about 20 a day. However, the full familiarity with student's capabilities, and the professional level of their knowledge which is obtainable with this approach, should make it possible for the teacher to select suitable individuals to teach the subject which they have just completed. This possibility opens up a virtually unlimited source of the best quality teachers, thus making this approach not only a practical proposition, but, above all, a most powerful educational tool.

Of greatest importance for a conventional teacher using this approach is the switch in attitude from regarding oneself as the source of information, to becoming a sink for it; from dealing with the class, to dealing with individual students; from relying on student's assumed knowledge to taking nothing about it for granted.

The method of work resulting from the application of this approach is not unlike a supervision of research and gives the teacher a powerful and fascinating tool for exploring his own subject with the aid of students. It provides a strong driving force for the development of the teacher's scholarship and professional knowledge and frees him from a narrow field of specialization to teaching practically anything that he would like to teach.

Teaching, from an uncontrolled process resulting in a product of random quality—the conventional graduate—can thus be made into one in which scholars can be shaped precisely, and whose academic level can be brought to any desired height. Teaching through the use of Announced Repetitive Tests, seems to be applicable to any discipline and at any level of teaching.

32

HUMANS REDISCOVERED OR, NO THERE WON'T BE A TEACHER SHORTAGE IN THE YEAR 2000

Sivasailam Thiagarajan

One of the most recurrent themes I have encountered in the educational-technology literature is that knowledge explosion, population explosion and the alarming increase in learning force will soon create a pedagogical crisis. Unless one half of the world teaches the other half, there will be a critical teacher shortage. Hence we should make more use of PI, CAI, IPI, CTTV or some other panacea the particular author is selling. The punchline in this logic (everybody having to teach everybody) never struck me as being particularly frightening or absurd or undesirable. "Each one, teach one" has been an ancient and successful slogan in such fields as adult literacy drives. I believe that the idea of everybody teaching everybody could be one of the best solutions to all these explosions. I also believe that we should seriously look into the technique of using untrained nonspecialists for teaching. This belief is based not on a sentimental reaction to automated learning but on the unemotional calculation of cost-effectiveness.

Let's take a look at some paradoxes in the current relationship between human teachers and instructional materials. When Miss Jones uses a film on ecology by Dr. Smith in her third-grade classroom, who is the real teacher? In Heinich's (1970) terminology, the former is the classroom teacher (one who is physically present in the instructional setting) and the latter, the mediated teacher (one whose instructional efforts are preserved in a mediated form). It is obvious that the mediated teacher does the real "teaching" in this particular situation because Miss Jones could be replaced by anyone else who could operate the projector and babysit her class. But it is Miss Jones who wields instructional authority in this situation because she could turn the projector off anytime she wants to, or say, "You kids don't have to remember that!" To remove such tyrannical power from the classroom teacher, more and more programmers and instructional developers are designing completely automated systems and calling them euphemistically "teacher-independent" or "teacher-free" in public and "teacher-proof" in private.

ENTER THE HUMAN

It has been obvious to serious instructional developers from the early days of programmed instruction that complete automation is as inefficient as total dependence on the classroom teacher. What is needed are materials which are deliberately designed to mix the "canned" teacher and the "live" teacher in optimum proportions. There are some instructional functions for which media are superior and some for which men are. Unfortunately, there is a dangerous misconception that media are good only for mechanical teaching and humans are superior for such noble things as guiding, inspiring and teaching higher-level cognitive skills. But, as Heinich (1970) points out, the truth is closer to the opposite. Heinich quotes Riley to the effect that the classroom teacher is not well informed in such areas as child guidance; Bruner to the effect that media have greater motivational power and the necessary flexibility to teach such higher-level skills as problem solving; and Hoban, Dale and Finn to the effect that media are far superior to classroom teachers in facilitating conceptual thinking and development of meaning.

I am not recommending the combination of media and teachers along the lines of the cliche that the former should take care of the dull, routine chores and relieve the latter to truly inspire and guide. Nor am I thinking of a superteacher in the classroom using a slave inside the television tube. I am thinking of a decision process similar to that of media selection in instructional development. There are many instructional functions which human beings can perform more effectively and less expensively than media. For example, even a naive native speaker could serve the *instruction presentation* function with more versatility than any language-laboratory recordings. A parent could decode frowns and other nonverbal expressions of hesitation and confusion and provide the right amount of *prompting* at the right time while even the most sophisticated computer has to wait for the child to make an overt error or a public confession of ignorance. In the related area of providing *feedback*, no computer could monitor oral responses which are so obviously essential in teaching such subject-matters as beginning reading or oral speech. Human beings are also superior in providing a *context for responding* with interpersonal skills. There is obviously something wrong in developing group discussion skills through self-instructional materials. Social praise is a more flexible and a more generalizable *reinforcer* than the candy or the trinket doled out by a machine.

FROM PROGRAMMED INSTRUCTION TO PROGRAMMED INSTRUCTORS

Nowhere has this need for the human touch been more keenly felt and so systematically utilized than in programmed instruction in beginning reading. All popular programmed instructional materials have integrated the nonspecialist human in their instructional system. The teacher's manual for Buchanan's (1963) pre-reading program has carefully sequenced lines for a dialogue with the children. The teacher is warned not to improvise or add to her prescribed lines. Woolman's (1967) teacher's manuals contain precise specifications of desired learner responses and step-by-step procedures for eliciting each of them. The teacher's manual for the *Michigan Successive Language Discrimination Program* (Smith, 1965) programs human instructional behavior without any apologies. The Parent-Assisted Learning Project at California (Niedermeyer, 1969) systematically trains the parent-tutor to work with instructional materials. This technique reaches its maximum efficiency in Ellson's programmed-tutoring systems (Ellson, Barber, Engle and Kempwerth, 1965).

PROGRAMMED TUTORING: HOUSEWIVES AS TUTORS

The programmed tutoring technique has been developed by Dr. Ellson and his colleagues at Indiana University. It is currently being used for the teaching of beginning reading and basic arithmetic to children.

During each 15-minute tutoring session, the tutor interacts with a single child. *What* the child is taught is determined by a content program and *how* he is taught is determined by an operational program. For beginning reading, the content program is based on an existing basal reader and contains sight-reading, comprehension and word-analysis material. The operational program specifies the procedure to be used for helping the child to learn these skills. There are ten different operational programs and each begins with a statement of the criterion behavior to be attained by the child. Following this is a brief description of what the tutor has to do and say to get the child started. This is followed by the *correct* and *incorrect* protocols. The former contains instruction for the tutor if the child accomplishes the task at an acceptable level. The tutor in this case is usually asked to reinforce the child and move on to the next frame. The incorrect protocol uses a branching strategy. It lists different actions to be taken depending upon the type of error made by the child. For example, if the task is to point to a correct multiple-choice alternative, these are the different types of errors:

a. the child does not point;
b. the child points ambiguously; and
c. the child points to an incorrect alternative.

Each type of error is handled with a specific set of prompts. If the child responds correctly during this prompting procedure, the tutor shifts to the correct protocol. If the child makes another type of error, the tutor makes a corresponding shift to a new set of prompts. If all prompts are exhausted before the child gives an acceptable response, the tutor moves to the next *step* of the operational program. This step requires the presentation of the same task to the child, but in a simplified form.

The high degree of the tutor's responsiveness to the individual child's performance suggests that programmed tutoring would be more effective than traditional tutoring procedures. This was found to be indeed true in a comparative study between this technique and another based upon expert opinion (Ellson, Harris and Barber, 1968). Programmed tutoring produced significant improvements in reading achievement scores while the other method had no measurable effect.

The original programmed tutoring team at Indiana University has trained more than 1500 tutors (mostly inner-city housewives) who in turn have tutored more than 15,000 children. The validity of this technique has been established by the fact that it has produced comparable, if not better, results at various centers throughout the country (Hawkridge and DeWitt, 1969). Programmed tutoring kits are now available for almost all major basal-reader series. A basic arithmetic course employing the same technique has recently been field-tested in Indianapolis schools.

Techniques for the preparation of programmed tutoring materials have been outlined elsewhere (Thiagarajan, 1972). The effectiveness of such materials is due mainly to the generation and communication of specific objectives and simplified procedures. Its success is based upon planned cooperation between mediated teachers—reading specialists who develop the programs—and contact tutors—the vast untapped teaching manpower of parents, brothers, volunteers and even the children from the next higher grade.

FROM INDEPENDENT LEARNING TO INTERDEPENDENT LEARNING

Any effective instructional material trains the student in a situation which closely resembles the situation in which he is eventually to perform. A paper-and-pencil program which claims to teach the reader how to swim usually receives the distrust it deserves. But it takes the instructional developers more time to realize the inappropriateness of teaching interpersonal skills to an individual learner in isolation. Israel (1966) has provided a strong rationale for the use of observer-mediated programs in which a second party provides objective feedback on interpersonal skills. Berlin and Wyckoff (1963) discuss diadic teaching programs which are taken by two people in interaction with each other. The *General Relationship Improvement Program* (Human Development Institute, 1963) which deals with perception of feelings in self and others is an example of this type of program. Balakrishna's (1967) program on sex techniques is another diadic program in which two learners—husband and wife—learn together. One of my early programs on how to play cribbage uses a stacked deck and a dual-track program. The learners play through the game, making decisions on which card to play and checking it with the program. Each player's move sets up the "frame" for the next player to analyze. Thus the presence of more than one learner provides a realistic environment for the practice of interactional skills. This fact is systematically utilized in instructional materials which we have labeled "grouprograms."

GROUPROGRAMS: LEARNING TEAMS

Even in the most homogeneous classroom, each student is more "advanced" in some respects than some other students. This suggests the possibility of organizing instructional materials to force a small group of learners to learn from each other. Grouprograms are deliberately designed to exploit individual differences in entry skills and experiences; they have been found especially effective with sophisticated adult learners. Grouprograms are especially useful for helping learners attain higher-level cognitive objectives and decision-making skills. They are equally useful in affective areas. Fink and his associates (1972) have recently developed a series of roleplay exercises and discussion questions which enable small groups of teacher trainees to experience a wide variety of such classroom control techniques as punishment, criticism, demand, use of authority, reinforcement, empathy, humor, probing and interviewing from the points of view of the teacher, the deviant student, the "good" student and the outside observer. The discussion questions enable members of the group to compare their feelings and emotions, discuss the advantages and disadvantages of each control technique and come up with an individual repertoire of behavior management skills. Grouprograms are also useful for integrating individual study of different texts and readings. Following individual study of developmental-testing skills from a programmed text on programming (Thiagarajan, 1972) my students go through a grouprogram simulating such testing situations. This activity bridges the gap between an abstract discussion of skills and the realities of an actual testing situation.

The process of designing and developing grouprograms has been discussed in another article (Thiagarajan, Russell, Babick and Sheppard, 1970). The strategy used in a grouprogram is based upon the fundamental programming principle of successive approximations. In our original grouprogram to desensitize family-planning workers in India toward sex-related terms, we used a set of inexpensive "dirty" pictures and a printed script (Krishnamurty and Thiagarajan, 1967). The first picture shows textbook diagrams of sperm and ova and the script requires one of the group members to lecture on fertilization. The pictures become progressively more "embarrassing," ending up in realistic drawings of the genetalia. Similarly, topics for discussion change from minimal cues to explicit roleplay directions like this one:

> Assume that a woman from the village wants to know how to use a foam tablet. Play the role of a family-planning worker explaining the technique. Use the picture on the opposite

page in your explanation. Remember to use common, everyday terms for sex organs and processes. The other members of the group will take turns playing the role of the woman and ask you questions.

In our recent groupprograms a group of five to eight members participate. The content of their discussion is controlled by a discussion booklet and the mechanics of the discussion, by audiotape. The discussion booklet contains relevant information and lists topics for discussion. The audiotape begins by assigning the role of the discussion leader to one of the members by some random-choice procedure (e.g., the tallest member). This role is reassigned to a different member at the end of each discussion. This leader initiates the discussion, attempts to encourage equal participation by all and keeps the group on task. He adjusts the pace of the discussion to suit the allotted time. He also takes notes and summarizes the conclusions of the group. The audiotape acts as a timer and stops the discussion at the end of the given time. Feedback is obtained by projecting a slide which usually provides a checklist for the group to evaluate the process it went through or a model answer to evaluate the final product.

THE MADRAS SYSTEM: THE LEARNER AS TUTOR

The use of advanced students as tutors for the less advanced is a time-tested device. Ellson (1968) quotes a historic testimonial from James Cordiner's *Voyage to India:*

> On entering the school, you can discover no individual unemployed, nobody looking vacantly around him. The whole is a picture of the most animated industry. . . . The system creates general activity and attention; it gives, as it were, to the teacher the hundred hands of Briarcus, the hundred eyes of Argus, the wings of Mercury.

To explain the mechanics of the system, Ellson (1968) quotes Narendra Nath Law's description from *The Promotion of Learning in India by Early European Settlers:*

> Dr. Bell had for a long time watched the system pursued in the village schools in southern India, and the system which he prescribed for the school in his charge was a variation of this indigenous method. The system is called the Madras System or the Pupil-Teacher System. It consisted in the elder or more advanced

students teaching the younger pupils. The teachers promoted to the next higher class became the taught, and at the next promotion became teachers of the newcomers.

A similar system called the "Monitor System" flourished for some time in England. Eventually both systems were abandoned mainly because of their high cost-effectiveness and resultant abuse.

With the development of effective techniques for generating and communicating specific instructional objectives and for programming tutorial behavior, it is no surprise that the Madras System has been rediscovered in a number of places. Keller (1968 [Article 1]) has independently arrived at a similar method through an analysis of neglected reinforcers in the classroom. A complete system for teaching experimental analysis of behavior at the college level has been developed by Ferster and Perrot (1968) and successfully used by many others in a number of courses. Upon completing a chapter of the textbook, each student demonstrates his fluency with the material by orally paraphrasing it to the instructor or to another student who has been tested out earlier. The content for these tutorial interviews is suggested by study guides, lists of technical terms, outlines and specific behavioral objectives accompanying each chapter. Detailed instructions for the interview procedure are provided in the introduction to the text and illustrated with a number of examples. These instructions cover such topics as how and when to intervene and prompt, how to record errors and omission, how to discourage digressions and rote recitations and how to probe a weak response.

In a course which I assisted in teaching at Indiana University, student-interviewers consistently reported deeper understanding and keener insights. They were motivated to master the chapter in order to ask intelligent questions. The interview provided a review for them. Hearing the same concepts and principles explained from slightly different points of view deepened their understanding. Anecdotal and experimental data from a number of other studies confirm that both the learner and the tutor benefit from the experience.

The Keller Method, or to use its current label, Personalized System of Instruction, has been applied to a wide variety of subject-matter areas, mostly at the college level. I have been experimenting with "something like it" for use in my teacher training workshops and by my colleagues in a high school in India. This variation is yet to be field tested with an entire course. It is currently limited to one or two modules within a course. The system requires *each* student to learn, teach and test the module thus extending the motivational and instructional benefits to those other than the above-average (who usually do not need it). In this system, each student learns the first unit of the module from another student who has acquired the status of a tutor. The learner then takes a criterion-referenced test from a third student who has the tester status. If he fails he returns to the tutor for a session of remedial instruction; if he passes he is promoted to tutor status, his tutor to tester status, and the tester to learner status in the next unit. When there are no more units to be learned, the tester receives the final grade for the module. Of course, the teacher has to prime the entire chain reaction by tutoring the first student on each unit. Further details of this system will be found in a forthcoming article (Thiagarajan, in press).

There are very few brilliant teachers in the world, but a lot of ordinary people. Instead of packaging mediocre instruction in the hope of relieving a part of a superteacher's time and effort, let us multiply him with media and leave the mundane but essential tasks to ordinary people. This should increase the cost-benefit of both regular and alternative forms of education. More importantly, techniques like programmed tutoring, groupro-gramming and the Madras System suggest exciting solutions to the challenge of teacher shortage in the future.

REFERENCES

Balakrishna. *A guide to better love life.* Hyerabad: Center for Educational Technology, 1967.

Berlin, J. I., and Wycoff, L. B. "The teaching of improved interpersonal relations through programmed instruction for two people working together." Paper read at the American Psychological Association, Philadelphia, August 1963.

Buchanan, C. D., *Programmed pre-reading.* St. Louis: Webster Division, McGraw-Hill, 1963.

Ellson, D. G., *Programmed teacher.* Bloomington, Indiana: Psychology Department, Indiana University, 1968.

Ellson, D. G., Barber, L. W., Engle, T. L., and Kempwerth, L. "Programmed tutoring: A teaching aid and a research tool." *Reading Research Quarterly,* 1965, 1 (1).

Ellson, D. G., Harris, P. L. and Barber, L. W. "A field test of programmed and directed tutoring." *Reading Research Quarterly,* 1968, 3(3), 307–367.

Ferster, C. B., and Perrot, M. C. *Behavior principles.* New York: Appleton-Century-Crofts, 1968.

Fink, A., Briggs, A., and Thiagarajan, S. *A simulation program for training teachers in behavior management.* Center for Innovation in Teaching the Handicapped, Indiana University, Bloomington, Indiana, 1972.

Hawkridge, D. G., and DeWitt, K. M. *An evaluation of the programmed tutoring technique.* Palo Alto: American Institute for Research in the Behavioral Sciences, 1969.

Heinich, R. *Technology and the management of instruction.* Washington: AECT Publications, 1970.

Human Development Institute. *General relationship improvement program.* Atlanta: HDI, 1963.

Israel, M. L. Observer-mediated programming: "A strategy for providing response detection for behaviors that are interpersonal and conceptually defined." *Journal of Programmed Instruction,* 1966, 3(3).

Keller, F. S. "Goodbye, teacher . . ." *Journal of Applied Behavior Analysis,* 1968, 1(1), 79–89. [Article 1]

Krishnamurty, G. B., and Thiagarajan, S. *A groupprogram for the desensitization of family-planning workers.* New Delhi: USAID, 1967.

Niedermeyer, F. C. *Parent-assisted learning.* Inglewood, California: Southwest Regional Laboratory for Educational Research and Development, 1969.

Smith, D. E. P. *Manual for the Michigan successive language discrimination program.* Ann Arbor, Michigan: Ann Arbor Publications, 1965.

Thiagarajan, S. *The programming process: A practical guide.* Worthington, Ohio: Charles A. Jones Publishing Company, 1971.

Thiagarajan, S. "Programming tutorial behavior: Another application of the programming process." *Improving Human Performance,* 1972, 1(2), 5–16.

Thiagarajan, S. Madras system revisited: A new structure for peer tutoring. *Educational Technology,* in press.

Thiagarajan, S., Russell, J., Babick, A., and Sheppard, A. "The design and development of groupprograms." *NSPI Journal,* 1970, 9(4).

Woolman, M. *Reading in high gear: Instructor's manual.* Chicago: Science Research Associates, 1967.

33

LEARNING BY TEACHING: A STUDENT-TO-STUDENT COMPENSATORY TUTORING PROGRAM IN A RURAL SCHOOL SYSTEM AND ITS RELEVANCE TO THE EDUCATIONAL COOPERATIVE [1]

Robert F. Morgan and Thomas B. Toy

Before and after testing on the Wide Range Achievement Test (WRAT) over a four month period assessed gains for student tutors and their pupils in a rural school system. 13 tutored pupils (grades 2 to 5) showed a mean net growth advantage of from 3 to 5 months on WRAT subtests over 14 comparable control untutored pupils. 10 student tutors (grades 8 to 12) showed a mean 9 month edge over controls, a gain of 13 months achieve-over 10 comparable control non-tutors. On the three WRAT subtests all experimental means exceeded control means, but only the reading subtest was significant at the 5% level (tutors held a mean 9 month edge over controls, a gain of 13 months achievement in 4 months). Implications discussed include suggesting a much more institutionalized role reversal between teacher and student, student tutoring, and an educational cooperative with graduated salaries and personal involvement for all participants.

Compensatory education often is needed to offset the disadvantage of having participated in traditional education. It is paradoxically true that children have suffered in the last decade both from deprivation of schooling (Green, Hoffman, & Morgan 1967; Green & Morgan, 1969) and exposure to schooling (Kozol, 1967; Neill, 1966, 1960). One contemporary conclusion is that (a) some form of organized education is essential, and (b) a prevalent form of traditional education seems inadequate and damaging.

With growing awareness of these points on the part of parents, educators, psychologists, and youths themselves, recent years have witnessed impressive educational experiments and programs, fresh approaches based on bodies of thought held unapplied by social scientists for decades. As is often the case, the proliferation of such creative efforts far outdistanced systematic evaluation procedures for their assessment (Morgan, 1969).

One approach to building fresh, more effective systems of education is to build entirely outside the traditional school system (Scott, 1969). For example, it is quite likely that much of the success of the Head Start program in its early years stemmed from the independence of its classes and procedures from the regular school's taboos, procedures, and vested interests. Other poverty programs which shared clients with traditional systems were often seen as threatening, especially when more effective, and therefore met enough resistance to make program effectiveness difficult. Without exceptionally skillful direction, such programs became compromised or extinct. The Follow Through program, Head Start placed in regular school grades, has had some rough going in this regard.

---

[1] The study presented in this discussion was conducted by the second author and Mary Toy, under the supervision of the first author, as a Master of Arts thesis at St. Bonaventure University in 1969.

From *The Psychological Record, 20,* 1970.

It has, however, been argued that it is worth difficulty of working within traditional educational systems in order to have some effect on changing the traditional system for the better. While the newer experimental approach may fall short of its goals, the older approach may nevertheless see enough of new procedures to be influenced. What is critical is to distinguish between a compensatory program which retains enough of its innovations to effect meaningful change and a compensatory program so hopelessly compromised that it remains only a financial feeder for the larger system. The present study appeared to be the former case: a program approach, formerly successful outside the school system, incorporated within a highly traditional one. In addition, a systematic attempt was made to evaluate its effectiveness, both for clients and practitioners.

The central focus of the program approach evaluated here was the process of one student tutoring another. This approach is based on a concept of the school child as capable of participating in a meaningful, dignified way in his education. He is seen as capable of learning more than specific content in coursework, but rather as a learner of how to learn. Additionally it was felt that learning how to learn means learning how to teach. Teaching oneself should be enhanced by learning how to teach others. We would therefore be interested in assessing academic progress of the tutors as well as the children taught by them.

Another bias of the authors, undoubtedly permeating the conduct of the program assessed, was the conviction that the school has a responsibility to *all* its children, not just to those who adjust best to the traditional school procedures. For example, student tutors and their control counterparts were volunteers; none were members of the Future Teachers of America. This bias was in general opposition to traditional professional programs in the community (and in education generally) which attempted to isolate certain categories of student for special procedures: classes for the emotionally disturbed, for the retarded, for the disadvantaged, for the "dull," "average" and the "bright" (these last three groups were referred to as the "turtles," the "dogs," and the "rabbits" respectively in one community). The prevalent "weeding out" approach to education, historically rooted in less democratic philosophies than we espouse nationally, results in a fair education with magnificent self concept for a minority at the expense of the majority. Our feeling was that all the children in the system were capable of learning and it was the school's responsibility to bring this about.

Another orientation of the authors which affected the tutoring program was our encouragement of positive reinforcement and internal controls in teaching. The student tutor was not an authoritarian replica of a controlling pedant. Rather, he was encouraged to teach as he would like to be taught—flexibly with participation by both parties. The tutoring method was in distinction to the prevalent practice (although not universal) in the community described by students as fitting Skinner's (1968) conception:

> . . . the child at his desk, filling in his workbook, is behaving primarily to escape from the threat of a series of minor aversive events—the teacher's displeasure, low grades, a visit to the principal's office . . . in this welter of aversive consequences getting the right answer is in itself an insignificant event, any effect of which is lost amid the anxieties, the boredom, and the aggressions which are the inevitable byproduct of aversive control . . . For the child one of the easiest forms of escape is simply to forget all he has learned, and no one has discovered a form of control to prevent this ultimate break for freedom.

Our student tutors were interested in teaching, not in control or punishment. Being older than their students yet sharing their status meant the tutors received both respect and attention from the beginning.. They had no need to force it. This in contrast to adult teachers in many traditional systems whose 'needs for regimentation or power are so immense that even access to the bathroom is given on a timetable or as a reinforcement for good behavior.

The student tutorial program presented here was preceded by several other such projects within the last five years (Cloward, 1966; Goben, 1967; Lippitt & Lohman, 1965; Melaragno & Newmark, 1967; National Commission on Resources for Youth, Inc., 1969, 1968).

The National Commission on Resources for Youth, Inc., (1968) ran a 6 week summer tutorial program in ghetto areas with underachieving 14 and 15 year olds as tutors. The tutoring was loosely structured and the initiative remained with the young tutor. Tutors were paid. On the basis of feedback from the tutored, the tutors, and the community, the program was viewed as successful. Further, the tutor seemed to derive at least as much satisfaction from his experiences as his younger pupil. Goben (1967) reports on a similar program carried on in the East Palo Alto black community. The teaching staff included volunteers from the ranks of teenagers as well as professional teachers. Other community cooperative education projects are illustrated by Lohman (1967) and the growth of "free universities" toward the end of the 1960s.

A pioneering attempt to introduce youth-tutoring-youth programs into a regular educational system is reported by Melaragno and Newmark (1967). Fifth and sixth grade students tutored first grade students in reading. Both tutors and their students were of Mexican-American background and rapport was reported as excellent. Again, benefits were claimed for tutors as well as their younger pupils. Several of the tutors ceased to be "diciplinary problems" to the school. The investigators concluded·

> The tutorial process has great potential for planned development as an educational force . . . However, its impact is likely to remain limited as long as it is a piecemeal program, an appendage to the regular curriculum and teaching procedures, a procedure used mainly for remedial work; rather it must be a means to change the total atmosphere of the classroom in order to eliminate some of the conditions that made remediation necessary in the first place.

Cloward (1966) found his underachieving "homework helpers" identified with their underachieving pupils and made good use of their common perspective. Lippitt and Lohman (1965) ran a program in which sixth graders tutored children in the first four grades of school. They too felt identification facilitated learning. They also felt the tutor's lack of membership in the category of adult professional teacher ruled out his association with past punishments received from some teachers (and generalized to all). Finally, the fact that tutoring on an individual basis greatly increases the time and attention expended on each pupil is pointed out. All of these factors were used to explain what was seen as a successful educational intervention. Unfortunately, neither this program nor many of the others mentioned here were designed for systematic reliable assessment. An exception was Cloward (1966) who both used and recommended objective performance measures. On the other hand, the 1969 report of the National Commission on Resources for Youth, Inc., stated it was "not possible" to accurately evaluate their data as many program participants had dropped the program before post-testing and, further, their program was too brief in duration. They did, however, term future statistical evaluation "essential."

Despite its brief duration (4 months) and occasional drop-outs, the present study was designed from the outset to include some structured methods of assessing effectiveness. It was not felt that control groups and before and after testing necessarily undercut a creative program. Such testing would be included in an evaluation of the following hypotheses:

1. The student-to-student tutoring approach can be systematically evaluated.

2. This approach can be effective in a very traditional rural school system, at least in the case of supervision from within the regular staff (provided in this study by the second author, a part-time school psychologist).

3. This approach can demonstrate significant achievement gains both for the pupils *and* their tutors, as compared to control students, even over a brief four month period.

4. This approach can be effective for the pupils tutored even though the tutors are selected randomly from volunteers of average achievement.

PROCEDURE

Those volunteering to teach and those who were to be taught were each divided into experimental and control groups. For both groups the experimental children were comparable in age and pre-test achievement to the control children. All Ss attended the same rural New York State school system of 12 grades, 479 students. Of the 141 students in grades two through five, 32 were selected by their teachers as needing tutoring. Half (16) were randomly assigned to the student learner group (by random number tables) and half (16) to the control group for student learners. Groups did not differ significantly in age or achievement. Of the 180 students in grades eight through twelve, 26 volunteered to tutor the younger students. Using random number tables, half (13) were assigned to the student aide-teacher group and half (13) to their control group. Again, groups did not differ significantly in age or achievement.

During the course of the study, several students were forced to drop out because of illness, schedule conflicts, or teacher resistance to tutoring in her classroom (two younger children lost in latter case). The final tally of subjects was: Student learners 13, Student learner control 14, Student aide-teacher 10, Student aide-teacher control 10 (there are more student learners than aide-teachers as a few aide-teachers had more than one pupil).

Student aide-teachers were assigned to their pupils on the basis of mutual scheduling convenience for themselves, their pupil, and their pupil's teacher. During the aide-teacher's study hall periods he would spend 20 to 40 minutes per day on an average of 3 days per week with his pupil. Sessions were held in the student learner's regular class rooms behind a two sided screen (4' x 5' to a side) built by the high school wood working shop.

The student aide-teachers received brief initial instructions. They were told their pupils would need a warm, friendly, and accepting atmosphere rather than the heavily structured traditional teaching atmosphere. They were to consult with the regular adult teacher of their pupil to determine what content areas needed most assistance (and to grant the regular teacher some sense of involvement with the tutoring). The aide-teachers were advised as part of their instructions that their pupils would not respond on some days as well as others and that on these days they might relax their focus: just reading or discussing something of interest to their student. Their own ideas on methods of teaching were encouraged within this framework. The psychologist giving these instructions made himself available to discuss these methods as well as to resolve any difficulties possibly arising between the student-aide-teacher and the regular teacher. Teachers, in turn, were requested to maintain a flexible attitude to the aide-teacher invading her classroom, allowing him to use his own methods. Teachers were also given access to the psychologist for those times when these instructions seemed intolerable. (Actually, this wasn't often; most teachers were cooperative if not initially convinced). Finally, the aide-teachers were instructed that their pupil had something to teach them as well as learn from them. Indeed, their pupil was the world's leading authority on *himself* . . he therefore should be allowed to help structure sessions in terms of his own needs.

Those whose random assignment placed them in the control group for student aide-teachers were initially disappointed their volunteering would not lead to immediate teaching. They met with the psychologist and were told assignment was random and had nothing to do with their capabilities. They were assured that they were next in line for a teaching assignment as the program was a continuing one (at this writing it still is). This appeared satisfactory. During the assessed tutoring program's duration, these control students remained in study hall when they were scheduled there.

The control children for the younger student learners also needed some attention (as did their teachers). They too were assured selection was like "tossing a coin" and that they were next in line (for most this turned out to be the case the following year). In some cases teachers appeared to give the control children extra attention to compensate for their deferred tutoring (or as resistance to the experiment). This was not unacceptable to the authors since while benefitting even more children than expected it also biased the results against the hypotheses: significant results would be even more striking (only in the case of two children for whom actual outside tutors were brought in by the teacher were they dropped from the study).

The children in the classroom in which tutoring took place adjusted quite readily to the interruption of routine; teachers felt this created no problem. Further, children who were tutored were regarded by their classmates as lucky; *not* as someone so dumb they needed tutoring. Attention from high schoolers had much status value to the grade schoolers.

Assessment instruments were given on a before and after basis with a 4 month interval in between. School had already been in session over a month when the study began and was terminated before the school year ended, thus not concluding in time with any regularly scheduled exam sessions.

Prior to assignment to groups, all of the subjects were given the 1965 revision of the Wide Range Achievement Test (WRAT) (Jastak & Jastak, 1965) and the Michigan State University Self-Concept of Ability questionnaire (Brookover *et al*, 1962). Four months later this testing was repeated. A questionnaire similar to Brookover's was completed by the homeroom teachers on their personal evaluation of the academic ability of the visiting student aide-teacher. The student aide-teacher's own homeroom teacher also filled this out. Both assessments were made at the end of the study and were scaled for comparison with the student aide-teacher's own self concept of academic ability.

RESULTS

The WRAT subtest raw scores showed significant (t test) gains at the 5% level for both experimental and control groups of student learners. The WRAT subtest raw score gains over 4 months were also significant for the experimental group of student aide-teachers. WRAT subtest raw score gains were not significant for the control group of student non-aide-teachers with the exception of the arithmetic subtest. On all subtests the experimental groups showed greater mean raw score gain than their controls. This was true for the aide-teachers as well as their pupils (see Table 1).

TABLE 1
Change of Tested WRAT Raw Scores: Means by
Group and Subtest Over the Four Month Period

Children selected by their teachers to be tutored (Grades 2-5)

	Reading Subtest		Spelling Subtest		Arithmetic Subtest	
	Pupils	*Control*	*Pupils*	*Control*	*Pupils*	*Control*
Pretest	49.2	48.3	31.7	32.1	27.2	27.7
Posttest	53.2	50.4	35.2	33.8	31.4	29.7
Change	+4.0°°	+2.1°°	+3.5°°	+1.7°°	+4.2°°	+2.0°°
Ss:	13	14	13	14	13	14

Children who volunteered to be student aide-teachers (Grades 8-12)

	Reading Subtest		Spelling Subtest		Arithmetic Subtest	
	Aides	*Control*	*Aides*	*Control*	*Aides*	*Control*
Pretest	55.8	52.7	30.9	31.4	29.0	30.1
Posttest	60.9	54.9	33.9	32.5	32.2	31.7
Change	+5.1°°	+2.2	+3.0°°	+1.1	+3.2°	+1.6°
Ss:	10	10	10	10	10	10

° change is significant at $p < .05$
°° change is significant at $p < .01$

Raw scores of the WRAT were converted into grade level scores for each subtest (see Table 2). The mean grade level increase over 4 months for the experimental group of student learners ranged from 5

TABLE 2
Change in Mean Grade Level in Months on the WRAT
by Group and Subtest Over the Four Month Period

Children selected by their teachers to be tutored (Grades 2-5)

	Reading Subtest	Spelling Subtest	Arithmetic Subtest
Tutored Pupils	5.1	7.1	9.0
Control Group	2.0	2.4	4.4
Net Advantage Tutored	+3.1	+4.7	+4.6

Children who volunteered to be student aide-teachers (Grades 8-12)

	Reading Subtest	Spelling Subtest	Arithmetic Subtest
Aide-teacher Tutors	12.9	9.4	15.6
Control Group	3.9	3.6	10.1
Net advantage Tutoring	+9.0°	+5.8	+4.6

° Change for experimental is significantly greater than change for control at $p < .05$.

months on the reading subtest to 9 months on the arithemetic subtest. The non-tutored control group showed a mean grade level increase of from 2 months on the reading subtest to nearly 4½ months on the arithmetic subtest. Thus, the controls were at or below what growth level would be expected in four months of schooling while the experimental group of learners exceeded by far what growth we might ordinarily expect in that time (nearly twice as much on the arithmetic subtest, for example). The net advantage in growth of mean grade level for the experimental group of learners ranged from 3 to nearly 5 months.

The evidence was therefore that the student aide-teachers were effective in their primary mission of tutoring. What of their own gains? The data show even more dramatic advantage for the teachers than the taught. The mean grade level increase over 4 months for the aide-teachers ranged from more than 9 months (spelling) to nearly 16 months (arithmetic). Their non-tutoring control group showed a mean WRAT grade level increase of less than the expected 4 months on two subtests (reading and spelling) but did show more than 10 months for the arithmetic subtest. In other words, the process of tutoring in just four months showed a mean net advantage of from 4 to 9 extra months achievement for the tutors over their control classmates. There was, however, much variability in the growth rates of individual tutors over the 4 month period of the program; only the 9 month net advantage in grade level for reading was significant at the 5% level.

The group self concepts of academic ability were relatively stable over the 4 months of schooling and did not tend to differentiate the groups either before or after the program. However, the self concept of academic ability of the visiting student aide-teacher is compared in Table 3 with the evaluations made of him by the homeroom teacher of the pupil he visited and with the evaluation made of him by his *own* homeroom teacher. The evaluation of his academic ability made by himself and by the teacher of his pupil are roughly the same. The evaluation of him by his own high school homeroom teacher is significantly lower, on the average, than either of them. Despite very real achieve-

TABLE 3

Comparison of Student Aide-Teachers' Mean Self Evaluation
With Their Evaluation by Their Own Teacher and Their Evaluation
by the Teacher of Their Pupil: Posttest Assessment

Evaluation by	Mean Score	t-test
Themselves	28.9	—
Their pupil's teacher	28.3	0.32
Their own homeroom teacher	23.2	4.39°

Note.—The larger the self evaluation score, the higher the estimated academic potential. Scores can range from 8 to 40 with the average 24.
° significant difference between the two teacher evaluations at $p < .01$

ment gains as measured by WRAT the home room "image" the tutors had in their own teacher's eyes was lower than in their own minds or in the mind of the "colleague," the adult teacher in the homeroom they taught in. Were the tutors more convincingly intelligent when teaching? Was their behavior far different under program conditions than in traditional class context? Was their own home room teacher hopelessly biased by past behavior or stereotyped thinking and unable to see the change? All are possible (probable) but it is an open question.

The program is continuing under the direction of a regular member of the teaching staff. A student is co-director. The rural school itself may properly be labeled conservative and traditional. Yet the emotional feeling toward this ongoing program is positive and encouraging in the main. All four hypotheses stated earlier appear to have been supported.

DISCUSSION

The striking achievement gains of tutors, even greater than for their pupils, needs some thought and further exploration. In this study it seemed identification with the problems and process of teaching someone else did help the tutors motivationally and behaviorally back in their own classrooms. Yet more seemed to be occuring than this stimulus generalization and role reversal of teacher-pupil identity. The tutor also had the opportunity to review content material he had not seen in years in order to teach it, this time to master it fully. Without second chances like these, small deficits in reading or math snowball over the years. They make further education even less rewarding with each succeeding year. This compensatory ploy of teaching content to *really* learn it is highly familiar to the college professor.

Whatever the reason, teaching facilitated learning. It is proposed here, in fact, that children *need* the opportunity to teach *in order* to learn effectively. The time our student tutor spent away from his study hall forwarded his education and his pupil's. Now who will help the adult teacher waiting for him back at the home room?

One such approach is the total change in classroom atmosphere discussed earlier. Something expanding on the shared roles of student and teacher illustrated here such that the undeclared war of mistrust between class and mentor reaches an honorable peace. To do this the teacher must acknowledge her responsibility to all her students while at the same time acknowledging their potential ability to guide their own growth. We propose an educational system which is a joint enterprise between children and adults. Responsibilities, roles, and rewards are shared. The unused pool of talented teaching manpower, the children themselves, are tapped into the learning process. As much as half a child's time in school would be devoted to teaching and related duties (including administration or services). He would teach children younger than himself, and, in the other half of his class time be taught by children older than himself. The adult teacher retains her value to the system: she is the class organizer, curriculum chief, catalyst, and professional consultant to this corporate enterprise (she even maintains an interest in keeping up on her subjects, including learning from her junior teachers). For true sharing in such a system rewards are relevant as roles and responsibilities. Morgan (1969) suggested a graduated pay scale for school systems; one that would increase for all on a seniority basis (number of years in school) and with increments for additional duties or special achievements. Thus, in the system proposed here, they would share everything of concern to their teachers including a paycheck. An unsupported guess is that the drop-out and morale problems would be minimal in such a system. In fact, the huge manpower pool tapped plus the increased outside revenue (for holding more students in school longer) should make such salary payments pay for themselves.

Naturally, teachers in such a system would have to be (or become) unusually secure, confident, intelligent, and creative professionals. Since our children often are limited by the capacities of their teachers, such broad capacity will surely be reflected in all the beneficiaries of the system, particularly the children. It might well be one of the few systems built around the needs of the child *and* the teacher instead of one to the exclusion of the other.

Half the waking hours of life for millions of teachers and children are spent in structured activities which seem devoid of personal meaning or fulfillment. The educational cooperative is one system which attempts to add meaning and purpose to education, something that seems more than a little needed these days.

REFERENCES

BROOKOVER, W. B., PATTERSON, A., & THOMAS, S. 1962. *Self-Concept of ability and school achievement.* Cooperative Research Project 845, Department of Health, Education, and Welfare, United States Office of Education.

CLOWARD, R. D. 1966. *Studies in tutoring.* Social Work Research Center, Columbia University, New York.

GOBEN, R. D. 1967. A school outside of school. *Southern Education Report,* 3, 31-33.

GREEN, R. L., & MORGAN, R. F. 1969. The effects of resumed schooling on the measured intelligence of Prince Edward County's black children. *Journal of Negro Education,* 38, 147-155.

GREEN, R. L., HOFFMAN, L., & MORGAN, R. F. 1967. Some effects of deprivation on intelligence, achievement, and cognitive growth. *Journal of Negro Education,* 36, 5-14.

JASTAK, J. F. & JASTAK, S. R. 1965, *The Wide Range Achievement Test,* revised edition. Wilmington, Delaware: Guidance Associates.

KOZOL, J. 1967. *Death at an early age.* Boston: Houghton Mifflin.

LIPPITT, P., & LOHMAN, J. E. 1965. A neglected resource: cross-age relationships. *Children,* 12, 3, 113-117.

LOHMAN, M. A. 1967. *After school tutorial and special potential development in I. S. 201 — Manhattan.* New York: Center for Urban Education.

MELARANGO, R. L. & NEWMARK, G. 1967. *A pilot study to apply the evaluation-revision strategy to reading instruction in first grade classrooms, interim report.* Santa Monica: Systems Development Corporation.

MELARAGNO, R. J. & NEWMARK, G. 1969. *A study to develop a tutorial community in the elementary school.* Santa Monica: Systems Development Corporation.

MORGAN, R. F. 1969. Compensatory education and educational growth. In R. L. Green (Ed.), *Racial crisis in American education.* Chicago: Follett Educational Corporation, 186-219.

NATIONAL COMMISSION ON RESOURCES FOR YOUTH, INC. 1968. *Youth tutoring youth — it worked.* Neighborhood Youth Corps in-school demonstration project, Manpower Administration Contract No. 42-7-001-34, United States Department of Labor Report.

NATIONAL COMMISSION ON RESOURCES FOR YOUTH, INC. 1969. *Youth tutoring youth.* Final report, Neighborhood Youth Corps in-school demonstration project, Manpower Administration Contract No. 42-7-001-34, United States Department of Labor.

NEILL, A. S. 1960. *Summerhill: a radical approach to child-rearing.* New York: Hart

NEILL, A. S. 1966. *Freedom not license!* New York: Hart.

SCOTT, J. P. 1969. A time to learn. *Psychology Today.* 19, 2, 66-67.

SKINNER, B. F. 1968. *The technology of teaching.* New York: Appleton-Century-Crofts.

34

INDIVIDUALIZED INSTRUCTION IN A LARGE INTRODUCTORY PSYCHOLOGY COLLEGE COURSE [1,2]

C. B. Ferster

This report describes an experiment which applies general principles of operant reinforcement to creating and maintaining new verbal behavior in the classroom. An application of these principles in a class of 79 students of the author's introductory psychology course at Georgetown University has led to an instructional program in which the student completes the course of study at his own pace. The course is reactive to those study behaviors leading to fluent understanding of the subject matter and which guarantees mastery of one part of the syllabus before the student goes on to the next.

The instructional procedures of the course are similar in concept to those reported by Keller (1967 a,b; 1968 a,b) and Ferster and Perrott (1968). The primary procedure of the course is the interview which one student schedules with another after reading a part of the assigned text, usually ten to fifteen pages. The interview is a formal arrangement in which the listener, who has already read that part of the text, uses a timer and listens to the speaker without interruptions. Both students refer to text or notes as they speak. After the speaker finishes talking, the listener comments on how the speaker covered the topic of the text, mentions important omissions, corrects inaccuracies of concept or language, or converses on some aspect of the subject matter. If both students are satisfied that the interview shows mastery of the text, they record the results on a class chart and the speaker finds another student to whom he speaks; if not, the speaker restudies the part and repeats the interview. Each student is required to listen once for each time he speaks. At the end of three to five sections (a chapter), the student takes a brief quiz to demonstrate his mastery of the course. There are five or six versions of each quiz, called written exercises to avoid the pejorative connotations of an examination. The quizzes are taken from essay study questions of which there are typically 10 or 15 for each part or 60 for each chapter. The study questions also give the students a rough guide as to the detail and penetration of study required. The written exercises are graded by the section assistant, and if the essay is satisfactory, the student goes on to do interviews on the next chapter. If it is not, a remedial procedure is discussed with the instructor or section assistant. There is a brief conference with a course assistant or instructor following each written exercise.

The student's grade is determined by how much of the course of

[1] This research was supported, in part, by Grant 32-20-7515-5024 from the Office of Education.

[2] The present experiment grew out of the training program of the Linwood Project (Ferster, 1967) and a course for a small number of graduate students at the College of Education of the University of Maryland. Subsequent to these experiments, the same procedure described here was used successfully by Dr. John J. Boren teaching the same course at the University of Maryland. Similar procedures are being used by the author in all of his courses at Georgetown University. Enrollment in the introductory course is planned for 120 students for the 1968-69 academic year.

From *The Psychological Record, 18,* 1968.

study he completes. A grade of "C" required approximately three-fourths of the amount of study needed for an "A". Complete mastery, however, was required at any level for course credit. There were no penalties for review or repetition of a written exercise. A student who failed to achieve mastery was given special help until the difficulty was diagnosed and mastery achieved. A final examination, a two-hour essay taken from the hundreds of study questions which the student had used in his study of the text, served as a final check on the student's mastery and to formally certify the student for course credit to the registrar.

The course content was defined by 8 Chapters of *Behavior Principles* (Ferster & Parrott, 1968), a text describing general principles of operant reinforcement, articles covering a range of general topics in psychology from the *Scientific American* and chapters on Personality (Lundin, 1966), Measurement (Horowitz, 1966), and Child Development (Smith, 1966). At first the four-credit course met for an hour on each of four days. Later, at the students' request, class time was extended for an additional hour on two of the class periods. One of the weekly class hours was designated for lecture and discussion, but attendance was optional and students could do interviews and written exercises during lecture periods. Lecture periods were spent discussing topics of general interest to the students such as psychoanalysis, study procedures, psychotherapy, and child rearing problems. These discussions served as occasions to demonstrate the use of the experimental language about behavior which the student was learning.

The students were assigned to one of five sections (approximately 17 students in each), each led by an upperclass psychology major who had already been through the course. These course assistants kept the records of the students' progress through the course, scheduled interviews, graded and discussed the results of written exercises, discussed problems and content with students, and kept the course instructor informed about the events in their sections. The course instructor observed all of the class procedures, answered questions or discussed content with individual students, and sought out students who were behind schedule or had special problems. The course assistants met with the instructor weekly to discuss special problems, exchange experiences and consider changes in course procedure.

The course met in a large lecture room with approximately 250 seats. The five sections of the room were identified by large placards suspended from the ceiling at the rear. The course assistants sat at tables in the front of the room or in one of the seats in the classroom. Students moved about the room freely and sat in neighboring seats to carry out interviews. Two students seated close together were not disturbed by the overall noise level of the room; if the noise level was unusually high they put their heads closer together. A nearby classroom was available, however, as a quiet room in which students could study or take written exercises. Three to six students were seen daily in the quiet room. The noise level of the class, a continuous low hum, was not very difficult to overcome. Many of the students read and took written exercises right in the classroom.

RESULTS

Of the 91 students who enrolled for the course, 81 remained after 2 weeks, and 79 completed the course for credit; 90% with A's, 4% with B's and 6% with C's. The final examination, 2 hours long and composed of short essay questions selected from the several hundred study questions the student used in the study of the text, was intended to certify the student for course credit. Although the examination questions were very detailed, nearly all of the students answered them technically and in the same detail as in their original study. Only two people had unsatisfactory final examinations and both difficulties cleared up on retest.

Students went through the course at different rates. Thirty-six percent of the class finished the course including final examination 3 weeks before the end of the semester. Seventy-two percent of the class finished the course including the final examination before the last day of class.

Figure 1 shows the percentage of students doing one, two, or more than two interviews on each of the class days of the course. Taking the class on the average, the frequency of interviews (hence, study) increased as the course progressed. Figure 2 shows percentage of students absent from class during the semester. Although attendance ranged widely, the modal attendance was of the order of 60% or 70%. The day-to-day cycle of absences was probably a result of the students' overall study schedule. The largest number of absences occurred on Fridays and the fewest absences on Tuesdays. Course attendance clearly reflected mid-term and other examinations in other classes. Figure 3 shows the frequency of those students who came to class but did not interview. These students may have read, listened to another student or carried out a written exercise. Except for the two days before and the one day after Christmas, attendance was substantially higher after Thanksgiving than it was for the first 30 class periods. Conversely, attendance at lectures and conversation with the course instructor decreased during this period. The large number of people present but not speaking during the final session were taking the final examination.

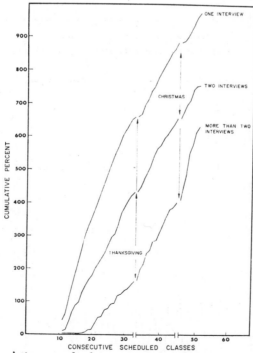

Fig. 1. Cumulative record of interviews showing the percentage of students doing one, two, or more interviews.

Figure 4 contains records for six students who exemplify the range of individual performances that was encountered. Each curve, for an individual student, shows the cumulative number of interviews plotted by consecutive scheduled class periods. Fifty-nine interviews were required to complete the course. A student working at constant rate and finishing the course on the last day of the semester would produce a straight line begining at origin and ending at the intersection of the 50th class period and the 59th interview. To conserve space and to make comparisons between the students easier, all of the curves are placed on the same coordinate by displacing them slightly in the vertical direction. The bottom record is that of a student who dropped the course. For the first month he attended class regularly but for the most part

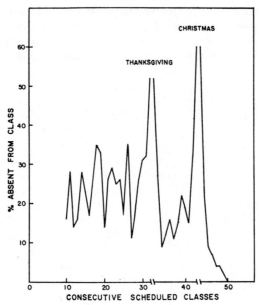

Fig. 2. Percentage of students absent from class.

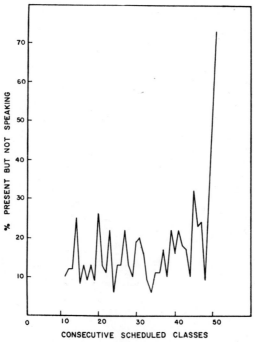

Fig. 3. Frequency of class attendance without interviews.

sat in the rear of the room reading. The course instructor had several conferences with him, in which the student appeared very depressed and anxious, and to be having difficulties with all of his courses. The course instructor introduced him to several of his classmates who were at the same stage of the course as he, inquired of his progress weekly, and discussed study habits and methods with him. The rate of progress through the course increased as did his mood and level of social activity in class, but his rate of progress was still not high enough to complete the course by the end of the semester without jeopardizing the rest of his courses which he possibly could pass by studying for the examinations. For this student there would have been merit in extending the course limit indefinitely. The experience of study leading to mastery

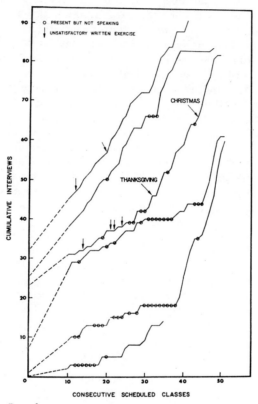

Fig. 4. Cumulative curves of interviews for individual students.

and the successful completion of a course at the "A" level might have been a significant experience for this student.

The second curve from the bottom is for a student who did very little during the first half of the semester, finishing the course with a sustained period of activity near the end. The open circles on the first part of the graph show that this student did most of his studying in class for the first part of the semester. When asked, during the 38th class period, about his performance, he replied that he was occupied with "other things" and that he would soon begin working on the course.

The third curve is for a student who decided to settle for a "C," or who increased his rate of work too late. The large number of classes which the student attended but in which he did not interview suggests that he was doing little out-of-class study during most of the course.

The fourth curve is characteristic of most of the students. Progress is slow but steady until Christmas when the students hit a rate of work which completes the course approximately on the last day of classes. These students appear to be pacing themselves.

The top two curves are for two students who worked at a sustained pace from the start. The student represented in the top curve finished the course several weeks before the end of the semester. The student represented in the 5th curve was absent from class for several weeks just before the end of the semester, probably to study for another course.

When a written exercise given after a chapter did not show mastery, the section leader conversed with the student about the topics in the written exercise. If the student appeared to be competent orally he was allowed to go on, despite the incomplete or inaccurate written exercise, to the interviews of the next chapter. Since the student's deficiency was in written communication rather than content, he was asked to do another exercise on the material he had just mastered orally to give him practice in writing. Most of the students quickly learned to do written exercises that matched the level of their oral fluency. Conversely, those students whose written exercises did not show enough mastery of the course were also unable to speak competently in conversation about the content covered by the written exercise. With these students, the section leaders discussed the interview procedure and the student's study activity and asked that the interviews on the chapter in question be repeated. If the student continued to have difficulty in speaking accurately and fluently about the current chapter, the section leader or the course instructor listened to an interview and helped the student restudy (on the spot) those parts of the sections not adequately enunciated during the interview. For most students several experiences at this level developed the study behavior needed to speak fluently about the course content. For a few students it was necessary to reduce the assignment to half sections (about 1200 to 1500 words) so as to give them the experience of mastery after sustained intensive study behavior. Otherwise it would have been impossible for these students to complete the course within the semester. These students were also having great difficulty in completing assignments in their other courses.

DISCUSSION

The interview is probably the experience in the course primarily responsible for the student's fluent active speaking repertoire. It provides an experience, closely following study activity, which exposes the new performances acquired as a result of study of the text. Because the student speaks in detail about a small amount of text (approximately 3,000 words), there is a fine-grain relationship between the student's interview performance and the study behavior that preceded. The speaking student is his own listener and reacts to small differences in the fluency, accuracy, and depth of coverage of his presentation. This differential reactivity of the student to his own speech reinforces those aspects of his study activity with the text which produce a competent vocal essay. Most students developed improved study skills which they extended to other courses. Besides providing fine-grain differential reinforcement of study behavior, the interview also is a motivational device. The interview helps maintain the student's overall activity in the course because it exposes at frequent intervals his progress through the course. Many students reported that the speaking experience during the interviews increased their ability to express themselves elsewhere and improved their social ease.

The listener's role in the interview is mostly to make it possible for the speaker to speak, since it is almost impossibe for most people to speak alone. The listener cannot reinforce the speaker's behavior in as much detail as the speaker himself, who is reacting to his own speech continuously as he speaks. Therefore, the decision about the adequacy of the interview came from the speaker rather than from the listener. Most students improved their style of study as they noticed small deficiencies in their performance during the interview. When the quality of the interview did not improve over several chapters, some kind of remedial experience was used, such as restudy or study methods. The student's perceptiveness about his own performance was probably due in some part to the absence of penalties in the interview.

Just as the speaker is his own listener, the listener may be talking to himself as he listens. The listener is particularly able to take part in such a silent conversation because he has himself just been engaging in the same behavior as the speaker and hence could have as easily said the same things. Because of these latent verbal behaviors, verbal stimuli from the speaker can prompt verbal performances which would otherwise need to be composed and emitted. The listener, therefore, is free to combine verbal behaviors from a wide variety of past experiences with those prompted by the student who is speaking. Students often report that they combine behaviors from their common personal experience with the vocabulary and content of the interview in a way that would not have been likely otherwise.

It was important that the speaker not be interrupted during the interview lest the frequency and fluency of the speaker's behavior be progressively reduced. The speaker's behavior is weakened by interruptions because they are aversive or because they supply prompts which shift the control of the speaker's behavior away from the preceding study behavior with the text. The listener took written notes to remember the interview and commented freely after the interview, refraining however from tutoring the speaker. Comments were consciously limited to attempts to strengthen, rearrange, recombine, or supplement behaviors already in the speaker's repertoire. Otherwise, the interaction would weaken the speaker's subsequent study behavior.

The Written Exercise

The written exercise given after each chapter was a conventional test rather than an exposure of the entire repertoire as in the interview. Although these tests were given frequently, they provided only a sample of the student's language from which the instructors could judge technical accuracy and fluency. The tests were used, therefore, as diagnostic information for certifying the student's progress through the course, and as a basis for suggesting remedial procedures. Because the written exercise only sampled the student's performance, it was not designed to reinforce the actual study behaviors that are required for proper comprehension of the course content. There was not sufficient point to point correspondence between the study behavior and the written exercise to produce such a delicate result.

The main point of personal contact between the student and the section leader was the conferences about the student's test essays. These conferences were effective because they occurred frequently enough that the student could adjust his conduct in stages and a part at a time. The undergraduate assistant, recently a student himself, contributed to an effective interaction because he had a repertoire very close to that of the student. The interaction between the student and course instructor over the written exercise probably prevented a drift in the student's criterion of course mastery.

The Role of the Course Instructor

Much of the course instructor's work needed to be done before the course started. The student assistants had to be appointed and trained; texts that could generate mastery without rote memorization needed to be selected; the amount of text required of the student needed to be defined carefully because the student was required to master it all at a high level of comprehension; study questions needed to be written for all of the materials and their frequency and thematic content designed to define the depth of penetration that was expected of the students; criteria for grading needed to be established and procedures arranged for introducing the students to the course procedures; record forms and charts had to be prepared for taking data of the student's progress in the course, for a permanent record, and for display to the students.

Once the course began, the course instructor's time was used flexibly. Free time was needed to observe the class and to listen to selected interviews. Individual students aproached the instructor in class with questions or for an opportunity to converse, but most students were concerned largely with acquiring mastery and credit for the course through study, interviews, and written exercises. Lectures were well attended at the start of the course, perhaps as a carry-over from students' past course experience and because of interest in the instructor's style. Attendance for lectures finally settled at 8-15 persons, usually those who were on schedule. It is probably best to schedule lectures and free discussion at a time that does not compete with the course activities that bring the student toward completion of the course requirements.

Just as students who were making good progress through the course sought out the instructor in lecture, discussion and casual conversation, the course instructor sought out those students who were lagging or otherwise having difficulty. Discussions were held individually with these students to find out why progress through the course was slow, or to find the reason for other difficulties. When a particular problem was identified, the course instructor continued to monitor the student's behavior by direct observation and interviews, and by conversation with the section leader.

The Design of the Text

Although the basic operation of the course did not depend on any special textual material, almost half of the course was based on *Behavior Principles,* a textbook whose design came from a self-conscious application of principles of reinforcement. *Behavior Principles* was composed under close control of an actual reader, who interviewed students who had studied a draft of a chapter of the text. When it appeared that an incomplete interview was due to a defect in the text rather than student's study behavior, a tutorial was carried out which then served as a guide for rewriting or adding to the text. Often the tutorial provided the actual language for the text revisions. The behavior generated by the interview put the writer closely under the control of the reader since he had detailed evidence of the behavior that the text generated in the student. The division of the chapters into parts, topographically by headings and page separation, and functionally by the study questions and interviews, had significant motivational effects. The small sub-units within chapters made the study experience more reactive than would be the case if the study unit were larger. Theoretically, each interview reinforced a small fixed-ratio schedule of reinforcement, and the successive interviews within a chapter were conditioned reinforcers leading to completion of the chapter.

Most of the study questions were in the form, "After reading this part, you should be able to . . . ." They were designed to instruct the student how to study each part of the text. At one stage of study, for example, a student would be expected to describe a reflex and an operant technically. At another stage the student might be expected to comment theoretically about operants and reflexes, saying just how they differ, what sources of confusion are, and reasons for making the distinctions. The actual facts the student analyzes might be very similar in the two cases, the differences being mainly in what kind of study behavior the student engages in. The study questions were numerous enough so that they had a point to point relation to part of the text, sometimes as small as a paragraph or two. Like the interview, each study question served as a conditioned reinforcer for the part of the text it defined, contributed to the reactivity of the study experience, and served as an instruction for the kind of study required of the student.

Abstract thinking was developed first by teaching the student the component performances and then rearranging them under the control of general statements. Thus, when the concept of chaining is introduced in Chapter 7, the student can already speak fluently about many sequences of performances and stimuli. For example, he can describe a pigeon pecking a key as a sequence in which only pecks of a certain form are followed instantly by a stimulus. He can say why it is necessary for the stimulus to follow the exact performance which is to be reinforced, and he can describe the behaviors which are controlled by this stimulus and which make possible the next performances in the sequence. When the student can discribe these and other similar sequences of performances and stimuli, new verbal stimuli such as "a chain," "conditioned reinforcer," and "discriminative stimulus" are introduced and his existing verbal repertoire is brought under their control by rearrangements appropriate to the concepts. In other words, the direct objective description of the behavioral events in plain English precedes the description of these same events in technical language. Theory is introduced even later, after the student has fluent control of the technical terms. A theoretical article by Skinner (1953) in Chapter 13, for example, was designed as a reinforcer for all of the chapters that preceded. The student could read such a chapter easily and meaningfully because he had already acquired all of the component behaviors from the preceding chapters. The article, which would be very difficult for the beginner, was easy and familiar for a student who had been properly prepared by the preceding text. Such a way of developing abstract thinking is the reverse of the procedure of many texts which state a principle first and then generate a few examples to illustrate it.

Each part of the text was designed to reinforce the behavior developed from the parts that went before. This was done by carrying the repertoire from each chapter forward with increased levels of abstraction and interaction with other terms and concepts. The development of abstract terms in stages, as described above, contributed to the cumulative effect of the text, in which the behavior that the student acquired in one chapter or section contributed to or even made possible this behavior in the text. Thus schedules of reinforcement from one chapter is a necessary repertoire for the chapters on stimulus control, which describe procedures in which intermittent reinforcement is an important component.

The course which is described here changes the usual role of the student and professor. The student, who in the conventional classroom listens to the professor, now becomes an active participant who demonstrates the competence he acquires from his study of the course materials. The professor, instead of conveying the course content to the student by speaking to him, arranges a verbal environment that recognizes the student's achievement and is reactive to it.

Although it was not necessary to lecture to the student to convey the course content to him, a limited number of lectures proved to be useful as a model of the repertoire that the student is trying to achieve and as a way of exhibiting the professor's style. Experience in this course confirms F. S. Keller's (1968) observation that about four or five lectures of 20-40 minutes each is an optimal amount of exposure of the professor's repertoire. Testing has a role different from the traditional lecture-examination teaching environment. Instead of a small sample of the student's behavior designed to test differences among students, the tests and interviews examine the student's repertoire in detail and depth so that he may go on to a next part of the course when he achieves competence in an earlier part.

An important by-product of the experimental classroom was the positive identification it encouraged with the professor and the course assistants and the acceptance of the objectives of the instructional system. In such a course, the role of the professor is that of an ally who helps the student to master the content and concepts needed to certify him. Since the criterion for certifying the student involves a single high level of quality it was seldom necessary to take disciplinary action and the occurrence of a low grade was the student's decision, not the professor's. Informal contact with the teaching staff also contributed to students' positive identification with the course. Because the professor was continuously in the classroom and not occupied conveying the content of the course, he was free for casual and informal interaction with the students during class. Many student contacts also occurred with the course assistants. As a result there were very few visits to the professor's office despite an open door policy.

REFERENCES

ARMINGTON, JOHN C. 1966. *Physiological basis of psychology.* Dubuque, Iowa: William C. Brown Co.

FERSTER, C. B., & PERROTT, M. C. 1968. *Behavior principles.* New York: Appleton-Century-Crofts.

HOROWITZ, LEONARD M. 1966. *Measurement.* Dubuque, Iowa: William C. Brown Co.

KELLER, F. S. 1967. Engineered personalized instruction in the classroom. *Revista Interamericana de Psicologia,* 1, Pp. 189-197. (a)

KELLER, F. S. 1967. Neglected rewards in the educational process. Proceedings of the 23rd American Conference of Academic Deans, Los Angeles. (b)

KELLER, F. S. "Good-bye, teacher . . ." *J. appl. behavior Anal.,* 1, 1968, Pp. 79-89. (a) [Article 1]

KELLER, F. S. In press. New reinforcement contingencies in the classroom. In *Programmierte Lernen* (Wissenschaftiche Buchgesellschaft, Darmstadt, Germany). (b)

SKINNER, B. F. 1959. Some contributions to psychology as a whole. *Amer. Psychol.,* 8, Pp. 69-78.

SMITH, CHARLES P. 1966. *Child Development.* Dubuque, Iowa: William C. Brown Co.

35

STUDENTS ARE A LOT LIKE PEOPLE!

S. N. Postlethwait

Professor Postlethwait has achieved wide recognition for his work in designing audio-tutorial programmes of instruction in biology. The system was started several years ago as an attempt to make some adjustment for the diversity of backgrounds of students in a freshman botany course (S. N. Postlethwait *et al., The Audio-Tutorial Approach to Learning,* Burgess 2nd Ed. 1969).

Using Mager's work (R. F. Mager, *Preparing Instructional Objectives,* Learon 1962) as the educational basis of his programmes Professor Postlethwait has designed with his colleagues a number of courses and has stimulated others to experiment in other fields. However, it is evident to those of us who have discussed his work with him that Professor Postlethwait's success is largely due to his readiness to appreciate the students' problems and points of view. As the article that follows indicates, he has himself adapted to the new methods and feels that both he and the students benefit from the change.

If audio-visual methods are to have any lasting beneficial impact on teaching, teachers must be prepared to adapt themselves to changes in their own methods when these are appropriate. Professor Postlethwait's experience shows what can be done and the difficulties which must be overcome in the process.

Bernard Chibnall
University of Sussex

The technological revolution is met with mixed emotions by both educators and students. The reason is relatively simple—people do not like to be replaced by machines and people do not like machines as a replacement for people. Education is more than an information dispensing and absorbing process. It requires a comradeship of sharing and exchanging of experiences and an excitement that grows from common interests and hopes between teacher and student. Most of us can trace our interest in a specific topic to the inspiration derived either directly or vicariously from some other human being.

Does this mean that one must reject the utilization of all technical devices in the development of an educational system? Far from it! Properly used equipment may very well enhance the personal relationship between student and teacher. Some of our most effective and powerful lessons are learned from teachers whom we have never seen but with whom we have a fellowship derived through some spanning medium such as the written word. Clearly this written 'bridge' between teacher and student has been a great boon to all of mankind and, until recent years, has been our only link to many of the great teachers of the past. Fortunately, technology has expanded our potential for even more intimate access to great teachers and with greater facility. The dimensions of audio and visual now can be preserved and retrieved in fantastically convenient vehicles. The imagination of man for utilization of these devices individually or in combination with the written word and/or tangible items is one of the major limiting factors in education today.

If one uses the educational model proposed by Hopkins of a 'student on one end of a log and a teacher on the other' the role of technological devices becomes more clear and less foreboding to many of us. The purpose of technology in this context is to 'capture' to the greatest degree possible the events or activity between the 'good teacher' and student in a one/one relationship, so that the product can be duplicated to accommodate many students in a close approximation of the original situation. With today's audio and visual devices it is possible to involve the student with nearly every exposure to the subject conceivable. The programme can contain tangible, printed, audio and visual materials in any combination in which the 'good' teacher wishes to use them. The only limitation is the capacity of the

From *University Vision,* No. 8, January, 1972.

teacher and student to relate to the simulated situation.

In 1961 at Purdue University a programme was begun which has been called the Audio-Tutorial system. The basic philosophy of this system is very simple. A 'good' teacher is asked to assemble the items he would use to teach one student and, while sitting among these items, to record on audio tape the conversation he would have with one student as he tutored that student through a sequence of learning activities. The product—the tape, tangible items, visuals and printed materials can be duplicated as many times as necessary to accommodate any number of students. Obviously the programme produced in this way will be limited by the cleverness of the teacher but the corollary is also true—a clever instructor can intimately involve the student in important and useful learning activities. The student now has access to the clever instructor in more ways than through the written word. Subtle communication through connotations by inflections in the voice are provided by the audio tape and the tangible, visual and printed materials assembled can exhibit the full skill of a great teacher to involve a student in a sequence of learning activities or a 'symphony of learning.'

The Purdue programme evolved slowly. The first programmes were mere lectures on tape and relied on audio as the sole medium of communication. Later, other media were added including tangible items (live plants, models and equipment for experiments), printed materials (textbooks, study guides and journal articles), and visuals (2 × 2 slides, 8 mm film and photographs). Study programmes were set up in booths in a learning centre which was open from 7:30 am until 10:30 pm Monday through Friday. Students came in at their convenience and spent as much time as necessary for them to master the lesson. An instructor was available at all times to help students on an individual basis if necessary. This study session was referred to as an independent study session (ISS).

Two other study sessions were included in the system: 1. a general assembly session (GAS) and 2. a small assembly session (SAS).

The GAS was scheduled on a weekly basis for one hour. It included several hundred students in a large lecture hall and involved them in the kinds of activities best done in a large group. Specifically, this assembly was used for major tests, long films, help session and an occasional lecture.

The SAS included eight students and an instructor and was scheduled on a weekly basis and used primarily for short written and oral quizzes. It served in an administrative role and for the identification of students with a specific instructor in the large unstructured course.

The course structured in the above pattern provided a full range of learning activities and situations. The ISS permitted students to enjoy some important features of a learning system that are not commonly available in a conventionally taught course. Some of these include:

1. *Repetition.* There is little question but that the nature of many objectives requires repetition for their achievement. However, repetition ought to be engaged in in an intelligent fashion and adapted to the individual needs of a particular student. In a course with 500 students the teacher cannot possibly make the adjustments in repetition for individual student need. Only the student can determine intelligently how much repetition is necessary.

2. *Concentration.* Most classrooms are not organized to permit students to concentrate during their study. Students are distracted by one another, and other dissociated events which may be occurring tend to distract the student's attention from the subject at hand. The audio-tutorial system permits the student to isolate himself from the surrounding environment by covering his ears with the earphones and by the use of other media to reduce his awareness of his surroundings.

3. *Association.* In a study of plant science the major objective is to learn about plants. It makes sense therefore, that a study of plants should be conducted where plants are available for observation. Diagrams, charts, models, photographs, and other such devices should be a means to the end so that students' attention is directed to the actual plant. The audio-tutorial system provides an opportunity for the student to have an object available at the time he reads about it, does experiments, etc.

4. *Appropriate sized units of subject matter.* People vary considerably in the amount of subject matter that can be grasped in a given amount of time. Programmers have demonstrated that most people can learn almost anything if it is broken into small

enough units and the student can take time to become informed about each unit before proceeding to the next. Any programme of study therefore should provide each student with an opportunity to adjust the size of the unit to his own ability to assimilate the information, so that those who can absorb large quantities of information may do so in an unrestricted fashion, whereas others who must proceed more slowly are permitted to do so. The audio-tutorial system allows the student to proceed at his own pace and to break the subject matter into units commensurate with his ability.

5. *Adapt the nature of the communication vehicle to the nature of the objective.* It is logical that no simple vehicles such as lecturing or a textbook can achieve the full spectrum of objectives for a complex subject. The student's experiences should not be confined to any particular vehicle as film, audio tape, text book, or lecture. In cases where the development of a procedural skill is necessary, there is no substitute for the student doing this procedure himself. A properly structured course, therefore, would carefully define objectives and not try to mould objectives to fit a favourite medium (lecture, for example) but instead would use the medium best adapted to the nature of the objective.

6. *The use of multi-media.* Individuals differ in their responsiveness to different kinds of communication devices. Some people learn well through reading, some can learn best by auditory communication, and others can learn best by literally handling specimens and performing experiments. The audio-tutorial system thus provides an opportunity for subject matter to be covered in a great variety of ways with the student exploiting the medium which communicates most directly and effectively for him.

7. *Finally, and most important, the integration of learning activities and situations.* It stands to reason that if learning events are to be complementary and to have some relationship, they should be brought into close proximity and properly sequenced. The conventional structuring of a lecture, recitation, and laboratory does not take this into consideration but rather may expose a student on Monday to a lecture concerning a given subject; perhaps on Wednesday the student does experiments related to that subject; on Friday a recitation will involve the student in some exposure to the subject: and then on Sunday night, late, the student may read on this subject from the text. The audio-tutorial system permits the student to bring all of these learning experiences into an integrated sequence so that each learning event may enhance or complement the adjacent ones and thus result in a 'synergistic' effect.

The individual nature of human beings cannot be over emphasized. Any good educational system must be based on the fact that 'learning must be done by the learner.' It must involve him (the student) in the process and must always provide a high degree of flexibility and adaptation to individual needs. However, superimposed over this quest for individuality is the dependence of each student on teachers to guide, facilitate and stimulate him to engage in appropriate learning activities. Today's technology provides new dimensions to accomplish this and, when these new tools are used properly, they provide more intimate access to the teacher—they do not dehumanize!

36

SELF-PACED INDIVIDUALLY PRESCRIBED INSTRUCTION

Lee Harrisberger

Self-paced individually prescribed instruction is an optimized learning activity in which 90% of the students can earn an A level of achievement—a cost-effective program of high quality that provides a creative challenge and rewarding experience for the faculty.

What! 90% Get A's?

Absolutely! What should one expect of the top 10% of the high school class? Engineering has been privileged to attract the top students, yet engineering teachers find it hard to accept the fact that the best brains in the country should all be able to make A's. It is almost unbelievable that engineering educators can take this highly selected, intellectually superior group of students and decree that they are capable of averaging only a C level of attainment in any engineering course. It is common practice to accuse a professor of offering a "snap" course if more than 10% make the top score, and it is not uncommon to count the number of failures at the end of the term as a figure of merit for the quality and rigor of the class.

Everyone laments the decline in engineering enrollment and agonizes over the reduction of engineering graduates in the face of the increasing demand for them. Engineering teachers shake their heads in dismay because half of the engineering freshmen quit the first year. They get upset when some tactless counselor tells engineering freshmen: "Take a good look at the guys on either side of you, because only one of you is going to make it." But, it is true that only one out of three engineering freshmen will get an engineering degree!

What if it were possible to devise a teaching scheme that would guarantee success for at least 90% of the students? Pure chaos would result. The grade-point average would be out. The national honorary societies would be of no consequence, because almost everyone would qualify. Industry recruiters would have to find some other way to identify "the top men." The faculty would be hard pressed to decide who should be "permitted" to work for a graduate degree.

More significant than upsetting the traditional index of social stratification are the consequences of having 90% of all engineering students doing A work! Practically no one would fail, and few would be motivated to transfer to some other field. Therefore, with little change in the number of entering freshmen, the graduating class would increase almost 300%! And the graduates would be A students! This phenomenal increase in production and quality of accomplishment might even be achieved with the existing staff and facilities. In most engineering schools, the upper-level courses have only about a third of the enrollment of lower-level courses. Obviously, administrators will immediately recognize a huge potential for "cost effectiveness." On might as well speculate that faculty salaries could be doubled, too! There are even some fringe benefits to having an entire class of A students—material and enrichment activities there was never time for before. The challenges would be without precedent.

Enough of this idealistic daydreaming. Anyone who has taught in an engineering school knows that 90% of the class will never make A's. It has been demonstrated over and over again that the most conscientious efforts at planning, lecturing, and writing good examinations result in an almost symmetrical distribution of performance, with the class average centered at the C level. No matter whether the students have above-average college entrance scores, 7-10% will fail, 7-10% will make A's, and the rest will be at the "mean" level of performance, in spite of the teacher's best efforts. No one can deny this inevitability; it is apparent that as long as educators continue to teach as they do it will exist.

Dr. Harrisberger is Head of the School of Aerospace and Mechanical Engineering, Oklahoma State University. He is also Editor of ERM, the newsletter of the Educational Research and Methods Division of ASEE. Professor Harrisberger currently is a member of the ASEE Board of Directors as Vice President and Chairman, Council of Sections West, and is the immediate Past-Chairman of the Publications Policy Committee.

There is a Way

There is a motive behind this speculation of a fantasy world wherein most of the students can succeed with a *A* level of achievement. Ample evidence now exists to prove that there *is* a teaching model that will indeed make it possible for 90% of the class to achieve an *A*. It has been successful at all levels, from kindergarten through senior level in college. Over 200 public schools involving more than 200,000 students are now using this new teaching approach to learning. A number of universities and colleges have one or more courses converted to this model. It appears to be one of the most revolutionary teaching concepts in the past 4,000 years.

This new technique is called "self-paced, individually prescribed instruction (IPI) or "The Process Approach to Teaching." It succeeds because it is explicitly tailored to the basic learning characteristics of the student. Educators have finally discovered that they are teaching *students*, not courses! The IPI course is not designed logically, but psychologically! Its sole objective is to create the most efficient path for the student to follow in order to make a lasting change in his behavior.

The Basic Strategy

What brought all this about? Psychologists have been watching students. They noticed that the students acted and reacted in certain patterns. Forthwith came a flood of learned reports documenting some fundamentals of education:

1. The lecture is dead! Investigations show that information communicated verbally without involvement has a short retention span; students who attend lectures perform no better than students who do not; lecture classes fail because students are in a passive, nonparticipating role; and lectures in courses requiring higher cognitive skills are notably less effective.
2. Instructor-dominated student discussions are less effective than student-dominated discussions.
3. Students have different learning styles. This refutes the age-old premise that all students in a given classroom are identically equal in background and ability to learn and therefore should be able to learn at the same rate. A student learns best when given an opportunity to explore the topic in more than one way and at his own speed, starting at his own point of preparation.
4. All learners must have frequent reinforcement and rewards. Learning efficiency increases with frequent and repeated opportunities to evaluate progress, with immediate diagnosis of the results.
5. A student's peers are more effective tutors than his professors.
6. Retention increases with involvement. Hence, student team-project activity involving problem solving of real situations is a powerful means for enhancing the relevance of acquired information and developing lasting synthesis technique.
7. Audio-tutorial tapes as a self-study aid are more effective than interviews with the instructor. There is no social pressure or embarrassment in admitting stupidity to a tape deck; it is also more accessible and repeatable than a live professor.

These are at least some of the highlights. An excellent source for more information is W. J. McKeachie's, *Teaching Tips* (Wahr Publishers, Ann Arbor, Michigan).

The Fiendish Plan

The effective, self-paced IPI course is developed by constructing "a hierarchy of behavioral objectives." Translated, this means that the whole course is divided into a group of minicourses, or units. Each minicourse has a clearly stated objective. There is a simple strategy in the writing of good statements of these objectives. Each objective must be described in performance terms, indicating what the student must do that can be observed and measured to show that he knows. All statements can be written with only a few "do" verbs such as demonstrate, describe, list, derive, select, etc. The key is developing an objective that requires the student to perform an observable act.

Actually, self-paced IPI is analogous to the Boy Scout merit badge approach: to get the Eagle (*A* grade), a Scout has to demonstrate competence in 21 merit badges (minicourses). Each merit badge has an instruction manual describing what the Scout must be able to do (performance objectives). It outlines practice and suggests ways to get help, outlining the practice exercises to do and the standards that have to be met when the Scout tries for the badge (competency test). It is totally self-study. The Scout can get all the help he wants from anyone. He can take as long as necessary to get ready, and he can take the test when he thinks he can pass it. He can take the test over again until he can do it right, and he can take the test for as many badges as he is competent to earn, any time he is ready.

A flow chart of all the minicourses is designed to arrange each of the study tasks in proper sequence. This assures that first things are learned first and that the following tasks capitalize on and reinforce the material learned earlier. A good reference for learning to define instructional objectives is *Preparing Instructional Objectives* by Robert F. Mager (Fearon Publishers, 1963).

For each minicourse the instructor constructs a series of *assessment items* and a *learning activity package* (LAP). The assessment items are just a list of things for the student to do to show that he has learned something, i.e., practice tests which help the student check his competency. The LAP is a batch of materials containing all the things to practice in order to meet the objective of the minicourse. Actually, it is a "do-it-yourself" manual. It provides the unique opportunity to devise more than one way to succeed.

The student should have anything that will help him. More than one self-study aid should be provided—audio tapes, models, video tapes, laboratory demonstrations, library references, programmed instruction materials, computers, sample tests, seminars, etc. Where differences in student learning styles can be accommodated, mechanized self-study aids and media can be effectively and efficiently employed to assist the learning process, instead of the teaching process.

Getting It Done

Equally as important as the design of a self-paced IPI course is its management. The first reaction to the idea of all students going along at their own pace with no scheduled classes is that it will degenerate to chaos and that students will procrastinate and never do anything. This will happen if the instructor does not pay attention to his role of programmer, counselor, manager, and chaplain.

Here are some clues on how to operate an effective, self-paced IPI course. Let the student work at his own pace, but require him to see the teacher at least once a week to report progress and competency. Keep a progress chart for counseling him and evaluating his success rate. Punch a card for each minicourse completed and let the computer keep track of it (an excellent opportunity to use computer managed instruction techniques). Give him a work contract:

(a) When he finishes all tasks, he gets an *A*. Permit him to take the test on all of them the first day or any day up to two full terms.

(b) At the end of the first term, if he has not completed all the tasks, he may receive a lesser grade based on the percentage of tasks completed, with an option to try for the *A* by an agreed-upon deadline. If he does not accomplish a minimum number of tasks by the end of the term, he receives a *W*. If he elects to try for the *A*, he gets an *I* until he completes all the tasks. If, by the contract deadline, he has not yet completed all the tasks, he may receive a final grade based on the number completed.

(c) He must show continuous progress or receive a *W*. There are no *F*'s in IPI courses—only non-achievement.

Everybody Wins

This is a system in which everybody benefits: the students, the faculty, and the administration. Self-paced IPI optimizes the learning opportunity for the student, provides a means for documenting teaching effectiveness for the faculty, and is an economical program of high quality.

From the student's point of view, it provides a host of opportunities and benefits:

1. He can pretest through the course hierarchy until he reaches his level of proficiency. That is, he can begin where he is ignorant.
2. He can move at his own pace, with unlimited opportunity to practice and develop the skills required.
3. He can test his competency at any time and as often as he needs with immediate diagnostic feedback.
4. He has more opportunity for personal contact with his professor.
5. He is graded on the basis of achievement only.

6. It is a no-fail learning environment, with no penalty for not achieving. It is success-oriented, ego-building, morale-boosting, and attitude enhancing.

This unique teaching program also provides a challenging and rewarding creative experience for the faculty:

1. The hierarchy of minicourses makes it possible to create multiple learning paths for each learning task. All available resources can be used to enrich the learning experience.
2. There is tremendous flexibility. Since the course is divided into many study units, a variety of media can be employed as learning aids.
3. The individualized diagnostic evaluation of student performance in each learning task provides continuous feedback on the effectiveness of the instructional strategy. Weak programs can be continuously upgraded.
4. Self-pacing creates an opportunity to use computer management routines to monitor student progress and course effectiveness.
5. The individualized evaluation techniques provide more opportunity for one-to-one interaction between the instructor and the student.
6. It provides an excellent opportunity for documenting teaching effectiveness and certifying the achievement of the students.

From an administrative point of view, this teaching model is also most efficient:

1. Effective IPI courses can be designed and implemented on a "do-it-as-you-go" basis. Most IPI courses are developed by repacking available materials.
2. The use of media is optimized, being used only for those units where it can be effective. There is little waste from ineffective utilization.
3. The reduction in mortality and the increase in level of achievement show a significant increase in the productivity of the course.
4. The efficiency of using peer students as proctors makes it possible for one professor to handle 100 students per course with essentially the same investment of time required for teaching one conventional course of 20 students.
5. The highly organized nature of the IPI model provides an excellent opportunity to develop a reward system for recognizing teaching effectiveness.

Join the Crowd

The motive behind all this verbiage is to get teachers to believe that if they do not take this opportunity to improve their teaching, they will be obsolete. It takes courage to change one's teaching methods, but more and more educators are using IPI courses in universities. There are over a dozen self-paced courses at Bucknell University, four physics courses at the Massachusetts Institute of Technology, several courses in engineering at the University of Texas, Kansas State University, University of Arkansas, University of Missouri at Rolla, University of Nebraska, and the United States Naval Academy, among others. Oklahoma State University has implemented a continuing series of three-day faculty workshops to prepare its faculty to implement the self-paced IPI model. To date over 200 faculty members have attended the workshop, and a host of IPI courses have been and are being instigated. The feedback from the instructors involved in these pioneering efforts is almost frightening:

1. When there is a choice between an IPI class and a lecture class, the students who have been in IPI will choose IPI.
2. One IPI course was examined by a national panel of professors and was found to contain the equivalent of two semesters of high-quality content. The students taking the course completed it successfully in an average of 57 contact hours. Even more frightening, five of the students decided to change their major to that of the course!
3. On the average, 75% of the IPI students will complete the course with an *A* level of achievement 2-6 weeks before the end of the term. The remaining 20% complete it within a 6-week period beyond the term.
4. Retention studies have shown significant increases in ability among IPI students when compared to students in the conventional teaching model.
5. IPI students show a reinforcement of positive attitudes toward the course, higher motivation, and increased level of performance.

It is obvious that self-paced IPI shows a tremendous potential. It involves a set of fundamental premises that are applicable to any discipline and any instructional objective. The implementation allows unlimited opportunity for the instructor to accommodate every resource that is available or that he can create. It can be implemented with the administrative pattern of any university without any special legislation of new rules or procedures. It can be designed, implemented, and operated within current budget limitations.

Because of its flexibility and its dependence on the professor for its design and implementation, its success or failure depends heavily on the ability of the professor. The truly dedicated teacher who believes that student achievement is the goal of the educational process, and who is motivated to try harder, should use the self-paced IPI method. △

Section V

History and Theory

The last five papers recount the background, historical and theoretical, of how PSI developed. There are some obvious changes between the first and last papers in this section, both in procedure and theoretical emphasis.

The attempt to design an instructional system which specified procedural details within the context of a theoretical base was deliberate. The ingenious specific examples of gifted teachers generally fail in translation as no more than eclectic gimmicks. Broad inspirational goals, *cum* philosophy, too often fail as procedural maps for teachers who simply ask "what do I do now?" We need specific suggestions linked to a *system* that allows extrapolation and transformation. The appropriate blend of specific prescription and general theory is a tricky mix for which we did not then, and do not now, have a formula. We were convinced that a teaching method which did not contain something as detailed as procedure sheets on the one hand and as abstract as learning theory on the other would be insufficient.

I would only add that these papers unfortunately slight the contributions of three individuals. Two of these, Carolina Martuscelli Bori and Rodolfo Azzi are Brazilian professors and were our colleagues during the early 1960s. They considered themselves our students but were in many ways our teachers during the Brazilian years. The passing reference to them in these papers is in no way appropriate to the important role they played in the development of PSI. It should be clearly acknowledged that their contribution was equal to ours. In a speech entitled "Snapshots from the Album of a Behavior Modifier," delivered at the Third Annual Southern California Conference on Behavior Modification in Los Angeles in October, 1971, Keller gives us an intimate account of that collaboration:

> The entry in my diary for the 29th of March, 1963, reads as follows: "Rodolfo, Carolina and Gil arrived yesterday . . . from Washington. . . . They were all filled with their trip, which seems to have been quite a success.

At Boston and Cambridge they talked with BFS [B. F. Skinner], Dick Herrnstein, Murry Sidman, Peter Dews and Og Lindsley. . . . At Brown, they met Posi Pierrel, Harold Schlosberg, Don Blough, Loren Riggs, and others; at Washington, they visited I.B.R., Walter Reed, Maryland U., and talked with many—Ferster, Boren, Brady, Findley, Mausi [nickname of a Brazilian at I.B.R.], *et alia.* We discussed the trip and ended with an exciting session on the problem of 'how to teach.' Rodolfo's presentation of Charles F[erster]'s thinking led us around to a tentative decision on the procedure to be used in Brasilia—a procedure that combines the features of Psychology 1-2 [Columbia's first course] with . . . BFS's Natural Science course at Harvard and CBF[erster]'s Behavioral Technology set-up at I.B.R. Details must be worked out, but the course of training promises to be one of the most exciting and most radical ever given in a university setting."

This entry doesn't half convey the action of that evening—the arguments, the quiet spells, the slow emergence of a plan, the final agreement, the elevation of our spirits, and the sleeplessness that followed. That evening, if you will pardon the expression, I was hooked. I struggled against it as best I could. After my friends had gone, I tried to do some work in the animal laboratory, but the odds against me were too great.

The third person who should be singled out is Dr. Charles Ferster, mentioned above in the section from Keller's diary. He met us often, listened for longer than we had any right to expect, and then unfailingly pointed out the critical points in our rambling discourse. It was in large part his patience and insight that led us from undifferentiated notions to an articulated system.

37

A PERSONAL COURSE IN PSYCHOLOGY

Fred S. Keller

I would like you to imagine that you have recently agreed to help establish a department of psychology. It is to be complete in every respect, with all the major specializations and at every level of training from the first course to the most advanced, in a university that is just being formed, and in a country where no such department now exists. Together with four young psychologists and former pupils as co-workers, you are expected to take a constructive part in procuring a complete staff, purchasing equipment, outfitting a library, designing a department building, and—especially—developing a curriculum of study. You have been assured of financial and moral support, and you have been told to be as bold and experimental as you wish in the program you adopt.

Imagine, too, that in a few months, you will have awaiting you, at the university's opening, a group of perhaps 100 students, fairly well grounded in language, mathematics, arts, and the other sciences, who want basic psychological training. You and your colleagues, with a few assistants, working in temporary quarters and with limited facilities, are expected to introduce them to psychology and to carry them thereafter as far as they may want to go.

To start you on your way, you and your colleagues have spent a month or more in visiting colleges, universities, hospitals, and research centers, where psychology is taught in one way or another. You have talked with interested teachers and researchers about your problem; you have examined shops, laboratories, libraries, classrooms, and clinics. You have taken notes on everything and tried to extract from every experience something of value for your project. You have bought some books and ordered some equipment. And you have sat down together at the end of your travels to decide upon your next objective. What is it going to be?

Under such conditions, I suggest that your first concern would be the introductory course and those 100-odd students who will be enrolled therein. There is only *one* introductory course, and it is, or should be, a key course and a foundation for the work to come. While teaching it, you and your co-workers can prepare for the courses that immediately follow. At the same time, you can begin your search for a distinguished staff of teachers at the more advanced levels. These new teachers will, in turn, help you design and equip your workshops and laboratories, stock your library, give form and clearer purpose to your program, and, finally, help you design your building. Right now, your job is to get ready for those 100 young men and women who will be there to greet you when the school bell rings.

But what sort of first course will you teach? There's much talk today of an educational re-awakening; much dissatisfaction throughout this country with our aims, our methods, and the results we now achieve. Will you try to export a course that is under fire at home? Perhaps you, yourself, have complained about the failure of your teaching—talked about the inefficiency of the lecture system, the evil of examinations, the meaninglessness of letter and number grades, the short-term retention of course content, and the rigid frame of hours, days, and weeks within which each course of study is presumed to fit. Perhaps you have even expressed a willingness to change these things, if you could only escape from the "system." Now you have your chance. What are you going to do?

The kind of course I'm going to suggest has never been taught. It won't work. It conflicts with the natural tendencies of man. It has nothing new about it. Even if it worked, it could only teach reinforcement theory. It might be all right somewhere else, but it won't go here. And I think you will find, in the last

Paper read at American Psychological Association, Philadelphia, August, 1963.

From *Control of Human Behavior*, Vol. 1, R. Ulrich, T. Stachnik and J. Mabry (eds.), Scott, Foresman and Company, 1966.

analysis, that it is against the law. So, having anticipated some of your criticisms, let me tell you more about it.

It is a course with lectures, demonstrations, discussions, laboratory hours, and "homework." The lectures and demonstrations are infrequent and primarily inspirational: Ideally, they are interesting, informative, and memorable—even entertaining. Once the course has started, they are provided at suitable places along the way, but only for those students who have reached a point that guarantees an appreciation of their content. For students who do not qualify until a later date, a recording of the lecture and, if possible, the demonstration, is available. Attendance at either lectures or demonstrations, however, is entirely optional, and no examination is based upon them.

Discussions, with one's peers or with an instructor, or both, are provided at certain times for those students who desire them and, as in the case of lectures and demonstrations, if they have earned the privilege. These discussions are also recorded and may be listened to again by any of the participants. Needless to say, the discussions are never to be used as examining devices by the teacher. They are primarily for the student, who has won the right to ask questions or to express himself with respect to the work he has been doing in the laboratory or at home.

The laboratory work itself begins on the second or third day of the course, and is its most important feature. Each student has his own private and well-equipped little room or cubicle, for a certain time each day (say an hour and a half), on five or six days of the week. There he works alone, or perhaps with a partner, under the general supervision of a laboratory assistant who has no more than nine other students in his charge at the time. The student's daily task begins when he has qualified for it—for example, when he has turned in a report of the preceding day's experiment, answered two or three questions on the last reading assignment, studied a description of his laboratory mission for the day, or done all of these things.

The experiments themselves are carefully planned to let each student discover for himself the operation of certain well-established principles of behavior; to teach him some basic skills in the use of equipment and the treatment of data; and to lead him from minimal to maximal responsibility in the writing of reports.

When a laboratory task has been completed (and *only* then), the student receives the assignment that will prepare him for the next. This is his "homework." It may include textbook study—plain or programmed; the reading of an article or technical report, carefully edited or supplemented to make it fully clear, and provided with a few key questions like those he may be asked at the beginning of his next laboratory session; and other readings may be given solely as a reward for work completed and to whet the appetite for more.

Besides preparing him for further laboratory missions, lectures, demonstrations, and conferences, this "homework" is intended to broaden the student's perspective by teaching him to generalize from the laboratory to many other situations of human life. It aims to encourage thinking in the direction of both research and practical application. And, finally, it is meant to provide the student with at least a nodding acquaintance with the great variety that goes by the name of psychology today.

The assistant's functions in such a course are very important. He is the one who prepares and checks equipment, collects reports, passes out work material and assignments, and records, in each student's individual log-book, each important step along the route—including the time of arrival and the number of set-backs, if any, before reaching port. He will also collect any student complaints, requests, comments, or suggestions (in writing), which he then passes on to the course director or other designated person.

The teachers, in a course like this, are not as conspicuous as they were under the old order. Their work-load and responsibility, however, are as great as before—especially during the first year's operation. They are the ones who design, in every minute detail and, initially, for just one student, each day's teaching program; and they are the ones who re-design this program in the light of student performance and assistants' reports. They must also stand ready to give an occasional lecture or preside at a demonstration; they must sometimes be available for conference or discussion with qualified students; and they must be prepared to read an occasional student paper. Their general loss in visibility to their students, which might be aversive to long-time performers on the classroom stage, is perhaps offset by the improved reception of their messages when given and, more generally, the increased status of their academic position.

When all the course requirements have been met, the course is at an end. At this point, the student's log-book is examined by the course director, who records the achievement, places the book in the department files, and takes a few moments, perhaps, to offer his congratulations. No final examination is given, no course grade, no reward for speed of attainment, and no punishment for delay. Examining and teaching were inseparable parts of the same educational process; and something better than a letter or a number is available, in a list of the goals that were reached and the time it took to reach them. The student is ready for Course No. 2, a new log-book, a new cubicle, a new assistant, a new body of fact and skills, and, probably, a new teacher. But this is not, at the moment, our concern.

I have sketched for you, during the past few minutes, a more or less imaginary first course in psychology, and I have suggested its more or less imaginary origin. More or less. Pilot research in this kind of teaching is already going on at several places in this country, although not exclusively aimed at first-course needs; and a full-scale test is now being planned for the first course itself, along the lines I have suggested here, at the new University of Brasilia, in Brazil, beginning in 1964. If success attends these ventures, it might well be that some such personal-course method of instruction could be applied in other sciences and at other levels of education.

38

NEW REINFORCEMENT CONTINGENCIES IN THE CLASSROOM?[1]

Fred S. Keller

In 1963, at the Philadelphia meetings of this Association, I outlined a new type of introductory course in psychology. I suggested how the plan for this course originated; and I mentioned that several try-outs of its basic procedure were either in process or prospect. Today, you have heard of the first attempt to teach such a course within a regular academic curriculum, at the new University of Brasilia, in 1964. It will be my part in this symposium to describe a similar application of reinforcement theory to the problem of teaching, but within a different academic framework.

When the plans for the Brasilia venture were made, it was felt that the time was not ripe for a similar effort within a North American setting. We thought the obstacles would be too great. We did not see how we could circumvent the "laws" prescribing the number of lectures and class meetings per term, the amount of compulsory attendance, the frequency of grade reports, or the dates of examination. Even if such rules were held in abeyance, we did not see how such a course could be taught without a strain upon the budget—without a corps of costly assistants, an expansion of working space and facilities, and at least a temporary reduction of the standard teaching load.

We now know that some of these fears were groundless, and that most of the obstacles were surmountable. With a few changes in one's thinking about the basic course requirements; with a reasonable degree of departmental flexibility and permissiveness; and with a well-disposed university administration, it *is* possible to offer a highly individualized mode of instruction within our own brand of mass education.

During the past semester, at Arizona State University, two variations of such a course have been taught—one by Professor J. G. Sherman, who had an active initiatory role in the Brasilia program, and the other by myself. These two try-outs

were designed, like the one in Brasilia, to let each student advance, at his own pace, throughout the entire course, mastering each successive part to the level of perfection, without losing any of the educational values that presumably accrue from lectures, demonstrations, conferences, discussions, and laboratory exercises. Our try-outs led to similar results, but since they differed in details of procedure, course content, and staffing, I shall describe here only my own attempt.

Ninety-four students, from two sections of a one-term laboratory course in elementary psychology, made up the original group to be instructed. Most of these students were in their first or second university year, and all of them had chosen to take the systematic course designed primarily for departmental majors. The group included both men and women and supposedly represented a wide range of intellectual capacity and achievment.

The staff for this course, in addition to the instructor himself, included a laboratory assistant and a classroom assistant, the normal complement for two class sections. To these were added ten proctors—five men and five women—selected from the top twenty of the preceding term's best students in a course having the same subject-matter, but taught in a conventional manner. They were fully acquainted with the background and aims of the new course, and they expected to work without pay. (Their services were later recognized by the University with a small hourly wage.) Eight of them served for the entire term, but two were forced to withdraw from the group in order not to fall behind in their own course work.[2]

In preparing for this venture, the textbook material of the preceding term's course was broken

[1] Paper read on September 5, 1965, at the Chicago meetings of the American Psychological Association.

[2] I cannot omit naming these faithful abecedarians, whose work proved so vital to the successful operation of our course: Stuart A. Culbertson, Joanna D. Driskell, Donald D. Eklund, Kenneth K. Graham, Norman D. Hamer, Heather J. Koger, Jacob J. Seyffer, Jr., and Helena B. Verhave. Also to be recognized with gratitude is the splendid work of our graduate assistant, Susan Anderson.

down into 20 units of work, as nearly alike in difficulty as could be estimated in advance. Each unit corresponded roughly to a standard homework assignment. An informal, one-page handout was prepared for each of these assignments, suggesting things of special importance to be looked for in the reading, clarifying ideas that might cause difficulty, and linking the unit to those that had preceded or would follow. For each assignment, also, a "readiness" test was constructed, with at least one alternate form. For the early units, such tests usually included 15 to 40 items of a true-false or fill-in type, with perhaps one essay question added. With the later ones, nothing but short-answer essays might be called for. Finally, for many of the units, mimeographed "bonuses" were prepared: Pavlov's autobiography, a selection on memory and its improvement, a readable article on behavior therapy, and so on. These were "enrichments," not assignments; no examinations were based upon them.

A series of lectures and demonstrations was also planned, with each one to be given at some natural break in the course, and only to students who had earned the right to attend by passing a given number of units. Arrangements were also made to record the lectures and hold over some of the demonstrations, so that late qualifiers could get them if they wished. No quizzes were based on either the lectures or demonstrations. Their aim was "motivational," with attendance optional.

No provision was made, in this first attempt, for incorporating laboratory exercises within the program of units. Instead, the procedure was the same as that used regularly for other sections of the course. Each student's laboratory work was condensed within a two-week period at some time during the semester. It was conducted and evaluated independently of other parts of the course.

At the first meeting of the class, a lecture was given on the course's origins, aims, and expectations. Each student was then given a mimeographed *Foreword*, telling him how the course was to be run, what the duties of the staff would be, and how he might best behave in order to guarantee success. Then he was introduced to his proctor, from whom he received his first reading assignment. He was encouraged to use the classroom as a study-hall when no lecture or demonstration was being given, and he was told to report to his proctor whenever he felt he was able to pass his first test with a perfect score.

With this much introduction, we got under way. We met our students on Tuesdays and Thursdays, for 75-minute periods, as in the preceding semester. After a few weeks, however, these meetings were supplemented, at the students' request, with a two-hour session of study and testing every Saturday morning. At about the same time, a box for questions, comments, or complaints was introduced within the study-hall. Students were encouraged to use this box with complete assurance that their contribution would go directly to the instructor and receive his personal attention.

The course testing was done by the proctors, usually in a nearby classroom, but sometimes in the study-hall itself. Immediately after each test, the questions were taken back and the answers examined. If all were correct, the student was given his next assignment, along with any bonus material he might have earned. If one or two errors were made, he was given a chance to defend his answers before being turned down. In case of any dispute at this time, which was rare, the matter was passed on to the assistant for a ruling. If the test was failed, the proctor discussed it briefly with the student and sent him away to prepare for an alternate examination, usually with advice on areas that were in special need of more study. An account was kept of each test and each decision. This was passed on, at the end of each class period, to the classroom assistant, who had charge of all records, tests, assignment sheets, and other materials. Each proctor ordinarily tested his own students; but during periods of increased demand, or on Saturdays, he was sometimes replaced by another proctor or by the classroom assistant.

When a large enough number of students (say 50% of the class) had passed a certain number of units, a lecture or a demonstration was provided for them. As I mentioned earlier, attendance at such performances was not compulsory and no quizzes were based on them. They were usually announced several days in advance. Ten lectures or demonstrations were provided during the term. In addition to these, two discussion meetings were held for a small number of students whose progress seemed to entitle them to special attention.

To conform with University practice, a final examination was given at the end of the term, and letter grades were provided for all students. The examination questions were drawn entirely from the readiness tests, with each of the 20 course units equally represented. Twenty-five percent of each student's grade was based on this examination; 25% more was based on his laboratory work; and 50% of his grade depended on the number of units passed during the term. If all 20 units had been passed, his course-unit grade was *A*; if 19 units, it was an *A-minus*; if 18, it was a *B-plus*; and so on. Students were given the option of taking an *Incomplete* in the course if they had passed less than 20 units by the end of the term. This Incomplete could be removed during a special two-week post-Commencement session of study and testing, or during the next University term.

Shortly before the end of regular classes, a questionnaire was constructed and given to all those students in attendance. Twenty items were included, to each of which a student could respond without revealing his identity; and an opportunity was afforded at the end for further expressions of opinion by anyone who so desired. Additional opinions of the course methods were solicited by the instructor in brief interviews with students who completed the course prior to the semester's end.

The outcome of our study can be described in different ways and from different points of view. If we begin with letter-grade results, we find the following distribution. Forty-one of our original 94 students received a grade of *A*; 13 received *B*'s; one received a *D*; and three got *E*'s—that is, they failed. There were no *C-* students in the group, although two members of the class who transferred to another section did receive this rating. Fifteen of the group never showed up, or withdrew at an early date for reasons not all of which are known. The remaining 19 took Incompletes, 10 of which were changed to letter grades during the special two-week session. Nine students will presumably take up the course again in the fall, at the point where they left off.

The more important revelations of the *questionnaire* were as follows. This method, in comparison with that of the usual lecture or lecture-and-laboratory course, requires a greater mastery of work assignments—46% of the group said *much greater*, 45% said *greater*, and 9% said *about the same*. It requires as much or more memorization of detail—19% said *much greater*, 38% said *greater*, and 22% said *about the same*. It involves greater understanding of basic principles—44% said *much greater*, 41% said *greater*, and 14% said *about the same*. It generates a greater feeling of achievement—33% said *much greater*, 46% said *greater*, and 13% said *about the same*. It gives greater recognition to the student as an individual—55% said *much greater*, 33% said *greater*, and 4% said *about the same*. And it is enjoyed to a greater extent—48% said *much greater*, 32% said *greater*, and 17% said *about the same*.

It also appeared that, as the course progressed, there was an improvement in study habits; an increased confidence in ability to master assignments; an increased desire to hear lectures; and a positive change in attitude towards test-taking. The percentage values, in terms of the five-point scale, are almost as convincing on these matters as on those already mentioned.

With respect to the study-proctor relation, 94% of the class reported that the discussion of tests with the proctors was helpful, or very helpful; 79% said that the proctor's non-academic, personal relation to them was important or very important; and 90% felt that the use of proctors in giving, grading, and discussing tests was desirable (64% said *very* desirable).

Thirty-four students added comments at the end of their questionnaire. Three of these can be construed as negative, at least on minor issues. The remainder were positive in tenor, often enthusiastically so. Eight students suggested that other courses should be conducted in a similar way. In general, these comments simply confirmed their responses to the questionnaire items and gave further support to opinions already conveyed to the staff in one way or another during the semester.

It now seems quite clear that our method, even in its rudimentary, unpolished form, produced an unusually high degree of educational control. Initially, this control had aversive overtones, associated with the inevitability and the rigor of the unit tests, the strangeness of the new procedure, and, perhaps, the new freedom from customary constraints. Within a few weeks, however, it took a more positive form. The prevailing atmosphere of the course became one of industry, cooperation, good humor, and self-respect. There was an obvious pride of accomplishment, for the slow students no less than the fast ones. The testing itself appeared to be welcomed, even enjoyed; and each new assignment was treated as a badge of distinction. In fact, the interest in passing tests and securing fresh assignments got to be so great as to interfere with attendance at lectures. The *privilege* of listening to a lecture seemed to be a more important reinforcer than the actual listening, and many pearls of wisdom were not collected by those who had won them.

There are many reinforcement contingencies that operate to bring about this educational control in the classroom situation I have just described. No one of them is really new, although the combination is perhaps unusual. Very significant, it seems to me, are those that pertain to the student-proctor relation. The role of the proctor is vital and, in some respects, to be envied. As an upper-classman, he enjoys a status, both academic and social, which is denied to graduate students and faculty. It is easy for him to be the kindly, understanding, big brother, whose good will is much desired, whose advice is seriously taken, and whose word can be law. With every test that he prepares to give, and with every discussion of its outcome, his own knowledge is strengthened and his counsel is made more effective. He cannot be blamed for difficult assignments or badly-constructed tests; he simply helps repair the damage that they may have done. If he is severe in grading, it is for the student's own good, either in later tests or on the final examination. And he is curbed from over-leniency by the awareness that his success depends finally upon the success of his charges. A better method of teacher-training is hard to imagine. It is not surprising that last year's students want to be this year's proctors, and last year's proctors want to be proctors again.

Other contingencies should be obvious. One of these is the stepwise procedure, whereby each work unit follows upon success with the one preceding and takes the student one step closer to his goal. Another is represented by the systematic nature of the course material, wherein each new concept is based upon others to which the student has already been exposed. And so very few, if any of the positive contingencies found within conventional teaching procedures are absent from this one.

On the other hand, many of the *negative* features are missing, or greatly reduced in degree. Among these are the threats that arise from half-understood lectures, from partially-mastered reading assignments, from periods of classroom inattention (or thought), from class absences (for whatever reason), from 'grading on the curve,' from prior test failures, from an interest in extra-curricular activities, or from impersonal treatment by those in whose hands one's educational fate may rest.

Many improvements in our method can still be made. The laboratory exercises must be integrated within the sequence of units; the conflict between lectures and test-taking must be avoided; the tests must be increased in variety and must include more review questions; study-hall and testing conditions must be bettered; and so on, and on. We have just begun.

As for the range of application of our method, the future will define the limits, but recent short-term try-outs (by Professor J. L. Michael) suggest that it may be used successfully with students both above and below the college level. With respect to further developments, it is premature to speak. Yet, you will forgive me, perhaps, if I dream of a day when education for all students—old or young, bright or dull, in our own country or abroad—will no longer be wasteful, ineffective, and hated; and when teachers everywhere will merit respect and affection.

39

APPLICATION OF REINFORCEMENT
PRINCIPLES TO A COLLEGE COURSE [1]

J. Gilmour Sherman

To speak before this audience, it would be comforting to have prepared a new theory of education or a data-rich analysis of current instructional methods. I have neither. I can only describe for you a course we have been teaching in a somewhat unorthodox way; which is still in transition; which relates directly to an experimental analysis of behavior but is shot full of hunches; and which we are at a loss as to how to evaluate with anything approximating even the minimum standards of rigor we demand in our own research laboratories. However, those of us involved are excited by what we see—namely, students working and learning—an experience we now find we had seen very rarely in the past.

It is difficult to describe what we are doing now, apart from a brief account of the rather strange route by which we arrived at our current practices. In 1962, while teaching at Columbia, I was invited to go to Brazil to teach at the University of São Paulo. During the previous year, Professor Fred Keller had taught at São Paulo, offering there for the first time a course in learning-reinforcement theory. The Brazilians proved to be a receptive audience, and while psychology as an experimental science departed from their traditional presentation of the material within the context of philosophy, an animal laboratory was established and supported with enthusiasm.

During my second semester at São Paulo I was invited, with two Brazilian colleagues, to organize a department of experimental psychology at the new University of Brasilia in Brazil's new capital. Two aspects of the Brasilia situation provided a unique opportunity to take a fresh look at our normal habits of teaching. First, no economic limits restricted our thinking and money was made available in large quantities. Second, since the very notion of the new university was to depart radically from traditional Latin American educational institutions, all rules had already been broken. No established university regulations of any kind existed to confine our procedures. The President of the University made it very clear that we were free, in fact encouraged, to do exactly as we pleased, to be as bold, radical and experimental as we wished. An unusual challenge, I think you will agree.

The first thing that pleased us was to come to the United States, re-enlist Professor Keller in the service of the Brazilian flag and set out on a tour of North American universities to observe, question, gather suggestions and listen to complaints. If our month of conferences uncovered anything approaching a unanimity of opinion, it was an expression of general dissatisfaction with the traditional ways of teaching. Some of our colleagues questioned the packaging of knowledge in lecture-hours, weeks, and semesters, arguing that these units bear no relation to specific stages in the learning process. A bewildering array of deficiency "make-up" examinations and advanced-placement tests (to take two extremes) indicates that our timing system is not working very well. Many questioned the efficacy of the lecture method itself. Others questioned the usefulness of examinations, claiming that efficient teaching should produce nearly equivalent performance in all students, there remaining perhaps some trivial differences in acquisition time. Still others commented that few textbooks appear to be entirely satisfactory when adopted as a whole, that the grading system is used largely as a punitive device, and courses present bits of information at rates and in orders that can claim no relation to established characteristics of the learning process. The result of these failures is that a substantial number of students are lost at some crossroad along the path to knowledge, and we do not know at what point they went wrong. These criticisms are not new. Probably some are overstated. However, there appeared to be good reason not to replicate abroad conditions which produce so much dissatisfaction at home. After a consideration of the kinds of problems I

[1] Paper presented at American Educational Research Association, February 17, 1967, New York.

have just mentioned we designed a course which was first started at Brasilia, and with variations, is the course Keller and I have been teaching at Arizona State University for the past three years. The course is perhaps most easily described by reading to you part of the material given to the student the first day of a new semester. Here I will quote at length:

This course is an attempt to develop a rather different way of teaching psychology at Arizona State University. In general terms, the objective of this new procedure is to offer *individual* instruction and attention within the framework of mass education. The hope is that each person will in fact master the basic material appropriate to a first course in psychology.

Two special characteristics of this method merit immediate and special attention. First, each student should be able to move at his own pace through the entire course. The rapid worker should not be held back by a slower student nor forced to waste time listening to several repetitions of information he has already learned. Equally important, the student lagging behind should not be forced to move ahead at the sacrifice of comprehension. Some of you may finish this course before the end of the semester. That is fine. You will merit the free time that this will make available. Others may not finish the course within the time marked off as a normal semester unit. This may create special problems. How fast you go depends on you.

Secondly, material will be presented only as you are prepared to deal with it. The student who "missed the point" but is allowed or forced to proceed, soon compounds his slight misunderstanding into total confusion—the stuff that E's are made of. The subject matter of this course is broken up into a series of units. You will be required to show mastery of each unit before moving on to the next. This way a small mistake can be corrected before it results in ultimate disaster. Sophocles wrote "one must learn by doing the thing; for though you think you know it, you have no certainty until you try." You will be asked to try often. To demonstrate your mastery of each unit, you will be required to pass a "readiness" test before proceeding further. For those who are willing to put a little effort into the job there can be no such thing as failure in the normal sense.

The information you will be asked to acquire will come in five kinds of packages— reading, laboratory, discussions, demonstrations, and lectures. These, however, will not occur merely because it is Monday, Wednesday or Friday. Some material is more appropriate for one type of presentation than another, and none of it is appropriate until you have mastered what goes before. There will be periods of concentrated reading and other periods of little or no reading at all. A reading assignment should not be undertaken until you have passed the readiness test associated with the end of the previous unit. Likewise, laboratory experiments can only be done when you demonstrate you are prepared to profit from them, by passing the previous unit. All of the necessary (i.e., required) material of the course comes labeled "reading" or "laboratory."

The lectures and demonstrations in this course will have a different relation to the rest of your course work than is usually the case. They will be provided only when you have demonstrated your readiness to appreciate them; no examination will be based upon them; and you need not attend them if you do not wish to do so. When a certain percentage of the class has reached a certain point in the course, a lecture or demonstration will be available at a stated time, but it will not be compulsory.

The teaching staff of your course will include a proctor, a classroom assistant, a laboratory assistant, and your instructor. The proctor, a fellow undergraduate, has been chosen for his maturity of judgment, for his understanding of the special problems that may confront you as a beginner and for his willingness to assist. He will provide you with all your classroom study-material except your textbooks. He will check all your readiness tests, and he will be the first to pass upon them as satisfactory or unsatisfactory. His judgment will ordinarily be law, but if he is ever in serious doubt he can appeal to a higher court for a ruling—to the instructor if necessary. Failure to pass a test on the first try, the second, the third, or even later, will not be held against you; better too much testing than not enough, if your final success is to be assured.

Your work in the laboratory will be carried out under the direct supervision of a graduate laboratory assistant, whose detailed duties cannot be listed here. In addition, there is a graduate classroom assistant, upon whom your proctor will depend, for various course materials (assignments, tests, special readings, etc.) and who will collect, and keep up to date, all progress records for all course members. The classroom assistant confers with the instructor daily, aids the proctors on occasion, and acts in a variety of ways to further the smooth operation of the course machinery.

The instructor will have as his principal responsibilities: (a) the selection of all study materials used in the course; (b) the organization and the mode of presenting this material; (c) the construction of tests upon the material; and (d) the final evaluation of each student's progress in the course. It will be his duty, also, to provide lectures, demonstrations, and discussion opportunities for all students who have earned the privilege; to act as a clearinghouse for requests and complaints; and to arbitrate in any case of disagreement or misunderstanding between students and proctors or assistants.

A great deal has been said about the "readiness" tests. These are not examinations in the usual sense. Your grade will not depend upon them. Their only function is to indicate your degree of understanding to you and indicate to us where you are having trouble and need help. If you fail a readiness test you will be required to redo the unit and try again before you proceed—but there is no penalty in terms of a grade for failing these tests, even two or three times. The only relation between the readiness tests and your final grade will be the total number of units you have passed at the end of the semester (i.e., what proportion of the total course you have mastered). The total number of units you have finished will determine 50% of your grade for the course— all 20 units as A, 19 units an A-, 18 units a B+, etc.

There will be a final exam at the end of the course which will cover the reading and laboratory work of the entire semester. The final exam will count 25% of your grade. An assessment of your laboratory work will count the remaining 25%.

As well as the above material, the student also receives his first reading assignment at this initial meeting of the course. The assignment sheets typically specify selected sections from the two course textbooks, hints as to certain terms or data

that require special attention, a series of study questions, some comments that relate one unit to the next or bring an issue up to date where the texts are beginning to show their age.

From this point on, the student is free to work at his own speed at home or in the classroom, which becomes a study hall. When prepared, he appears at any hour when a proctor is on duty and takes a quiz. If passed, he enters the fact on the class progress chart and receives his next unit assignment—more reading or a laboratory experiment. If failed, he discusses the problem with his proctor, or sometimes the instructor, goes off to review the unit and comes back to try again with an alternate form of the test. Since there is no penalty for failure, other than not being allowed to proceed, a pass means being 100% correct. An uncorrected error leads to trouble later on and so we demand perfection. Our call for excellence seems to be respected by the student—but more of that in a moment. There are 20 reading units and 10 laboratory exercises in the program which is intended as a one semester course.

Let me report on some changes in the behavior of the students and the instructor. If the late Harold Schlosberg were here, I am sure he could quantify the dramatic changes in facial expression shown by nearly every student sometime within the first two weeks. They are a happy, friendly group. The next unusual event occurs when a student appears to report that he passed unit three on the first try but still feels unsure of the material and requests permission to take a second test. To keep the proctors' work load within reasonable limits we had to pass a law that no more than two successes with a single unit were allowed! Soon the instructor finds he knows nearly every student by name, which he never did before. The students talk freely with the instructor, but the character of these conversations has changed. Instead of a petty discussion of the possibility of receiving partial credit on a near miss, our interactions are not only pleasant but almost always directed toward the informational content of the course. Next, nearly every student who finishes the program expresses an interest in becoming a proctor. Finally, and this is perhaps what counts, the distribution of grades is radically changed. For good or bad, the normal curve disappears. This past semester, my grade sheet showed 41% A's; 9% B's; 11% C's; there were no D's and no failures, but 30% Incomplete. There, of course, is the rub. You can recapture the normal curve by taking a speed measure—for example the number of units completed by mid-semester. It is possible that this is the basis for the normal curve we so typically find? In any case, if you allow the student whose progress has been slow (for whatever reason) to take an incomplete and return the following semester (and I see few other than bureaucratic reasons why you shouldn't) he too eventually finishes the 20 units, takes the final and receives an A or B. The student has learned the material and this is what we set out to accomplish.

The proctors are another happy story. They receive two points of academic credit for their work and *earn* it several times over. They come early, work late, learn even more than their students, and go on to take the top grades in the advanced courses (as yet traditionally taught). At weekly meetings they play an important part in program revision, suggesting a unit which is too large, a textbook passage that is unclear or a test question that is ambiguous. The behavior of the students clearly reveals that *the proctors provide a kind of reinforcement, however subtle and ill-defined, which has yet to be built into a programmed text.* I think they are the key to whatever successes they have had.

As I sat trying to describe the changes in the instructor's outlook on life, I found I could not begin to be as eloquent as Professor Keller was a year ago when he described our course to the A.S.U. faculty. I would like to quote him.

> The instructor of such a course works harder than he did before, but he profits more. He finds a new appreciation of his labors and a new dignity in his profession. He is no longer dogged with the feeling that he gives his all to those who don't understand it, don't want it, and don't deserve it.

> But his job is more difficult than before. Initially he must state his goals, in rather concrete form. He must make a tentative analysis of his course content and put it in suitable units of instruction. He must know his chosen textbook or books more intimately than he ever has before. He must construct a greater variety of questions on his assignments, and they must be better questions—unambiguous and fair, not tricky or show-offish. If he designs them well enough, they will help him teach. He must learn to give lectures that are interesting enough to attract a non-captive audience and help make worthwhile the completion of course units. He must learn to write clear supplements to unclear or over-difficult reading assignments, pointing up areas of special importance and suggesting the kinds of questions that may be asked about them. He must be alert to the progress of every student, the slow as well as the fast, and be ready with a kind word when it seems merited. He must keep an eye on the work of his subordinates, lest they over-step the bounds of their function. Everywhere he must be ready to reward good conduct and prevent the bad from occurring. And so on. The instructor of such a course is a very busy man.

Finally, just a brief word about the relation of our procedures to current learning theory. I am sure most of you have already spotted the more important characteristics—most of which have been discussed frequently in recent years since the advent of programmed instruction and the teaching machine. Our procedures share the following with more traditional programming: placing the student in a position where he must respond, where he receives nearly immediate feedback from his efforts, where he may proceed at his own pace, where punishing contingencies are made minimal, and where his individual work is monitored at every step as he proceeds through a carefully designed sequence of material requiring an increasingly complex performance. We feel that the design of this course establishes a behavioral repertoire more complex than what is generally attempted by a programmed text. All the traditional tools of instruction are present—textbook reading, laboratory, lectures, discussions and tests. The important point is that the tools stand in a different (contingent) relation to the student's behavior. The procedures, then, bring the advantages of programmed instruction in contact with most aspects of the normal process of education. While in no position to offer a perfected method, or a standard formula, I am convinced that adaptations of such a course can prove useful at other levels and in different disciplines. From similar courses now being constructed at other universities and in different departments, we are encouraged in our hope that the procedures I have described are not *inherently* limited in applicability to an introductory undergraduate course in experimental psychology.

40

PSI: AN HISTORICAL PERSPECTIVE

J. Gilmour Sherman

When Fred Newman first wrote me about this symposium he simply asked if I would be willing to talk and left the door open to me to suggest topics. I responded suggesting three activities concerning the Personalized System of Instruction that have occupied my PSI time during the last year. Fred wrote back and said "Gil, I have found an appropriate role for you in the symposium. I have put you on the program to talk about history—and you have ten minutes." I assumed that when Fred looked through my "new" ideas he realized there was little new there, and it would be less embarassing for all concerned if it were labeled history so no one would expect very much. Fred has taken me off the hook and I thank him for it. I was asked to talk about the history of PSI and so I will. I have talked about it several times before but never quite as I will today, as recently I have some new feelings about what was important. While speaking to history directly, I plan to distort it just enough to work in one of the three things I really wanted to talk about.

Certainly the story begins at Columbia in the 1950's, although we did not know it at the time. Keller and Schoenfeld had earned a reputation for innovation for their textbook and the introductory-lab course which became famous. Innovation was in the air. At the same time all of us at Columbia were very very aware of programmed instruction and the teaching machine; Skinner published his paper "The Science of Learning and the Art of Teaching" in 1954. In the middle and late 50's Skinner came to Columbia several times, each time talking about teaching machines. As graduate students, we were all well versed in discussing the virtues, advantages, and characteristics of programmed instruction. We could recite its advantages—the student responds, there is immediate reinforcement or feedback, the student progresses at his own rate, material is presented in small steps all carefully sequenced, the program leaves a

record leading to the possibility of improvement, the desired terminal behavior is clearly specified and punishment is minimal. Those who know Fred Keller will know why the latter was appealing. Those familiar with PSI will recognize this list as important aspects of the Personalized System of Instruction. This, then was the first major influence.

At about this time I became so interested in programming, it was so much a part of our lives and conversation, that I bought an early model of a teaching machine with research money given to me for other purposes. With a colleague I set out to write a program on relay circuits to train our research-lab assistants. I had acquired some sophistication with relay devices which I am still proud of in face of the onslaught of solid-state equipment. The teaching machine unhappily was mechanical, where my skills were zero. The machine persisted in taking my carefully programmed cards, crumpling them into small balls and spitting them out on the floor. Keller is not particularly noted for any greater mechanical ability. The machine was not to be our direction.

I am skipping a lot, but about this time a series of accidents led first Keller, and then myself, to Brazil. We have both told that story in many places and in many ways, but only recently have I come to realize how important Brazil was in determining some of the characteristics of PSI. The Brazilians taught us a great deal about the importance of the individual, and a respect for each person's human dignity. When first hearing about PSI there have been those who criticized it on the grounds that it is mechanical, cold and automatic. Anyone who has been a student, or a teacher, in such a course knows that if there is *any* merit in such a system it is that it allows a humane, personal, individual interaction that respects the dignity of all involved in a way none of us have experienced before. There is a flavor and style in the approach for which we owe a debt to Brazil and the Brazilians who left such a personal mark. This was

1 Paper read at the Rocky Mountain Psychological Association, May 13, 1971.

the second major influence.

One other Brazilian event provides an important link in this too rapid and increasingly biased account. As the procedures developed, it was our notion to give frequent tests which would be graded immediately by a proctor. I may be wrong but I think Keller's first proctor was an illiterate who solved the problem of comparing the student's test with an answer key in a way that we would now describe as "matching to sample." In any case, we did not get too far before they had a revolution in Brazil. That ended this part of the story.

We both moved to Arizona State University and set out to do what the Brazilian revolution had frustrated. We kept the essential characteristics of Skinner's programming, brought in the Brazilian influence of personal individual interaction, and hired proctors to serve in the system (they were not necessarily illiterate).

I have assumed the audience is at least somewhat familiar with the kind of course I am talking about. In essence, the normal lecture format is replaced by an emphasis on written material. Carefully prepared assignments consisting of sections from standard textbooks, articles and specially prepared supplements are given to the student along with study questions and other instructions as to what to read, in what order and for what information. When the student thinks he has mastered the material he comes in to take a brief quiz. This is immediately corrected by a proctor. If there are errors, the proctor indicates what part of the assignment needs further study, the student goes off to work some more and then comes back to try again. The tests are not exams in the normal sense, students are not penalized by a lowered grade because of an error. The tests are not graded at all, but rather are a device and an opportunity to demonstrate mastery, or detect confusions, the latter to be corrected before they lead to serious trouble. Since there is no penalty for mistakes, the student is free to keep trying until he learns. Excellence can be demanded and grades are determined solely on how much of the material is finally mastered. As a student masters a unit he then moves on to the next unit proceeding through the course at his own pace demonstrating his competence each step of the way.

There are other characteristics of the system which time will not allow me to describe. Increasingly I meet people who tell me they are "doing something quite similar"—except it turns out they require students to take one test a week, or they grade the tests, or have introduced some other "minor" modification. Some of these "small departures" produce profound behavioral results raising some questions that the new procedure should in fact be considered a PSI course. The time seems near when we are going to have to state the essential characteristics of PSI and decide what is and what isn't—but that is for another time.

In the moments remaining I want to pick out one characteristic—the proctors—and carry the history a bit further. Initially at A.S.U. I had few funds available and for a semester I acted as a proctor alongside a single graduate student assistant. That kept me too busy answering repetitions of the same questions and left me no time for the interesting questions, personal attention, and unique interactions the system makes possible between student and teacher. A year later there was a large staff of paid graduate students—all of whom immediately took to giving mini-lectures, the thing we were trying to avoid. Fortunately we ran out of money. For no good reason other than economy, we decided to have as proctors those undergraduates who had most successfully completed the course the previous year. This proved to be an improvement. The students worked for course credit in an upper level course concocted for the purpose and called "seminar in course programming." For the next few years the course thrived and grew and we started to give lectures about it at professional meetings!

Somewhere near the end of these talks there was always a paragraph that started with a comment something like "and the proctors are another happy story—they learn the most of all." There was a message there, but we were not listening. We did notice that a large percent of our students applied to be proctors the following year—but we never went on to say there must be something about that position that is reinforcing.

Eventually there was a revolution in Arizona and we moved on. Since one-trial learning was never my specialty, when I got to Georgetown I immediately hired advanced students to be proctors and repeated all our earlier procedures. Again the proctors did too much teaching, but before I could work out something better the money ran out again. This time my colleagues looked unfavorably on giving course credit, the system was in ruins and I would probably have gone back to lecturing, if it hadn't been that in the meantime I had forgotten how.

Out of desperation we decided to make proctors out of some of the students taking the course. My one assistant and I corrected the first few tests for any given unit. The first ten students to pass with a perfect score become proctors and take on the function of grading, guiding and interviewing classmates with an extensive proctors' manual to guide them. Students who missed the chance to become a proctor on unit one become a proctor by being among the first ten to pass unit two—essentially bumping one of the existing proctors, all of whom in the meantime are working like mad to retain their position. We essentially have a constantly changing group of ten proctors who are always those students furthest out in front.

Clearly this solves the money problem—and the course credit problem if anyone is squeamish about that. But like earlier accidents this too turned out to be more important than simply saving money. As we had noted before, the position is reinforcing and a substantial part of the class worked to get into the lead and become a proctor. Almost exactly one-third of the class held the position sometime during this past semester.

Next, the proctors are clearly only one unit ahead of the student being examined and they are not expected to be as wise as a more advanced student. With less reputation to protect they are less liable to start giving lectures or worse, making up answers when pressed. They find it easier to admit they don't know and send the student on up the line when an unusual question makes this appropriate. Even more important, as we had noted earlier, proctors learn the most of all. We

have all heard the saying "you don't learn something until you teach it." "Practice makes perfect" might have led us to predict a happy result from this permutation on an innovation. The data on overlearning and massed versus spaced practice might have led us to the same prediction from a more solid data base than an old adage. Alternatively one might say that since the proctors are exposed to nearly every conceivable error, the additional S^Δ training sharpens their discriminations.

I have the decided feeling there is a more important reason than any of the above for the success of this procedure. But now I am passing the limits of my thinking and will defer further comments to a later time.

So that I can claim to have included a bit of data, let me quickly report that this past semester, while some students who were not proctors received over 90 on the final, no proctor fell below 90. Seven of the 32 proctors scored 100 on the final—a score not attained by any student who went through the course without proctoring. This seems to be a useful procedure for learning—and learning to the point of near perfection at that.

So much for history. My colleagues are about to give you more data and more leads to what the future holds than I am able to give. I would suggest that the position of the proctor in the PSI approach is one with an importance, a promise, and a future we have only begun to explore.

41

THE THEORY BEHIND PSI[1]

J. Gilmour Sherman

It is both a pleasure and a bit frightening to stand here today. It is always exciting to find so many people open to, interested in, or seeking, new styles of teaching. It seems to be happening in many places.

I returned only four days ago from Brazil where there was a similar meeting and great enthusiasm. Many of you will have read the Carnegie Commission's report, "The Fourth Revolution: Instructional Technology in Higher Education." That report describes a very different educational system for the future. It is you, in groups like this in both countries, who will bring about the projected diversity that presumably will characterize education in the year 2000. It is a privilege to have this opportunity to share some thoughts with you.

It is also a pleasure to see several old friends, leaders in the development of PSI, and to make new acquaintances here, of people who have been teaching PSI courses. However, these knowledgable individuals make me slightly uncomfortable. There *are* topics I would like to discuss with them, but that is for another time. They have heard or read most of what I am going to say now. The only thing I can do is express my delight that they are here and now proceed to ignore them! For my remarks are intended for those who today are making their first contact with PSI. It is impossible to resist, first, pointing to this problem of speaking to a heterogenous audience, second, wondering how often we are ignoring or boring a segment of our audience in the classroom, and third, apologizing for the blatant hypocrisy of now launching into a speech condemning the lecture method. However, I won't talk long, a question period is probably more productive.

Two final fears. One is that when I am done some will comment that I didn't say anything. It would not be totally inappropriate, for the remark-

able fact is that PSI is a simple idea. There is little that is new; the traditional activities and tools of education are all there: Textbooks, tests, labs, demonstrations, and even occasionally, lectures. It has all been tried before, or so Keller and I are told about once a week, via letters that claim that the writers invented PSI many years ago. Probably they did. If there is anything new about PSI it is that old, standard materials and traditional educational practices *stand in a new relation to the behavior of the student.* Telling is not teaching. This is the key—that the students are active and their activities have consequences.

My last fear couples the fact that PSI is *not* new, with an earlier experience I recently learned of, the work of Frederic Burk who developed one of the first systems of instruction at the San Francisco State Normal School in 1912. He and his faculty rewrote courses of study to permit learners to advance at their own rate. Self instruction bulletins were written, published and distributed for courses in math, grammar, history, language and geography. Over 100,000 bulletins were sold without any advertising or profit to the authors. (Parenthetically, this author notes that the later practice persists.) In 1917 a ruling of the California attorney general abruptly stopped their publication, as the power to publish textbooks or printed instructional materials was judged to rest entirely with the State Board of Education. (Since I don't know if that ruling has been changed, I can only hope that your current attorney general is a more friendly sort.)

If there is nothing new about PSI one can only say that a visit to a PSI classroom certainly looks very different from what is normally seen on most campuses. Let me paint a verbal picture of the scene.

One's first impression may well be one of a very ordinary classroom (for no special equipment is necessary) but one that has yielded to chaos for there is a considerable amount of movement and even noise. Students are coming and going, indi-

---

[1] Paper read at West Coast PSI Conference, California State University, Long Beach, California, September 18–19, 1972.

viduals are talking with one another. The professor is on the floor wandering around, perhaps the only normal link to a classroom is that no one is paying much attention to him.

A second look is quite remarkable—everyone is working. This is truly stunning. Since in a PSI course there are no regular, required hours, only those who are ready, willing and able to work are there. It is a busy, friendly, impressive sight. Students come in to pick up unit materials— essentially assignments, but assignments that are specially prepared by the instructor—they refer to standard text segments, specify the objectives of the reading, clarify some uneven parts of the text, perhaps contain the flavor of the opinions of the instructor with regard to specific points, and provide study questions which the student can use to judge his own comprehension. A student may choose to study in this environment where the instructor and proctors are available to answer questions, or he may choose to study elsewhere. Another student will arrive having finished a unit's reading and request a "test." Typically it will contain ten questions; some true-false, some multiple choice, one matching, one complete the sentence, and a short essay question; all of it designed to take 10-15 minutes. When finished he will go immediately to a proctor, a fellow student. The proctor, consulting his materials, will correct the test, ask a few additional verbal questions, and indicate one of three possible outcomes. One, that the material has been mastered and the student may proceed to the next unit. Congratulations are in order. Two, that there are problems, these are described, with suggestions as to which parts of the unit assignment need review before a second form of the test is attempted, or three, that the difficulties are beyond the competence of the proctor, and the student should consult the instructor.

The last view of the classroom then shows some students arriving, picking up materials, and leaving immediately. Others are studying, still others are taking tests. Some are sitting with a proctor, and a few are conversing with the professor. No one is asleep, no one is embarrassed, no one is surpressed with fear, wearing a dunce cap, trying to argue that they should receive half credit, or explaining away a previous absence on the grounds of ill health—real or imagined. Now all of this is indeed very different from someone standing in front of a room giving a speech. As chaotic, esoteric, or capriciously Rube Goldberg-like as the system may seem, let me assure you, it is not. Before going into that let me digress for a moment to things that are not quite so apparent—the function of the teacher; recording, logistics and test scoring.

The professor contemplating such a course should recognize he is about to change his role—he is about to become a manager and a critic rather than an author and performer. He has decisions to make regarding course policies, grading, procrastination, selection of proctors, and record keeping that will make or break his course. If he looks upon it as a way to reduce his work load, avoid teaching, or automating his course to the point where he can walk away from it, he has missed the point of the term *personalized* system of instruction, and he is headed for a disaster. The professor has changed his role, but he is more important than ever. He is about to meet his students perhaps for the first time in his career.

The tests are not exams in the normal sense. Students are not penalized by a lower grade because of errors. The tests are not graded at all, but rather are a device and an opportunity for the student to demonstrate mastery, or detect confusions, the latter to be corrected before they lead to serious trouble.

Roughly, rather than starting with 100, counting errors and subtracting points that are forever lost, the procedure is to count successes and add. The difference is not trivial; for it leaves the student free to try; free to fail; and therefore eventually more likely to succeed. It is the amount he masters that determines his grade. We judge our art masterpieces, not by the number of preliminary sketches discarded along the way, but by the final product produced.

Again the method did not grow quite like Topsy. There were historical, philosophical, and psychological reasons for the format as it stands. PSI was the product of the effort of four people, Fred Keller and myself plus two Brazilians— Carolina Martuscelli Bori and Rodolpha Azzi. The original plan was developed ten years ago in Brazil, for the new University of Brazilia. While none of us have said this before, having just returned from Brazil filled with pride over my command of Portuguese which has taken a decade to acquire—in retrospect I wonder (half in jest) how much of our de-emphasis of the lecture was dictated by the fact that ten years ago neither Keller or myself could speak more than a few words in the language of the country where we were called upon to teach.

The philosophy behind the method was one of striving for mastery and excellence. That goal is clearly debatable; there are legitimate educational occasions when mastery is not the goal, and as a corollary PSI is not appropriate.

When mastery *is* the aim, then I suggest the normal curve's projection of a C is an insult to the student, hardly conducive to fostering dignity, creativity and achievement. With a goal of mastery the characteristics of PSI follow, quite automatically. Mastery is synonymous with unit perfection. Perfection can *not* be controlled by the calendar and the clock—it demands a self-paced system. It appears to be a law of education that *we can not hold both time and quality constant*. When students are at different points in the course, lectures become impossible and an emphasis on the written word (or other audio-visual material) is inescapable as the source of information. Finally, the different rates of progress inevitably resulting from individualized instruction requires we *amplify* the instructor, via either machine or proctor. The five characteristics of PSI as set down by Keller indeed appear essential.

The psychological data indicates learning is not a spectator sport, the student is not a sponge. Rather learning results from performance and the consequences that follow it. Clearly punishment which suppresses behavior should be avoided. Until recently there seemed to be only two choices—maintaining standards through punishment (a practice which produced a notable absence of any widespread love-for-learning in the adult population) or a permissive system which sacrificed quality. Only as a sophisticated theory of learning developed, were we in a position to both avoid the crippling consequence of punitive systems and still maintain a standard of excellence. This requires constructing adequate systems built on positive consequences. It is that theory of learning, the experimental analysis of behavior, that is the theory behind PSI.

What I have tried to do is give you a rapid view of the format of a PSI course, and how and why it functions as it does. (Later speakers will give you more details—and they are important.) Individualized instruction is quickly becoming so popular a phase, it runs the risk of becoming a slogan, and even outmoded, without ever having really been tried. PSI is not only a goal, it is a plan, a specific method, a suggested procedure for the implementation of a kind of learning most now agree is desirable.

In closing I would stress the fact that the system is related to an underlying theory. The method is not the answer to all of education's ills, it is not offered as a final solution. It should not become the new orthodoxy or be slavishly followed. Hopefully someone here today, after several trials, will devise a variant of the basic procedure that is superior to anything any of us have yet attempted. I would encourage experimentation. On the other hand, again, the system was not devised by chance. It should not be changed for reasons of whim or fancy. The *form* is not important, some of the *functions* are, to the extent that they reflect what we know about the process of learning. Perhaps *the* major virtue of PSI is that it makes the ingredients of learning visible. The results of modifications are immediately apparent in the behavior of individual students. I would urge those who are now happy in their classrooms to continue whatever they are now doing. Those with the desire and time to experiment, might well choose PSI as an alternative. After an initial tryout following the "formula" they will be ready to strike out on their own. I could wish for nothing more than to someday sit in an audience and hear one of you describe a system of instruction, perhaps designated by a quite different name, which evolved from the possibility for experimentation PSI makes possible. Whatever the format and details of the next generation-system, I only hope it preserves the dignity for each individual, student and staff alike, that PSI provides. That is the final impression from a PSI classroom: it is a place of learning and knowledge, mutual and self respect, can all increase together. It is not only the kind of classroom, but the kind of world we are all seeking.